The ADIRONDACK Book

Book

A Complete Guide

Nancie Battaglia

THE ADIRONDACK BOOK

A Complete Guide

Third Edition

Elizabeth Folwell
with Neal S. Burdick

Berkshire House Publishers
Lee, Massachusetts

On the Cover and Frontispiece: Photographs by Nancie Battaglia
Front Cover: *Climbers on Whiteface Mountain.*
Frontispiece: *Elk Lake.*
Back cover: *Breakfast setting at Lake Placid Lodge; the telemark — a challenging and elegant turn; travel by carriage — a relaxing way to go.*

The Adirondack Book: A Complete Guide
Copyright © 1992, 1996, 1998 by Berkshire House Publishers
Cover and interior photographs © 1992, 1996, 1998 by Nancie Battaglia and other credited sources
Maps © 1992 by NRC Graphics Inc.

Library of Congress Cataloging-in-Publication Data

Folwell, Elizabeth, 1953–
  The Adirondack book : a complete guide / Elizabeth Folwell with Neal S. Burdick. — 3rd ed.
      p.   cm. — (Great destinations series, ISSN 1056-7968)
    Includes bibliographical references (p.   )and index.
    ISBN 0-936399-92-9
      1. Adirondack Mountains Region (N.Y.)—Guidebooks. 2. Adirondack Park (N.Y.) —Guidebooks. I. Burdick, Neal S. II. Title. III. Series.
  F127.A2F55   1998
  917.47'50443—dc21   97-31633
                                                   CIP

ISBN: 0-936399-92-9
ISSN: 1056-7968 (series)

Editor: Sarah Novak. Managing Editor: Philip Rich. Design and composition: Dianne Pinkowitz. Original design for Great Destinations™ series: Janice Lindstrom. Cover design: Jane McWhorter.

Berkshire House books are available at substantial discounts for bulk purchases by corporations and other organizations for promotions and premiums. Special personalized editions can also be produced in large quantities. For more information, contact:

Berkshire House Publishers
480 Pleasant St., Suite 5; Lee, Massachusetts 01238
800-321-8526
E-mail: info@berkshirehouse.com
Website: www.berkshirehouse.com

Manufactured in the United States of America
First printing 1998
10 9 8 7 6 5 4 3 2 1

No complimentary meals or lodgings were accepted by the author and reviewers in gathering information for this work.

GREAT DESTINATIONS™ Series

The Berkshire Book: A Complete Guide
The Santa Fe & Taos Book: A Complete Guide
The Napa & Sonoma Book: A Complete Guide
The Chesapeake Bay Book: A Complete Guide
The Coast of Maine Book: A Complete Guide
The Adirondack Book: A Complete Guide
The Aspen Book: A Complete Guide
The Charleston, Savannah & Coastal Islands Book:
    A Complete Guide
The Gulf Coast of Florida Book: A Complete Guide
The Central Coast of California Book : A Complete Guide
The Newport & Narragansett Bay Book: A Complete Guide
The Hamptons Book: A Complete Guide
Wineries of the Eastern States
The Texas Hill Country Book: A Complete Guide

The Great Destinations™ series features regions in the United States rich in natural beauty and culture. Each Great Destinations™ guidebook reviews an extensive selection of lodgings, restaurants, cultural events, historic sites, shops, and recreational opportunities, and outlines the region's natural and social history. Written by resident authors, the guides are a resource for visitor and resident alike. The books feature maps, photographs, directions to and around the region, lists of helpful phone numbers and addresses, and indexes.

Acknowledgments

Just as the Adirondack Park is a combination of many different places, the third edition of *The Adirondack Book* represents the efforts of many good people who contributed in all sorts of ways.

I'm indebted to Neal Burdick, director of publications at St. Lawrence University, in Canton, New York, and editor of *Adirondac* magazine, for writing the comprehensive *History* and *Transportation* chapters that introduce the region so well.

Special thanks are in order to Lake Placid photographer Nancie Battaglia for the evocative and informative images that appear on and between the covers.

To my intrepid team of restaurant reviewers, hats off and cheers for once again seeking out an eclectic selection of eateries. Thank you, Sue Halpern and Bill McKibben, Barbara McMartin and Alec Reid, Joan and Roy Potter, Lohr McKinstry, Amy Godine and Jack Nicholson (no, not that Jack Nicholson), Dennis Aprill and family, and Peter O'Shea.

A word of appreciation is due my *Adirondack Life* magazine co-workers: publisher Tom Hughes, art director Ann Hough, associate editor Galen Crane, and advertising sales director Jo'el Kramer for their interest and support. At the Adirondack Museum, in Blue Mountain Lake, director Jackie Day, librarian Jerry Pepper, and publications editor Alice Gilborn were helpful from the earliest stages of this project.

My husband, Tom Warrington, once again proved to be the best companion imaginable when we were in search of yet another great barbecue joint and an honest cup of coffee and was a source of down-to-earth advice.

I'm grateful to the Berkshire House staff: Jean Rousseau, publisher; Philip Rich, managing editor; Sarah Novak, editor; Liz Rousseau, marketing director; and Mary Osak, office manager.

The last word of thanks goes to all Adirondack innkeepers, restaurateurs, craftspeople, shop owners, antique dealers, guides, and others who add the human dimension to this wild and wonderful place.

Contents

CHAPTER ONE
The People's Park
HISTORY
1

CHAPTER TWO
Over the Rivers and Through the Woods
TRANSPORTATION
19

CHAPTER THREE
Rustic, Classic, and Basic
LODGING
31

CHAPTER FOUR
From Folkways to Fine Arts
CULTURE
109

CHAPTER FIVE
Always in Good Taste
RESTAURANTS & FOOD PURVEYORS
150

CHAPTER SIX
A Land for All Seasons
RECREATION
213

CHAPTER SEVEN
Woodsy Whimsy to Practical Gear
SHOPPING
291

CHAPTER EIGHT
Nuts, Bolts, and Free Advice
INFORMATION
334

GEORGE E. PATAKI
GOVERNOR

Dear Friends:

From its incredible glacial beginnings to its spectacular beauty today, New York's Adirondack region offers a remarkable diversity that few places in the world can rival.

As one of the largest and oldest state parks in America, the Adirondack Park is a unique resource. Created more than 100 years ago, its six million acres include public land protected as "forever wild" by the New York State Constitution and private land where careful forest management, tourism and other natural resource-based industries support some ten million visitors annually. The park is home to 130,000 permanent residents and 70,000 seasonal residents.

The Adirondack Park provides countless places to experience and things to see. Its 46 mountains over 4000 feet, 2600 lakes and ponds and 1800 miles of river, millions of acres of forest and abundant wildlife provide endless recreational opportunities. From scenic drives along mountain roads to week-long hikes in the back country, from bird-watching to fishing, the Adirondack Park is an exciting and sometimes challenging place to live, work and visit.

The Park's small towns, historic sites and museums are gateways to the Adirondacks' rich culture and history of military conflict, rustic architecture, logging, hunting, fishing, trapping and natural resource conservation.

From my own experience visiting the Park with my children, I have found that the Adirondacks are a place of discovery and renewal -- discovery of the working of nature, history and tradition; renewal of our own spirit and enthusiasm for life as we walk majestic mountain trails and canoe in clear lakes surrounded by a timeless forest.

I welcome you to share these experiences and to use this comprehensive guidebook when you visit the Adirondacks this year and for years to come.

Very truly yours,

Gyp E. Pataki

Introduction

New York's Adirondack Park is a big park: bigger than Yellowstone and Yosemite put together and larger than any of the national parks in the lower forty-eight. This park is better than national parks in many ways, too. You don't pay an entry fee when you cross the so-called Blue Line, the park's boundary; you don't need a permit to hike, climb a mountain, canoe, or explore the backcountry. People make this park their home and have lived here for many generations, giving this region a distinctive culture and offering an array of services to visitors.

The park covers six million acres, about the size of the state of Vermont. Land owned by New York State is approximately 2.5 million acres, and large landowners, especially timber companies, own about a million acres more and contribute significantly to the local economy. The year-round population of the Adirondack Park is about 130,000 residents, although Hamilton County, where I live, has only three or four people per square mile.

I've lived in the Adirondacks all my adult life, and I've enjoyed visiting many different communities, exploring wild places, and learning about the region. Although the landscape appears timeless, human endeavors change frequently. That's the impetus behind the third edition of *The Adirondack Book* — to supply information about new places and updates on classic spots. I hope that these pages encourage you to explore this great place.

Betsy Folwell
Blue Mountain Lake

THE WAY THIS BOOK WORKS

There are eight chapters in this book — History, Transportation, Lodging, Culture, Restaurants and Food Purveyors, Recreation, Shopping, and Information — and many maps and indexes. Within each chapter, you'll find subheadings — "Fishing," for example — and under that topic is general information that's true for the whole park. Then specific services and businesses are grouped geographically by region: **Lake George and Southeastern Adirondacks, Champlain Valley, High Peaks and Northern Adirondacks, Northwest Lakes,** and **Central Adirondacks** (which includes the southwestern Adirondacks). Towns are listed alphabetically in the regions. So, Bolton Landing may be the first town listed in the Lake George area, and pertinent businesses in that town will then be listed alphabetically.

Many of the entries have "information blocks" on the left side of the page, listing phone numbers, addresses, and so forth. We've checked these facts as close to the book's publication date as possible, but businesses do change hands and change policies. It's always a good idea to call ahead — a long-distance call is a whole lot cheaper than a tank of gas.

For the same reason, you won't find specific prices listed for restaurants, lodgings, greens fees, and so forth; we indicated a range of prices, which you'll find at the beginnings of the chapters or directly under the specific heading. Lodging prices are based on a per-room rate, double occupancy, during the high season, so that we had consistent standard for comparison; off-season and mid-week rates are generally cheaper. Restaurant price ratings show the cost of one meal including appetizer, entrée, and dessert, but not cocktails, wine, tax, or tip.

	Lodging	*Dining*
Very Inexpensive	Under $40	
Inexpensive	$40–$70	Up to $15
Moderate	$70–$100	$15–$20
Expensive	$100–$200	$20–$35
Very Expensive	Over $200	Over $35

Credit Cards are abbreviated as follows:

AE — American Express   DC — Diners Club
CB — Carte Blanche   MC — MasterCard
D — Discover   V — Visa

The
ADIRONDACK
Book
A Complete Guide

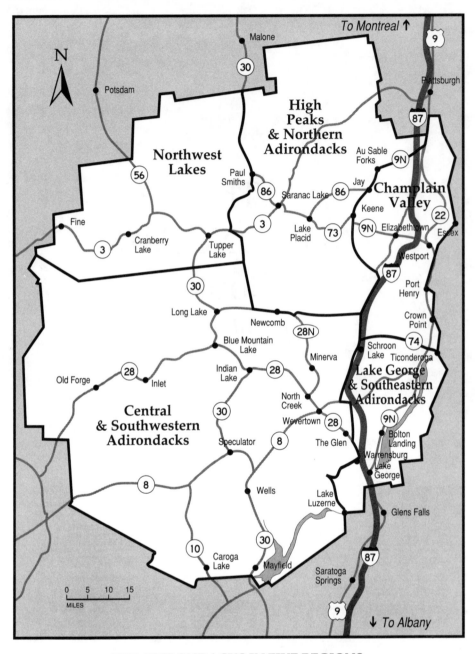

THE ADIRONDACKS IN FIVE REGIONS

CHAPTER ONE
The People's Park
HISTORY

To 19th-century painters and photographers alike, the Adirondacks offered a romantic vision of wild nature. This photograph by Katherine McClellan shows the Johns Brook Valley, in Keene.

Against the backdrop of deep forests, majestic mountains, and sparkling clear lakes, explorers, patriots, fortune hunters, dreamers, and schemers all tried to shape the Adirondacks into something that could be managed and subdued, but the wilderness resolutely resisted their attempts. As small settlements flourished in the Northeast and great cities grew along the Atlantic coast, this region remained a blank spot on the map. Along Lake Champlain's western shore, military outposts and clusters of homes were built in the mid-18th century, but only a few trappers, scouts, hunters, and surveyors penetrated the woods and waters beyond the lake's gentle valley. Slightly more than two centuries ago, when New York City was the political and commercial center of our new nation, mapmaker Thomas Pownall labeled the state's upper corner as "the Dismal Wilderness," and in 1784 fretted, "It is said to be a broken, unpracticable tract. I own I could never learn any thing about it."

Within a hundred years, all that changed dramatically. By 1884, there were thriving towns, a network of roads, railroads, and steamboats, and a tourism business that rivaled that of any Gilded Age destination. Numerous guidebooks and publications trumpeted the scenic beauty and fine accommodations to be found in the Adirondacks. The region's rare beauty, so close to the urban centers, stirred new ideas of conservation and preservation: a *New York Times* editorial suggested that "Within an easy day's ride of our great city . . . is a tract of country fitted to make a Central Park for the world"; another writer said, "Had I my way, I would mark out a circle of a hundred miles in diameter and throw around it the protecting aegis of the constitution. I would make it a forest forever." At the same time, the vast natural resources — timber, minerals, and waterpower — led to bursts of activity and economic boom. How humans first came into the country and made their own discoveries about this place is best understood in the context of the region's natural history, so we'll begin our own exploration there, with the very roots of these mountains.

NATURAL HISTORY

A common misperception about the Adirondacks is that they're part of the Appalachian Mountain range. In fact, the Adirondacks are the only Eastern mountains that are not Appalachian. They're of a completely different geologic family, twice as old as the Appalachians and more resistant to the forces that perpetually wear mountains down.

THE ADIRONDACK DOME

The Adirondacks are a southern appendix of the great Canadian Shield, a vast complex of billion-year-old Precambrian igneous and metamorphic rock shaped like a knight's shield that is the nucleus of the North American continent. While most of it underlies Canada, a portion dives under the St. Lawrence River in the vicinity of Alexandria Bay, New York, where it becomes visible as the Thousand Islands, and surfaces as a dome-shaped uplift, the Adirondacks.

Today, this dome lies generally between 1000 and 2000 feet above sea level, with higher mountain peaks; the surrounding valleys (Champlain on the east, Mohawk River on the south, Black River on the west, and St. Lawrence on the north) range from less than 100 to more than 500 feet above sea level. While the slope of the dome is quite gradual from most directions, the eastern elevation change from Lake Champlain (95 feet above sea level) to the summit of Mt. Marcy (5344 feet) occurs more abruptly, in about 25 air miles.

The uplift gives rise to dozens of rivers — 6000 miles of them — which more or less radiate out from its center like spokes on a wheel. The Hudson, whose highest source is the lyrically named Lake Tear-of-the-Clouds, on the upper

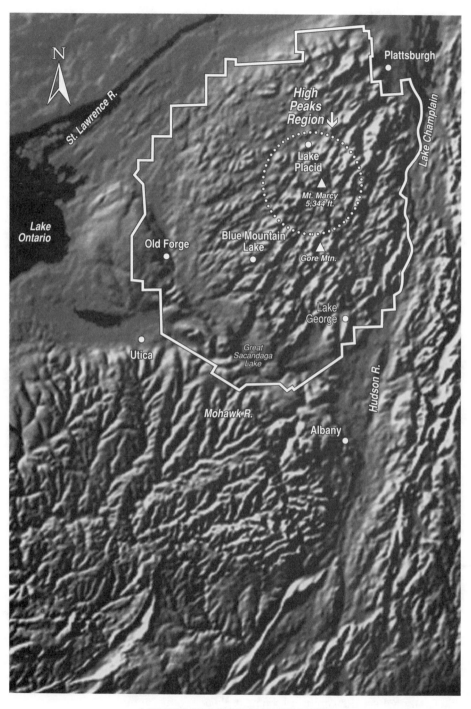

ADIRONDACK TOPOGRAPHY

slopes of Mt. Marcy, flows southeast before turning due south as it leaves the Adirondack Park. The Raquette (French for "snowshoe") begins virtually dead center in the park at Blue Mountain Lake, only a couple of miles from a tributary of the Hudson, and drains much of the northwest Adirondacks into the St. Lawrence River. Not too far away the Saranac and Ausable rivers start their tumble through the northeast quarter. The Sacandaga flows south; the West Canada, Moose, Independence, and Beaver drain the southwest and west. Around the clock from about 10am (northwest) to 2pm (northeast) are the Oswegatchie, Grass, St. Regis, Salmon, Chateaugay, and Chazy rivers.

The Adirondack dome continues to rebound from the weight of glaciers, at the rate of a few millimeters a century. This upward thrusting has eroded the younger rock cover and exposed the ancient bedrock, which is among the oldest exposed bedrock in the world. Part of the bedrock is composed of anorthosite, a rare feldspar nearly identical to some of the rocks brought back from the moon; it has a bluish cast that you can pick out in some highway rock cuts.

Rounded mountains surrounding the Saranac lakes were sculpted by glaciers 10,000 years ago.

Nancie Battaglia

In contrast to the ancient skeleton of the region, the face of the Adirondacks you see today is remarkably young by geologic standards, having been most recently carved by glaciers only about 10,000 years ago. The southwest-to-northeast trend of many rivers and lakes is the result of this latest glacial action, as are such features as the shapes of the mountains and the locations of ponds. You may spot eskers — tall, narrow, sandy ridges created when meltwater tunneling beneath the glaciers left sediment in its wake.

From the roads and trails you can also see immense boulders that appear to have been plopped down where they sit. In fact, that's just how these "erratics" got there, carried by the glaciers and left behind when the ice receded. They're completely unrelated to the rock upon which they repose, and they'll likely stay where they are until the next glacier comes along.

FLORA AND FAUNA

The Adirondacks straddle the border between the northern, largely coniferous boreal forest (from Boreas, the Greek god of the north wind) and the midcontinental mixed forest. Dominant tree species of the boreal forest are spruces and firs, while the mixed forest is characterized by maples, beeches, ashes, birches, and pines. Along the frontier between these forest types their representative species mingle, presenting an ecologically complex and visually pleasing mix. In the Adirondacks, you can find within a few miles of each other oak groves suggestive of the southern states and bogs typical of northern Canada. Adirondack slopes in autumn are decorated not only by the brilliant reds, oranges, and yellows of the maple and beech woods but also by the deep, rich, everlasting greens of the conifers.

You can cross ecological zones by gaining elevation, also; a rise of 1000 feet in altitude is equivalent to driving about 300 miles north. A drive up the Whiteface Memorial Highway or a hike to the top of a comparably high peak will carry you through vegetation bands until at the summit you would find yourself above timberline in an arctic zone inhabited only by mosses, lichens, and tundra-hardy plants.

In the past 20 years, several moose have moved back to the Adirondacks; some are being monitored with radio collars.

Nancie Battaglia

Wildlife is abundant in most of the Adirondacks, ranging from that ubiquitous picnic interloper, the chipmunk, to the reclusive moose, which has reintroduced itself into the region slowly over the last few years. Among the larger animals, you're most likely to see the prolific whitetail deer, all too frequently in the middle of the road directly ahead of you. Black bears have learned where humans camp, and often rummage for food near campsites. (While generally harmless, they are wild animals and should not be approached.) Species such as the mountain lion and wolf were hunted out of the region in the 1800s; some environmentalists would like to see them reintroduced, as has hap-

"Where Are the Mountains??"

Many people think the whole Adirondack region is mountainous. Not exactly true, as you'll discover if you enter from anywhere except the east. Only about a quarter of the 6.1-million-acre Adirondack Park is what most of us, by Eastern standards, would consider mountainous. That's the northeast sector, the area around Lake Placid and home of the High Peaks — the highest, Mt. Marcy; the most famous, Whiteface (fifth highest, not first as some people think); and other 4000-footers such as Gothics, Giant, Skylight, Haystack, and so on. The rest of the park is mostly rolling upland forest, with collections of lower peaks (around Lake George and in ridges from Indian Lake to Old Forge, for example) and several isolated summits such as Crane Mtn. in the south, the Jay Range in the east, and Azure Mtn. in the north.

pened, with only mixed success, with the lynx. The opportunistic coyote has filled the niche vacated by the wolf; you may hear its call some night.

Of more concern to you will be considerably smaller beasts, particularly blackflies and no-see-ums, which appear as if on cue on the second warm day of spring and can make pests of themselves until around the first of July. The secret is to keep moving, stay where there's a breeze, pursue indoor activities, or muster your resolve to ignore the creatures.

Loons, revered for their haunting songs, inhabit many Adirondack lakes and ponds. With luck you may see an osprey, peregrine falcon, or bald eagle soaring on warm air currents over a lakeshore or cliff. Hawks are fairly easy to spot; songbirds — especially warblers — are plentiful during warm weather; and at least ten varieties of ducks nest near the waterways of the park.

Fishing used to be not just popular but downright famous in the Adirondacks, but overfishing and acid-rain pollution have dramatically diminished the size and number of fish in recent years in formerly productive lakes and rivers. However, anglers still catch fine brook, brown, and rainbow trout; landlocked salmon; walleye and northern pike; and large- and smallmouth bass. In many areas, aggressive scientific stocking programs by the Department of Environmental Conservation have helped bring back sportfishing; research continues in park ponds and streams on how best to cope with acid precipitation.

While most of the Adirondacks do not harbor snakes of any number or consequence, Tongue Mountain, overlooking Lake George, shelters colonies of Eastern timber rattlesnakes. While they should be treated with respect, the snakes should not be a compelling reason to avoid this area with its excellent hiking and marvelous views. Take proper precautions (wear sturdy boots and long pants and stay on the trails), and remember that the mountain is their home and you're the intruder.

SOCIAL HISTORY

HUNTERS, EXPLORERS, TRADERS, AND SETTLERS

Adirondack wildlife, notably deer, attract hunters by the thousands each fall, and animals were what attracted the first humans to the region, so far as we know. Conventional wisdom holds that no Native Americans lived year-round in the heart of the Adirondacks; they apparently avoided these peaks

---

What's the Adirondacks?

What do we mean when we say "the Adirondacks?" Here are some possibilities:

• **The Adirondack Park:** Established in 1892, it covers 6.1 million acres of public and private land in a polygonal configuration occupying much of the northern third of New York State. It's the largest state park in the nation, larger even than our smallest states. Its boundary is known as the Blue Line because it was first drawn on a state map with a blue pencil. It's not all wilderness: everything within, from the summits of the highest peaks to the most remote bog to Main Street in Lake Placid, is in the park. It will probably show up as a great green lumpy circle on your road map.

• **The Adirondack Forest Preserve:** Established in 1885, this is now the 42 percent of the Adirondack Park that is public land and preserved as wilderness. It's many scattered parcels of land, not one contiguous unit, and it won't appear at all on your road map. In a nutshell, if you're on Forest Preserve land you're free to hike, hunt, fish, canoe, and do whatever else you want, although some parts are off-limits to motorized vehicles (e.g., snowmobiles and motorboats). If you're not on public land, you're trespassing on somebody's property, unless you have permission to be there. Odd as it may seem to come across private land inside a state park, please respect it. If you want to go for a walk in the woods, look for trailheads with state Department of Environmental Conservation signs; they are on public land.

• **The Adirondack Mountains:** For the most part they occupy the northeast quarter of the Adirondack Park. Not all of them are on public land. Forty-plus are more than 4000 feet above sea level, although this number changes each time some of the borderline summits get re-measured.

• **And . . .** There's a town called Adirondack near Schroon Lake. There's a Loj called Adirondak (the spellings attributable to Melvil Dewey, champion of simplified spelling, who owned the site in the early 20th century) near Lake Placid. And there's a magazine called *Adirondac* — no one knows why it's spelled like that, although a long-since-abandoned mining town near Mt. Marcy was so spelled. There's a different magazine called *Adirondack Life*, and these are the two best periodicals specific to the region.

and forests except for seasonal forays to hunt or fish or gather special plants such as berries, herbs, sweet grass, and bark and roots for baskets and boats. Evidence of more permanent camps has been found in the Champlain and Sacandaga valleys, to the east and south of the mountains.

The Native Americans who penetrated the region hundreds of years ago were enemies (the Iroquois from the south and the Hurons and Algonquins from the north), and they fought at any chance encounter. Artifacts from the scenes of their battles, and from their campsites along the waterways, are the principal record of their presence in the region. Their legacy resides mostly in names, such as Oswegatchie (a long river in the northwestern Adirondacks, meaning "black water" or "'orse, we got ye," attributable to some settlers whose horse had unsuccessfully tried to escape, if you prefer tall tales); Couchsachraga, which roughly means "dismal wilderness" (the 18th-century mapmaker mentioned at the beginning of this chapter was not alone in his assessment); and Ticonderoga, supposedly "the place where waters sing as they swiftly cascade over the rocks into the lake." One should be careful of these names, though; the supposed "Indian" name for Mt. Marcy, Tahawus ("cloudsplitter"), was apparently invented by a disgruntled New York City newspaperman shortly after the peak was named for a governor of the state.

Dominating the view from the junction of Adirondak Loj Road and Rte. 73 between Keene and Lake Placid is Algonquin Peak, second highest in the Adirondacks; just beyond it to the south and hidden from view is Boundary Peak. South of that, barely visible over a shoulder of Algonquin, is Iroquois. Perhaps apocryphal, the story is that the two nations named the two prominent summits as "border monuments" to their parts of the Adirondacks, the Algonquins in the north and the Iroquois in the south, with the lesser peak between them marking the actual boundary.

To the best of our knowledge, the first European to see the Adirondacks was Jacques Cartier, who in 1535 climbed what later was named Mont Royal, now in the heart of Montreal in the Canadian province of Quebec. He noted in his journal that he could discern "hilles to the south." It took 74 years for another

---

A Little Traveling Etymology

Most people think "Adirondacks" is a corruption of an Iroquois word for their enemies the Algonquins, whom they called "rat-i-ron-tacks" or "eaters of bark" in derisive reference to the Algonquins' supposed inability to hunt or farm well. This, of course, has never been proven, and some Native Americans of this writer's acquaintance dismiss it as white man's fantasy. The word was first applied by a surveyor, Ebenezer Emmons, in 1837.

Singular or plural? Depends if you're talking about the region (singular) or the mountains in it (plural), which are interchangeable in many people's minds. But "Adirondacks is . . ." sounds strange, so most people use the plural form.

European to see the Adirondacks. In 1609 Samuel de Champlain, another French explorer, journeyed south from Canada up the lake that he named for himself (south is upstream on Lake Champlain, to the distress of those who believe water must flow down a map) and reported on the marvelous rocky scenery spilling at times directly into the lake.

Near Ticonderoga, Champlain and his Huron guides came upon a party of Iroquois. A battle ensued; Champlain, armed with an arquebus, killed several warriors and vanquished the astonished Iroquois. They never forgave the French for violating a cardinal rule of Eastern Woodland Native American warfare (don't use a weapon your opponent doesn't know about) and sided with the British against the French in later contests for control of North America.

It's possible that a third European explorer, Henry Hudson, spied the Adirondack foothills on the northern horizon from the future site of Albany in that same year of 1609. Whether he did or not, for the next century and a half the Adirondacks went virtually ignored while the perimeter valleys filled slowly with settlers, and wars came and went. Lying north of the Mohawk Valley, which was the most northerly travel route to the interior of the continent, the mountains were largely bypassed by the westering pioneers. Those few who did penetrate the interior were interested not in settling but in extracting resources: beaver for fur and white pines for ship masts.

In fact, these white pines helped spur the Americans to win their independence. After the British drove the French forever into Quebec in 1759, the Crown sent timber cruisers into the Adirondack forests to mark the tallest and straightest white pines. These were to be used for British naval and commercial ships' masts and the colonists were not to touch them. That the colonists not only could not harvest these giants but also had to stand by and watch while they were taken, perhaps to be turned against them in naval battles, was more than they could accept. The "king's trees" became a rallying point for the region's freedom fighters.

Although little Adirondack land was known in the late 18th century, most of it was owned. First the British and then the American government, short of cash, used this "waste and unappropriated" real estate as payment to soldiers, the idea being that the soldiers would either settle it or sell it. Few settled here; most sold their holdings to other nonresidents or speculators. In one such transaction in 1771, two ship's carpenters named Totten and Crossfield, acting as front men for a coalition of financiers, came into possession of nearly a million acres in what is now the middle of the Adirondack Park. The tract was never properly surveyed, and even now the "Totten and Crossfield Purchase" confounds assessors and real-estate agents.

Emblematic of the problems faced by those who did try to civilize their holdings is the case of John Brown (not the abolitionist; he comes later), who in 1798 purchased some 200,000 acres of literally trackless wilderness west of Old Forge. He and his family struggled there for years. Farming proved futile against a cold climate and soil whose most reliable issue was rocks. Lumbering didn't pan out; it was too far to markets and roads were abysmal. Iron ore was discovered and a forge built, but that enterprise also failed. Later, one of Brown's sons-in-law, Charles Frederick Herreshoff, attempted to revitalize the "old forge," but after a series of setbacks put a bullet through his brain in 1819. He had told his family he would settle the land or it would settle him.

LUMBERJACKS AND RIVER DRIVERS: LOGGING

Adirondack lumberjacks pose for photographer Seneca Ray Stoddard, 1888.

Courtesy of the Adirondack Museum

It was the forest itself, at first a hindrance to settlement, that finally brought human progress into the Adirondacks. As the nation's demand for wood grew in the early 1800s, loggers advanced farther into the region. Little known in 1830 (the source of the Nile River was discovered before the Hudson's, and Pikes Peak was climbed before Mt. Marcy), by 1850 the Adirondacks made New York the leading lumber-producing state in the nation. Lumber barons sought the white pine for its strength and straight grain, and were so successful at finding it that today only a few isolated tracts retain old-growth white pines. Hemlocks were stripped of their bark for its tannin, critical in the leather tanning industry, and the logs left behind in the forest to rot. When in 1867 it was discovered that spruce made the best pulp for paper, that species was doomed to the ax and saw.

Elsewhere, logs were lashed together to form rafts and floated to markets, but Adirondackers discovered you could simply push the logs into the rivers, particularly at "ice out" in the spring, and let the current carry them to mills. Thus was the river drive born in 1813. For the rest of the 19th century, and into the 20th, Adirondack rivers — declared public highways for the purpose — were choked with tumbling logs every spring.

Later, railroads penetrated even the most remote parts of the wilderness to haul out logs year-round. Tupper Lake, a hub of logging activity in the northern Adirondacks, also became a major railroad center, with main lines extending in several directions and branches reaching out from them like tentacles.

Not surprisingly, the harvest of timber was so successful in that pre-conservation era that by 1910 the Adirondack forest was almost a memory. Miles of woodland lay in waste, clearcut and buried in brush. Slopes denuded of vegetation were washed away by rain. Railroad locomotives started conflagrations when sparks from their smokestacks landed on the dead "slash" left behind.

Adirondack visitors now see mile after mile of mature mixed hardwood forests with very little evidence of this wholesale cutting. How the woods recovered is part of a later story of enlightened ideas of forest management. Today, the forest products industry ranks second behind tourism as an economic force in the Adirondacks. Furniture, pallets, and the famous Adirondack baseball bats, as well as raw lumber and pulp for paper, are among the products of this enterprise.

DAYS OF ORE: MINING

Meanwhile, mining was another important element in the 19th-century opening of the Adirondacks. Iron was always a temptress in the Adirondacks — it was there, sometimes in abundance, but hard to get at, hard to transport, and full of an impurity that rendered it costly to process. Mining operations sprang up near Port Henry, Lyon Mountain, Chateaugay Lake, Lake Placid, and Star Lake. All of these forges have since ceased, in some cases leaving behind declining "company towns."

Yet another operation's misfortunes seemed to prophesy the fate of the entire mining industry in the Adirondacks. Iron ore was discovered near Sanford Lake in 1826, and for decades the operators fought against bad roads, lack of water (necessary in the ore-separation process), too much water in the form of floods, economic ups and downs, the accidental shooting death of one of the principals at a spot ever since called Calamity Pond, and most of all, that maddening impurity.

Ironically, this contaminant turned out to be ilmenite, the ore of titanium, and when this was discovered to have applications in the paint and aerospace industries, the mine flourished for a period in the mid-20th century. Iron was then the unwanted component. In the face of declining markets and competition from abroad, the mine shut down in 1989. The story is not all bad for mining, though: garnet near North Creek, zinc and talc in the northwest, and wollastonite near Willsboro have been profitably extracted in recent years.

Presidents in Residence

Although we can't claim that George Washington slept here, the father of our country was certainly aware of the vital importance of fortifications at Ticonderoga and Crown Point along Lake Champlain's western shore. **Thomas Jefferson** and **James Madison** visited Lake George in 1791, on a summer reconnoiter to Vermont that doubled as a vacation; Jefferson, a seasoned world traveler, described the lake as one of the most beautiful he'd ever seen.

In 1817, **James Monroe** skirted the wild edge of what would become the Adirondack Park in a trip from Champlain to Sackets Harbor, on the St. Lawrence River. **Andrew Jackson**, who served in Congress from 1827-1829, was a close friend of Richard Keese II, after whom the village of Keeseville is named. Jackson ("Old Hickory") went north to see Keese, and in honor of the occasion, a hickory sapling was sought to plant in the front yard of the homestead. But no hickories could be found for miles around, so a bitter walnut was substituted. It thrived.

Chester A. Arthur stayed at Mart Moody's Mount Morris House, near Tupper Lake, in 1869, and slept on the floor like everyone else. When he was president, in 1881, Arthur named the guide and innkeeper postmaster of a new settlement named — surprisingly enough — Moody.

Grover Cleveland also knew Moody as a guide. While hunting near Big Wolf Pond, Cleveland reportedly said to him, "There's no wolves, here, darn it! But — there ain't a hundred pencils here, either, goin' every minute to take down everything I say." The president returned to the Adirondacks for his honeymoon, and also stayed at posh places like the Grand View, in Lake Placid, and Saranac Inn.

President **Benjamin Harrison** visited his vice-presidential candidate Whitelaw Reid at Loon Lake during the 1892 campaign, and he whistle-stopped in Crown Point, Lyon Mtn., Bloomingdale, and Saranac Lake. Along the way, he was feted with band concerts and pageants, and given gifts of iron ore and wildflower arrangements. In 1895, Harrison built a rustic log camp named Berkeley Lodge on Second Lake, near Old Forge.

William McKinley made a special trip here to John Brown's grave in 1897, but it was his assassination that led to one of the most exciting footnotes in Adirondack history. **Theodore Roosevelt**, who first came to the mountains as a teenager in 1871, was climbing Mt. Marcy when news of McKinley's imminent demise was cabled north. A guide scrambled up the peak to tell T.R., who made it down in record time. Three relays of teams and wagons whisked him in the murk of night from the Tahawus Club to North Creek, and Roosevelt learned he had become the twenty-sixth president on September 14, 1901, in the North Creek railroad station.

Calvin Coolidge established a summer White House at White Pine Camp, on Osgood Pond, in 1926. This was at the height of Prohibition; silent Cal's place was a mere stone's throw away from Gabriels, a hotbed of bootleg activity. He never knew.

Franklin D. Roosevelt was no stranger to the North Country. He officiated at the opening of the 1932 Winter Olympics, dedicated the Whiteface Memorial Highway in 1935, and celebrated the fiftieth anniversary of the Forest Preserve in Lake Placid that same year.

ADVENTURES IN THE WILDERNESS: THE RECREATION INDUSTRY

By far the major player in Adirondack economics is, as it has been for more than a century and probably will be for the foreseeable future, tourism. This industry came about as the result of a fortuitous combination of a number of factors: a changing attitude toward wilderness, more affluence, and the increasing acceptability of leisure activities following the Civil War.

Early in the 19th century, as had been true for most of human history, wilderness was a thing to be subdued, an enemy of progress, the abode of darkness and evil. Europeans brought this notion to the New World with them; it justified the conquering of the wilderness, along with its animal and human inhabitants. But by the 1840s, as the frontier was pushed farther from most people's consciousness, and life became more than a struggle to stay alive, Americans — particularly Easterners — became less antagonistic toward wild nature. Indeed, as conditions in the cities worsened, folks became nostalgic for a simpler, cleaner time.

Simultaneously, the philosophical movement called Transcendentalism took hold of a small but significant portion of the population. One of its principal tenets was that nature, especially wild nature, is the source of spiritual, emotional, and even physical well-being. Leading lights of Transcendentalism such as Henry David Thoreau and Ralph Waldo Emerson glorified nature. Emerson, Louis Agassiz, James Russell Lowell, and several others spent part of the summer of 1858 in the Adirondacks, in an idyllic setting later dubbed "The Philosophers' Camp," and Emerson's poem "The Adirondacs" was one of the most popular pieces of writing during its time. Meanwhile, artists such as Charles Ingham, Thomas Cole, and A.F. Tait brought visual images of the Adirondacks to the public.

The economic boom in the North during and after the Civil War provided expendable cash for such pursuits as vacations, and as the Puritan work ethic was tempered over time the idea of relaxation became socially acceptable. It remained only for someone to suggest that people visit the Adirondacks.

That someone was a Boston minister, William H.H. Murray, who in 1869 published *Adventures in the Wilderness*, a boldly embellished account of his experiences camping, fishing, and canoeing in the Adirondacks. Although not the first to extol the virtues of such an outing, this book was a hit, the rush was on, and, for better or worse, the region was forever changed. An entire industry was born, spawning rustic inns with guides who took the "city sports" hunting and fishing, then more lavish hotels and better transportation.

The 1870s through 1910 have been called the golden age of the vacation business in the Adirondacks. Hotels rivaled those in major cities for their opulence; the first one in the world to have electricity throughout was the Prospect House, overlooking Blue Mtn. Lake. Along Lake George, Lake Placid, the Saranacs, and into the interior, the fashionable summer scene was on a par with Newport or Saratoga, although here the emphasis was not on sailing or spas, but the great outdoors. Men hunted, fished, told lies, and smoked cigars;

Courtesy of the Adirondack Museum

The Prospect House, built in Blue Mountain Lake in 1881, was the first hotel in the world to have electric lights. Thomas Edison designed the dynamos that powered the building.

ladies took to the woods and waters shaded by parasols, gloves, hats, and veils. For some women, that backwoods experience translated into a quiet cruise across a peaceful pond with a patient guide pulling at the oars, but for the more adventuresome, tramping on the trails was perfect sport.

Families came for the entire summer, bringing trunkfuls of fine china and linen as well as household servants; some stayed in their own "camps," actually veritable villages of well-appointed buildings along a remote lake. U.S. presidents relaxed in the region. Most people came and went via luxurious overnight trains from New York and Boston. Steamboats plied Adirondack lakes, making regular stops at the lodges on their shores.

Decorative touches in an Adirondack "Great Camp" included everything from twig furniture to Japanese lanterns, as this interior view of Camp Cedars shows.

Courtesy of the Adirondack Museum

THE ADIRONDACK CURE

O thers came to the Adirondacks not for fun, but literally to save their lives. Thanks to the pioneering work of Dr. Edward Livingston Trudeau, the Adirondacks became a mecca for tuberculosis sufferers. Trudeau, himself a victim of the disease, believed the best treatment was rest and clean air. Sanitariums in the Saranac Lake area were the destination of thousands of people from the 1880s to the 1950s. By the mid-20th century, antibiotics made treatment easier, but medical research remains a significant part of Saranac Lake life in the 1990s. Robert Louis Stevenson, Philippines president Manual Quezon, baseball great Christy Mathewson, gangster "Legs" Diamond (who brought his bodyguards), composer Béla Bartók, and Mrs. Fiorello LaGuardia were among those who came to "take the cure."

THE CONSERVATION MOVEMENT

New York State Surveyor Verplanck Colvin and his crew explored the unmapped Adirondack wilderness.

"Mount Haystack" from the *Seventh Report of the Adirondack Survey*, 1880

W hether seeking game, a sunny hotel veranda, or a sanitarium, people came to the Adirondacks not to see burned-over wastelands of clearcut forests, but green and healthy woods. They began to clamor for some sort of protection for the Adirondack wilderness.

Indeed, such a movement had begun almost simultaneously with the beginnings of the recreation industry. Conservation was alien to most Americans, living in the midst of such superabundance, but in Europe, where a denser population had put more pressure on fewer resources for much longer, it had become a necessity. A bookish Vermont lawyer named George Perkins Marsh, U.S. ambassador to Italy, saw what steps the Italians had taken and what value they had for an America fast churning its way through its natural resources. In 1864 he published *Man and Nature*, a daunting tome that is credited as the first salvo of the American conservation movement. In it he suggested that Americans adopt European conservation practices, such as forest management, and that the Adirondacks would be a good place to start.

Earlier, a few voices had appealed for some action to stem the destruction of the forests. But Marsh's book provided a practical reason to do so: healthy forests, he said, retained rainfall, regulating its runoff into streams and rivers that supplied "Downstate" with water. "Downstate" meant not only New York's cities, but also its commercial lifeline, the Erie Canal. Suddenly the state's powerful business community had a reason for conservation.

Marsh's call was taken up by many, none more eloquently than Verplanck Colvin, who from 1872 until 1900 took it upon himself, with the irregular support of the state, to survey the entire Adirondack region. In annual reports to the state legislature he argued passionately for creation of some sort of "park or preserve" to save the forests for watersheds and, almost as an off-the-cuff aside, recreation. Eventually, he got both, plus a little more:

• In 1885, the state established in the core of the region the Adirondack Forest Preserve to protect the supply of water to cities and the Erie Canal.

• In 1892, in large part because of continuing abuses of the Forest Preserve by logging interests, the state provided a second layer of armor, the Adirondack State Park, which encompassed the Forest Preserve and thousands of acres of private lands intermingled with it. Thus the park consisted of a mix of public and private lands, an unusual situation that continues to this day.

• In 1894, because abuses still had not ceased, the legislature allowed the voters of New York to amend their constitution to dictate that the Forest Preserve should remain "forever wild." In other words, there would be not conservation but preservation in the Forest Preserve. The woods would not be managed; they would be left to nature. Nowhere else in the world does wilderness have such a triple-ply sheath of protection.

THE ADIRONDACKS IN THE 20TH CENTURY

After the excitement of the 1880s and 1890s, the Adirondacks went into relative dormancy for the first few decades of the 20th century. Ironically, in the years immediately after protective steps were implemented, rampaging fires destroyed much of whatever forest the loggers had left. The careful observer can still find scars from these fires, although the forests have largely recovered. Reforestation and other elements of scientific forestry gradually caught on.

Tourism grew steadily, particularly after World War I, as other industries receded. Although towns such as Saranac Lake and Lake Placid celebrated the coming of cold weather in carnivals replete with ice palaces, parades, and innumerable sporting competitions, it was Melvil Dewey's Lake Placid Club that launched winter as a time for tourism, too. The club's full roster of organized programs, from tobogganing and skating to skiing and sleigh riding, packed visitors' days and nights with action that anyone — athlete or not — could enjoy. The 1932 Winter Olympics in Lake Placid, in which Sonia Henie once again took the gold for figure skating, and the Americans triumphed in bobsledding, also put the Adirondacks on the map for skiers.

By the 1920s, Lake Placid
was a haven for snow lovers.

Courtesy of *Adirondack Life* magazine

More and more people came to camp, hike, and climb the mountains, departing from the sedate vacationing style of the late 1800s. The state responded by building campgrounds near principal highways, along with wilderness trails with three-sided log shelters called lean-tos. The Adirondack Mountain Club was formed by outdoor enthusiasts in 1922. In the booming 1950s and '60s, the notion of vacation homes came into vogue, and the Adirondacks, within a day's drive of millions of urbanites and suburbanites, was a choice location.

However, by the late 1960s, overconsumption, this time by vacationers, was as real a concern as overconsumption by loggers had been 80 years earlier. Completion of Interstate 87, the Adirondack Northway, in 1967, promised only to exacerbate the problem.

Since then, Adirondack affairs have been dominated by a debate, sometimes heated, over how the region should be managed to serve the best interests of residents, visitors, and the environment. In broadest terms, those concerned most about the future of the Adirondack ecosystem have promoted levels of controls on growth by various government agencies, and have supported additional wild-land purchases by the state, while advocates of free-market economic growth and home rule have fought such proposals.

The proliferation of vacation homes prompted conservationist Laurance Rockefeller to propose a national park in the Adirondacks in 1967. That unpopular idea went nowhere, but it did spur his brother, Governor Nelson Rockefeller, to appoint a state commission to study the region's future. Among the commission's proposals for better management released in 1970 was an Adirondack Park Agency (APA) to regulate land use by zoning all land in the park.

When the APA brought out its plan for zoning on state land, which included such steps as banning motorized vehicles in some areas, there was an outburst of protest. A state agency, it was argued, should not tell people what they could and could not do on public property. But when in 1973 the APA issued its plan for restrictions on the use of private land, the outburst became an eruption. This time, the state was telling people what they could and could not do with their own land. Much of this control was vested in zoning laws that regulate the density of buildings per square mile. Other regulations included building setbacks from shorelines and permitted economic activities within different zoning areas. Towns were encouraged to draft their own local zoning ordinances, but very few actually did, due to lack of funds to draft the plans.

The existence of the APA, and more abstractly its role as guardian of the character of the Adirondacks — a definition on which there is no agreement — has colored all subsequent discussions about what to do with the region. Some argue that development can, and should, increase to bolster local business, while others counter that the area's natural assets should not be sacrificed for short-term gain.

As the disagreement over the fundamentals of managing the Adirondack Park has waxed and waned, one thing has remained constant: the undeniable beauty of the landscape. Behind all the wrangling, that stays a basic truth, and something that folks on all sides of the issue can agree on.

In this second century of the Adirondack Park, there's much to discover and appreciate about this special place, regardless of the bugs, rain, ice, snow, and political discussions you may encounter. Read on; if you don't already, perhaps you'll learn to love the Adirondacks, too. Not just in summer, or when the leaves blaze away on the hillsides, but during mud season, blackfly hatches, and when the cold winds blow off Whiteface. If this were an easy place to love, well, it just wouldn't be the Adirondacks.

Nancie Battaglia

An aerial view of Lake Placid and Whiteface Mountain.

CHAPTER TWO

Over the Rivers and Through the Woods

TRANSPORTATION

From Lake George to Raquette Lake, steamboats once sailed Adirondack waters.

The rivers were the first travel corridors in the Adirondacks. By canoe or by snowshoe over the ice, Native Americans and the first Europeans followed these paths of least resistance. Although no river provided passage through the entire immense and rugged region, it was possible to travel from the southwest to northeast corners via the Moose, Raquette, and Saranac river systems with but a few short "carries," the Adirondack word for "portage." The importance of the rivers is underscored by the fact that in the early 1800s they were declared public highways for the purpose of floating logs to market on them.

The first roads were literally hacked out of the forest in the early 1800s, usually to transport iron ore. Later, some of these dirt tracks were corduroyed (paved with logs), but they were never very good, being not much more than wide trails. A stagecoach ride on one could be a life-threatening experience.

Even into the beginnings of the tourist era, the waterways remained the principal routes of conveyance. Craft indigenous to the Adirondacks were designed to suit their environment: the guideboat, light, fast, and maneuverable, with oars rather than paddles, marvelous for fishing and hunting on Adirondack ponds; and tiny steamboats, built to fit the small lakes of the interior.

The first popular overland means of movement was the railroad. Originally built to haul timber out, the railroads quickly became a profitable and convenient way to haul tourists in. In the heyday of the vacation era, a spider web of lines throughout the region saw several passenger trains a day speeding north from East Coast cities to destinations in the park. One of the most popular targets, Blue Mountain Lake, could be reached by a remarkable trip that involved an overnight train ride from New York via Utica, transfer to a steamboat, change to the world's shortest standard-gauge railroad (less than a mile long), and a final transfer to another steamboat for delivery to your hotel of choice.

With the growing popularity of the automobile as the 20th century progressed, roads were gradually improved until they eventually surpassed the railroads, although such special offerings as ski trains enabled passenger service to struggle along until well after World War II.

The late 1960s were a watershed time; the last passenger train serving the interior, the Adirondack Division of the New York Central (the Utica-to-Lake Placid line), rolled to a stop in 1965, and the Adirondack Northway, the only interstate highway in the region, was completed along the eastern edge of the park in 1967. This event seemed at once to assure that the family car would be the way the vast majority of people would travel to the Adirondacks for years to come, and to discourage the development of a public transportation system.

So, if you want to get around in the Adirondacks, heed this advice: buy, rent, beg, or borrow a car. Even if you get here by some other means, once you arrive it can be difficult to do much without one, and renting a car is no mean feat in most places. The region has fewer people than a few blocks in Manhattan do, yet it takes in all or part of 12 counties. Thus, public transportation comes in one of two stripes — slim and none — so be forewarned.

The following information gives you the best routes for access to the Adirondacks, and for getting around once you're here. We start with the most practical means of transportation — your car — and also provide details on bus, train, and air service. Routes that incorporate a ferry crossing are also described. A selection of taxi services in principal communities is listed as well. For car rentals within the Adirondacks (the service has greatly improved as of 1997), we suggest you contact the chamber of commerce or visitor information center of the area you plan to visit; you'll find phone numbers and addresses in this book's Information chapter under "Tourist Information."

BY CAR

HIGHWAYS TO GET YOU HERE

Major highways can get you to the perimeter of the Adirondack Park from all points:

• *From New York:* Take I-87 north. This is the New York State (or Thomas E. Dewey) Thruway, a toll road, to Albany (Exit 24); then it becomes the toll-free Adirondack Northway. Principal exits off the Northway for the interior are 21 (Lake George), roughly four hours from metro New York; 23 (Warrensburg, North Creek, and Blue Mtn. Lake), about 15 minutes farther north; 28 (Schroon Lake, Paradox Lake, and Ticonderoga), about five hours from New York; and 30 (for Lake Placid, Saranac Lake, and the High Peaks), another 15 minutes up the line.

• *From Philadelphia and South:* Take the Northeast Extension of the Pennsylvania Turnpike and then I-81 north to Syracuse. From Syracuse take I-90 east to entry points such as Utica and Amsterdam, or I-81 farther north and then east on Rte. 3 at Watertown to reach the northern areas. Either way, it's not as far as you might think — you can reach the southwest edge of the park in about six hours from Philadelphia. Or you can take I-88 from Binghamton to Schenectady, go east two exits on I-90 and head north on I-87 from Albany; see above, "From New York." And there's always the Garden State Parkway to the New York Thruway, then proceed as above.

• *From Buffalo, Cleveland, and West:* Take I-90 east to Syracuse, then proceed as directed above ("From Philadelphia"). From Buffalo to the edge of the park north of Utica is a little over four hours.

• *From Toronto and Detroit:* Take Rte. 401 toward Montreal. Three toll bridges cross the St. Lawrence River. The one that provides the most direct access not only to the edge of the park but also to such interior locations as Lake Placid and Blue Mtn. Lake leaps from Prescott (Highway 16 exit) to Ogdensburg; the toll is $2.00 U.S. one way. On the U.S. side, take Rte. 37 west a couple of miles to Rte. 68 south to Colton, and Rte. 56 into the park. From Toronto it's about five hours to the edge of the park and seven to the center.

• *From Ottawa:* Take Highway 16 to the Prescott–Ogdensburg toll bridge and proceed as directed above ("From Toronto"). Allow two hours to the edge of the park, four to central points.

• *From Montreal:* Take Highway 15 south; this becomes I-87, the Adirondack Northway, at the border. Principal jumping-off exits for the interior are 38 (Plattsburgh), only an hour (plus customs wait, which can be lengthy) from the outskirts of Montreal; and 34 (Keeseville), 20 minutes south of Exit 38.

• *From Boston:* Take the Mass. Pike, I-90, to I-87, then head north and follow the directions given under "From New York," above, to get past Albany. Or, take I-93 north to I-89, to one of the Lake Champlain ferry crossings described below. Via Albany, the Adirondacks are about four hours from Boston; via the ferries they're closer to five, but the ferries are fun.

HIGHWAYS TO GET YOU AROUND ONCE YOU GET HERE

North and South

Not surprisingly, four of the five north-south highways that traverse the Adirondacks do so in the narrow corridor between Lake Champlain and the

ADIRONDACK ACCESS

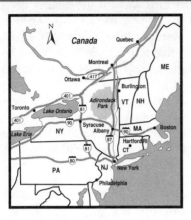

Blue Mtn. Lake is central — it's $1 \frac{1}{2}$ to 2 hours to the edge of the park in every direction — so this location will serve as a reference point in determining about how long a drive to the Adirondacks will take:

CITY	MILES TO BLUE MTN. LAKE	APPROXIMATE TIME TO BLUE MTN. LAKE
Albany	105	2 hrs
Binghamton	220	4 hrs
Boston (via Albany)	270	$5 \frac{1}{2}$ hrs
Buffalo	280	$5 \frac{1}{2}$ hrs
Burlington, VT	100	3 hrs (involves ferry)
Montreal	165	$3 \frac{1}{2}$ hrs*
New York	260	$5 \frac{1}{2}$ hrs
Ottawa	150	$3 \frac{1}{2}$ hrs*
Philadelphia	390	8 hrs
Rochester	210	$4 \frac{1}{2}$ hrs
Syracuse	140	3 hrs
Toronto	320	7 hrs*
Utica	90	2 hrs

*plus possible delays crossing border

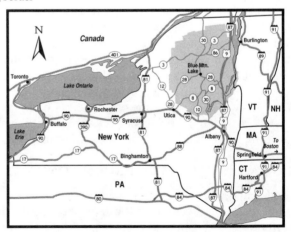

mountains. This is where much of the region's population and many of its attractions are located, and it's also on a direct line between two dense concentrations of population: New York City and Montreal. These routes are:

• *NY Rte. 9N,* which makes a scenic ramble from Saratoga Springs northwest to Corinth and Lake Luzerne, then east to Lake George village, then up to Hague, and to Lake Champlain at Ticonderoga, where it meets . . .

• *NY Rte. 22,* which hugs Lake Champlain all the way from Whitehall, up to Ticonderoga, where it joins 9N. The combined routes have magnificent views of the lake on the east and farmland in the valley beneath the High Peaks on the west, passing through Crown Point and Port Henry. At Westport, Rte. 22 follows the lake valley north to Willsboro, while 9N heads west to Elizabethtown, over Spruce Hill and on to Keene. This historic route passes through Upper Jay, Jay, and Au Sable Forks, paralleling the Ausable River, and connects again with Rte. 22 at Keeseville.

• *U.S. Rte. 9* begins in the park just north of Glens Falls and skirts Schroon Lake and the Schroon and Boquet rivers, but its route has been mostly supplanted by . . .

• *I-87,* the Adirondack Northway, a full-blown interstate highway that won an award as "America's Most Scenic Highway" in 1966-1967.

• *NY Rte. 30,* the fifth north-south route, bisects the region from Gloversville via Speculator, Indian Lake, Blue Mtn. Lake, Long Lake, Tupper Lake, and Paul Smiths to Malone. It's famous for some unexpected extra-wide segments between Long Lake and Tupper. The remote and lightly populated western half of the region has no north-south highways.

East and West

Reflecting the reality that most travel in the Adirondacks is and always has been north-south, only three highways traverse the entire region on the east-west axis, and two of them cover some of the same territory. These are:

• *NY Rte. 28,* which forms a huge semicircle from Warrensburg through North Creek, Indian Lake, Blue Mtn. Lake, Inlet, Old Forge, and down to Utica.

• *NY Rte. 8,* which zigzags west from Hague, on Lake George, through Brant Lake, Chestertown, Johnsburg, Speculator, Lake Pleasant, Piseco, Hoffmeister, and southwest to Utica.

• *NY Rte. 3,* which crosses the northern part of the park from Plattsburgh, to Cadyville, Redford, Vermontville, Bloomingdale, Saranac Lake, Tupper Lake, Piercefield, Childwold, Cranberry Lake, Star Lake, and exits the Blue Line west to Watertown.

Additional Routes

Other shorter but scenic routes in the Adirondacks include:

• *Northeast on NY Rte. 73* from Underwood (Exit 30 of the Northway) to Lake Placid, which offers a 45-minute panorama of the High Peaks.

• *West on NY Rte. 86* from Jay, past the foot of Whiteface Mtn. and through dramatic Wilmington Notch to Lake Placid, then on to Saranac Lake and Paul Smiths.

• *East on NY Rte. 374* from Chateaugay, past the Chateaugay lakes and Lyon Mtn. to Plattsburgh, which, in addition to views of the Adirondacks, provides a long-distance scan across silvery Lake Champlain to the Green Mountains of Vermont as it drops down Dannemora Mtn.

• *Northwest on NY Rte. 28N* from North Creek on Rte. 28 to Long Lake. Be sure to stop at the roadside rest area at Newcomb, where a display identifies the High Peaks arrayed to the north.

• *East on the "Number Four" Road* from Lowville, past Stillwater Reservoir and on to Big Moose and Eagle Bay, which is on NY Rte. 28. This drive offers not so much great views as a sense of the forest depths of the western Adirondacks. About half of the 45 miles is unpaved, and there are no services over the full distance.

The Adirondack North Country Association (ANCA) has designed several driving tours both in and around the Adirondacks. These are arranged so as to hit scenic vistas, historic markers, craft shops, and so on. You can pick up a map of these routes at tourist centers and chambers of commerce, or call ANCA at 518-891-6200.

BY BUS

Considering the size of the Adirondack region — you could fit Connecticut inside it — it's astonishing how little bus service exists. There's only one round trip a day that's of any use, and once you get off the bus you're dependent on traveling by foot, or finding sparse taxi service and even sparser rental car possibilities. If you do plan to use bus service, however, here are your options:

• *Greyhound Lines, Inc.,* plies the I-87 ("Northway") route on the eastern edge of the park several times a day, but declines to stop anywhere within the Blue Line. The best you can do is Glens Falls or Plattsburgh. For more information: 518-434-8095 (Albany terminal).

• *CHAMP Express* offers service within Essex County and between Lake Placid and Plattsburgh, connecting with Greyhound buses there. For more information: 518-523-4431.

• *Adirondack Trailways* is your best bet for bus access, and offers the following routes:

Daily trips into the interior: You can escape Manhattan as early as 10am from the Port Authority Bus Terminal, from even-numbered gates 28-36 for Lake George, Schroon Lake, Keene Valley, and many other Adirondack towns.

Adirondack Trailways bus stations are found in restaurants and diners across the region.

Nancie Battaglia

Allow five hours to reach Warrensburg, one of the southernmost Adirondack stops. Other Trailways buses leave at 1, 2, and 4pm; call ahead for a schedule. A one-way ticket from New York City to Warrensburg cost $50 in 1997. South-bound trips leave Canton at 8:45am daily and arrive in New York at 6:50pm.

Some of the stops on this run help you realize you're not in urban America anymore. The "bus station" in Keene Valley, for example, is the Noon Mark Diner; in Lake Placid, it's the Main Street Deli.

The weekend special also operates on this route as far as Saranac Lake, where it splits off to end in Tupper Lake. It goes north on Friday only, leaving New York at 5:45pm and arriving in Tupper Lake at 12:55am, and returns on

---

Deer Crossing

Keep your eyes peeled for deer as you drive through the Adirondacks — not only to see them, which will be a pleasant memory of your trip, but also to avoid hitting them.

Deer are most active in the late afternoon and evening, and particularly just after sunset, when they're also hardest to see. They often travel in pairs or small groups; if one crosses the road ahead of you, others are likely to follow. They're especially mobile during the fall "leaf-peeping" season, for several reasons: that's their breeding season; they have to travel more to find food; and hunters disrupt their daily routines. In winter they seek out plowed roads since the going is easier.

One more thing: the instinctive reaction of a deer caught by car headlights is to freeze, not to scramble out of the way. It's up to you to miss, if you have time and can do it safely. Your best bet: drive alertly, obey speed limits — and take those "DEER CROSSING, X MILES" signs seriously.

Sunday only, leaving Tupper Lake at 4pm and arriving in New York at 11:20pm.

Five other buses from New York/Albany north: Two penetrate the Adirondacks as far as Warrensburg and the other three give it up in Glens Falls, just outside the Adirondack Park. There's also summer-only service along the west shore of Lake George to Ticonderoga.

For more information: Adirondack Trailways, 1-800-225-6815, or at the New York City number, 212-947-5300.

In Chapter Three, *Lodging*, accommodations within walking distance of local bus stops are noted.

BY TRAIN

Courtesy of the Adirondack Museum

The New York Central's Adirondack Division station at Thendara, circa 1927.

AMTRAK

Amtrak operates one train a day each way between New York City and Montreal, which was brought to national attention in the 1997 PBS special *America's Scenic Rail Journeys. "The Adirondack"* leaves each city in the morning and reaches its destination the same evening (schedules are different on Sundays), closely following the west shore of Lake Champlain for the better part of 90 miles through the park. The New York departure is from Penn Station (212-582-6875), not Grand Central as it was for years. It makes several stops in the Adirondacks, but how to get around once you are deposited at these places is problematic. You can arrange, *in advance,* for shuttle service from the storybook Victorian depot in Westport to Lake Placid (or Elizabeth-town or Keene) by calling 518-523-4431 or 518-523-1475. It may not be what it once was, but compared to buses and puddle-jumper airplanes, this remains the snazziest way to get to the Adirondacks.

The trip is spectacular, involving tunnels, high trestles, rocky ledges 150 feet above the waters of Lake Champlain, and vistas of farm and forest, river, lake, and mountain that simply cannot be had any other way. The Champlain Valley Heritage Network has published a descriptive map of the route (available from the Essex County Visitors Bureau, 1-800-PLACID), which also lists local taxi service. The least expensive Fort Edward–Plattsburgh round-trip fare was $28 in 1997.

In addition, **Amtrak's Empire Service** leaves New York's Penn Station several times a day and stops in Albany-Rensselaer, Schenectady, and Utica, where you can arrange to rent a car by calling 1-800-654-3131 (Hertz) or 1-800-331-1212 (Avis). One train a day from Boston hooks up with this route at Albany-Rensselaer. Coming from the west, Empire Service originates in Buffalo; Chicago–Boston/New York and Toronto–New York Amtrak trains also ply this route.

For more information: 1-800-USA-RAIL (872-7245) or 1-800-523-5700.

THE SKI TRAIN

The ski train still exists, although not actually as a distinct route anymore. Special deals to Whiteface Mtn. from several Northeast cities are available, with pick-up and return to the Westport station. For more information: 1-800-899-2558.

BY FERRY

The only way to get to the Adirondacks from the east is to cross Lake Champlain, largest freshwater lake in America after the Great Lakes. You can do

The ferry from Essex, New York to Charlotte, Vermont is one of four car ferries that cross Lake Champlain.

Nancie Battaglia

Winter Driving

All those feet of snow the Adirondacks are famed for may be great news for skiers and snowmobilers, but what about the road conditions, you might wonder. Throughout the park, the state and county highway departments have prowling fleets of snow plows that toil night and day to keep roads clear; it's probably a good bet that Adirondack roads after a deep snow are in better condition than suburban streets after a modest flurry. For several years, a "bare roads" policy has been in effect for the North Country, meaning that sand and salt are applied liberally when roads may be slippery. Another plus for winter driving these days is the prevalence of four-wheel and front-wheel-drive cars, which both handle better on slick roads than the traditional rear-wheel-drive vehicles. (If you're coming to the wintry Adirondacks in a pick-up truck, van, or passenger car with rear-wheel drive, try putting at least 150 pounds of weight — concrete blocks, sandbags, whatever — over your rear axle to help traction.)

The worst driving scenarios often occur at the beginning or end of winter, when temperatures hovering at the freezing point can cause a mixture of snow, rain, and sleet, with perhaps a little fog near lakes and low cold spots. Then it's best to consider your options: can you wait out the storm at your lodgings, or are you prepared to rest at a remote pull-out if conditions deteriorate? Every winter traveler's car should carry a sleeping bag, a small shovel, a snow scraper, extra windshield-washing fluid, a powerful flashlight, and some candy bars, just in case you need to dig out of a snowbank, or sit quietly beside the road for a few hours as the weather takes its course.

---

that on the bridge at Port Henry, which has a nice view that lasts for about 30 seconds, but why not enjoy yourself and take one of the Lake Champlain ferries? The views last for up to an hour and you don't have to steer. Three of the four crossings are operated by the oldest continuously running inland navigation company in America. Rates vary depending upon type of vehicle, number and age of persons in it, etc.; those shown are for car and driver, one way, in 1995.

• *From Charlotte, Vermont, to Essex:* This may be the most scenic route, seeming to deliver you truly into the mountains. Crossing time is 20 minutes; trips run from approximately April 1 to New Year's, departing Charlotte on the hour and on the half hour, from 8:30am to 7:30pm during the summer season. $6.75. For more information call 802-864-9804.

• *From Burlington, Vermont, to Port Kent:* This is almost as scenic, and delightful for its relaxing one-hour crossing of the widest part of the lake. Trips run several times a day from mid-May through mid-October. Snacks and light meals, including a continental breakfast, can be had on board. $12.00. 802-864-9804.

• *From Grand Isle, Vermont, north of Burlington, to Plattsburgh:* A ways north of the Adirondacks, this route provides a decent if long-distance view of them. It operates year-round, blasting through ice packs in even the coldest snaps, generally every 20 minutes from 5am to 1:20am. Crossing time is 12 minutes. $6.75. For more information: 802-864-9804.

• *From Orwell, Vermont, to Fort Ticonderoga:* This crossing is a living museum. Following a route that's been in use since the British army arrived in the 1700s, it brings you to the foot of the promontory on which the restored fort reposes. This is one of the few cable-guided ferries left in America: The cable is attached at each landing and power is provided by a tugboat. Crossing time is six minutes; the one-way fare is about $6 per car, and trips run from 8am to 6pm, from early May through late October, and until 9pm, from July 1 through Labor Day. There's no schedule; "We just go back and forth," the captain says.

For more information: 802-897-7999.

BY AIR

COMMERCIAL AIRPORTS

In all this vast territory there's only one commercial airport: Adirondack Airport at Lake Clear, about 15 minutes from Saranac Lake and 30 from Lake Placid. In early 1997 it was served by USAirways (1-800-428-4322), flying 19-seat Beechcraft planes that look like cigars with wings. Service consisted of three direct round trips (one morning, one afternoon, one evening) from Albany, scene of USAir connections. Forget weekends, though; none of these goes on Saturdays, and only one on Sunday nights. Fares are all over the lot, depending on the time of year, how far ahead you purchase your ticket, and so forth. Nonrefundable prices for 1997 for a flight from Albany were $277 round trip or $215 one way, with 21-day notice.

As these commuter airlines come and go like fireflies on a summer night, it's best to call first to make sure this one's still airborne. The airport number is 518-891-2290. If you're calling another airport or a travel agent, ask about "Saranac Lake," not "Adirondack." Car rentals are available at the airport: USAirways can help you book with Hertz or call the agency at 1-800-654-3131.

Cities just outside the Adirondacks that offer air service are Albany, Syracuse, and Burlington, Vermont (amenities such as jets and a wider variety of rental cars), and Watertown and Plattsburgh (puddle-jumpers). The best source of up-to-date information about these options is your travel agent.

PRIVATE AIRPORTS

Private airports, ranging from a paved strip down to a patch of grass in the woods, can be found scattered about the Adirondacks. Consult a good navigational map to locate these. Perhaps the most significant is on the outskirts of Lake Placid, with a 4300-foot runway and complete facilities: 518-523-2473.

Another is at Piseco, at which pick-up can be arranged by calling Don Bird's taxi service, fifty miles away in Inlet, 315-357-3631. Better be prepared to be met at most of the others; taxi service and cars to rent are nowhere to be found in most cases. For the truly adventuresome, you can charter a seaplane to pick you up on the East River, at 23rd St. and Waterside Plaza, New York City; check under "Scenic Flights" in Chapter Six, *Recreation*, for seaplane services.

BY TAXIS AND SUCH

Taxi and other livery service in the Adirondacks varies radically in terms of availability (or even existence). Services in principal communities do include the following:

Lake George	Lake George Taxi, 518-668-9600
	Adirondack Limousine, 518-668-5466
Lake Placid	Liberty Taxi, 518-523-3333
	Jan's Taxi, 518-523-1891
	Thomas Pelkey, 518-523-9797/2324
Saranac Lake	Lavigne Taxi, 518-891-2444
	Corrow Taxi, 518-891-5082
	Northway Limousine, 518-891-0338
Tupper Lake	Kennedy's Taxi, 518-359-2193
	Lucky 8 (taxi and limo), 518-359-3849
Inlet/Old Forge area	Don Bird, 315-357-3631

BUMP!

As winter runs its course, and longer, sunnier days warm the black asphalt highway surfaces, the frost begins to melt below the roads. During cold nights, underground moisture freezes again, and a cycle of expansion and contraction in the ground begins. With bedrock not too far beneath the soil, the ice can only expand upward, sometimes pushing rocks along with it, and "frost heaves" in the roads are the result. These bumps can range from minor humps that are barely noticeable to deep dips that can send cars airborne. Usually, the bumps occur in roughly the same spots each year, and highway crews are diligent about marking these hazards. Watch for the large diamond-shape "BUMP" signs as a warning to slow down; the treacherous spot itself may be marked with orange flagging on sticks placed on the shoulder of the road, or smaller, plain yellow diamonds set back on the right-of-way. Be alert; try to brake well before you reach the bump.

CHAPTER THREE
Rustic, Classic, and Basic
LODGING

Holland's Blue Mountain Lake Hotel circa 1886. This massive lodge stood near the present-day intersection of Rtes. 28, 28N, and 30.

Travelers to the eastern Adirondacks in the early 1800s were welcomed at inns and taverns, although accommodations occasionally felt short of expectations: a visitor to the Pavilion, a hotel near Ticonderoga, described the place in 1855 as "noisy and ill-conducted . . . The food is bad, the cooking worse, the rooms are small, the bedsteads large, and you have your choice between a feather-bed and one made of corn-husks, with now and then a corn-cob thrown in by way of variety."

After the Civil War, and the publication of *Adventures in the Wilderness* by William H.H. Murray, the entire Adirondack region — from the High Peaks to the lake country — became popular as a tourist destination. The demand for lodging — luxurious lodging that could compare with hotels in Newport or Saratoga Springs — grew, and huge hotels multiplied on lakeshores from Blue Mtn. Lake to Westport, Bolton Landing to Lake Placid. Lake George's Fort William Henry Hotel had scores of rooms and tiers of piazzas; the Mansion House, in Elizabethtown, boasted rooms for 200 guests; Paul Smith's St. Regis House was described as "first class in every respect, and patronized by the very best class of people in the country."

Those vast hotels succumbed to fire and/or the changing tastes of the traveling public. The Adirondacks in the late 19th century were an exclusive place, a destination that was difficult to reach, and with the advent of modern steamship travel, the spas of Europe became accessible to the wealthy. At the same time, the middle class was increasing in numbers, automobiles were becoming affordable, and ordinary people started taking vacations. They eschewed stodgy old hotels and headed for tent campgrounds, resorts, and roadside cabins.

Covewood, on Big Moose Lake, was built in the 1920s and featured a main lodge for socializing plus private sleeping cabins.

Nancie Battaglia

Resorts of the 1920s combined planned activities like dances, waterfront contests, and games for kids with amenities such as common dining rooms and private cabins. The housekeeping-cottage colonies — groups of buildings without a central dining facility — took that notion of privacy a step further, and were popular because families could prepare all their meals. Motels, designed for people who just wanted a clean place to rest for a few hours, were built on the edges of many towns.

The 1980 Winter Olympics in Lake Placid led economic planners to worry that not enough rooms would be available for the legions of spectators. Many homeowners took the plunge into accommodating guests, and the Olympic legacy is many freshly converted bed & breakfasts. B&Bs continue to thrive, with a flurry of businesses opening in 1997, as owners of historic properties in the Champlain Valley and the central Adirondacks began taking in guests.

A word here differentiating the various lodging terms: generally, in New York, a *bed & breakfast* is defined as a place that holds 10 or fewer guests. Breakfast is served and the owner usually lives on the premises. An *inn* is larger, often serves dinner or lunch as well as breakfast, and has to comply with state codes for public safety and food service. Then there is the *bed-&-breakfast inn*, which is a place that's bigger than a B&B, is regularly inspected by the state, and offers the morning meal in the price of a night's stay. As long as we're on the subject of definitions, a *housekeeping cabin* includes a kitchen or kitchenette, so guests can cook meals.

Nowadays the variety of Adirondack lodgings covers the full spectrum: there are country lodges that offer hearty meals and access to hiking or cross-country skiing; vast old hotels filled with antiques; lakeside resorts with a full roster of activities; housekeeping cottages nestled by the beach; and motels. For many visitors, the classic Adirondack vacation is a week on the lake in the same housekeeping cottage that they enjoyed as a child. Some families come back the same week every year, and for that reason, many of the nicest places are booked years in advance. If you want to try a housekeeping cabin and have some flexibility in your vacation time, consider May–June or September–October.

Listed in this chapter you'll find a whole range of accommodations. Our criteria for selection was to seek out places with a special approach — an individual personality — that offer comfort, cleanliness, and hospitality. For some listings, the setting is a primary consideration; in others, it's wonderful architecture; some sites offer first-class amenities and services; in still others, it's the hosts and hostesses that set the place apart. With this kind of intuitive categorization, you'll find positive notes on a few modest, inexpensive places that succeed at what they're trying to do, just as you'll find perhaps briefer mention of the highly acclaimed spots. Above all, we try to offer a range of prices and options.

At the end of the chapter, you'll find a listing of motels. There are many, many more places to stay in the Adirondacks than you'll read about in this book (if we listed all the places in Lake George village alone that would fill this entire chapter); phone numbers and World Wide Web addresses for tourist information offices can be found in Chapter Eight, *Information*.

ADIRONDACK LODGING NOTES

RATES

Some cottages and resorts are available by the week only in July and August, and this is indicated in the "Min. Stay" section of the information box. Extrapolate the per-night, double-occupancy rate by six, and you should get an idea of what a week's visit costs. It's possible for a single woman to stay at Wiawaka Holiday House, on Lake George, for $200 per week, just as a couple can spend upwards of $800 for a single night at The Point.

Rates quoted are for per-room, double occupancy during the prime tourist season, which in most cases is July and August. Some places that are open year-round charge more during January–March because of increased heating costs. You can usually expect lower rates for midweek stays, off-season rentals, or package deals; it's definitely worthwhile to ask. In places described as bed & breakfasts, you can expect that breakfast is included in the price of your room; many resorts and inns offer full or modified American meal plans.

Some places add ten or fifteen percent gratuity to the bill and motel and hotel rooms are subject to New York's seven-percent sales tax. The rates that are listed here don't reflect those additional charges.

Very Inexpensive	Under $40 per night, double occupancy
Inexpensive	$40–$70
Moderate	$70–$100
Expensive	$100–$200
Very Expensive	Over $200

MINIMUM STAY

Many of the resorts and housekeeping cabins rent units by the week only in the summer, with guests arriving and leaving on a Saturday or Sunday. In the winter, some accommodations ask for a two-night minimum stay in order to make it worthwhile to turn up the heat in the cabin. Midweek in the off-season many places will happily welcome overnight guests; if no minimum stay is specified, you can assume that one night is fine.

DEPOSIT/CANCELLATION

Reservation arrangements vary greatly from place to place. Some resorts and cottages that rent by the week ask for a 50-percent deposit; some winter-season places have a "no-snow" cancellation policy so that guests don't get stuck if the weather fails to cooperate.

PRIVATE RENTALS AND RESERVATION SERVICES

Most real-estate agents handle private summer-home rentals. These places might be anything from backwoods camps to new condominiums to lovely old houses with private lakefront, boats, and all the up-to-date creature comforts. *Adirondack Vacation Home Rentals* (Richard Knight; 315-369-6242; PO Box 190, Old Forge NY 13420) offers scores of spotless private camps and houses year-round in the Old Forge, Big Moose, and Inlet area. The Mt. Marcy Marketplace classifieds, found in the bimonthly *Adirondack Life* magazine (518-946-2191; PO Box 410, Jay NY 12941), can be a terrific source for vacation rentals throughout the region. For the Lake Placid area, try *Brief Encounters Realty* (518-523-3433; PO Box 390, Lake Placid NY 12946). Securing private accommodations takes considerable planning, but can be ideal if you're traveling with pets or have a large family in tow.

The parkwide *Adirondack Bed & Breakfast Reservation Service* (Nadia Korths; 1-800-552-BNBS; 10 Park Pl., Saranac Lake NY 12983) can help you set up an inn-to-inn tour. About 20 high-quality bed & breakfasts (including a few outside the Adirondack Park) are offered; special bicycling, boating, and spa weekends are scheduled. New in 1997 is the *Bed & Breakfast Adirondack Collection* (1-888-222-9789), which markets ten lodges in the eastern Adirondacks.

Some private campgrounds are listed in this chapter, but a list of all of the Department of Environmental Conservation campgrounds in the Adirondack Park can be found in Chapter Six, *Recreation*.

CREDIT CARDS

Credit cards are abbreviated as follows:

AE: American Express
CB: Carte Blanche
D: Discover

DC: Diners Club
MC: MasterCard
V: Visa

LODGING IN THE ADIRONDACKS

LAKE GEORGE AND SOUTHEASTERN ADIRONDACKS

Bolton Landing

HILLTOP COTTAGE BED & BREAKFAST
Owners: Anita and Charlie Richards.
518-644-2492.
6883 Lakeshore Dr.
Open: Year-round.
Price: Inexpensive.
Credit Cards: MC, V.
Special Features: No pets; no small children; no smoking.

The Bolton Landing to Lake George road was originally known as "Millionaires' Row," and Hilltop Cottage belonged to a caretaker for one of the grand estates. It's directly across the street from the Marcella Sembrich Memorial Studio, a museum honoring the Romanian-born diva, and once housed her music students. The clapboard cottage has three guest rooms upstairs; one has a queen-size bed and a private bath, while the other two share a bath. Anita, a former German teacher, and

Charlie, a retired guidance counselor, bought the 11-room house in 1985 and opened as it a B&B three years later. Hilltop Cottage is a friendly, homey place, and after a breakfast of German apple pancakes on the screen porch, you can walk over to Bolton's tennis courts and lakefront parks.

The Sagamore Hotel occupies a prime spot on Lake George; the Morgan, *shown in the foreground, offers cruises for guests.*

Nancie Battaglia

THE SAGAMORE HOTEL
Managing Director: W.
    Robert McIntosh.
518-644-9400.
www.thesagamore.com.
Sagamore Rd.
Open: Year-round.
Price: Expensive to Very
    Expensive.
Credit Cards: AE, DC, MC,
    V.
Handicap Access: Several
    units; elevators in hotel.
Special Features: 2 gourmet
    restaurants; spa; fitness
    center; tennis courts;
    conference facilities;
    children welcome; no
    pets.

For more than a century there's been a Sagamore Hotel overlooking Lake George. Completed in 1883, the grand lodge has survived two fires and weathered the Depression, but gradually declined during the seventies. In 1983 the island property was bought by a real-estate developer who launched extensive renovations. Today the Sagamore Hotel is the pride of the community and winner of numerous awards for excellence in serving the traveling public.

The elegantly appointed public areas include a conservatory with lake views, the Trillium Dining Room, the Sagamore Dining Room, a casual pub, an art gallery, and a gift shop. Guests have 350 deluxe units to choose from, including suites, hotel bedrooms, lakeside lodges, and executive retreats with lofts. The list of Sagamore amenities is impressive: a huge indoor pool, spa and fitness center, miniature golf, an indoor tennis-and-racquetball facility, outdoor tennis courts, playground, a beautiful sandy beach, docks for guests' boats, and a Donald Ross–designed championship golf course two miles away.

The Sagamore Hotel is a popular spot for conferences, offering excellent facilities for large and small groups. There's no need to leave the kids at home if one or both parents are attending meetings: the social department has plenty of supervised activities for children.

Chestertown

The Chester Inn is a handsome Greek Revival home in Chestertown.

Nancie Battaglia

THE CHESTER INN
Owners: Bruce and
  Suzanne Robbins.
518-494-4148.
Main St./Rte. 9, near the
  town hall.
Open: Year-round.
Price: Moderate.
Credit Cards: MC, V.
Special Features: No pets;
  children over 12
  welcome; smoking in
  designated areas only.

One of Chestertown's beautiful homes that is listed on the National Register of Historic Places, this Greek Revival inn dates back to 1837. Beyond the grand hall, with its mahogany railings and grain-painted woodwork, there are four lovely second-floor guest rooms with private baths, including the Victorian Suite, which has its own sitting room and bath with a deep, old-fashioned tub. Downstairs is a common room with a TV/VCR and plenty of books. Guests are welcome to explore the 13-acre property, which has gardens, a horse barn, smokehouse, and an early cemetery, and it's a short walk to the Main Street Ice Cream Parlor or to a movie at the Carol Theatre. Nondrivers take note: Chestertown is a regular stop on the Adirondack Trailways bus line, and this inn is just a block from the station.

**THE FRIENDS LAKE
  INN**
Owners: Sharon and Greg
  Taylor.
518-494-4751.
Friends Lake Rd.
Open: Year-round.
Price: Expensive, MAP;
  Moderate, B&B.
Credit Cards: AE, MC, V.

For most of its 130-year history, the Friends Lake Inn has been a hostelry of one kind or another, although its first tenants, the tannery workers, would marvel to see people rather than cowhides soaking in the enormous wooden hot tub outdoors. Sharon and Greg have completed extensive renovations on the building and guests now enjoy 14 comfortable rooms and small suites, all with private baths. Bedrooms have brass or

Min. Stay: 2 nights on
weekends; 3 nights on
holiday weekends; 1
night midweek.
Special Features: Outdoor
hot tub; cross-country-ski
trails; mountain-bike
rentals; guide service for
outdoor treks; gourmet
restaurant; extensive
wine list.

iron bedsteads, patchwork quilts, and antiques;
many have fireplaces, whirlpool tubs, and views
of Friends Lake.

Truly an inn for all seasons, guests can enjoy
sleigh rides and cross-country skiing on 32 kilometers of groomed trails here in the winter; fishing in the spring; swimming and mountain biking
in the summer; hiking in the fall. From time to
time, there are wine-, Scotch-, or beer-tasting dinners and murder-mystery weekends. Small busi-
ness conferences are easily accommodated. There's no need to travel far for
dinner — the restaurant on the first floor is delightful. Inquire about seasonal
packages that combine lodging with golf, rafting, or skiing; midweek bed-&-
breakfast stays and two-night romantic getaways are reasonably priced.

**LANDON HILL BED &
BREAKFAST**
Owners: Judy and Carl
Johnson.
518-494-2599.
Landon Hill Rd.
Open: Year-round.
Price: Moderate.
Credit Cards: MC, V.
Min. Stay: 2 nights on
weekends
Special Features: Children
welcome; no pets; no
smoking.

In 1995 this lovely Victorian home set among
rolling hills on a country lane was opened as a
bed & breakfast. The place is peaceful and comfortable. A beautiful oak spiral staircase leads you to
the four tastefully decorated guest rooms upstairs
(two with private baths), and downstairs are a
guest room and bath that are handicap accessible.
Before breakfast, have coffee and fresh muffins by
the wood stove, then, after stoking up on homemade quiche and fresh fruit, explore the Johnsons'
89 acres, or head for Chestertown's historic district
or the nearby Schroon River for fishing and canoeing. Landon Hill is just a mile from I-87, the North-
way, so it's a convenient jumping-off spot for further adventures. Inquire about
art workshops occasionally offered here.

Diamond Point

CANOE ISLAND LODGE
Owners: Jane and William
Busch.
518-668-5592.
Lake Shore Dr.
Closed: Mid-Oct.–mid-
May.
Price: Expensive.
Min. Stay: 3 nights.
Credit Cards: None.

Back in 1943 Bill Busch financed the down payment on Canoe Island with a couple hundred
bushels of buckwheat, and in June 1946 he welcomed
the first guests to his lodge. The 21-acre, 25-building
complex now offers all kinds of family-vacation
options from quaint log cabins to modern suites and
private chalets. There are clay tennis courts, a sandy
beach on Lake George, hiking trails, and numerous
boats to sail. Perhaps the best part of a stay here,

Special Features: Private island; sand beach; sailboats; rowboats; windsurfers; tennis; children welcome.

though, is the chance to enjoy the lodge's very own 5-acre island, about ³/₄ mile offshore. Regularly scheduled shuttle boats take guests to the island where they can swim, snorkel, fish, sunbathe, and explore a beautiful, undeveloped part of the lake.

The Busch family takes great pride in offering hearty European-style meals with home-grown vegetables, homemade bread and pastries, and treasured old-country recipes. On Thursdays, there are island picnics and on Sundays, gala buffets; dances, movies, and special children's programs are also on tap, although there's no pressure to join in. Memorial Day weekend features a traditional Maifest with dancing and a costume party; Columbus Day weekend has an Oktoberfest with live music followed by midnight buffets.

The lodge accommodates 175 people at peak capacity. In spring and fall, rates include breakfast, lunch, and dinner; from July 1–Sept. 7, a modified American plan is in effect.

Hadley

SARATOGA ROSE INN
Owners: Nancy and Anthony Merlino.
518-696-2861,
1-800-942-5025.
Rockwell St.
Open: Year-round.
Price: Moderate to Expensive.
Min. Stay: 2 nights on weekends.
Credit Cards: MC, V.
Special Features: Fireplaces; no children under 12; smoking permitted downstairs only.

In its heyday Hadley was a bustling community with a variety of waterpowered businesses relying on the Hudson River. Well-to-do mill owners built elaborate mansions in town, and today, one of them has been restored to its former glory by Nancy and Anthony Merlino. Saratoga Rose — on sedate, tree-lined Rockwell Street, it's a surprising sight in exuberant shades of buff, shocking pink, and mauve — is now a bed-&-breakfast inn with four second-floor guest rooms, each with private bath and air conditioning. The Queen Anne Room has a king-size bed and working fireplace; the Garden Room has a private sun porch and spa tub. The Carriage House has a very private large chamber with a queen-size canopy bed, fireplace, and a secluded deck with jacuzzi. All rooms are decorated with period antiques and prints.

Two-night packages are available to inn guests, with perks like clubhouse passes to the Saratoga harness-racing track, guided horseback-riding trips, scenic airplane flights, or a visit to Saratoga Springs for a mineral-water bath and relaxing massage.

Saratoga Rose has a very good restaurant (see Chapter Five) that's open to the public year-round (ask about "Gourmet-to-Go" options), and a small pub room; in the summer, the wide, geranium-draped veranda is a pleasant spot to enjoy supper.

Hague

THE LOCUST INN
Innkeeper: James Coates.
518-543-6035.
Rtes. 9N & 8.
Open: Year-round.
Price: Moderate.
Min. Stay: 2 nights.
Credit Cards: D, MC, V.
Special Features: 1 handicap
access room; art gallery;
beach; boat ramp; chil-
dren welcome; no pets.

A graceful homestead built in 1865, the Locust Inn was renovated in 1992 and launched as a bed & breakfast. It's conveniently next to the town beach and boat ramp on Lake George; Hague Brook flows next to the property and offers good fly-fishing in the spring.

The three attractively appointed guest suites — all with lake views — have queen beds, private baths, sitting areas, and TV/VCRs. The carriage house is a separate cottages located on Hague Brook. Innkeeper Jim Coates can arrange for casual dinners such as lobster bakes, barbecues, and such; ask him about a guided sunset cruise of the peaceful end of Lake George.

**RUAH BED &
BREAKFAST**
Owners: Judy and Peter
Foster.
518-543-8816.
Lake Shore Dr.
Open: Year-round.
Price: Moderate to
Expensive.
Credit Cards: D, MC, V.
Special Features: Hiking
trails; fireplace; bal-
conies; children under 12
by special arrangement.

Such an appealing place naturally has amusing legends: this stone mansion was designed by Stanford White; part of the estate was won in a poker game; the Lake George monster — the biggest hoax ever seen in northern New York — was created in the studio of the original owner, artist Harry Watrous. Visit Ruah and you'll have your own stories to tell — about visiting a lovely inn overlooking a beautiful lake.

The four guest chambers are all upstairs and have private baths. The Queen of the Lakes is outstanding, quite spacious, with access to the balcony and views from every window. The Watrous Suite is a separate wing with two adjoining bedrooms and balconies.

Common rooms downstairs include a vast living room with a fieldstone fireplace and an antique grand piano, a cozy library, and an elegant dining room. To give you an idea of the scale of this inn, the veranda stretches across the front of the house and measures about 80 feet long.

**TROUT HOUSE
VILLAGE RESORT**
Owners: The Patchett
Family.
518-543-6088,
1-800-368-6088.
www.trouthouse.com.
Lake Shore Dr./Rte. 9N.
Open: Year-round.
Price: Moderate.

One of the few four-season resorts on the quiet northern portion of Lake George, Trout House is a handsomely maintained complex of log cabins and chalets. Many of the cabins have fireplaces, decks, and complete kitchen facilities (including dishwashers); there are numerous suites and rooms in the main lodge, all with private baths. In the summer, there are canoes, rowboats, sailboats, kayaks, bikes, and even a 9-hole putting green for

Min. Stay: 2 nights on
  weekends.
Credit Cards: AE, D, MC, V.
Special Features: 400-foot
  sandy beach; boats and
  bikes for guests; fire-
  places; cable TV with
  HBO; children welcome;
  no pets.

guests. Trout House is a short distance from historic
sites like Fort Ticonderoga and Crown Point, while
the Ticonderoga Country Club — a challenging 18-
hole course — is just up the road.

By January, the atmosphere changes from that of
an active resort to a quiet country inn. Cross-country skiers, snowshoers, skaters, ice fishermen, and
snowmobilers can go out right from the front or
back doors to explore miles of countryside.

*Log cabins and private
lakefront make Alpine Village
a pleasant destination for
families.*

Nancie Battaglia

Lake George

ALPINE VILLAGE
Owners: Lil and Ernest
  Ippisch.
518-668-2193.
Rte. 9N.
Closed: Dec. 1–May 1.
Price: Moderate.
Min. Stay: 3 nights.
Credit Cards: D, MC, V.
Special Features: Private
  beach; tennis; children
  welcome; no pets.

The sitting room of the main lodge is an Adirondack gem, and log cabins of all sizes, from the
spacious main lodge to cute duplex cottages with
fireplaces, characterize this lakeside resort. The
grounds are nicely landscaped, leading down to a
private beach; other amenities include rowboats
and canoes for guests, a recreation room, tennis
court, and some dock space for visitors' boats. In
the summer, breakfast is included in the room rate.
Folks here will even pick you up at the bus station
if you make advance arrangements.

CLINTON INN
Manager: Steve Swanson.
518-668-2412.
Lake Shore Dr.
Open: May 15–Oct. 15.
Price: Moderate.
Credit Cards: MC, V.
Special Features: Beach;
  children welcome.

At this new lakefront resort, there are 16 one-
and two-bedroom housekeeping cabins and
numerous deluxe motel rooms. There's a heated
pool plus a sandy beach on Lake George, clay tennis courts, basketball and volleyball courts, boat
docks, and an 18-hole putting green. The staff here
will help arrange babysitters, and there's a self-ser-
vice laundry on the premises.

Housekeeping cabins, with complete kitchens, barbecue grills, picnic tables, and cable TV are rented by the week only in high season, and may be reserved for shorter periods in spring and fall. After Labor Day, motel rooms are offered at 3-nights-for-the-price-of-2 rate.

DUNHAM'S BAY LODGE
Managers: Kathy and John
　Salvador.
518-656-9242.
Rte. 9L, on the east side of
　the lake at Dunham's
　Bay.
Closed: Mid-Oct.–late May.
Price: Expensive.
Credit Cards: AE, MC, V.
Min. Stay: 3 days on sum-
　mer weekends.
Special Features: Sandy
　beach; tennis; pool; play
　area; restaurant; children
　welcome; no pets.

The centerpiece of this stylish resort on the less-developed side of Lake George is a massive stone lodge built by a well-to-do Glens Falls dentist in 1911. Inside the lobby and restaurant, Dunham's Bay is spacious and sunlit; there's a new indoor/outdoor pool complex with a jacuzzi, and for a cool drink at the end of the day, there's a swank cocktail lounge with a pool table.

Accommodations range from one- or two-bedroom housekeeping cabins in a shady grove to large modern rooms in the main lodge or motel. Cottages rent by the week only in the summer, while during the off-season, from Memorial Day to mid-June, there's a two-night minimum stay and daily rates are considerably less. There's a restaurant and snack bar on the premises offering breakfast, lunch, and dinner.

**FORT WILLIAM HENRY
　MOTOR INN**
Manager: Sam Luciano.
518-668-3081,
　1-800-234-0267.
www.fortwilliamhenry.
　com.
Canada St./Rte. 9.
Open: Year-round.
Price: Inexpensive to
　Expensive, depending on
　season.
Credit Cards: AE, D, DC,
　MC, V.
Handicap Access: Yes.
Special Features: Restau-
　rants; pool; in-room
　phones; cable TV; handi-
　cap-access rooms; chil-
　dren welcome; small pets
　accommodated.

For more than 125 years there's been a hotel named Fort William Henry on this bluff overlooking Lake George. The current version is a brand-new complex with 288 rooms, an indoor pool, a heated outdoor pool, and 18 acres of manicured grounds. The motor inn has four restaurants, including the Lookout Cafe, serving lunch in a pleasant outdoor setting, and the Trolley, which specializes in steak and seafood. Interesting package options are available, such as a two-night bicycle adventure that includes breakfast, dinner, bike rentals, and a trail map, or a golfer's getaway. Note also that rates for Labor Day–late June are less than half price compared to the summer season.

Right next door is the Fort William Henry museum, portraying French and Indian War history on the site of the original fort; cannons boom, muskets blaze, and uniformed soldiers go through their drills. If modern amusements are more to your taste, there's miniature golf and the Million Dollar Beach a short walk away.

ROARING BROOK RANCH & TENNIS RESORT

Owners: The Garry Family.
518-668-5767,
1-800-882-7665.
Rte. 9N.
Closed: Mid-Oct.–late May.
Price: Moderate.
Credit Cards: MC, V.
Special Features: MAP;
horseback riding; sauna;
indoor and outdoor
pools; tennis; in-room
phones; cable TV.

ROCKLEDGE

Owners: Jack and Pat
Barry.
518-668-5348.
Lake Shore Dr.
Closed: Mid-Sept.–June 1.
Price: Moderate to
Expensive.
Credit Cards: MC, V.
Special Features: 540 feet of
lakefront; sandy beach;
pool; children welcome;
no pets.

STILL BAY

Hosts: Carolyn and Bob
Brown.
518-668-2584.
www.adirondack.net/tour
/stillbay.
Rte. 9N.
Closed: Oct.–May.
Price: Moderate to
Expensive.
Credit Cards: None.
Special Features: Beach;
dockage for guests'
boats; children welcome;
no pets.

WIAWAKA HOLIDAY HOUSE

518-668-9892.
Rte. 9L; RR 1 Box 1072.

Route 9N was once a little bit of the Wild West, lined with more than a dozen prosperous dude ranches that appealed to singles and families. Most of the guest ranches had closed by the 1970s, but Roaring Brook made the successful transformation into a more modern facility. The main lodge still reflects a half century of rustic cowboy charm, but suites and motel rooms have been upgraded throughout. To help you improve your game, there's a tennis pro on staff; to help keep the kids occupied, there's entertainment most nights. And you can ride that cayuse to your heart's content.

The original "Rockledge," a three-story mansion built in 1886, stands guard under the pines on this 14-acre lakefront property. Although the historic house isn't open to guests, the building's gracious presence adds a special touch to this otherwise thoroughly modern resort.

Rockledge offers one- or two-bedroom housekeeping cottages, motel rooms, and suites. Cottages are generally available by the week only. There's an outdoor pool, a sandy beach, and room for badminton, volleyball, and shuffleboard.

The lovely white-pillared boathouse at Still Bay gives a clue to the property's past — it also was part of a turn-of-the-century estate along Millionaires' Row. Now the seven acres are home to modern motel and efficiency units and housekeeping cottages.

There's a 325-foot-long swath of natural, sandy beach; nicely landscaped grounds; dock space for guests' boats; a play area; and a recreation room for rainy days and evenings. During July and August, guests receive complimentary continental breakfasts, and rowboats, canoes, and pedal boats are available free, too.

Founded in 1903 as a place where working women could take inexpensive vacations, Wiawaka offers clean, simple accommodations in three pretty Victorian cottages, a rustic dormitory

Closed: Mid-Sept.–early
June.
Price: Very Inexpensive.
Credit Cards: None.
Special Features: Private
beach; dockage; primar-
ily for women.

reputedly designed by Stanford White, and a motel. Set on 60 unspoiled acres on the east side of Lake George, the place is remarkably peaceful and relaxing.

Vacationing at Wiawaka is a bit like staying at a YWCA camp: no smoking or alcohol is allowed on the premises; guests are expected to make their own beds and sweep out their rooms; swimming, boating, and horseshoe pitching are part of the fun. Three meals a day are included in the room rate; taking a room without meals is not permitted. In 1990 the first male guests were welcomed here (before that, they had to stay elsewhere in Lake George), and children are not allowed.

Lake Luzerne

**THE ELMS WATER-
FRONT COTTAGES
AND LODGE**
Owners: Denise and Dave
Paddock.
518-696-3072, winter:
518-696-3246.
Closed: Oct. 15–May 1.
Price: Inexpensive.
Credit Cards: None.
Special Features: Sandy
beach; children welcome;
inquire about pets.

Families have been returning to the Elms every summer for more than 40 years, and it's no wonder why they come back. There's a nice sandy beach on a tranquil bay of the Hudson River, rowboats, and 15 housekeeping cabins and suites. For a couple of families vacationing together, the Sacandaga Lodge has three two-bedroom units. Nearby is the Waterhouse Restaurant, and for amusement, there's horseback riding, whitewater rafting on the Sacandaga River, golf, and small museums all within a short drive.

In summer, cottages are available by the week only; from May–Father's Day and Labor Day–Columbus Day special group rates are available for five cottages or more, for school, church, or social groups, and family reunions.

**THE LAMPLIGHT INN
BED & BREAKFAST**
Owners: Linda and Gene
Merlino.
518-696-5294,
1-800-262-4668.
www.adirondack.net/tour
/lampinn.
2129 Lake Ave.
Open: Year-round.
Price: Moderate to
Expensive.
Min. Stay: 2 nights on
weekends.

Prominently featured in the December 1993 issue of *Country Inns* and voted "Inn of the Year" for 1992 by readers of *The Complete Guide to Bed & Breakfasts, Inns and Guesthouses in the United States and Canada* by Pamela Lanier, the Lamplight Inn is an elegant, tasteful retreat. Built a century ago as the bachelor "cottage" for a wealthy lumberman, the inn has been painstakingly refurbished by Gene and Linda Merlino. The public room has rich chestnut wainscoting; high, beamed ceilings; two fireplaces; Oriental rugs, lace curtains, and lots of antiques. The spacious, sunny

Courtesy of the Lamplight Inn

The guests' parlor at the Lamplight Inn, a home built in the 1890s as the bachelor cottage for a wealthy lumberman.

Credit Cards: AE, MC, V. Special Features: Fireplaces; no pets; smoking permitted in parlor only; children over 12 welcome.

dining room, although a recent addition, is entirely in keeping with the Victorian style. Breakfast is open to the public on Sunday mornings, and the dining room is available for private parties and meetings.

An ornate keyhole staircase leads upstairs to the 10 guest chambers (all with private baths), and five of the rooms have gas-burning fireplaces. The furniture and decor are quite different and delightful in each room: for example, the Skylight Room has a high coffered ceiling, skylight, and a high-back old-fashioned oak bedstead, while the Victoria Room has a queen-size canopied four-poster bed. The handsome carriage house has five suites, all with queen-size beds, gas-burning fireplaces, phones, cable TV, and air conditioning. Breakfast, which is included in the room rate, includes fresh fruit and sweet breads or cake, homemade granola, omelettes, and daily specials like apple crêpes or Belgian waffles.

In 1994, the Merlinos bought the property next door and renovated the house into two lovely suites with fireplaces, TVs, and phones. Trails linking the Brookside Guest House and the Lamplight Inn have been cleared for walking and cross-country skiing. Recently the inn acquired a beer-and-wine license, and you can have a bottle of champagne sent to your room.

The Lamplight Inn is close to the Saratoga Racetrack and tends to be quite busy during the month of August. During November through April room rates are offered at special savings, with packages for leaf-peepers, holiday shoppers, cross-country and downhill skiers, and couples hoping for a romantic break during dreary mud season.

Paradox

LAKE PARADOX CLUB RENTAL HOUSES/ RED HOUSE BED & BREAKFAST
Owner: Helen Wildman.
518-532-7734.
Sawmill Rd. & Rte. 74 (Paradox); Box 125 (Severance NY 12872).
Closed: Most cabins mid-Oct.–mid-May; 2 cabins & B&B open year-round.
Price: Inexpensive to Moderate.
Credit Cards: None.
Min. Stay: 1 week for houses July–Aug.
Special Features: Children welcome; pets accommodated with prior arrangements for cabins; private sand beach; boats; no smoking at Red House.

Helen Wildman's family has owned hundreds of acres on the western end of Paradox Lake for more than a century; eight of the 11 lakefront rental houses were built by her grandfather. These places are big — four to six bedrooms — and have full kitchens, old-fashioned stone fireplaces, and screened porches. There's nice swimming at the club's private beach, canoes and rowboats for exploring pretty Paradox Lake, plus tennis, horseshoes, hiking trails, and a baseball field. Guests can rent outboards for fishing, or Sunfish for sailing around the lake. Helen says, "Many of our tenants return regularly, year after year, but there's always room for newcomers, especially if your vacation plans are flexible."

In spring and fall, weekly rental rates are about half the July–August fees. Two of the houses are completely winterized, great for ice fishermen and cross-country skiers who'd like to discover nearby Pharaoh Lake Wilderness Area.

Nearby, and under the same ownership as the Lake Paradox Club, is a charming old farmhouse now operating as a B&B. The Red House on Sawmill Road is next to Paradox Brook; guests here can enjoy the club's waterfront amenities, too. Sixteen miles down the road is Fort Ticonderoga, and Schroon Lake is just four miles away.

ROLLING HILL BED & BREAKFAST
Owners: Jewel and Lou Ady.
518-532-9286.
Rte. 74 (Paradox); Box 32 (Severance NY 12872).
Closed: Nov.–Mid-May.
Price: Inexpensive.
Credit Cards: None.

A restored 1840s-vintage farmhouse near Paradox, Pyramid, and Eagle lakes, Rolling Hill offers country hospitality and a hearty homemade breakfast. Guests share bathrooms for the four pleasant, antique-filled rooms upstairs, and just off the dining room there's a spacious screen porch, a real plus during bug season. For hikers and fishermen, the action is east (Paradox Lake) or west (Pharaoh Lake Wilderness), with miles of trails and dozens of trout ponds. This is good terrain for bicyclists, too, with lots of quiet back roads to explore.

Putnam Station

LAKE CHAMPLAIN INN
Innkeepers: Nancy and Joe Hoell.
518-547-9942.
Box 105, Lake Rd.
Open: Year-round.
Price: Moderate.
Credit Cards: None.
Special Features: Access to Lake Champlain.

A stately 1870s farmstead in the midst of 275 rolling acres, this newly opened bed & breakfast has four handsome rooms, all with double beds and private baths. Original chestnut mouldings, Oriental rugs, and antiques throughout make this a pleasant base for exploring nearby Vermont and the quiet east side of Lake George; boaters on the Champlain Canal will find this to be an excellent break from a night at a mooring.

Schroon Lake

SCHROON LAKE BED & BREAKFAST
Innkeepers: Rita and Bob Skojec.
518-532-7042.
Rte. 9.
Open: Year-round.
Price: Moderate.
Credit Cards: MC, V.
Min. Stay: 2 nights on weekends.
Special Features: Fireplace; no smoking; no pets; children over 12 welcome.

Only minutes off the Northway (I-87) is this lovely country inn with five attractive guest rooms, all with sparkling private baths. The living room has a stone fireplace, shelves of books and magazines, and comfortable sofas for curling up with the novel of your choice. Chambers have polished hardwood floors, Oriental rugs, fine antiques, patchwork quilts, and thick terrycloth robes in the closet. Just across the lawn is a gourmet restaurant serving lunch and dinner.

SILVER SPRUCE INN
Innkeepers: Phyllis and Cliff Rogers.
518-532-7031.
Rte. 9.
Open: Year-round.
Price: Moderate.
Credit Cards: D, MC, V.
Min. Stay: 2 nights on weekends; inquire.
Special Features: Fireplaces; no smoking; no children.

This historic home is a true gem. Encompassing more than 8,000 square feet and containing 28 rooms, the place manages to be luxurious and unpretentious, rustic and elegant, at the same time. At present there are two guest rooms with queen beds and two large suites with king-size waterbeds; all accommodations have wonderful oversize bathrooms with deep porcelain tubs that date back to the days when the building belonged to the owners of a major plumbing-supply company. Silver Spruce would be an ideal setting for a group of friends traveling together or a small corporate retreat.

Silver Spruce Inn (circa 1820) mixes historic architecture with modern comforts; the private bathrooms are spacious and sunny.

Nancie Battaglia

The lovely great room spans the entire width of the building, with plenty of couches and chairs, a piano, and an electric organ clustered by a huge fireplace. Running the length of the building is a spacious sunporch with wicker furniture. In the basement is an intriguing surprise, a rustic tavern that dates back to Prohibition days, complete with bookshelves that hide secret stashes of liquor and a back bar that once graced the Waldorf Astoria Hotel.

Restoration of a huge barn is ongoing, with plans to offer a few more suites in the future.

WOOD'S LODGE
Innkeeper: Catherine
    Wood Querns.
518-532-7529.
East St.
Closed: Mid-Oct.–May 10.
Price: Moderate.
Min. Stay: 2 nights on
    summer weekends.
Credit Cards: None.
Special Features: Private
    beach; children welcome;
    no pets.

The Lake House, a Steamboat Gothic hotel perched over Schroon Lake, is just one part of the four-acre complex at Wood's Lodge, a waterfront hostelry that's been owned and operated by the same family since 1912. The Lake House has two tiers of delightful gingerbread-trimmed porches wrapping around the building, and antiques in every room. There's also a chalet with several suites and private rooms, a main lodge with two-room suites, and five lakeside cabins. Many of the accommodations have kitchen facilities, but for those without, there's a modern community kitchen and an elegant dining room with a beautiful lake view.

Wood's Lodge is a short walk from what downtown Schroon Lake has to offer (barbecue at Pitkin's, weekly square dances by the lake), and there's a private beach, tennis court, and shuffleboard court on the property.

WORD OF LIFE INN
Manager: Don Lough.
518-532-7771.
www.wol.org.
Rte. 9.
Open: Year-round.
Price: Inexpensive to
 Expensive.
Credit Cards: D, MC, V.
Handicap Access: 6 rooms
 available.
Special Features: Indoor
 pool; children welcome;
 Christian atmosphere;
 recreational facilities;
 summer camps for
 youth.

A full-service Christian resort, the Word of Life Inn offers all kinds of accommodations from chalets and rustic lakeside cabins to deluxe executive and honeymoon suites. There's a complete roster of activities, concerts, and inspirational speakers, plus tennis, miniature golf, swimming, boating, hiking, and special events. Besides the inn, which is just south of Schroon Lake village, there's a family campground farther down the lake with sites for tents, travel trailers, and motor homes (some sites have electrical, water, and sewer hookups), plus several housekeeping cabins. Videos showing the facilities are available for a small fee.

Silver Bay

**NORTHERN LAKE
 GEORGE RESORT**
Owners: The Martucci
 Family.
518-543-6528.
Rte. 9N.
Open: Year-round.
Price: Inexpensive to
 Expensive.
Credit Cards: MC, V.
Handicap Access: Some
 accommodations.
Special Features: 400 feet of
 lakefront; sandy beach;
 free rowboats and
 canoes; hiking trails
 nearby; children
 welcome; dive shop.

Opened as the Hotel Uncas in 1896, the Northern Lake George Resort bills itself as the last of the lake's original old hotels still open to the public. The main lodge has been changed significantly over the years, though: the third floor with dormer windows was removed in the 1950s, and balconies and porches were added. The Great Room still maintains the appeal of an old Adirondack lodge with its stone fireplace and polished wood floors.

Inn guests can select from rooms on the lodge's second floor with private balconies providing views of the lake; new, winterized lakeside villas with fireplaces, kitchens, cable TV, and decks; or motel rooms. There's a cocktail lounge and public restaurant on the premises, open from late June through early September.

The depths of Lake George hold numerous wrecks from French and Indian War bateaux to sidewheel steamboats. The Northern Lake George Resort has a full-service dive shop offering tank fills and supplies; special dive charters to underwater historic sites can be arranged for groups.

**SILVER BAY
 ASSOCIATION
 YMCA CONFERENCE
 CENTER**
518-543-8833.
Silver Bay Rd., off Rte. 9N.

With nearly a square mile of picturesque property on Lake George and 65 buildings, Silver Bay Association is an awesome complex. Many of the structures hark back to the turn of the century in graceful Victorian architecture, yet meals and

Open: Year-round.
Price: Inexpensive to
   Moderate.
Credit Cards: MC, V.
Handicap Access: Yes.
Special Features: Full con-
   ference facilities; planned
   activities; waterfront.

amenities are thoroughly modern. The list of activities is almost endless, from swimming and fishing
to crafts and aerobics classes. Hiking and cross-
country-ski trails weave among the hillsides, and
there's ice skating on the lake. A day-care center,
open weekdays, is part of the complex.

Accommodations run the full range from tidy
double rooms in old-time lodges to cozy cabins; it's
possible to stay here without being part of a work-
shop or conference by joining the association, which costs about a hundred
dollars a year for a family or $50 for an individual.

Warrensburg

BENT FINIAL MANOR
Owner: Patricia Scully.
518-623-3308.
194 Main St.
Open: Year-round.
Min. Stay: 2 nights on
   holidays & summer
   weekends.
Price: Moderate to
   Expensive.
Credit Cards: None.
Special Features: Fireplaces;
   conservatory; children by
   prior arrangement.

A gracious Queen Anne–style mansion with three
fireplaces, dozens of stained-glass windows,
glorious woodwork, a wraparound porch, conservatory, circular tower, and the trademark "bent finial,"
this Main Street bed & breakfast is classy indeed.
There are five guest rooms with private baths and
queen-size beds: the Master Chamber has a wood-
burning fireplace and a secluded veranda overlooking the garden in the back of the house. The Eastlake
Chamber is decorated with Eastlake furniture, while
the Turret Room has curved walls, lovely windows,
and plenty of ruffles and lace. The new Country
Suite accommodates six in three bedrooms that
share a bath and an efficiency kitchen.

**COUNTRY ROAD
   LODGE**
Owners: Sandi and
   Steve Parisi.
518-623-2207.
www.adirondack.net/tour
   /countryroad.
Hickory Hill Rd.
Open: Year-round.
Price: Inexpensive.
Credit Cards: None.
Special Features:
   Cross-country-ski trails;
   no pets.

In 1974, Steve Parisi began transforming an old
farmhouse on the banks of the Hudson River
into a year-round bed & breakfast and a haven for
cross-country skiers. Country Road Lodge is decidedly off the beaten path, well suited to birdwatch-
ers, hikers, and others who want to explore the
secluded 35-acre property and adjacent state lands.
Hickory Hill downhill ski center, a low-key facility
with an impressive vertical drop, is right next door,
and Warren County's cross-country ski and hiking
trails start at the back door.

There are four comfortable guest rooms, two
with private baths. Special winter weekend packages include meals plus après-ski treats. There's no
TV at Country Road Lodge, but plenty of books, magazines, a piano, board
games, and a panoramic view of the Hudson River and Sugarloaf Mtn.

Donegal Manor dates back to the 1820s, when James Fenimore Cooper was a guest.

Nancie Battaglia

DONEGAL MANOR BED & BREAKFAST
Owner: Dorothy Dill
  Wright.
518-623-3549.
117 Main St.
Open: Year-round.
Price: Moderate to
  Expensive.
Min. Stay: 2 nights on
  holiday and some
  weekends.
Credit Cards: MC, V.
Special Features: Fireplace;
  children over 6 welcome;
  no pets.

James Fenimore Cooper was a guest at Peletiah Richards's house when he was researching _The Last of the Mohicans_, and according to one of Richards's children, Peletiah reportedly grumbled, "That young man has made some mistakes in describing the journey of the Munro-Hayward party that was guided by Uncas." In those days, the house was among the grandest in town, and later in the 19th century this place became more elaborate still, with the addition of an Italianate tower, a long veranda, and a bay window. Details inside Donegal Manor are lovely: there's an ornate fireplace in the parlor, a beautiful coffered wood ceiling above the staircase, and antiques throughout.

Two guest rooms with private baths are upstairs. A section of the house that dates to 1820 has been renovated into a handsome suite with a corner fireplace in the living room, queen-size bed, and spacious bathroom. Downstairs is an antique shop and more collectibles can be found for sale in the barn.

The best part about Donegal Manor can't be described in architectural or decorative terms — it's Dorothy Dill Wright, the innkeeper, and her genuine Irish charm. We suspect she's the real reason that folks return time and again to this bed & breakfast.

THE HOUSE ON THE HILL

Owners: Lynn and Joe Rubino.
518-623-9390,
1-800-221-9390.
Rte. 28.
Open: Year-round.
Price: Moderate.
Credit Cards: CB, D, DC, MC, V.
Special Features: No smoking; antique shop on premises; French and Italian also spoken.

A few miles outside Warrensburg is a nicely restored 14-room Federal-style farmhouse set on 176 acres. Joe and Lynn Rubino bought the place in 1969 and have spent years fine-tuning the property. Throughout the parlor, hallways, and living room, there are Victorian-era antiques and interesting ephemera, especially opera items such as autographed scores, playbills, and letters. There's an eclectic assortment of artwork on the walls from signed Salvador Dali and Peter Max lithos to 19th-century engravings.

Five spacious guest rooms and baths are on the second floor. One room, with its own kitchenette and private staircase, can be combined with another bedroom to form a suite. There's a spectacular Venetian porcelain chandelier in the Rose Room. In the mornings, Lynn slips upstairs to leave fresh pastries; coffee makers and tables for two are in each chamber.

The Rubinos pride themselves on offering a dust-free, smoke-free, relaxed atmosphere. Breakfast — as much you'd like and whatever you please — is served at any time up to 11am, and dinners may be arranged by special request. "Romantic getaway" packages are available, and the Rubinos know just when to light the candles and disappear.

THE MERRILL MAGEE HOUSE

Innkeeper: Florence Carrington.
518-623-2449.
2 Hudson St.
Open: Year-round.
Price: Expensive.
Credit Cards: AE, D, MC, V.
Min. Stay: 2 nights on holidays and weekends.
Handicap Access: 1 room.
Special Features: Restaurant; tavern; pool; hot tub.

Until Florence and Ken Carrington purchased this lovely Greek Revival house in the center of town in 1981, the property had remained in the same family all the way back to 1839. The oldest part of the original house is now the tavern and reception rooms; the back portion of the restaurant, circa 1812, actually came from another homestead some miles away. Merrill Magee House is listed on the National Register of Historic Places.

Upstairs is the Family Suite, which accommodates five in two bedrooms and a sitting room. The new Peletiah Richards Guest House, behind the inn, combines 20th-century conveniences, like private baths and a glassed-in spa room, with 19th-century decor: each room has its own fireplace, brass or four-poster bed, and handmade quilt. These rooms are all named after herbs, and "Parsley" is wheelchair accessible.

Merrill Magee's grounds are beautifully landscaped, with flower gardens, shady nooks, and a swimming pool. In the summer, you can sit on the porch and listen to evening concerts held in the bandshell just on the other side of the white picket fence. Special events include an annual Beaujolais Nouveau celebration that features wild game on the menu; conferences and meetings are cheerfully accommodated.

RIDIN'-HY RANCH
Managers: Andy and Susan Beadnell.
518-494-2742.
Sherman Lake, several mi. N. of Warrensburg & W. of Bolton Landing.
Closed: Dec. 1–26.
Price: Moderate.
Credit Cards: AE, D, MC, V.
Min. Stay: 2 nights.
Special Features: Horseback riding; indoor pool; restaurant; children welcome; no pets.

Western-style dude ranches were once abundant in the southeastern Adirondacks, but many have closed in the last few years. Ridin'-Hy, an 800-acre complex on Sherman Lake, continues to prosper, offering everything from a private intermediate-level downhill ski area to rodeos. There are 50 miles of trails for snowmobiling, cross-country skiing, or horseback riding: you can ride Old Paint year-round, for as many hours or days as you please. In warmer weather, guests can swim, row, or water-ski on Sherman Lake, and fish in Burnt Pond or the Schroon River.

The centerpiece of the ranch is an enormous two-story log cabin that contains a cocktail lounge, living room, game room, and restaurant. Accommodations include new chalets, lodge rooms, and motel units, all finished with natural wood. Numerous midweek and off-season packages are available.

CHAMPLAIN VALLEY

Crown Point

Crown Point Bed & Breakfast is an elegant mansion built in the 1880s by a local banker.

Nancie Battaglia

CROWN POINT BED & BREAKFAST
Owners: Sandy and Hugh Johnson.

Built by a banker in 1887, this stately 18-room mansion is a testament to Victorian craftsmanship. The woodwork — made of cherry, mahogany, oak, chestnut, walnut, and pine — gleams in panel-

518-597-3651.
3A Main St.
Open: Year-round.
Price: Inexpensive to
    Moderate.
Credit Cards: AE, MC, V.
Special Features: Children
    welcome; no smoking;
    no pets.

ing, window trim, pocket doors, floors, and an ornate staircase. There are three parlors, three porches, four fireplaces, and five acres of gardens and grounds for guests to enjoy. It's a five-minute walk to Lake Champlain or a short bike ride to the ruins at Crown Point.

There are five guest rooms, all with private baths and decorated with antique bedsteads and dressers. Guests can gather in the new Adirondack room, which has a wood stove, TV/VCR, lots of books and games, and a casual, rustic atmosphere.

Elizabethtown

DEER'S HEAD INN
Innkeepers: John de la Rue
    and Mark Ormiston.
518-873-9903/9995.
Rte. 9 (Court St.).
Open: Year-round.
Price: Inexpensive.
Credit Cards: AE, MC, V.

This landmark lodging was commandeered by the Army as a hospital following the Battle of Plattsburgh in 1814, and presidents Grover Cleveland and Benjamin Harrison both were guests. In recent times the Deer's Head has been renovated inside and out, upstairs and down. Three simple guest rooms with private baths are upstairs; a charming pub and restaurant are on the first floor. Note that the inn does not serve breakfast (restaurants are within walking distance), but lunch and dinner are available.

**OLD MILL BED &
    BREAKFAST**
Owners: Beki Maurello-
    Pushee and Bruce
    Pushee.
518-873-2294.
Rte. 9N.
Closed: Mon.–Thurs.
    fall–winter; inquire.
Price: Moderate.
Credit Cards: AE, D, MC,
    V.

In the thirties and forties this lovely property — bounded on two sides by the Boquet River — was an art school run by landscape painter Wayman Adams. Now it's a lovely bed & breakfast packed with antiques, Oriental rugs, paintings, and sculpture. Four guest rooms (three with private baths) are in the main house; students from the Meadowmount School of Music often bunk in the studio building during the summer.

Breakfast is decidedly a highlight here. On sunny, warm mornings it's served on the enclosed patio that has a fountain as its centerpiece, and the rest of the time the feast is presented in the formal dining room. Muffins, juice, poached pears with cream or baked grapefruit with honey are the starters, followed by bourbon French toast, lemon soufflé pancakes, or perhaps quiche with garden-fresh tomatoes.

**STONELEIGH BED &
BREAKFAST**
Owners: Rosemary
  Remington and William
  Ames.
518-873-2669.
Water St.
Open: Year-round.
Price: Inexpensive.
Credit Cards: AE, MC, V.
Special Features: Fireplace;
  older children welcome.

Richard Harrison, a Boston-based architect, designed this imposing Germanic-looking castle for New York State Supreme Court Justice Arthur Smith in 1882. The house has a fine library, as befits a country judge, and several porches and balconies under the tree-shaded, secluded grounds. There's also a TV room and a living room for guests.

Downstairs, there's a suite with private bath that is wheelchair accessible; upstairs, four spacious rooms share a bath and a half.

**STONY WATER BED &
BREAKFAST**
Owners: Winifred Thomas
  and Sandra Murphy.
518-873-9125,
  1-800-995-7295.
Roscoe Rd.
Closed: 2 weeks in Apr. &
  Nov.
Price: Moderate.
Credit Cards: AE, MC, V.
Special Features: Fireplace;
  library; pool; gardens;
  dinner available to guests
  by special reservation
  (except July & Aug.);
  children welcome; no
  smoking; inquire about
  pets.

Robert Frost slept here. Rockwell Kent designed the library. Louis Untermeyer owned the place. Stony Water, a beautifully restored Italianate house on 87 acres in the rolling hills outside Elizabethtown, is simply wonderful.

In the main house, a grand piano in the parlor invites guests to play and a new screen porch makes late-spring evenings free of insect pests. Upstairs are two guest rooms decorated with antiques, and over the garage, there's a comfortable, sunlit apartment that accommodates up to four people. Off in the woods is Untermeyer's former writing studio, which has been attractively redone as a two-bedroom house. In the backyard a former gardener's shed has been charmingly transformed into a wheelchair-accessible cottage.

Stony Water is on a very quiet country road ideal for mountain biking; there are hiking trails on the property to explore, and even an in-ground pool. The perennial and herb gardens are lovely from late spring through fall.

Essex

CUPOLA HOUSE
Manager: Donna Lou
  Sonnett.
518-963-7222.
S. Main St.
Open: Year-round.
Price: Moderate to
  Expensive.
Credit Cards: MC, V.
Special Features: Boat slips;
  no smoking; children
  welcome.

A prim and proper Greek Revival with wonderful two-story porches, Cupola House has two handsome apartments decorated with antiques and Adirondack furniture that are just a quick walk up from the Essex Marina. Both have complete kitchens and full baths and access to the upstairs porch; rates include a boat slip at the marina. The south apartment nicely accommodates two couples or a family; the north apartment has one bedroom with a wood stove.

If you need transportation to or from the Westport train station or nearby airports, it's available at no charge. Cupola House is just two blocks from the ferry to Vermont and conveniently close to all of Essex's shops and restaurants.

ESSEX INN
Owners: Trish and John
    Walker.
518-963-8821.
Lake Shore Rd.
Open: Year-round.
Price: Moderate.
Credit Cards: AE, MC, V.
Handicap Access: 2 down-
    stairs suites.

Stretching along Main Street with two tiers of porches is this lovely, carefully restored inn. The building is surprisingly narrow — just one room and the hallway wide — with a cafe, courtyard, and dining room, plus two spacious guest suites downstairs. Upstairs there are three bedrooms, plus two more suites: one includes a bedroom, bath, and kitchenette, while the other has two bedrooms, a sitting room, and bath.

The hotel is full of antiques, plus handsome period engravings and photographs. In 1995 new owners took over the Essex Inn and set to work making the landmark as friendly as it is historic. The food's good, too.

The Essex Inn occupies a prime spot in the heart of the village's historic district.

Nancie Battaglia

THE STONEHOUSE
Innkeeper: Sylvia Hobbs.
518-963-7713.
Church & Elm Sts.
Closed: Nov.–Apr.
Price: Moderate to Expen-
    sive.
Credit Cards: None.
Special Features: Fireplaces;
    bikes for guests.

Step into this 1826 Georgian stone house and you feel as if you've entered a classic English country house. Tall windows suffuse dappled light into the living spaces; private gardens ring the property. Two lovely suites with private baths and two rooms with a shared bath occupy the second floor; in progress are renovations to the top floor, which will transform the space into an exceptional

20' x 30' room with exposed beams, exposed stone walls and French doors that open onto a rooftop deck with a view of Lake Champlain.

Breakfast could be categorized as first-rate continental, with fresh baked goods from Montreal, seasonal fruits and gourmet coffee and tea. Note that the Stonehouse is located across the street from one of Essex's historic churches and is available for receptions and private gatherings.

Port Henry

ELK INN BED & BREAKFAST
Innkeeper: Julia Hammond.
518-546-7024.
Rtes. 9N/22; HCR 1 Box 87.
Open: Year-round.
Price: Inexpensive to Moderate.
Credit Cards: None.

Just a mile and a half north of Port Henry, the Elk Inn has been in the same family for three generations. It's a very pleasant house with views of Lake Champlain from the wraparound porch and features five guest rooms, including a nice suite with a private bath and a pair of adjoining rooms that share a bath. The full breakfast (everything home-made) is a high point with guests.

THE KING'S INN
Innkeepers: Linda Mullin and Nancy Masher.
518-546-7633, 1-800-600-7633.
109 Broad St.
Open: Year-round.
Price: Moderate.
Credit Cards: AE, D, MC, V.
Special Features: Pub serving lunch and dinner; fireplaces.

Slowly but surely downtown Port Henry is re-furbishing neglected buildings from the town's heyday as an iron-mining center. One bright spot is the restored King's Inn, an 1893 mansion on a hill overlooking the lake. There are nine nice rooms, all with queen beds and private baths. Three have working fireplaces; two have views of the lake.

Folks traveling by train or boat take note: pick-up and delivery to the marina or depot can be easily arranged, and Port Henry's shops, historic sites, and waterfront are within walking distance.

Ticonderoga

STONE WELLS FARM BED & BREAKFAST
Hosts and owners: Erv and Marilyn Fries; Jeff and Susan Wells.
518-585-6324,
1-888-261-5800.
331 Montcalm St.
Open: Year-round.
Price: Moderate.
Credit Cards: AE, MC, V.
Special Features: No smoking or alcohol on premises.

A wonderful cobblestone facade sets off this sur-prisingly large Craftsman-style bungalow at the foot of Ticonderoga's main street. Inside, chest-nut woodwork, vest-pocket windows, and airy, comfortable rooms make an amiable haven for guests. Two rooms share a bath on the first floor, and three rooms and two baths are located on the second floor. Ask for the "blue room" if you'd like a private bath.

Hearty breakfasts are served from 7–9:30am., and you're off to spend a day at Fort Ticonderoga.

Westport

All Tucked Inn, on Westport's Main Street, has lovely perennial gardens.

Nancie Battaglia

ALL TUCKED INN
Innkeepers: Tom Haley and
     Claudia Ryan.
518-962-4400.
53 S. Main St.
Closed: 2 weeks in Mar.
Price: Moderate.
Credit Cards: None.
Special Features: Children
     over 6 welcome; dinners
     by prior arrangement.

A grand old Dutch Colonial home, All Tucked Inn occupies a prominent spot on Westport's Main Street. There are nine lovely rooms (all with private bath); five have views of Lake Champlain. A suite on the first floor has its own porch and fireplace. From the inn, you can walk to the Westport Yacht Club, the marina, Westport Trading Company, tennis courts, and even the golf course.

Tom Haley is a fine cook and will prepare dinner for guests by reservation; from November through April weekend packages with meals are available.

**THE GRAY GOOSE
     GUEST HOUSE**
Owner: Elizabeth Kroeplin.
518-962-4562.
Open: Year-round, by
     reservation.
Price: Moderate.
Credit Cards: None.

This sprightly Victorian has two first-floor rooms, each with private bath and a private entry off the front porch. There's one room upstairs with twin beds and its own bath, plus another bedroom that shares a bath. All of Westport's attractions, from good restaurants to swimming, tennis, and golf, are within strolling distance.

**THE INN ON THE
     LIBRARY LAWN**
Innkeepers: Susann and
     Don Thompson.
518-962-8666.
1 Washington St.
Closed: Mar.–Apr.
Price: Moderate.
Min. Stay: 2 nights on
     holiday weekends.
Credit Cards: AE, MC, V.
Special Features: No smok-
     ing; children welcome.

As you might imagine, this charming little hotel — which dates back to 1875 — is situated just across from Westport's wonderful old library. Extensive renovations in 1980 have created peaceful, refined public areas and 10 elegant, comfortable rooms, all with private baths. On the second floor there's a library and lounge area; a sitting room with fireplace welcomes visitors downstairs.

Breakfast (soufflés, waffles, pastries, and fresh fruit) is included with the room rate.

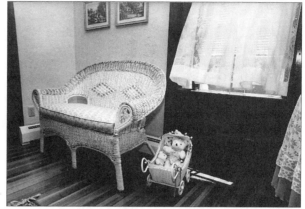

The Victorian Lady has gleaming wood floors and natural light throughout.

Nancie Battaglia

THE VICTORIAN LADY
Innkeepers: Doris and
  Wayne Deswert.
57 S. Main St.
518-962-2345.
Open: Year-round.
Price: Moderate.
Credit Cards: None.
Special Features: Children
  welcome; no smoking.

Three architectural styles are exuberantly (and successfully) combined at the Victorian Lady, a newcomer to Westport's list of fine lodgings. Inside, you'll see evidence of the original Greek Revival home, but outside, Second Empire shows up in a square tower and mansard roof. The full-length porch is Eastlake and offers a fine place for reading a novel or looking out over lovely gardens.

Three guest rooms all have private baths; there's a room with bunk beds that shares a bath. While in Westport, be sure to take the self-guided walking tour of historic buildings.

THE WESTPORT HOTEL
Innkeepers: Rita and Ralph
  Warren.
518-962-4501.
114 Pleasant St., Rte. 9N
  across from the Amtrak
  station.
Open: Year-round.
Price: Moderate.
Credit Cards: D, MC, V.
Special Features: Restau-
  rant; children and
  leashed pets welcome.

When the railroad came to Westport in 1876, Albert Gates opened his hotel on the other side of the tracks. Ever since, the spacious clapboard building has been operated as an inn. Guests can now choose from 10 refurbished rooms decorated with antiques and hand-stenciled walls; most have private baths. In warm weather, there's a breezy wraparound porch for watching the world go by on Route 9N or enjoying a meal from the hotel's fine kitchen.

Folks who are traveling without a car should note that there's daily Amtrak service to Westport, and many of the town's charms, from the Essex County Fair and Depot Theater to the lakefront, are nearby. From Columbus Day through Memorial Day, package deals with lodging, dinner, and breakfast for two are quite affordable.

Willsboro

CHAMPLAIN VISTAS
Owner: Barbara Moses.
518-963-8029.
183 Lake Shore Rd.
Open: Year-round.
Price: Moderate.
Credit Cards: None.
Special Features: 1 room
  handicap accessible.

This rambling homestead dates back to before the Civil War and was once the centerpiece of a thriving farm that produced wheat, milk, wool, and apples. Many of the original barns and buildings remain on the property. In 1993 the house was converted into a bed & breakfast and named Champlain Vistas for the marvelous sweeping views; one year later it became listed on the National Register of Historic Places.

Guests can stay in rooms with private or shared baths; one downstairs is handicap accessible. Nearby rolling back roads make for good biking, and there's storage available for bicycles.

1852 INN
Innkeepers: Lil and Isaac
  Iten.
518-963-4075.
277 Lake Shore Rd., Rte. 22
  bet. Essex & Willsboro.
Open: Year-round.
Price: Inexpensive.
Credit Cards: MC, V.
Special Features: Lake
  views; bikes; children
  and well-behaved pets
  welcome.

Just up the road from the historic settlement of Essex is a lovely Greek Revival home, operated by Lil and Isaac Iten as a bed & breakfast. The 1852 Inn has a sweeping view of Lake Champlain and four simple, appealing guest rooms upstairs that share baths. Three beaches are within a few miles of the inn; several golf courses are a short distance away in Willsboro, Westport, and Peru. Bicycles, cross-country skis, and a canoe are on hand for guests who'd like to explore.

From May through the fall, the perennial gardens are in glorious bloom, and some fresh treat from the vegetable patch will appear on your plate at breakfast. If you come with the kids, they can gather their own eggs from the hens in the morning.

HIGH PEAKS AND NORTHERN ADIRONDACKS

Elk Lake

ELK LAKE LODGE
Managers: Janet and Percy
  Fleming.
518-532-7616.
Elk Lake Rd., off Blue
  Ridge Rd. (Elk Lake);
  Box 59 (North Hudson
  NY 12855).
Closed: Nov.–early May.
Price: Expensive; includes
  all meals.
Credit Cards: None.

In a nutshell, Elk Lake Lodge is the quintessential Adirondack lodge. Set on a breathtaking private lake ringed by the High Peaks, in the midst of a 12,000-acre preserve, the place offers everything an outdoorsperson could ask for: great fishing, unlimited wilderness hiking, and canoeing on an island-studded lake that's off-limits to motorboats. Of course, if just hanging out, listening to the loons, and admiring the view are your kinds of recreation, this place has that in spades.

Min. Stay: 2 nights.
Special Features: Private
lake and pond; mountain
hiking trails; canoes &
rowboats for guests; fishing; children welcome;
no pets.

There are six rooms in the turn-of-the-century lodge, all with twin beds and private baths. Around the lakeshore there are seven cottages, ranging from Little Tom, a cozy spot under the trees for two, to Emerson Lodge, which sleeps up to 12. Several of the cabins are equipped with kitchens and have fireplaces, or have decks overlooking the lake; all are nicely decorated. The price of a stay at Elk Lake includes all meals, which are served in the dining room with huge picture windows showing the mountains and lake.

Nancie Battaglia

View of the High Peaks from Elk Lake Lodge's dock.

Jay

THE BOOK AND BLANKET
Innkeeper: Kathy Recchia and Fred Balzac.
518-946-8323.
Rte. 9N.
Open: Year-round.
Price: Inexpensive to Moderate.
Min. Stay: 2 nights on holiday weekends.

Rooms in this restored Greek Revival home are named for authors: the Jack London number has a north-woods ambiance, queen-size bed, and private bath with a whirlpool tub; the Jane Austen room has a queen-size bed and a quiet nook for reading; the F. Scott Fitzgerald room has a double bed and shares a bath. All of the rooms — upstairs and down — have lots of books, and guests are encouraged to browse and borrow at will. Or you

Credit Cards: None.
Special Features: Children welcome; inquire about pets.

Keene

ADIRONDACK ROCK & RIVER GUIDE SERVICE
Owner: Ed Palen.
518-576-2041.
Alstead Hill Rd.
Open: Year-round.
Price: Inexpensive.
Min. Stay: 2 nights on weekends.
Credit Cards: MC, V.
Special Features: Indoor climbing wall; instruction in rock and ice climbing and kayaking.

BARK EATER INN
Owner: Joe-Pete Wilson.
518-576-2221.
Alstead Hill Rd.
Open: Year-round.
Price: Moderate to Expensive.
Min. Stay: 2 nights on holiday weekends.
Credit Cards: AE, MC, V.
Special Features: Cross-country skiing; horseback riding; dinners available; children welcome; special packages.

can relax by the fire in the living room with Daisy, the basset hound, at your feet, as you watch a classic film on the VCR. The Book and Blanket offers a home-cooked breakfast in its pleasant dining room.

At the end of a peaceful road that crosses a gorgeous high valley, Rock & River has a spacious climbers' lodge (a handsomely renovated barn) that sleeps 12 in three private rooms and a bunk room, plus the new Guide's House, which has two rooms with private baths and two that share a bath. The climbers' lodge can be rented by a group; it has an indoor climbing wall for warming up before trying the excellent rock climbing nearby. Breakfast is included with the overnight rate.

Backcountry trips are Rock & River's forte, offering beginning and advanced lessons in ice- and rock-climbing and kayaking for all ages. The lodge is also conveniently located at the head of the Jackrabbit Trail, a cross-country-ski route that connects Keene with Lake Placid and Saranac Lake.

The stagecoach carrying folks from Lake Champlain to Lake Placid used to stop here more than 150 years ago; and, since the 1940s, members of the Wilson family have taken in guests. The main part of this country inn is a beautiful farmhouse with two stone fireplaces and wide board floors. There are seven rooms upstairs that share baths, plus four rooms in the new Carriage House with private baths. The Log Cottage has two three-bedroom suites and two guest rooms with private baths. Breakfast is served family-style in the dining room; dinners are available by special arrangement.

Guests seek out the Bark Eater not just for the marvelous views of the High Peaks and the friendly staff, but for horseback riding, hiking, and cross-country skiing. The lodge has dozens of well-mannered English and Western mounts and many miles of woodland trails. Polo games are held in a nearby field on summer Sunday afternoons. In winter the bridle trails become groomed ski trails; Bark Eater's 20 kilometers connect with the Jackrabbit system, so you could ski for days and never cover the same territory.

Keene Valley

HIGH PEAKS INN
Owners: Linda and Jerry
   Limpert.
518-576-2003.
Rte. 73.
Open: Year-round.
Price: Moderate.
Min. Stay: 2 nights on
   weekends.
Credit Cards: MC, V.
Special Features: Fireplace;
   pool table; children wel-
   come.

From 1929 to 1949 this substantial Italianate home was known to travelers as Beede Cottage; now it's a cozy inn with all the modern comforts in eight guest rooms. On the first floor, there's a suite with queen-size bed, full bath, and its own entrance; a highlight upstairs is the room with queen-size bed, big picture windows framing mountain views, and a private bath. Most of the second-floor rooms share baths, although two have sinks in the rooms. All are furnished with antiques and hand-stitched quilts. A full breakfast is included in the rate.

MOUNTAIN MEADOWS
Owner: Patricia Quinn.
518-576-4771.
Rte. 73
Open: Year-round.
Price: Inexpensive to
   Moderate.
Credit Cards: None.
Special Features: Children
   welcome.

The East Branch of the Ausable River curls through this lovely property and the pointy peak of Noonmark Mtn. looms to the west. Mountain Meadows is a mecca for hikers, cross-country skiers, and climbers; Pat Quinn will help you plan an outing and drop you off at the trailhead.

The bed & breakfast is actually two comfortable Adirondack-style houses that share a sunny deck. The bedroom wing has three large rooms with king-size beds that convert to twins and which share two baths. There's another chamber with private bath and a southern exposure.

**TRAIL'S END FAMILY
   INN & HIKER'S
   LODGE**
Owners: Karen and Frank
   Kovacik.
518-576-9860.
www.trailsendinn.com.
Trail's End Rd., off Rte.
   73.
Open: Year-round.
Price: Moderate.
Credit Cards: MC, V.
Special Features: Fireplaces;
   hiking trails; children
   welcome.

A gambrel-roofed house with eyebrow windows on a quiet road, Trail's End calls itself a hikers' lodge, implying that the accommodations aren't so fancy that you need to worry about blow-drying your hair before you come to breakfast. Downstairs, the lodge has a large comfortable living room with a fireplace and VCR plus a winterized sun porch full of toys and games for kids.

Guest rooms upstairs include Catamount, which has a corner fireplace, a private porch, and full bath; Jay, the largest room, with a private bath; and Marcy Suite, a two-room suite with king-size bed, TV, bath, and futons on a sleeping porch. There are four double rooms that share baths, plus a newly refurbished two-bedroom cottage with complete kitchen, TV/VCR, washer/ dryer, and stereo that accommodates up to six guests and even a pet. At times, hiking clubs or family groups take over the

An old-fashioned guest room at Trail's End.

Nancie Battaglia

entire place, which can hold about 40 comfortably. Meals can be arranged for large groups.

You don't need a car to enjoy Trail's End and vicinity. The bus stops every day at the Noon Mark Diner, a five-minute walk away, and from the inn, there's easy access to numerous High Peaks hiking trails.

Lake Placid

ADIRONDAK LOJ
Manager: Rob Bond.
518-523-3441.
www.adk.org.
Adirondak Loj Rd., off Rte. 73, 3 mi. S. of Lake Placid village.
Open: Year-round.
Price: Inexpensive to Moderate.
Credit Cards: MC, V.
Special Features: Hiking; outdoor workshops; tent campground; backcountry cabins; High Peaks Information Center.

With its sweeping panorama of Mt. Marcy and Indian Pass, the drive into Adirondak Loj sets you up for a visit to the Adirondack Mountain Club's (ADK) wilderness retreat. On Heart Lake in the midst of the High Peaks, the 1920s-era lodge is a rustic, comfortable place. In the living room, you can rock in an Old Hickory chair in front of the vast stone fireplace, and choose from the shelves practically any book that's ever been written on the Adirondacks. Breakfast — the wake-up bell rings bright and early — is served family-style at picnic tables in an adjoining room. Bag lunches are available, and plain, home-cooked dinners are served when the lodge is busy.

There are four private rooms, four bunkrooms, and a huge coed loft. The bunkrooms, which have four built-in log beds, are snug and cozy, like cabins on a ship; the loft can be a hard place to get a good night's sleep if there are any snorers in the crowd. The management refers to the bathrooms as "semi-private," but they're actually similar to facilities in a college dorm. You don't need to be a member of the ADK to stay at the Loj, but you must make advance reservations.

The Adirondack Mountain Club's Adirondak Loj is a great place for hikers and backcountry skiers to stay.

Nancie Battaglia

On Heart Lake are two cabins that accommodate four to 16 people during the fall, winter, and spring. For the intrepid traveler, ADK has three excellent backcountry cabins that are accessible by foot and available year-round: Johns Brook Lodge is a 3 1/2-mile hike in from Keene Valley. Further still are Grace Camp and Camp Peggy O'Brien, which have tiers of bunks, gas lights, and wood heat; they're excellent bases for hiking, snowshoe, or ski weekends.

BROOKS' SUNSHINE COTTAGE
Owner: Bernadine Brooks.
518-523-3661.
6 Maple St.
Open: Year-round.
Price: Moderate.
Min. Stay: 2-night minimum for suites in season.
Credit Cards: MC, V.

In a quiet residential neighborhood just a two-minute walk from Lake Placid's Main Street, this lodging features four large bedrooms with two baths in the main house plus three attractive suites (with kitchens, air conditioning, TV/ VCR, and living rooms) in an adjacent Victorian home. A breakfast buffet is served every day with fresh fruit, bagels, muffins, and a hot entrée on the menu.

HIGHLAND HOUSE INN
Owners: Cathy and Ted Blazer.
518-523-2377.
3 Highland Place., off Hillcrest Ave. near the Holiday Inn.
Open: Year-round.
Price: Moderate.
Credit Cards: MC, V.
Min. Stay: 2 nights on weekends.
Special Features: Children welcome; mountain-bike rentals.

Secluded but central, Highland House looks and feels like an authentic Adirondack inn, which it assuredly is. The main house, with antiques and rustic details, opened to guests in 1910. Downstairs, there's a large living room with a wood stove, a piano room, a dining room, and a deck with benches and a giant hot tub built around two big clumps of white birch trees. In nice weather, guests enjoy breakfast (which is included in the nightly rate) in a glass-enclosed garden room. It's only a two-minute walk from this residential neighborhood to Main Street.

The inn has seven rooms, all with private baths. Next door to the main lodge is Highland Cottage, a perky little spot complete with kitchen, fireplace, air conditioning, and deck; there's a two-night minimum reservation for the cottage.

THE INTERLAKEN INN
Owners: Carol and Roy
  Johnson.
518-523-3180,
  1-800-428-3269.
15 Interlaken Ave., around
  the corner from Mirror
  Lake Inn.
Open: Year-round; B&B
  only Apr. & Nov.
Price: Expensive, MAP;
  Moderate, B&B.
Credit Cards: AE, MC, V.
Min. Stay: 2 nights on fall
  and winter weekends.
Special Features: Fireplace;
  restaurant; children over
  5 welcome.

Walnut-paneled walls, tin ceilings, a fireplace, a winding staircase, and all kinds of antiques make the Interlaken a true gem. Built in 1906 by one of the founders of the Bank of Lake Placid, the secluded spot has been operated as an inn for most of its existence. Downstairs, the dining room is elegant, yet casual; guests can eat on the porch during nice weather. Off the living room is a cozy little bar, with club chairs, a card table, and TV/VCR — the perfect place for reliving that golf match or discussing the fall foliage.

There are a dozen lovely guest rooms on the second and third floors, most with queen-size beds, all with private baths, and decorated with antiques. The Honeymoon Suite has a canopy bed and its own private balcony. The third-floor rooms are especially charming; even the bathrooms, with clawfoot tubs tucked under the eaves, are romantic. During most of the year, rooms are available on the modified American plan. On Sundays and Mondays, except for holiday weekends, no dinner is served and the bed-&-breakfast rate applies.

The Interlaken Inn is a family affair. Carol, and her son Kevin, who graduated from the Culinary Institute of America, staff the kitchen, and dinners are delightful, with menus that change every day: you'd never find the same combination of gourmet soups, salads, entrées, and desserts if you'd stay here for months. Afternoon tea is served most every day; ask about gourmet picnic lunches.

LAKE PLACID LODGE
Manager: Kathryn
  Kincannon.
518-523-2700.
www.lakeplacidlodge.com.
Whiteface Inn Rd.
Open: Year-round.
Price: Very Expensive.
Credit Cards: AE, MC, V.
Special Features: Boats and
  bikes for guests;
  fireplaces in rooms;
  well-behaved dogs and
  children welcome.

First, a geography lesson: the village of Lake Placid is on tiny Mirror Lake; the lake named Placid is slightly west of town and it's a big body of water with a pair of islands and gorgeous views. Only a few lodgings are located on the secluded western banks of Lake Placid, with the Lodge in a particularly magical spot.

Built as a summer home at the turn of the century, the building has been enlarged over the years, adding a wing here and a porch there, changing the rooflines, and creating a dramatic staircase linking the guests' lodge with the dining room in

Nancie Battaglia

The rustic yet elegant log cabins at Lake Placid Lodge have stone fireplaces and views of the lake.

1994, but the heart of the building remains intact. In 1946, Mae and Teddy Frankel opened the place as a hotel, and for nearly 40 years ran it with a personal touch. Christie and David Garrett bought the Lodge in 1993 and transformed it into a stunningly beautiful resort that compares favorably to The Point, the Garretts' world-class hotel on Upper Saranac Lake. Actually, rates at the Lodge are a bit more within reach than The Point, and the restaurant (open to the public) offers marvelous selections for breakfast, lunch, and dinner.

Guests have 22 rooms from which to choose, such as Tamarac, with a king-size bed, cobblestone fireplace, and a cozy sitting alcove; St. Regis Suite, on the upper level of Lakeside Lodge, with two fireplaces, huge soaking tub, and porch overlooking the lake; and Pinnacle, which has the best views, king-size bed, and a stone fireplace. Beginning in 1996, the Lodge began renovating log cabins on the adjacent Whiteface Inn property, which offer privacy and handsome woodsy details. There's a postage-stamp-size sandy beach, and canoes, sailboards, pedal boats, and bicycles are on hand for guests. The beautiful and challenging Whiteface Inn golf course is an easy walk from the Lodge.

MIRROR LAKE INN
Owner: Edwin Weibrecht.
518-523-2544.

On a hillside overlooking Mirror Lake, this delightful resort hotel in the heart of town offers an inviting array of amenities and services. There's

The Mirror Lake Inn has a private beach as well as an indoor pool and spa.

Nancie Battaglia

www.mirrorlakeinn.com.
5 Mirror Lake Dr.
Open: Year-round.
Price: Moderate to Very
  Expensive.
Credit Cards: AE, D, MC,
  V.
Handicap Access: Yes,
  hotel rooms.
Special Features: Spa;
  tennis; heated pools;
  ice skating; restaurant;
  conference facilities;
  hair and skin-care salon;
  children welcome.

a spa with exercise equipment, aerobics classes, and personal trainers; a hair and skin-care salon open five days a week; even a nutritional counselor serves on the staff.

The best accommodations, "Placid Suites," are split-level rooms connected by an oak spiral staircase, with king-size beds, huge whirlpool baths, and private balconies overlooking the lake; suite guests receive champagne and flowers upon arrival, and nightly turn-down service. There are a full range of private rooms, from country-furnished doubles with private balconies, to the comfortable "Colonial Bedrooms," which give guests a chance to enjoy all that the inn offers at an economical price. Even the least expensive rooms have refrigerators, hair dryers, clock radios, cable TV, and magnifying make-up mirrors.

Mirror Lake Inn has a fancy restaurant (with a dress code for dinner and an extensive menu that includes low-fat choices), a cozy bar, and various nooks and crannies for guests to relax in. The inn is an exceptional facility for conferences, with plenty of attractive meeting rooms for large or small groups. Packages are available for early-season downhill skiing, midweek visits, and golf.

**MT. VAN HOEVENBERG
BED & BREAKFAST**
Owner: Wayne Failing.
518-523-9572.
Rte. 73, near the Mt. Van
  Hoevenberg Recreational
  Complex.

Four-season housekeeping cabins plus a three-bedroom, two-bath bed & breakfast would make Wayne Failing's facilities for guests appealing in any Adirondack setting, but the great attraction here is the place's proximity to excellent cross-country skiing and hiking. The B&B is next to the

Open: Year-round.
Price: Moderate.
Min. Stay: 2 nights on busy
  weekends.
Credit Cards: MC, V.
Special Features: Guide ser-
  vice; hiking trails; sauna;
  children welcome.

50 km of groomed tracks at the Olympic cross-country complex and connects with the Cascade Ski-Touring Center and Jackrabbit trails. You can head into the High Peaks Wilderness Area without parking your car at a trailhead and afterwards enjoy an invigorating wood-fired sauna.

Wayne himself is a licensed guide who leads fishing, rafting, hiking, and skiing trips.

South Meadow Farm has a working sugarhouse.

Nancie Battaglia

**SOUTH MEADOW FARM
LODGE**
Owners: Nancy and Tony
  Corwin.
518-523-9369,
  1-800-523-9369 outside
  518 area code.
Rte. 73.
Open: Year-round.
Price: Moderate.
Credit Cards: MC, V.
Min. Stay: 2 nights on holiday weekends; inquire.
Special Features: Farm animals; cross-country-ski
  trails; fireplace; meals
  available; working maple
  sugarhouse; children
  welcome; no smoking.

Also near Mt. Van Hoevenberg's cross-country-ski and biathlon facilities is a small family farm that operates as a homey bed & breakfast. The Corwins produce much of the food that appears on the table, including maple syrup. The lodge property contains ski trails that are part of the 50-km Olympic complex and is close to hiking trails up Cascade and Pitchoff mountains, making this is an ideal spot for outdoorspeople.

Accommodations include five rooms with half baths, rooms in the loft with shared baths, and four mountain cabins for the "soft camper," which have sleeping lofts, woodstoves, and candlelight, with running water and privies nearby. The lodge's living room is quite handsome and centers around a massive fireplace. Breakfast is included in the nightly rate; family-style dinners and trail lunches are available.

STAGECOACH INN
Owner: Peter Moreau.
518-523-9474.
370 Old Military Rd.
Closed: April.
Price: Moderate.
Credit Cards: MC, V.
Min. Stay: 2 nights, inquire.
Special Features: Fireplaces;
　children over 10; inquire
　about pets.

The first guests at this North Elba landmark checked in when Andrew Jackson was president. In the last 165 years, much care has gone into keeping this venerable lodge located on the edge of town handsome and inviting. Beaded-pine paneling gleams, rustic yellow birch trims the stairs and balcony, and a huge fieldstone fireplace beckons.

There are nine guest rooms, five with private baths; two rooms have their own fireplaces. Four rooms share baths. A full country breakfast is included in the rate.

Newcomb

AUNT POLLY'S INN
Owners: Maggie and Doug
　Alitz.
518-582-2260.
Rte. 28N.
Open: Year-round.
Price: Inexpensive to
　Moderate
Credit Cards: MC, V.
Special Features: Hiking
　trails; dinners available
　by prior arrangement.

Before the Civil War, Aunt Polly Bissell took in travelers at her home on the edge of the High Peaks, and in August 1995, Maggie and Doug Alitz opened the doors once again. Their house is lovely, packed with eclectic antiques; four nice guest rooms share two modern baths.

The 70-acre property includes hiking and cross-country-ski trails that lead back to a wild pond, and recreational opportunities abound in and around Newcomb. You can take the 10-mile trek into Santanoni Preserve on foot, bikes, skis, or by horse-drawn wagon, head off to climb in the High Peaks, or tour the Visitor Interpretive Center.

MURDIE'S BED &
　BREAKFAST
Owner: Raymond Murdie.
518-582-3531.
Rte. 28N.
Open: Year-round.
Price: Inexpensive.
Credit Cards: None.
Special Features: Children
　welcome.

Near Newcomb's town park, which has an awesome High Peaks vista, Ray Murdie has opened his simple home to guests. "Folks from all over the world — Israel, Holland, West Germany — have stayed here with me," he says. Three bedrooms, which share a bath, are all upstairs, and there's a shower downstairs for guests; the whole house is open to visitors, with the enclosed back porch a favorite spot for relaxing near the woodstove or watching the birds at the feeder. Murdie's is a convenient spot from which to hike, cross-country ski, check out the Visitor Interpretive Center, or explore the upper Hudson River.

Saranac Lake

AMPERSAND BAY BOAT
　CLUB
Hosts: Keti and John
　Zuliani.

A short distance from downtown Saranac Lake, but directly on beautiful Lower Saranac Lake, Ampersand Bay has several nice two-bedroom log

518-891-3001.
12 Ampersand Bay Rd.,
off Rte. 3.
Open: Year-round.
Price: Moderate to
Expensive.
Credit Cards: None.
Min. Stay: 1 week during
summer for suites &
cottages.
Special Features: Private
beach; canoes; boat
launch; children
welcome; no pets.

cabins with screen porches and complete kitchens; studio apartments; two two-bedroom boathouse suites overlooking the water; and assorted other cottages and rooms. If you're traveling with your own boat, you can handily launch and dock here; there's a fee for slips. The Zulianis' 40-acre retreat includes a private sandy beach and free canoes and sailboats so that guests can explore the many state-owned islands in the lake. From Lower Saranac you can travel through the locks to Middle Saranac Lake, or Oseetah, Kiwassa, and Lake Flower, with great fishing throughout.

THE DOCTOR'S INN
Innkeeper: Susan Moody.
518-891-3464.
Trudeau Rd., off Rte. 3.
Open: Year-round.
Price: Inexpensive to
Moderate.
Credit Cards: MC, V.
Special Features: Guide
service; children and pets
welcome.

At the foot of Mt. Pisgah, on five quiet acres at the edge of the village, is this bed & breakfast that opened in 1994. The Doctor's Inn — named for its historic connection to a renowned sanitarium — has been renovated throughout with polished hardwood floors and big stone fireplaces, and offers two spacious suites with lovely mountain vistas and two double rooms. Ask about hiring a licensed guide if you're interested in backcountry exploring; if you'd prefer golf or downhill skiing, the inn has attractive package rates. Five golf courses are within 15 miles of the place; cross-country skiing on backcountry or groomed trails is just moments away, and three alpine areas (Whiteface, Big Tupper, and Pisgah) are close by.

**FOGARTY'S BED &
BREAKFAST**
Owners: Emily and Jack
Fogarty.
518-891-3755,
1-800-525-3755.
37 Riverside Dr.
Open: Year-round.
Price: Inexpensive.
Credit Cards: None.
Special Features: Boat dock
for guests; swimming;
children welcome.

Built in 1910 as a cure cottage for tuberculosis patients, this attractive home overlooking Lake Flower has handsome woodwork, leaded-glass windows, wonderful porches, and five bedrooms sharing three baths. Although Fogarty's is a quick walk from Saranac Lake's business district and restaurants, it's in a very peaceful neighborhood and even has a dock on the lake for swimmers and boaters. Winter guests note that cross-country skiing at Dewey Mtn. is about a mile away, and in early February, when the winter carnival is in full swing, you can look over to the fabulous ice palace on the opposite shore of the lake. One point to keep in mind about Fogarty's: because the house is set on a steep hillside, you've got to climb a lot of steps (73 to be exact, says Emily) to get to the entrance.

**HARBOR HILL
COTTAGES**
Hosts: Denise and Wayne
   Bujold.
518-891-2784.
104 Riverside Dr.
Open: Year-round.
Price: Moderate.
Special Features: Sandy
   beach; fireplaces; boats
   for guests; dockage;
   children welcome.

A cluster of cabins on Lake Flower, Harbor Hill provides waterfront tranquility within a residential neighborhood. On a July or August Friday night, guests sitting on the docks can enjoy the outdoor folk music concerts from across the water, or they can canoe over to the bandshell. In the winter, you can ice skate right from the front door.

Four of the five winterized housekeeping cabins have fireplaces; they range in size from one to three bedrooms, and all have picture windows and decks overlooking the water. There's a private beach for swimming, dock space for visiting motorboats, and rowboats, pedal boats, bikes, and canoes for guests.

The second-floor lobby of the Hotel Saranac is a gracious, sunny space.

Nancie Battaglia

**THE HOTEL SARANAC
OF PAUL SMITH'S
COLLEGE**
518-891-2200, 1-800-937-
   0211, fax: 518-891-5664.
www.hotelsaranac.com.
101 Main St.
Open: Year-round.
Price: Inexpensive to
   Moderate.
Credit Cards: AE, DC, MC,
   V.
Handicap Access:
   Elevators; most rooms.

For more than four decades, hospitality-management students of Paul Smith's College have gotten on-the-job training at this landmark downtown hotel. As a result, the staff here is friendly and helpful at all hours of the day or night. There are 91 air-conditioned guest rooms, all with private baths; rooms are spotless and comfortable. The second-floor grand hall, with beautiful painted wood beams, a grand piano, and potted plants, is elegantly welcoming and true to architect William Scopes's vision of how a fine hotel should greet its guests. A.P. Smith's Restaurant, named after the

Special Features:
Restaurants; cocktail
lounge; children
welcome; inexpensive
golf and ski packages.

famed North Country hotelier and college founder
Paul Smith, is open from breakfast to dinner, while
the Boathouse Lounge — a quiet, congenial pub —
serves light meals as well. On the ground floor is a
gift shop featuring quality crafts and a full-service
travel agency.

The Hotel Saranac offers numerous packages for golf or skiing, tour groups or
conferences are cheerfully accommodated, and Canadian money is accepted at
par. Travelers wishing to see the Adirondacks via public transportation should
note that the Adirondack Trailways bus stops here, and it's quite easy to see
Saranac Lake on foot and take a cab to Lake Placid.

*Cruising Upper Saranac Lake
in one of The Point's classic
wooden inboards.*

Nancie Battaglia

THE POINT
Owners: Christie and
David Garrett.
Manager: Bill McNamee.
518-891-5674,
1-800-255-3530.
Mail: Star Rte., Box 65.
Closed: Mar. 15–Apr. 15.
Price: Very Expensive.
Credit Cards: AE.
Min. Stay: 2 nights on
weekends.
Special Features: Great
Camp; gourmet meals;
boats for guests; member
Relais et Chateaux; no
children under 18.

William Avery Rockefeller built a drop-dead
gorgeous Great Camp named Wonundra on
an Upper Saranac Lake peninsula in the thirties,
and if you've read any recent articles about the
Adirondacks, chances are you've seen The Point,
that Rockefeller place that's now open to guests. A
roundup of comments from the press gives you a
glimpse of what's so special here: "Absolutely, but
absolutely, lovely, a place in which everything you
see is total perfection," wrote Rene Lecler in *The
300 Best Hotels in the World*. "A private estate that
sweeps all honors as the most enchanting lakefront
sanctuary of its kind in America," stated *The Hideaway Report*. "It's rather like those European castles
where one can arrange to spend a week as the

guest of the duke and duchess," commented the *Yale University Alumni Magazine*; "The Point: the wilderness at its most luxurious," summarized *Vogue Magazine*.

The 11 rooms, in four different buildings, each have vast beds, lake views, and fireplaces, and are filled with an astutely planned mixture of antiques, Adirondack furniture, Oriental rugs, old prints, and stuffed beasts. The Boathouse is a special gem, with its own private dining alcove and wrap-around balcony, but all the rooms are divine.

In the Main Lodge, the Great Hall measures 30 by 50 feet; fireplaces of astonishing proportions blaze away. The atmosphere here is that of a truly elegant house party, with black tie suggested for dinner on Wednesday and Saturday nights. The food warrants that treatment too, with menus deftly combining native bounty, fine herbs, exquisite seafood, and imported ingredients in an imaginative kaleidoscope of flavors. The wine list is unsurpassed, the bar is always open.

All this elegance and hedonism comes at a price, with two nights for a couple at The Point costing about as much as a week for two at Elk Lake Lodge. But *Forbes* magazine sums it up well: "There are no telephones, no newspapers, and no menu choice. You partake of what is prepared each day and sit down to dine at the appointed hour. If you don't like the hosts, the food, the guests or the digs, tough luck . . . [yet] for those in search of sybaritic creature comforts, there is only one destination — The Point."

A final note: don't expect to be able to drive in for just a look at the place. No signs mark the way to The Point, and only registered guests get the secret directions.

Wilmington

WILKOMMEN HOF
Owners: Heike and Bert Yost.
518-946-7626, 1-800-541-9119.
Closed: Apr. 15–May 15; Oct. 15–Nov. 15.
Price: Inexpensive to Moderate.
Credit Cards: MC, V.
Special Features: Meals available; sauna; hot tub; children and pets welcome; midweek ski packages.

A newly renovated European-style guesthouse, Wilkommen Hof has three rooms with private baths, a three-room suite, and three rooms that share baths, to house a maximum of 24 guests. Full breakfasts and after-ski treats are included in the room rate; hearty dinners may be arranged.

The fabled Ausable River trout waters are nearby, as are numerous state-marked trails for cross-country skiing and hiking. (Heike and Bert can suggest trips off the beaten path on foot or by bike.) Wilkommen Hof is quite popular with Whiteface Mtn. downhill skiers since it's just minutes away from the slopes. After all that exertion, guests can wind down in either the outdoor hot tub or indoor sauna.

NORTHWEST LAKES

Cranberry Lake

AMETHYST B & B
Hosts: Barbara Slater and
   Joan Rabin.
315-848-3529.
Rte. 3.
Closed: Sept.–May.
Price: Moderate.
Credit Cards: None.
Special Features: For
   women only.

An old-fashioned screen porch on this well-kept 1930s-vintage summer home provides a tree-framed view of Cranberry Lake. Amethyst is an out-of-the-way retreat for women only, featuring paintings, books, music, and videos by female artists. Three double rooms share two modern baths, and breakfast is hearty fare: homemade waffles, real maple syrup, country sausage.

CRANBERRY LAKE INN
Owners: Genie and Mike
   Coleman.
315-848-3301.
Rte. 3.
Closed: Spring.
Price: Inexpensive.
Credit Cards: MC, V.
Handicap Access: Some
   units; inquire.
Special Features: Children
   and well-behaved pets
   welcome.

Look down the lake from the motel/restaurant complex and you get a feel for just how wild and vast the Adirondacks are. This clean, homey place is a good jumping-off spot for exploring Cranberry Lake or the Five Ponds Wilderness Area several miles to the southwest, or heading out on the network of nearby snowmobile trails. There are 23 units for guests including two apartments; many rooms have views of the lake. The restaurant here is one of the best in the immediate area, and the antiques, stuffed animals, and old photographs give a good introduction to this uncrowded part of the park.

WILDCLIFFE LODGE
Owners: Barb and Vern
   Peterson.
No phone.
Mail: Box 526.
Closed: Nov. 15–June 1.
Price: Inexpensive to
   Moderate; lodge rooms
   are MAP.
Credit Cards: None.
Special Features: Remote
   location; access by
   boat only; children
   welcome.

Unless you want to hike 13 miles, the only access to the Wildcliffe Lodge is across the lake by boat, a distance of about six miles. As a matter of fact, everything comes to this remote hostelry over the water, from steak to beer and the mail. Guests catch the water taxi from the Emporium, in Cranberry Lake. Forget about phones or TV; electricity is supplied by a generator.

The main lodge is a big log building, with dining room, a bar that's open to the public, and a long porch. There are four rooms upstairs in the lodge, sharing baths; rates include breakfast and dinner. Two log cabins are in the woods, which have full kitchens, baths, and gas heat.

(For the cabins, guests need to supply all bed linens, blankets, towels, and even some cooking gear.) The Petersons serve plain, honest fare such as steaks, pork chops, and ham; the annual Fourth of July chicken barbecue and the September pig roast are jolly affairs.

From Wildcliffe, there are miles of wilderness hiking trails. Fishing and canoeing are good in Cranberry Lake, and the lodge is open during the first couple weeks of big game season if you'd like to hunt deep in the backcountry.

Lake Clear

The parlor at the Lodge at Lake Clear.

Nancie Battaglia

THE LODGE AT LAKE CLEAR
Innkeepers: Cathy and Ernest Hohmeyer.
518-891-1489.
Rtes. 30 & 186; Box 46.
Open: Year-round.
Price: Moderate to Expensive.
Min. Stay: 2 nights in chalets; 2 nights on holiday weekends.
Credit Cards: MC, V.
Special Features: Fireplaces; restaurant; children welcome; pets allowed in chalets — deposit required.

The Hohmeyers have made the Lodge at Lake Clear highly acclaimed for home-style German cuisine, and overnight guests have enjoyed the family's gracious hospitality for more than four decades. On 25 secluded lakeshore acres, accommodations here combine modern conveniences with Old World charm.

There are four upstairs rooms in the inn, each with private bath. In 1995, an adjacent house was completely renovated for guests; it has a view of the lake, kitchen, fireplace, and whirlpool tub in the full bath. Two chalets built in 1991 are completely outfitted and sleep two to six. Also on the grounds is a one-bedroom summer cabin. All of these buildings are located away from each other so that families can enjoy some woodsy privacy.

Guests have use of canoes, rowboats, a picnic area, and beach, and Cathy is happy to arrange mountain-bike rentals, guide service, or overnight canoe trips for visitors. The lodge also offers packages ranging from wellness weekends to romantic getaways.

Paul Smiths

The boathouse at Northbrook Lodge once housed a millionaire's fleet.

Nancie Battaglia

NORTHBROOK LODGE
Manager: Laura-Jean
  Schwartau.
518-327-3379.
Osgood Lake, off Rte. 86.
Closed: Sept. 15–June 15.
Price: Expensive. MAP;
  special rates for families.
Min. Stay: 3 nights.
Credit Cards: None.
Special Features: Fireplaces;
  lakefront; sandy beach;
  children welcome.

Set on a magnificent secluded pine-shaded peninsula on Osgood Lake, Northbrook Lodge was constructed as a millionaire's retreat in the 1920s by the same builder as the magnificent Adirondack Great Camp, Topridge, a few miles away.

Sixteen rooms for guests are in appealing cottages connected by covered walkways and porches; all have private baths, refrigerators, and separate entrances.

Breakfast and dinner are included in the room rate, and meals — made completely from scratch — are served in the dining hall. The boathouse has a bar/lounge with a classic Brunswick Balke billiard table; canoes and rowboats are available for guests at no extra charge.

WHITE PINE CAMP
Manager: Lynn Witte.
518-327-3030.

Imagine a week spent at a real Great Camp, once the summer White House of President Coolidge. Four of the cabins along Osgood Lake are available

Osgood Lake, off Rte. 86.
Closed: Late Oct.–early
  May; inquire about
  winterized units.
Price: Expensive.
Min. Stay: 1 week in July
  and August. 2 nights in
  spring and fall.
Credit Cards: MC, V.
Special Features: Historic
  site; fireplaces; children
  welcome.

to guests by the week in July and August and for shorter visits in spring and fall; a couple of units will be available for winter rentals as well. All the cabins — furnished with an eclectic assortment of rustic and Mission-style antiques — have porches, fieldstone fireplaces, kitchens, and separate bedrooms that accommodate two to four people; one unit in the main lodge offers more flexibility. Guests can use the beach, boathouse, Japanese teahouse, croquet lawn, bowling alley, canoes, and rowboats, and enjoy the extensive grove of wild rhododendrons that covers the hillside.

White Pine Camp also operates as a historic site, with guided tours in the morning and evening, but innkeeper Lynn Witte says that tours unobtrusively avoid the cabins' private spaces.

Saranac Inn

**SUNDAY POND BED &
  BREAKFAST**
Owners: Lesley and Dick
  Lyon.
518-891-1531.
Rte. 30 (Saranac Inn); Star
  Rte., Box 150 (Saranac
  Lake NY 12983).
Open: Year-round.
Price: Inexpensive.
Credit Cards: None.
Special Features: Guide
  service available;
  children welcome.

Say you're a canoeist or hiker and you want to explore the St. Regis Canoe Area with its dozens of lakes and ponds, but you hate the thought of camping out. Look no further: Sunday Pond is located smack where you can start all those adventures right from the front door.

The Lyons' home — one of a very few in this corner of the park — is quite nice, with a long porch, skylights, a fireplace, and a big family room. Guests can choose from two rooms that share a bath, a room with a private bath, or a spacious sleeping loft with its own bath. Breakfasts are ample and healthy; hearty trail lunches and dinners (pasta primavera, sautéed chicken breast with wild rice, London broil, vegetarian lasagna, etc.) are available to guests by request.

Tupper Lake

COLD RIVER RANCH
Hosts: Marie and John
  Fontana.
518-359-7559.
Rte. 3, Coreys; mail:
  Coreys, Tupper Lake NY
  12986.
Open: Year-round.
Price: Moderate, B&B; MAP
  available.

Cold River Ranch is famous for wilderness trail rides and overnight pack trips into remote areas of the High Peaks, and the huge old farmhouse is a very comfortable bed & breakfast as well. Nine guests are accommodated in four rooms with shared baths. Breakfast, which John describes as "fancy home cooking," can include cheesecake still warm from the oven. Full board is an option, too.

Credit Cards: MC, V.
Special Features:
   Horseback riding; cross-country-ski trails;
   children welcome.

CURTIGAY COVE
Owners: Gail and Morris
   Weissbrot.
518-359-9612, winter:
   904-753-8296.
2 Delair Dr.; winter mail:
   508 Rainbow Blvd., Lady
   Lake FL 32159.
Closed: Fall and winter.
Price: Moderate.
Min. Stay: 1 week.
Credit Cards: None.
Special Features: Sandy
   beach; children welcome.

THREE PILLARS
Owners: Bob and Neil
   Shofi.
518-359-3093, winter:
   914-835-2900.
Moody Rd.; winter mail:
   231 Halstead Ave.,
   Harrison NY 10528.
Closed: Nov. 15–June 25.
Price: Moderate.
Min. Stay: 1 week in
   summer; 3 days in fall.
Credit Cards: None.
Special Features: Private
   beach; lakefront; children
   welcome.

THE WAWBEEK RESORT
Managers: Nancy and
   Norman Howard.
518-359-2656,
   1-800-953-2656.
www.wawbeek.com.
553 Panther Mtn. Rd.,
   off Rte. 30.
Open: Year-round.
Price: Moderate to
   Expensive; MAP
   available.

In the winter, the horse trails are endless backcountry ski trails. Guides, instructors, and rental equipment are available, and the Fontanas are happy to arrange custom ski tours for guests.

On a quiet bay of Little Wolf Lake, just east of Tupper Lake village, the Weissbrots offer four handsome fully equipped housekeeping cottages. "Our customers from the city always tell us, 'This is exactly what we were looking for,'" says Gail.

All the cottages have sun decks, picnic tables, and outdoor fireplaces; guests need to bring bed linens and towels. Curtigay Cove is the kind of place that families return to every year, with kids building friendships that last beyond the summer.

With about a quarter mile of shoreline on Big Tupper Lake, the secluded cabins at Three Pillars have a great view. The location, on the southern end of Big Tupper Lake and close to Bog River Falls, is one of the best you'll find on this large lake.

There are three pine-paneled, comfortably furnished housekeeping cottages with complete kitchens, fireplaces (wood is supplied), and screen porches, plus a three-bedroom apartment above the boathouse that offers the wonderful sensation of being right on the water. There's a nice sandy beach and a long dock for guests' boats. Ask about where to find the walleyes.

Sharing the same Upper Saranac bay as the classic Great Camps Wenonah Lodge and Sekon Lodge, the Wawbeek Resort has an authentic Adirondack style. The original Wawbeek, itself a Great Camp, burned in 1980, and new owners consolidated that property with a former boys' camp next door. One of the buildings, Mountain House Lodge, is a wonderful turn-of-century structure with double-deck porches, stone fireplace, and great room; it's the kind of place that would be ideal for several couples or an extended family to share for a

Min. Stay: 1 week in some accommodations in summer; inquire.
Credit Cards: All major.
Special Features: Lakefront; sandy beach; boats; boat launch and dockage for guests; tennis; restaurant.

week in any season. Scattered under the trees are comfortable one-bedroom log cabins, larger cottages, and a three-bedroom carriage house.

Guests have all of gorgeous Upper Saranac Lake to explore by sailboat, rowboat, or canoe. There's a beach, tennis court, game room, basketball court, and boat launch on the premises. In the winter, cross-country skiers can try the Deer Pond cross-country trails just a short distance away.

The Wawbeek's restaurant is in one of the most attractive settings — with a first-rate menu, to boot — in the Adirondack Park.

CENTRAL ADIRONDACKS

Arietta

AVERY'S INN
Manager: Darla Oathout.
518-835-4014.
Rte. 10 (Arietta); Box 48A (Caroga Lake NY 12032).
Closed: 1998 for renovations.
Price: Inexpensive to Moderate.
Credit Cards: MC, V.
Special Features: Restaurant and bar; access to snowmobile trails.

A big old hotel on a less-traveled stretch of highway, Avery's has been operated by the same family for more than a hundred years. The West Branch of the Sacandaga River is just across the road; snowmobile and hiking trails are nearby. It's an out-of-the-way spot, so much so that they have to generate their own electricity.

There are 17 rooms for guests, all with private baths. Special weekend packages with meals and lodgings are designed for leaf-peepers, cross-country skiers, and snowmobilers.

Benson

LAPLAND LAKE CROSS-COUNTRY SKI & VACATION CENTER
Owners: Ann and Olavi Hirvonen.
518-863-4974.
Storer Rd. (Benson); RD 2, Box 2053 (Northville NY 12134).
Open: Year-round.
Price: Moderate.
Min. Stay: 2 nights on winter weekends; 1 week in high summer.
Credit Cards: D, MC, V.

J ust when you think that you got the directions wrong to this rather remote spot, you see road signs in . . . *Finnish*? Quickly, the view opens up to a brand-new ski shop and a bunch of neat little cottages. Readers of *Snow Country* magazine recently rated the Lapland Lake — with 35 km of groomed trails, a restaurant, and a full ski shop — among the top ten Nordic ski centers in the East.

Summertime is nice at Lapland Lake, too. There's a small spring-fed lake on the 300-acre property where guests can swim, canoe, and fish. Trails here connect with state-owned hiking trails; you can pick up the Northville–Lake Placid Trail less than a mile away, or climb Cathead Mtn.

Special Features: Cross-country-ski trails; sauna; ski-rental shop; ski lessons; snack bar; live reindeer; children welcome; no pets.

Ten housekeeping cottages range in size from two to four bedrooms, and are called *tupas*, which means "cabin" in Finnish. They're spotless and comfortable; most have wood stoves or screen porches. The biggest place, *Lapin Tupa*, is the property's original farmhouse. It has a formal dining room with a nice view of the pond, a big eat-in kitchen, living room with piano, four bedrooms, and two full baths.

Trailhead Lodge is a comfortable old farmhouse near Silver Lake Wilderness Area.

B. Folwell

TRAILHEAD LODGE
Owner: John Washburn.
518-863-2198.
Washburn Rd. (Benson);
RD 2, Box 2047A
(Northville NY 12134).
Open: Year-round.
Price: Inexpensive to
Moderate.
Min. Stay: 2 nights winter
weekends; 3 nights
holiday weekends.
Credit Cards: MC, V.
Special Features: Guide
service; canoe rentals;
fireplace; outdoor-skill
workshops; children
over 6 welcome.

John Washburn's great-grandfather took in hunters and fishermen here more than a century ago, and guided them to the big ones; nowadays you can do much the same thing in a bit more comfort at Trailhead Lodge. On the outside, the building looks like a typical farmhouse and inside, the walls are finished off with new pine boards and Adirondack decor, like snowshoes, pack baskets, and such. Four guest rooms share baths; visitors may choose bed-&-breakfast or modified American plan arrangements.

John, a licensed Adirondack guide, is very knowledgeable about the woods and wildlife; he leads map-and-compass workshops for groups, or takes folks on hikes, canoe trips, backcountry ski adventures, and snowshoeing trips. By the roaring fire on a chill night, you might coax him to recite Robert Service poems or tall tales.

Big Moose Lake

BIG MOOSE INN
Innkeepers: Bonnie and
   Doug Bennett.
314-357-2042.
www.bigmooseinn.com.
Big Moose Rd.; mail: Eagle
   Bay NY 13331.
Closed: Apr., Nov.
Price: Inexpensive to
   Moderate; MAP available.
Min. Stay: 2 nights on
   weekends.
Credit Cards: AE, MC, V.
Special Features: Canoes;
   restaurant; snowmobile
   trails; lakefront; children
   welcome.

Mud season is about the only time you can't enjoy Big Moose Inn. In late spring, you can canoe and fish on Big Moose Lake; summertime you can hike around Pigeon Lake Wilderness Area or visit nearby towns like Inlet and Old Forge; in the fall you can see beautiful foliage or hunt; when the snows arrive, there's snowmobiling or cross-country skiing practically right to the front door.

There are 16 rooms upstairs in the inn, all recently refurbished and with private baths. Most chambers have a nice view of the lake; one includes a fireplace, king-size bed, and jacuzzi tub. Big Moose Inn's restaurant is one of the best in the neighborhood, worth a detour.

COVEWOOD LODGE
Owner: C.V. Bowes, Jr.
315-357-3041.
Off Big Moose Rd.
Open: Year-round.
Price: Moderate to
   Expensive; depends on
   cottage size.
Credit Cards: None.
Special Features: Sandy
   beach; lakefront; cross-
   country-ski trails;
   children welcome.

One of the all-time great woodsy Adirondack retreats, Covewood was built as a hotel back in the days when guests stayed all summer long. Even in today's busy world, you'd probably wish you could stay from Independence Day to Labor Day, the place is so peaceful. Major Bowes keeps it that way.

There are 17 housekeeping cabins along the lake and under the pines, ranging in size from one room to seven bedrooms plus kitchen, living room, and porches. All the cabins have fireplaces and furnaces. There's a big rustic lodge with a stone fireplace for guests to enjoy after they've explored the wild woods nearby.

THE WALDHEIM
Owners: Nancy and Roger
   Pratt.
315-357-2353.
Big Moose Rd.; mail: Eagle
   Bay NY 13331.
Closed: Columbus
   Day–Mid-June.
Price: Expensive, but
   includes 3 meals.
Credit Cards: None.
Special Features: Sandy
   beach; boats for guests;
   children welcome; rustic
   buildings; fireplaces.

The Waldheim was built in 1904 by E.J. Martin from trees cut on the property, and there's a wonderful old-time feel to the place. ("No phone, no TV, no clocks," says Nancy Pratt, the third generation of her family to run the place.) Many of the 15 cabins are made of vertical half logs and have twig-work railings on the porches. The places are aptly named "Cozy," "Comfort," "Heart's Content," and every one has a fireplace. Rates include three full meals a day, which are served in a gracious dining room furnished with antique chairs and tables.

The boathouse and cottages at the Waldheim are made of vertical half logs.

Nancie Battaglia

Just about when the cottages open, lovely wild azaleas bloom along the pathways. Guests can hike, canoe, swim, and fish; arrangements can be made to have a seaplane pick you up at the dock for a scenic flight. There are no planned activities except the weekly camp picnic, a moveable feast taken to a remote part of the lake by boat. The 300-acre property is adjacent to state land so the location is secluded indeed.

Blue Mountain Lake

CEDAR COVE COTTAGES
Managers: Helen and Bert Czawakiel.
518-352-7393.
Off Rte. 28.
Closed: Fall & winter.
Price: Moderate.
Min. Stay: 1 week.

Three housekeeping cottages hidden away in a secluded spot, Cedar Cove offers privacy and lovely views of the lake. Cabins all have fireplaces, picture windows, and docks; these places are generally booked for July and August by families who return every year. In June or September, though, real solitude can be found here.

CURRY'S COTTAGES
Owners: Mike and Bob Curry.
518-352-7354, winter: 518-352-7355.
Rte. 28.
Closed: Nov.–Apr.
Price: Moderate.
Credit Cards: None.
Min. Stay: 1 week in July–Aug.; weekends May–June, Sept.

These charming barn-red housekeeping cottages are a familiar sight to Blue Mtn. Lake visitors; photographs of the chorus line of white Adirondack chairs along the beach have appeared in numerous national magazines. Three generations of Currys have operated the cottages, and Bob, the current Curry, is always at work making improvements.

Nine cottages accommodate couples to families of six; four cottages are on the water, and the remainder are on the edge of the woods across the

Special Features: Boat
launch; children
welcome.

road. The beach at Curry's is a favorite with families; it's safe and shallow for kids.

FOREST HOUSE LODGE
Innkeeper: Anne LaForest.
518-352-7030.
Rtes. 28/30.
Open: Year-round.
Price: Inexpensive.
Credit Cards: None.

Year-round lodging near Blue Mtn. Lake has been hard to find — that is until recently, when Anne LaForest opened her restored Craftsman-style home to guests. The place is located on the state highway between Blue Mtn. and Indian lakes, next door to the Forest House restaurant (serving dinners on weekends fall through spring and daily in summer). Two good-sized bedrooms with antique or twig bedsteads share a bath upstairs, with plans to create a larger suite from a corner room.

Breakfast — homemade everything — is served on Portmeirion china at a table set with fresh flowers, with music from a huge collection of CDs that ranges from bluesman Delbert McClinton to classical music.

The main lodge at the Hedges is set on a quiet bay of Blue Mountain Lake.

Nancie Battaglia

THE HEDGES
Owners: Cathy and Richard
Van Yperen.

Colonel Hiram Duryea, a Civil War veteran and millionaire industrialist, began building the Hedges in 1880. The main house, with four won-

518-352-7325, 518-352-7672.
Closed: Oct. 10–June 15.
Price: Expensive; MAP.
Credit Cards: None.
Handicap Access: 2 cottages.
Special Features: Private
  sandy beach; boats for
  guests; tennis; meals;
  children welcome; no
  pets.

derful guest rooms all with private baths, has an unusual mansard roof line that sweeps onto a wraparound porch. The lovely Stone Lodge, built about 1890, has a three-bedroom suite with fireplace on the first floor, and six rooms with private baths upstairs. Antiques and fine woodworking are found throughout these two lodges.

There are a dozen one- to four-bedroom sleeping cottages along the secluded lakeshore. All accommodations are offered modified American plan; picnic lunches are available at a small charge. Guests have use of canoes, rowboats, a clay tennis court, and the library; the game room, a museum-quality gem of rustic detail, is worth a visit even if you don't play ping-pong.

Meals are served in the dining room lodge, another appealing old building, which has stamped-tin walls and ceilings and a stone fireplace. Guests get their own tables for the duration of their stay, so there's no need to try to make new friends over dinner every night. (Note that alcoholic beverages are not permitted in public areas.) After dinner, desserts and coffee are put out so that folks can linger over those treats in their own cabins or rooms.

Blue Mtn. Lake is a very beautiful, quiet lake; the Hedges is in a particularly lovely, private spot. Generations of families have returned since the hotel opened to guests more than 75 years ago; three generations of the Van Yperen family work hard at making sure folks feel comfortable.

HEMLOCK HALL
Owners: Susan and Paul
  Provost.
518-352-7706.
Maple Lodge Rd.
Closed: Mid-Oct.–mid-May.
Price: Moderate to
  Expensive; MAP.
Min. Stay: 3 nights in
  summer; as available
  spring and fall.
Credit Cards: None.
Special Features: Private
  beach; boats for guests;
  meals; children welcome;
  no pets.

On Maple Lodge Road, a mile off the main highway, is another stunning Adirondack hostelry. Hemlock Hall was carefully restored by Eleanor and Monty Webb in the 1950s, and their hard work still shows. The woodwork in the main lodge — a complicated pattern of wainscoting on the walls and ceilings — still gleams, and there are numerous antiques throughout. The stone fireplace has hearths on two sides, opening onto part of the living room and a wing of the dining room. There's even a fireplace in an upstairs hallway.

There are 23 rooms for guests in accommodations ranging from lodge rooms with shared baths to motel units to two- or three-bedroom cottages. The tower suite in the main lodge has its own private screen porch and charming window seats; several of the lodge rooms have nice lake views; you can even rent the top floor of the boathouse. Breakfast and dinner are included in the room charges.

The dining room serves wholesome, plentiful food in a family-style arrangement. There's one entrée offered each evening, with chicken and biscuits on

Wednesdays a great favorite. (Non-guests can dine with prior reservations.) Folks are seated at different tables each night so they get to mingle with the other visitors; alcoholic beverages, which might make all this mingling a bit easier, are not permitted in the dining room.

LAPRAIRIE'S LAKESIDE COTTAGES
Owners: Kim and Ernie LaPrairie.
518-352-7675.
Rte. 28/30.
Closed: Columbus Day–May 15.
Price: Moderate to Expensive.
Min. Stay: 1 week in summer; 3 nights spring and fall.
Credit Cards: No.
Special feature: Private beach and docks.

These two attractively renovated housekeeping cabins are so close to the shore of Blue Mtn. Lake that you can hear the waves washing up on the private beach. The Shanty can hold up to nine guests in three bedrooms and has a lakeside porch, fireplace, bath and a half, and complete kitchen; Crooked Cottage has a loft bedroom overlooking the lake and is comfortable for a couple or a small family. Traveling with teenagers? LaPrairie's cabins are among the only places in Blue Mtn. Lake with cable TV.

Rental canoes are available next door at Blue Mtn. Outfitters and there's swimming right out the front door.

POTTER'S RESORT
Owners: Laura and Ralph Faxon.
518-352-7331.
Rtes. 28 & 30.
Closed: Sept. 30–May 1.
Price: Inexpensive to Moderate.
Min. Stay: 1 week for housekeeping cottages July–Aug.
Credit Cards: MC, V.
Special Features: 1 year-round cottage; private beach; dockage for guests' boats; tennis; restaurant; children welcome; no pets.

As you enter the hamlet of Blue Mtn. Lake, Potter's Resort is one of the first places you'll see. Ten housekeeping cottages are available: most have porches; several have fireplaces; some are huge old log cabins with cathedral ceilings. There are 10 motel units near the road that all have porches, and four motel rooms with fireplaces.

Potter's has a great beach, dock space for visitors' boats, and a tennis court. The classic Adirondack dining room is open for breakfast, lunch, and dinner from late June through Labor Day, with a complete menu and liquor license. New in 1997 are a large year-round rental cottage, a gift shop — with Beanie Babies galore — and a four-wheel-drive rental car for stranded travelers.

PROSPECT POINT COTTAGES
Manager: Bob Webb.
518-352-7378.
Edison Rd., off Rte. 28.
Closed: Oct. 10–May 10.
Price: Moderate.
Min. Stay: 1 week July–Aug.; 3 nights spring and fall.

This beautiful peninsula on Blue Mtn. Lake was once the site of the mammoth 100-room Prospect House, the first hotel in the world to have electricity. (Never mind that technology went only so far; running water was not available.) Now five recently renovated two- and three-bedroom housekeeping cottages occupy the point; they're spot-

Credit Cards: None.
Special Features: Private
 sandy beach; children
 and pets welcome.

lessly clean and very quiet, set near a big, sandy beach.

The view of Blue Mtn. is simply magnificent. From Prospect Point, which is close to town, but off the highway, it's an easy walk to the arts center for a concert, the boat livery for a tour of the chain of lakes, or the post office to mail those picture postcards saying "Wish you were here."

Indian Lake/Sabael

BURKE'S COTTAGES
Owners: Rose and Bruce
 Burke.
518-648-5258, winter:
 516-281-4983.
Lake Shore Dr., Sabael.
Open: Year-round.
Price: Moderate.
Min. Stay: 2 nights; 1 week
 July–Aug.
Credit Cards: None.
Special Features: Private
 beach; dock; children
 welcome; no pets.

On Indian Lake a few miles south of the village, the Burkes rent six newly renovated housekeeping cabins throughout the seasons. Most have two bedrooms, fireplaces, picnic tables, and grills; some have decks or screen porches. You can see Indian Lake from each of the cottages.

There's a private beach for swimming, a dock for boats, and Rose and Bruce are around from spring through fall to help you select the perfect hike, that undiscovered restaurant, or something to do on a rainy day.

CAMP DRIFTWOOD
Owners: Doris, Jon, and
 A.E. Voorhees.
518-648-5111, winter: 941-
 355-3535.
199 Sabael Rd., Indian
 Lake; winter mail: 2712
 59th St., Sarasota FL
 34243.
Open: Year-round.
Price: Inexpensive to
 Moderate.
Min. Stay: 1 week
 July–Aug.
Credit Cards: None.
Special Features: Private
 beach; boats for guests;
 children and well-
 behaved pets welcome.

Indian Lake is about 13 miles long, with numerous bays and publicly owned islands to explore, and Camp Driftwood is a good base from which to plan day trips, or simply to relax in a secluded spot. Nick, Jon, and Doris Voorhees rent 10 housekeeping cabins all along the shore and tucked back in the woods. Maple Cabin is an old lodge, with three bedrooms, a fireplace, screen porch, and deck; Birch also has three bedrooms, and you can practically roll out of bed in the morning for a dip in the lake. All cottages have full kitchens and wood stoves for cool mornings, plus outdoor fireplaces for barbecues. Guests need to bring bed linens and towels.

There's a sandy beach for wading, a float for advanced swimmers, canoes and rowboats for guests, and genuine hospitality from the Voorhees family. This is the kind of place where families settle in for two weeks or more and pretend they're at home.

**CHIEF SABAEL
    COTTAGES**
Owners: Cynthia and
    Robert Kluin.
518-648-5200.
Lake Shore Dr., Sabael.
Cottages closed: Columbus
    Day–Memorial Day;
    efficiencies open all year.
Price: Inexpensive to
    Moderate.
Min. Stay: 1 week in
    cottages July–Aug.
Credit Cards: None.
Special Features: Private
    sandy beach; tennis;
    dockage for guests'
    boats; children welcome;
    extra charge for pets.

On a quiet stretch of the lake four miles south of the village, Chief Sabael Cottages offer privacy and convenience: it's a short walk to the Lake Store for resupplying the refrigerator. The Kluins rent six housekeeping cottages, which accommodate from two to seven people; many have fireplaces and porches with lake views. The cabins are available by the week only during July and August; visitors may arrange for shorter stays in spring and fall. Additionally, there are winterized efficiency units open year-round, so that skiers, snowmobilers, fishermen, whitewater rafters, and others can stay near all those activities.

This is one of the few places in the immediate area with a private tennis court. There's also a log lean-to by the lake, a sandy beach, and dock space available for guests' boats at an extra charge.

The 1870 Bed & Breakfast is within walking distance of Indian Lake's theater and restaurants.

B. Folwell

1870 BED & BREAKFAST
Host: Bill Zullo.
518-648-5377.
Main St.
Open: Year-round.
Price: Inexpensive.
Credit Cards: None.
Special Features: Fireplace;
    cable TV; children
    welcome; no pets.

Guestbooks from decades ago capture the flavor of this place: "Our stay here was wonderful as usual. In the past 16 years, nothing has changed," commented one repeat visitor 25 years ago. You'll still find real braided rugs on the floors, tatted spreads on the antique beds, ruffled curtains in the windows, family pictures dating back to the turn of the century on the walls, and a homey, quiet atmosphere.

There is one bedroom with a private bath on the first floor, and four nice rooms upstairs that share a bath and a sitting room. The living room has comfortable Grandma's-house-type furniture, a fireplace, cable TV, plus shelves of board games and puzzles. From the shady front porch, you can look out over the garden, and further back on the old 40-acre farm, there's a big raspberry patch that's open for grazing. Tennis courts (at the school) are kitty-corner; there are couple of new bikes in the barn that guests can use, and there's a private right-of-way to Lake Adirondack for fishing or canoeing about a half mile away.

GEANDREAU'S CABINS
Owners: Dotty and Bob
  Geandreau.
518-648-5500.
Rte. 28, Indian Lake.
Open: Year-round.
Price: Inexpensive.
Min. Stay: 2 nights.
Credit Cards: None.
Special Features: Children
  welcome; pets must be
  leashed at all times.

When you enter the hamlet of Indian Lake from the east, one of the first places that comes into view is Geandreau's cluster of well-kept cabins on Route 28 across from Lake Adirondack. In the summer, the border of bright red dahlias in the front yard might catch your eye. For more than 30 years Dot and Bob have built up a year-round business, accommodating everyone from adventure-seekers to folks looking for a peaceful place to rest.

The cabins sleep up to five people, and are fully outfitted with kitchen equipment, linens, towels, and so on. There are screened porches on all the cottages, making them particularly enjoyable during bug season. Rowboats and canoes for exploring the nearby lake are provided; there's a nice swimming beach about 200 yards away.

SNOWSHOE HILL COTTAGES
Owners: Helen and John
  Feeney.
518-648-5207.
Cedar River Rd.
Open: Year-round.
Price: Inexpensive.
Min. Stay: 2 nights.
Credit Cards: None.
Special Features: Children
  and pets welcome.

East of downtown Indian Lake is the gorgeous Cedar River valley, gateway to thousands of acres of state-owned wilderness. One place to stay near this rocky trout stream is Snowshoe Hill Cottages, two four-season, fully equipped housekeeping cottages, plus an apartment (with a private entrance) in the Feeneys' house. Just up the road is good fishing on the Cedar River Flow, good hiking up Wakely Mtn., or mountain biking along the dirt roads of the Moose River Recreation Area. In the other direction, about two miles away is Wakely Lodge Golf Course. In the winter, you can cross-country ski or snowmobile from the front door.

TIMBERLOCK
Owner: Richard Catlin.
518-648-5494, winter:
  802-457-1621.

Timberlock welcomed its first guests in 1898. Not much has changed since those early days: all the common buildings and the guests' log cab-

Nancie Battaglia

Timberlock, a series of log lodges and cabins, is on Indian Lake, miles from town.

On Indian Lake.
Closed: Sept. 20–June 23.
Price: Expensive; full American plan; special rates for families.
Min. Stay: 1 week.
Credit Cards: None.
Special Features: Private beach; boats; horseback riding; tennis; children welcome; no pets.

ins are still equipped with gaslights and wood stoves, so don't expect to find outlets for laptop computers. The atmosphere here is rustic, relaxed, peaceful, yet the resort offers a surprising variety of activities and amenities.

There are four Hartru tennis courts; gentle horses for guided trail rides; an excellent sandy beach; numerous boats to sail, paddle, or row on Indian Lake; and trails on the property for hiking and birding. Timberlock is home to fall Elderhostel seminars on Adirondack history and nature; there are adventure-camp sessions for teens and other outdoor-educational programs offered from year to year. If you'd prefer to discover the Adirondacks on your own, the Catlins have assembled a 120-page book outlining car trips, picnic spots, mountain climbs, museums, and other sites to explore.

"Timberlock is not for everyone," says Dick Catlin. "We are not a luxury place and have not paved away the wildlife." There are a dozen "family cottages," that have full baths, screen porches, and lake views, plus some small cabins without baths. Rates include three hearty meals a day and use of all the facilities and activities except horseback riding. There are no neighbors within miles of Timberlock, and your wake-up call in the morning may well be a loon's yodel from the lake.

Inlet

THE CROSSWINDS
Owner: Jan Burwell.
315-357-4500.

Located right on Fourth Lake are the Crosswinds' cabins, five attractive two-bedroom housekeeping units. All the places have completely

Rte. 28.
Closed: Oct. 15–May 15.
Price: Inexpensive to
  Moderate.
Min. Stay: 1 week
  July–Aug.; overnights
  welcome in off-season.
Credit Cards: None.
Special Features: Private
  beach; children welcome;
  no pets.

DEER MEADOWS
Owners: Linda and Robert
  Gordon.
315-357-3274.
Rte. 28.
Open: Year-round.
Price: Inexpensive.
Min. Stay: 2 nights on
  holiday weekends;
  cottages rent by the week
  July–Aug.
Credit Cards: D, MC, V.
Special Features: Private
  beach; children welcome.

HOLL'S INN
Innkeeper: Rosemary Holl.
315-357-2941, winter:
  315-733-2748.
South Shore Rd.; winter
  mail: 615 Ravine Dr.,
  Utica NY 13502.
Closed: Sept.–June.
Price: Moderate to
  Expensive; full American
  plan.
Min. Stay: 2 nights.
Credit Cards: None.
Handicap Access: 25 rooms
  have ramps.
Special Features: Private
  beach; restaurant and
  bar; library.

equipped, knotty-pine-paneled kitchens; guests need to supply their own linens and towels. There's a 200-foot private sandy beach, and a large dock for boats (small extra charge for dock space). It's a short walk from the Crosswinds to downtown Inlet, which has a movie theater, restaurants, tennis courts, outfitters, liquor store, and shops.

At Deer Meadows, there's a 10-unit motel with queen-size beds, cable TV, and in-room coffee on Route 28, and on a private drive across the highway, there are six pleasant housekeeping cottages ranging in size from one to three bedrooms. All the cottages have fireplaces and complete kitchens; guests need to bring bed linens and towels.

There's a nice little beach and picnic area on Seventh Lake, free rowboats for guests, and plenty of friendly mallard ducks to feed in the summer. The accommodations are open year-round, and snowmobilers appreciate Deer Meadows because the Gordons have a heated garage available for minor repairs.

Rosemary Holl says, "The way we were is the way we still are!" This spacious resort — 150 beautiful acres on the shore of Fourth Lake — dates back to the 1920s, and the Holl family has been in charge since 1935. The buildings and grounds are meticulously maintained and quite secluded; whitetail deer often cross the lawn to drink from the lake.

There are numerous rooms with private baths in the original hotel building; 25 rooms with private baths in the Annex, and two apartments in the Alpine House. Guests get three hearty meals a day in the lovely dining room, which is also open to the public with advance reservations. An especially charming nook of the inn is the Tyrolean Bar, done up in Dresden blue, yellow, and red, with cozy booths and hand-decorated plates commemorating all the honeymooners who have stayed at Holl's over the years. After all that food and drink, there are plenty of ways to work off the extra calories: swimming, tennis, rowing, or canoeing.

ROCKY POINT TOWNHOUSES
315-357-3751.
Rte. 28.
Open: Year-round.
Price: Expensive.
Min. Stay: 1 week July–Aug.
Credit Cards: MC, V.
Special Features: Docks for guests' boats; children and pets welcome.

The original Rocky Point, an enormous old lodge, was razed to make room for lakeside three-bedroom townhouses. Each one is nicely appointed and has a fireplace, three full baths, and cable TV; kitchens have microwaves, dishwashers, washer/dryers and new appliances. The beach is excellent, nearly a quarter-mile long, but if the water's too chilly there's a indoor pool and spa. Four tennis courts are on the property, and two excellent golf courses are within a 10-minute drive.

WOODHOLME
Owners: Muriel and Bill Campbell; Jean and Jean-Pierre Fortier.
315-357-2161, winter: 613-241-2459.
Seventh Lake; winter mail: 205 Daly Ave., Ottawa, Ont., Canada K1N 6G1.
Closed: Sept.–June.
Price: Moderate.
Min. Stay: 2 weeks.
Credit Cards: None.
Special Features: Private lakefront; boats; children welcome.

On the north shore of Seventh Lake, sharing a boundary with state lands, Woodholme is in a lovely, out-of-the-way setting. On the same property as the two large housekeeping cottages is a historic Adirondack lodge, which once operated as a hotel; although that building is not open to guests, it adds a distinctly rustic air to the place. There's private waterfront, with a boat and motor provided for each cottage, and a canoe is available for trips on Sixth and Seventh lakes. From Woodholme, there's a hiking trail up Black Bear Mtn. — take a container for the blueberries you may find along the way.

Johnsburg

GARNET LAKE LODGE
Owners: Joyce and Pete Parker.
518-251-2582, winter: 518-251-2273.
Garnet Lake; winter mail: Box 68, North Creek NY 12853.
Closed: Winter & spring.
Price: Moderate.
Min. Stay: 1 week July–Aug.; 2 nights off-season.
Credit Cards: None.
Special Features: Private beach; rowboats ; children welcome.

Garnet Lake is mostly surrounded by forever wild state lands and has only about two dozen residences around it. There's very good fishing, nice swimming, excellent hiking, and plenty of peace and quiet. The Parkers rent five two- and three-bedroom cottages, each of which comes with a rowboat for finding those lunker bass. The cabins are completely furnished except that guests need to bring sheets and towels.

Long Lake

ADIRONDACK HOTEL
Owners: Carol and Art
  Young.
518-624-4700,
  1-800-877-9247.
Rtes. 28/30.
Open: Year-round.
Price: Inexpensive to
  Moderate.
Credit Cards: AE, MC, V.
Special Features: Bar and
  restaurant; fireplace.

There's been a lodge at this spot overlooking Long Lake since before the Civil War, and portions of the current Adirondack Hotel date to the 1870s. Public spaces include a nice parlor and two dining rooms; the lobby includes a museum-quality turned-spindle cashier's booth. Taxidermy specimens (full-size black bear, giant moose head, and a goodly assortment of Adirondack mammals) add to the old-time feel.

Nineteen guest rooms are located on the second and third floors. Many have been renovated and have modern bathrooms, but some rooms share baths.

GREEN HARBOR
Owners: Ellen and Ken
  Schaeffer.
518-624-4133,
  1-800-845-5253.
Rte. 28/30.
Closed: Late fall–early
  spring.
Price: Moderate.
Min. Stay: 1 week in
  July–Aug.
Credit Cards: None.

Six well-maintained housekeeping cottages and a small motel are set on a private sandy beach at Green Harbor; cabins have cable TV and decks or porches with views of the water. Winter visitors can stay in three bed-&-breakfast rooms in the main house and venture out on Long Lake's miles of cross-country skiing or snowmobiling trails. There's a game room with ping-pong table, library, and large color TV.

LONG VIEW LODGE
Owners: Angela and Fred
  Fink.
518-624-2862.
Deerland Rd.
Open: Year-round.
Price: Moderate.
Min. Stay: 2 nights on
  weekends; 3 nights
  holiday weekends.
Credit Cards: MC, V.
Special Features: Private
  beach; children welcome.

A Long Lake landmark since 1929, the Long View remains comfortably true to its roots. The inn has 14 bedrooms, most of which have private baths; the adjoining rooms with shared baths are ideal for families. There are two sleeping cottages on the property as well.

Public spaces are airy and comfortable, with chairs, books, and cozy nooks. The restaurant serves breakfast, lunch, and dinner daily all year-round; the new Ice House Tavern, built in 1994, is a great spot for enjoying a light meal. There's a shady veranda overlooking the lake and a nice beach.

WATER'S EDGE CABINS
Owners: Lesley and Tom
  Knoll.
518-624-5825.

Tucked into a private nook on Long Lake but convenient to the highway, Water's Edge is a cluster of four housekeeping cottages, all recently redone and nicely decorated. The cabins are all

Deerland Rd.
Closed: Mid-Oct.–mid-
May.
Price: Inexpensive to
Moderate.
Min. Stay: 2 nights; 1 week
in July–Aug.
Credit Cards: MC, V.
Special Features: Private
beach; children welcome.

named after Adirondack birds, with Osprey a large two-bedroom unit, Sandpiper a cozy place for a couple, and Loon and Chickadee the in-between sizes. Each cottage has a full-size kitchen, fireplace or glass-doored woodstove, picnic table, and cable TV. There's a private beach and a dock; guests share an aluminum canoe and a pedal boat.

WHISPERING WOODS
Owners: Margaret and Bob
Sauerhafer.
518-624-5121,
1-800-822-2814.
Walker Rd.
Closed: Nov. 1–Apr. 30.
Price: Inexpensive to
Moderate.
Min. Stay: 2 nights; cottages
rent by the week
July–Aug.
Credit Cards: MC, V.
Special Features: Private
beach; children welcome;
leashed pets welcome.

The large sandy beach on a quiet shore of Long Lake is one of the major attractions at Whispering Woods, but the campground/cottage complex also has a well-stocked grocery store, game room, playground, and canoes and rowboats to rent. There are numerous options for lodging, from the five-bedroom Farmhouse and assorted cabins to apartments in the Main Lodge. All of the cottages have kitchens equipped with the basics; guests need to bring bed linens and towels. For recreational vehicles and travel trailers, there are wooded and lakeside sites with complete hookups available from May through October.

Minerva

MORNINGSIDE CAMPS
AND COTTAGES
Owners: Sandy and Frank
LaBar.
518-251-2694.
Minerva Lake.
Closed: Mid-Oct.–mid-
May.
Price: Inexpensive to
Moderate.
Min. Stay: 1 week in
summer; 2 nights
spring and fall.
Credit Cards: None.
Special Features: Private
beach; children welcome;
pets may stay in spring
and fall.

Set on 80 acres of land accessible by a private road, Morningside Camps offer waterfront seclusion on Minerva Lake. There are 10 nice log cabins with stone fireplaces and five chalets, all of which have complete kitchens, bathrooms, and decks or screen porches. The property features a private beach, a play area with a treehouse for the kids, a tennis court, docks for canoes and rowboats, and hiking trails through the woods that lead you to the general store, the town beach, or around the shoreline. Each cabin comes with its own boat.

Understandably, there's a waiting list for the LaBar's cabins in July and August, but places are available before the Fourth of July and after Labor Day. Don't be afraid to ask.

A cozy log cabin at Morningside, on Minerva Lake.

Nancie Battaglia

North Creek

THE COPPERFIELD INN
Manager: Laura Hollenbeck.
518-251-2500, 1-800-424-9910.
www.mediausa.com/ny/ cprfldin.
Main St.
Closed: Nov.
Price: Moderate to Expensive.
Credit Cards: AE, D, DC, MC, V.
Special Features: Heated pool; children welcome; no pets.

An elegant, tasteful motor inn that comes as quite a surprise after you've driven down North Creek's modest Main Street, the Copperfield has all the amenities you'd expect at a real ski resort: heated pool, health club, hot tub, tennis court, fancy restaurant, sports bar, conference facilities, shuttle bus to the slopes. Work completed in summer 1997 created the Trappers Tavern, beauty salon, and a state-of-the-art health club. All kinds of interesting package deals for whitewater rafters, golfers, senior citizens, and midweek guests are available. The 24 huge, luxurious rooms come with queen- or king-size beds, terrycloth bathrobes, and grand marble bathrooms.

GOOSE POND INN
Innkeepers: Beverly and Jim Englert.
518-251-3434.
Main St.
Open: Year-round.
Price: Moderate.
Credit Cards: None.
Special Features: Fireplace; wood-fired sauna; children over 10 welcome; no pets.

A beautifully restored Victorian home set back on a shady lawn off Main Street, Goose Pond Inn has four lovely bedrooms, each with its own bath. Antiques, old prints, and amusing details are found throughout. Jim cooks up superb breakfasts, such as brandied French toast with sautéed apples, crêpes with rhubarb sauce, or Belgian waffles with flambéed bananas. From the inn, it's a five-minute drive to downhill skiing at Gore Mtn., or to any of the whitewater rafting headquarters for trips down the Hudson Gorge. If adventure isn't your thing, you can always commune with the resident geese at their pond here, or curl up by the fire with a good book.

North River

GARNET HILL LODGE
Owners: Mary and George
    Heim.
518-251-2444.
Thirteenth Lake Rd.
Closed: Thanksgiving
    week.
Price: Expensive; MAP.
Credit Cards: MC, V.
Special Features:
    Cross-country-ski
    trails; ski shop;
    restaurant; fireplaces;
    private lakefront;
    children welcome; no
    pets.

Cross-country skiers flock to Garnet Hill: there are some 35 miles of groomed trails, a full shop, and reliable snow cover. In fact, readers of *Snow Country* magazine honored the place as one of the 10 best Nordic centers in the country.

But you don't have to ski to enjoy this country inn, and you don't have to wait for winter, either. In the early spring, you can observe maple-syrup making at the sugarbush. Later on, you can mountain bike or hike on the trails, plan a trip into Siamese Ponds Wilderness Area, or you can just watch the days pass in a beautiful setting from a comfortable chair near Thirteenth Lake.

The Log House, built in 1936, has 16 upstairs guest rooms, all with private baths. Downstairs is the restaurant, a game room, a massive fireplace made of local garnet, and two lounges for guests. Guests can also stay in Big Shanty, which was the home of Frank Hooper, developer of the original garnet mines in the area; this traditional Adirondack lodge has seven guest rooms, a stone fireplace, many rustic details, and overlooks Thirteenth Lake. A new building on the property, the Tea House, has just two luxurious rooms, with king-size beds and whirlpool baths, and its own private lounge.

Garnet Hill visitors can swim at the private beach, play tennis at the inn's courts, and rent canoes, rowboats, and sailboats for exploring Thirteenth Lake. Numerous packages are available for whitewater rafters, fishermen, inn-to-inn skiers, and groups.

HIGHWINDS INN
Innkeeper: Holly Currier.
518-251-3760,
    1-800-251-3760.
www.adirondack.net/tour
    /highwindsinn.
Barton Mines Rd.
Closed: Apr. 1–June 30;
    Oct. 15–Dec. 24.
Price: Moderate, B&B;
    Expensive, MAP.
Min. Stay: 2 nights on
    winter weekends.

The former home of the president of Barton Mines, Highwinds Inn is a surprisingly civilized place in a very out-of-the-way spot, some five miles off the main highway. The house is lovely, with a beautifully furnished living room centered around a rough-hewn garnet fireplace. Four guest rooms, each with private bath, are upstairs, and rooms all look out on a sweeping vista of the ponds and hills in the Siamese Ponds Wilderness Area. The elevation here is 2500 feet above sea level, so Highwinds is probably the highest accommodations you can find anywhere in the state.

Credit Cards: MC, V.
Special Features: Cross-country-ski trails; gourmet restaurant; wilderness cabin; children over 4 and pets welcome.

There are 1600 acres that guests can explore on foot over 25 km of cross-country trails, on mountain bike along old woods roads, or by canoe on small private ponds stocked with trout. Hikers are welcome to tour the old garnet mines with guides in the summer. On Pete Gay Mtn., which looks across at the downhill runs of Gore Mtn., there's a wilderness log cabin that's available for two-night stays.

One word summarizes the food at Highwinds: excellent (see Chapter Five, *Restaurants*). Breakfast is often whole-grain blueberry pancakes, sour cream waffles with maple syrup, or fresh-baked pastries. Guests can opt for a bed-&-breakfast plan or modified American plan.

Guest rooms at Highwinds Inn have views of the mountains and ridges of Siamese Ponds Wilderness Area.

Nancie Battaglia

Northville

INN AT THE BRIDGE
Owners: Lee and Dot Brenn.
518-863-2240.
641 Bridge St.
Open: Year-round.
Price: Moderate.
Credit Cards: AE, D, MC, V.
Special Features: Fireplace; lakefront; well-behaved children welcome; no pets.

A grand Queen Anne–style cottage with porches, gables, and a tower, the Inn at the Bridge is a stylish place. All six bedrooms are furnished with Victorian antiques and have new private baths; one room is accessible to the mobility impaired. There's a lovely fireplace in the parlor, which also has comfortable couches, television, and books galore. Breakfast includes an assortment of homemade breads, muffins, bagels, fruit, and so forth; the inn serves full dinners on weekends and by private arrangement on other days for parties of four or more. (Some diners cruise over in their boats.) There's a gazebo on the lawn overlooking Great Sacandaga Lake, docks for guests, and visitors can stroll through town to the Adirondack Country Store and other shops along Main Street.

Old Forge/Thendara

THE KENMORE
Owners: Joyce and Ron
  Leszyk, Dave Harradine.
315-357-5285.
Fourth Lake, Old Forge.
Off Rte. 28.
Closed: Apr.
Price: Moderate.
Min. Stay: 1 week July–
  Aug.; 3 nights in winter.
Credit Cards: None.
Special Features: Canoes
  and rowboats for guests;
  children welcome; no
  pets.

A cottage colony off the main highway on the north shore of Fourth Lake, the Kenmore welcomed its first guests in 1901. Fourteen modern housekeeping cottages ranging in size from one to three bedrooms are available by the week in summer and for three-night stays in spring and fall; four of the three-bedroom cabins are completely winterized and conveniently located for snowmobilers and cross-country skiers. Most of the cottages have lake views; many have fireplaces.

There's a shallow sandy beach and play area for the kids, free canoes and rowboats, picnic tables and outdoor grills, a volleyball court, and a campfire area. If the urge hits to explore farther afield, Old Forge's numerous attractions — from the Strand Theater to the Enchanted Forest/Water Safari park to the Fulton Chain of Lakes tour boats — are nearby.

**LEDGER'S LAKEFRONT
  COTTAGES**
Owners: Ellie and Terry
  Ledger.
315-357-5342.
On Fourth Lake, off Rte. 28
  bet. Eagle Bay & Old
  Forge.
Closed: Nov.–Apr.
Price: Moderate.
Min. Stay: 1 week in
  summer.
Credit Cards: None.

Three nicely maintained one- and two-bedroom housekeeping cottages are set around a spacious lawn on the north shore of Fourth Lake. Ledger's has a private sandy beach, docks for guests' boats, and a huge, friendly Newfoundland dog.

MOOSE RIVER HOUSE
Innkeepers: Kate and Bill
  Labbate.
315-369-3104.
12 Birch St., Thendara,
  off Rte. 28 behind Van
  Auken's Inne.

This stately Victorian home (circa 1884) on the banks of the Moose River was lovingly restored: on the first floor, there's a stately parlor with a baby grand piano; the living room has French doors that open out to a porch overlooking the river. The guest accommodations are first-rate:

Nancie Battaglia

The front porch at the Moose River House, Thendara.

Open: Year-round.
Price: Moderate.
Min. Stay: 2 nights on summer & fall weekends.
Credit Cards: MC, V.
Special Features: Children over 12 welcome; no pets; no smoking.

two rooms with queen-size beds have private baths; two rooms, each with vanities, share a bath, and there's a suite with its own living room, kitchen, and bath. The host and hostess are also first-rate: Bill and Kate go the extra mile to insure that guests are happy.

You can launch a canoe from the back door and noodle down the meandering Moose; ask about "River and Rail" trips, where you paddle one way and take the Adirondack Scenic Railroad back. State-marked hiking trails to Nick's Lake and Otter Lake are close by, as is McCauley Mtn. for downhill and cross-country skiing.

VAN AUKEN'S INNE
Innkeepers: Kathleen and Paul Rivet.
315-369-3033.
Forge St., Thendara, off Rte. 28 by the Adirondack Railroad station.
Open: Year-round.

This grand old inn was a year old when the Adirondack branch of the New York Central made its first stop in Thendara station in 1892. Since then, the trains have come and gone (and are back again for scenic excursions from Thendara to Minnehaha and Rondaxe), while Van Auken's has remained a constant presence across the way.

The exterior of Van Auken's Inne still looks the way it did a century ago.

Nancie Battaglia

Price: Inexpensive to Moderate; B&B.
Min. Stay: 2 nights on weekends in high season.
Credit Cards: MC, V.
Special Features: Restaurant and bar; children welcome; no pets.

The second floor — where 20 bedrooms used to share two baths — has been made into 12 nice guest rooms, each with private bath. Original details and antique furniture have been incorporated into these modern accommodations, and some rooms open onto the huge second-floor veranda. The public areas downstairs, like the taproom and the lobby, once again have polished wood floors, stamped-tin ceilings, and other elegant touches. The restaurant is open for breakfast, lunch, and dinner; see Chapter Five for a review.

Piseco

IRONDEQUOIT INN
Innkeeper: Andy Danec.
518-548-5500,
　1-888-497-0305.
Old Piseco Rd.
Closed: Apr., mid-Nov.–Dec. 26.
Price: Moderate.
Credit Cards: D, MC, V.
Special Features: Private beach; private island; tent campsites; canoes to rent; children welcome; no pets.

The Irondequoit Inn was founded in 1892 by a group of upstate New York businessmen as an outdoor getaway. Now the property covers 600 acres and spans nearly two miles of shoreline on Piseco Lake. From the front porches of the two main buildings, you can look down the lawns to see Oxbow, Rogers, and Piseco mountains. There's even a private undeveloped island in the lake that guests can canoe to for picnics, swimming, or sleeping out under the stars. Folks have described a stay here as like summer camp for families.

There are nine rooms which share three baths,

one-bedroom efficiencies, and housekeeping cabins. There's also a campground by the lake with tree-shaded sites.

Room rates for the main lodge include full breakfast. Dinners — good, simple family-style fare — are available to guests and the public by reservation.

Raquette Lake

RISLEY'S RUSH POINT
Owner: Barbara Risley
 Allen.
315-354-5211, school year:
 315-429-9239.
Rte. 28, Raquette Lake;
 winter mail: 3 E. Spofford
 Ave., Dolgeville NY
 13329.
Closed: During the school
 year.
Price: Moderate.
Min. Stay: 1 week; advance
 reservations only.
Credit Cards: None.
Special Features: Children
 welcome; no pets.

Several of the cottages here — part of the original 19th-century Adirondack camp — are rustic gems with stockade-style log siding, stone fireplaces, and long spacious porches under big pines and spruces. There are also three newer three-bedroom cottages, with eight cabins altogether on the 27-acre property. Each has a complete kitchen and bathroom; guests need to supply bed linens and towels.

A special attraction at Risley's is a natural sand beach that slopes gradually for a 100 yards into deep water. There's a dock for guests' boats, outdoor fireplaces, picnic tables, a playground, and two lean-tos.

Speculator

**ALPINE MEADOW
 CHALETS**
Owners: Chari and Chuck
 Smith.
518-548-5615.
Old Indian Lake Rd.
Open: Year-round.
Price: Moderate.
Min. Stay: 2 nights; inquire.

Just off the highway between Speculator and Indian Lake are a cluster of pleasant, winterized one- and two-bedroom chalets. They feature all the comforts of home: grills, picnic tables, microwaves, TVs, and have easy access to snowmobile trails, Lake Pleasant's waterfront, and the shops, restaurants, and activities to be found in "Sparkle City," as some call downtown Speculator.

BEARHURST
Owners: Helen and Dick
 Armstrong.
518-548-6427, winter:
 518-842-6609.
South Shore Rd.
Closed: Oct.–May.
Price: Moderate to
 Expensive.

Most folks associate Great Camps with Raquette Lake or the St. Regis lakes, but in other parts of the park, there are some smaller estates that are equally nice. One of these is Bearhurst, which was built in 1894 by Herman Meyrowitz (fashionable optical shops in Paris, Geneva, and Milan still carry his name), and it occupies a quarter-mile of lakefront on Lake Pleasant.

Bearhurst's main lodge and deck overlook a quiet corner of Lake Pleasant.

Nancie Battaglia

Min. Stay: 1 week July–
  Aug.; 2 nights June, Sept.
Credit Cards: None.
Special Features: Private
  lakefront; dockage for
  guests' boats; children
  welcome; no pets.

Guests stay in five of the original outbuildings including the icehouse, pumphouse, summer kitchen, and boathouse, all of which have been converted into delightful modern accommodations while still maintaining historical details and charm. The living rooms in each have fireplaces, and the fully outfitted kitchens even have dishwashers.

The centerpiece of the property is the main lodge, a stunning log building with lovely leaded-glass windows and gracious porches; the stonework is intricate, with spiral stone staircases leading down from the front porch. One fireplace even has an inset oval leaded-glass window on the second floor. The Armstrongs live in the main lodge, but guests can certainly enjoy the building from the outside.

There's a private beach, dock space for guests' boats, and a pretty little rustic gazebo for watching the sunset over the lake. If you visit in June, the grounds are covered with pinksters, the graceful wild azaleas.

**THE INN AT
  SPECULATOR**
Innkeeper: Neil McGovern.
518-548-3811.
Rte. 8.
Closed: Weds. fall, winter,
  & spring.
Price: Inexpensive; MAP.
Min. Stay: 2 nights on
  weekends.
Credit Cards: AE, MC, V.

Joe Buck, a German immigrant who had been headwaiter at Luchow's and maitre d' at the Waldorf Astoria, moved to Speculator in 1946. He built the inn, with a bar and restaurant downstairs, his apartment on the second floor, and tiny garret cells for hunters and fishermen on the third floor.

Neil McGovern bought the place in 1979 and has been working on it practically nonstop ever since.

Guests now stay on the second floor in homey, spacious quarters, some with private baths. There's a big living room with a fireplace, television, telephone, and a piano, just above the main dining room.

The inn's property includes frontage on Lake Pleasant, so there's easy access to the lake for canoeists and fishermen, and the ice is generally safe for cross-country skiing and snowmobiling from January through March.

Stillwater Reservoir

THE NORRIDGEWOCK III
Manager: Pat Thompson.
315-376-6200.
Beaver River, on Stillwater Reservoir; Box 232 (Eagle Bay NY 13331).
Open: Year-round.
Price: Moderate to Expensive; MAP.
Min. Stay: 2 days in cabins.
Credit Cards: None.
Special Features: Remote location; water taxi; children welcome; no pets.

Beaver River is a settlement on Stillwater Reservoir that's way off the beaten path — you can't drive here, although you can hike, cross-country ski, snowmobile, or canoe nine miles to reach the cabins and rooms at the Norridgewock. The Thompson family, who have run this unique lodge for three generations, also operate a water taxi that will pick up and deliver guests.

The place is quite self-sufficient, generating its own power and offering a modified American plan for overnighters. It accommodates between 25 to 35 people, "depending on how friendly you are," according to Pat Thompson.

STILLWATER
Owners: Marian and Joe Romano.
315-376-6470.
Stillwater Rd., Stillwater Reservoir; Star Rte., Box 258M (Lowville NY 13367).
Closed: Apr.
Price: Inexpensive.
Min. Stay: 2 nights in winter.
Credit Cards: AE, D, MC, V.
Special Features: Boat launch; restaurant; children welcome; no pets.

Stillwater Reservoir, which is several miles back from the main highways via a winding gravel road, has 117 miles of shoreline, 45 islands, and thousands of acres of public land for you to explore. There are more loons here than anywhere else in the Adirondacks, and the fishing's not too bad, either. Stillwater Hotel is understandably popular with snowmobilers since the snow cover is generally excellent and several trail systems are accessible right from the property.

Located at the western end of the lake is the Romano's hotel/restaurant complex, the only accommodations that you can drive to on the reservoir. There are seven winterized motel rooms, plus a restaurant and bar that are open to the public.

MOTELS & CAMPGROUNDS

For a list of public campgrounds, see "Camping" in Chapter Six, *Recreation.*

LAKE GEORGE AND SOUTHEASTERN ADIRONDACKS

For a complete list of accommodations in the Lake George–Chestertown–Warrensburg area, contact Warren County Tourism (1-800-95VISIT). A sampling of motel and campground accommodations is listed below.

Bolton Landing

Adirondack Park Motel (518-644-9800; Rte. 9N, Bolton Landing NY 12814) Price: Moderate. Pleasant, family-run motel with single and double rooms, efficiencies, two-bedroom cottages, and five-bedroom house on Lake George. Playground, pool, private beach. Closed: Columbus Day–Memorial Day.

Melody Manor (518-644-9750; Rte. 9N) Price: Moderate to Expensive. 40 rooms. Private beach; pool; boats; tennis; no pets. Closed Oct. 31–Apr. 30.

Victorian Village (518-644-9201; Rte. 9N) Price: Moderate. 30 units. Private beach; boats; tennis; no pets. Closed: Oct. 31–Apr. 30.

Diamond Point

Chelka Lodge (518-668-4677; Rte. 9N, Diamond Point NY 12824) Price: Moderate. Nice motel and efficiency units; private sand beach; continental breakfast included July and Aug. Min. stay 3 nights in summer. Closed: Nov.–Apr.

Sand 'n' Surf Motel (518-668-4622, 1-800-903-4622; Rte. 9N) Price: Inexpensive to Moderate. Motel rooms, some with water bed and hot tubs. Lake George charter fishing operation on premises. Closed: Nov. 1–Apr. 15.

Lake George

Balsam Motel (518-668-3865; 430 Canada St., Lake George NY 12845) Price: Moderate. Quiet family-run motel with non-glitzy housekeeping cottages. Heated pool; beach; no pets. Closed: Oct. 15–May 15.

Colonial Manor (518-668-4884; Rte. 9N) Price: Moderate to Expensive. Motel and cottages. Heated pool; playground; no pets. Closed: Oct. 15–May 1.

The Georgian (518-668-5401; Canada St.) Price: Moderate to Expensive. Huge, modern motor inn. Heated pool; private beach; docks for guests' boats; restaurants. Open: Year-round.

Tea Island (518-668-2776; Lake Shore Dr.) Price: Moderate. Motel, efficiencies, and cottages. Private beach; cafe. Closed: Oct. 15–Apr. 15.

CHAMPLAIN VALLEY

For a complete list of accommodations in the area, contact Essex County Tourism (518-597-4646; Crown Point NY 12928).

Keeseville

Ausable Chasm KOA Campground (518-834-9990; Rte. 9, Keeseville NY 12944) 89 tent and RV sites; some full hook-ups. Short walk to Ausable Chasm. Closed: Mid-Oct.–mid-May.

Port Kent

Yogi Bear's Jellystone Park Camp Resorts (518-834-9011; Rte. 373, Port Kent NY 12975) Numerous RV hookups and tent sites, overlooking Lake Champlain at the Port Kent Ferry. Pool; nature trails; activities for kids; camping cabins; playground; laundromat. Closed: Mid-Oct.–mid-May.

Ticonderoga

Ranchouse at Baldwin on Northern Lake George (518-585-6596; 79 Baldwin Rd., Ticonderoga NY 12883) Price: Moderate. Eight units, some with complete kitchens. Lakefront; near hiking trails to Rogers Rock; canoe and fishing boat for guests. Closed: Mid-Oct.–May 1.

HIGH PEAKS AND NORTHERN ADIRONDACKS

Lake Placid has lodging information available at 1-800-44P-LACI, or you can contact the Visitors Bureau (518-523-2445; Main St., Lake Placid NY 12946). A sampling of motels in the area is listed below.

Lake Placid

Best Western Golden Arrow (518-523-3353; 150 Main St.) Price: Moderate to Expensive. Modern motor inn on the lakefront in the heart of downtown. Health club; heated pool; private beach; shopping arcade. Open: Year-round.

Holiday Inn SunSpree Resort (518-523-2556; 1 Olympic Dr.) Price: Moderate to Very Expensive. 200+ upgraded, nicely appointed suites and rooms. Overlooking the Olympic Arena. Heated pool; access to Jackrabbit cross-country-ski trails; 2 championship golf courses; health club; lake view; restaurant and lounge. Open: Year-round.

Howard Johnson Lodge (518-523-9555; Saranac Ave.) Price: Moderate to Expensive. Tennis; indoor pool; near hiking trails. Open: Year-round.

Lake Placid Hilton (518-523-1120; 1 Mirror Lake Dr.) Price: Moderate to Expensive. Large, new motor inn complex across from the lake in downtown. Indoor and outdoor pools; restaurant and lounge; shops. Ask about packages for family vacations: kids may stay and eat for free. Open: Year-round.

Lakeshore Motel (518-523-523-2261; 54 Saranac Ave.) Price: Inexpensive to Moderate. Nice family-run place with eight double rooms and eight efficiencies on Lake Placid. Private beach; rowboats and canoes; picnic tables and grill for guests. Open: Year-round.

Mountain View Inn (518-523-2439; 140 Main St.) Price: Moderate to Expensive. Across the street from Mirror Lake and very convenient to the Olympic Center. Open: Year-round.

Prague Motor Inn (518-523-2587; 25 Sentinel Rd.) Price: Inexpensive to Moderate. Quiet, folksy Mom-and-Pop place with an amusing Queen Anne house in front of the motel units.

Northwoods Inn (518-523-1818; 122 Main St.) Price: Moderate to Expensive. Extensively renovated in 1994-95 with 89 suites. Try Dakota's Cafe Grille restaurant downstairs for steaks by the inch and pub fare; the selection of microbrews on tap is the best in town. Open: Year-round.

North Hudson

Blue Ridge Falls Campground (518-532-7863; Blue Ridge Rd., North Hudson NY 12855) Off the main highway; pool; walk to waterfalls. Closed: Winter.

Saranac Lake

Comfort Inn (518-891-1970; 148 Lake Flower Ave., Saranac Lake NY 12983) Price: Inexpensive to Moderate. Nice, new motel with pleasant grounds and a decent restaurant, McKenzie's Grill. Open: year-round.

Wilmington

Hungry Trout Motor Lodge (518-946-2217; Rte. 86, Wilmington NY 12997) Price: Moderate to Expensive. 20 rooms. Great view; nice restaurant and R. F. McDougal's Tavern; excellent fishing on private stretch of river; fly-fishing guide service, lessons, and tackle shop. Closed: Mid-Apr.–late June; Nov.–Dec.

Whiteface Chalet (518-946-2207; Springfield Rd.) Price: Inexpensive to Moderate. 18 rooms. Quiet, off-highway location. Tennis; cafe and lounge. Closed: Apr., Nov.

NORTHWEST LAKES

For a complete list of lodgings in the immediate area, contact the Tupper Lake Chamber of Commerce (518-359-3328, 1-800-640-6785; 60 Park St., Tupper Lake NY 12986).

Tupper Lake

Pine Terrace Resort (518-359-9258; Rte. 30) Price: Inexpensive to Moderate. Housekeeping units and motel rooms. Pool; clay tennis courts; private beach across the road; picnic area. Closed: Nov.–Apr.

Red Top Inn (518-359-9209; Rte. 30) Price: Inexpensive. 18 rooms. Lake view; private beach across the road; fishing dock. Close to Big Tupper Ski Area. Open: Year-round.

Shaheen's Motel (518-359-3384; 310 Park St.) Price: Inexpensive to Moderate. 33 motel rooms; heated pool; copier and fax service; continental breakfast. Open: Year-round.

CENTRAL ADIRONDACKS

The Central Adirondack Association (315-369-6983; Main St., Old Forge NY 13420) lists many accommodations in the Inlet, Eagle Bay, Old Forge, Raquette Lake, and Blue Mtn. Lake area. Information on lodgings in Hamilton County is available from the county tourism office (518-648-5239; White Birch Lane, Indian Lake NY 12842). For the Great Sacandaga Reservoir region and Caroga-Canada lakes, contact the Fulton County Regional Chamber of Commerce (518-725-0641; 18 Cayadutta St., Gloversville NY 12078). See Chapter Eight, *Information*, for individual town chambers of commerce.

A sampling of motels, campgrounds, and cottages is listed below.

Long Lake

Sandy Point Motel (518-624-3871; Rte. 28/30, Long Lake NY 12847) Price: Inexpensive to Moderate. Motel units and efficiencies. Private beach; docks; cable TV; rental boats for guests; cross-country skiing and snowmobiling. Open: Year-round.

Shamrock Motel (518-624-3861; Rte. 28/30) Price: Inexpensive to Moderate. Motel and neat-as-a-pin housekeeping cottages. Private beach; picnic area. Closed: Mid-Oct.–Memorial Day.

Old Forge

Best Western Motel (315-369-6836; Rte. 30, Thendara NY 13472) Price: Moderate. 50 renovated rooms. Indoor pool; tennis; jacuzzis; putting green. Open: Year-round.

Clark's Beach Motel (315-369-3026; Main St., Old Forge NY 13420) Price: Moderate. 42 units. Lake view; next to public beach; indoor pool. Open: Year-round.

The Forge Motel (315-369-3313; Main St., Old Forge) Price: Moderate. 61 units. Lake view, the best from Room 13; pool; next to public beach; walk to restaurants. Open: Year-round.

Old Forge KOA (315-369-6011; Rte. 28, Old Forge) Campground. 200 sites on 101 acres. Private lake; Laundromat; showers; convenience store; dumping station; canoes; movies. Open: Year-round.

Water's Edge Inn and Conference Center (315-369-2484; Rte. 30, Old Forge) Price: Moderate. 42 rooms. Lakefront; indoor pool; sauna; dock; family restaurant; across from Enchanted Forest/Water Safari park. Open: Year-round.

Nancie Battaglia

No matter where you stay in the Adirondacks, a lovely lake is usually nearby.

CHAPTER FOUR

From Folkways to Fine Arts
CULTURE

Culture viewed as the noble endeavors in human society — fine arts, literature, classical music, theater, ballet — may have been out of reach of the old-time Adirondack woodsman and his family, but the wild landscape inspired many a visiting painter, writer, and composer. It could be argued, too, that because of popular fiction, weekly national magazines like *Harper's* and *Every Saturday*, and Currier & Ives prints,

Courtesy of the Adirondack Museum

A fiddler entertains Raquette Lake Hotel guests in front of a campfire, 1888.

the Adirondacks were much better known as a particular place a hundred years ago than they are today.

Consider *The Last of the Mohicans*, for example. The harrowing trip from what's now called Cooper's Cave, in Glens Falls, to the fort at Ticonderoga went along the Hudson River, crossed over the Tongue Mountain range, skirted the west side of Lake George and reached Lake Champlain at its narrowest spot; the adventure is now firmly etched in American letters, but few of us connect the journey with actual sites that happen to be in the Adirondacks. James Fenimore Cooper visited Warrensburg and Lake George in 1824 to research his story and observe the landscape. Many of his landmarks are inaccessible today, but you may catch a few glimpses if you follow in his tracks, on modern-day Rte. 9.

Visual artists recorded the region in a state of bucolic grace, before the iron industry's charcoal kilns darkened the skies and lumbermen cut the forests; beginning in 1830, and on up through the turn of the century, the countryside practically swarmed with painters. Thomas Cole, Frederic Church, and other Hudson River School artists depicted perfect scenes of glowing mountains, shimmering lakes, and tiny villages. Frederic Remington, who was born just north of the Adirondacks, in Canton, New York, sketched trappers' cabins and lumber camps. The English painter A.F. Tait also showed the manly side of the

Courtesy of the Adirondack Museum

A Good Time Coming by A.F. Tait shows a 19th-century Adirondack hunting party and all their gear.

wilderness, in oil paintings of groups of hunters and fishermen and portraits of their prey. Many of Tait's images were used for Currier & Ives lithographs, but the popularity of those Adirondack prints also created demand for Tait imitators; more than 100 different Currier & Ives images illustrate scenes of the region, from maple-sugaring parties to ice fishing to humble log farmsteads.

Winslow Homer painted woodsmen in Keene Valley and at the North Woods Club, near Minerva, in a luminous, impressionistic style that helped cinch his career as America's premier watercolorist. His illustrations of hunters and lumberjacks that appeared in weeklies brought the backwoods to urban homes. Harold Weston, who lived most of his life in Keene Valley, made bold, burly oils of the High Peaks that were exhibited widely from the 1920s to 1970s, and now reside in major collections throughout the world. Rockwell Kent spent his last decades at his farm near Au Sable Forks, painting the Ausable River valley and designing houses. David Smith, one of the best-known sculptors of the modern age, lived in Bolton Landing; today, in a field overlooking Lake George, many of his abstract sculptures remain, but unfortunately, the property is rarely open to the public.

Composers found their muse in the woods and waters, too. A few parlor ditties made the rounds in the late 19th century, like "Floating for Deer" and "The Adirondacks: A Gallop," and the immense popularity of canoeing at the turn of the century created a whole new genre of songs celebrating the sport, such as "Paddlin' Madeline Home." But, more importantly, two of the finest modern composers, Charles Ives and Béla Bartók, both spent extended periods of time working in the Adirondacks. Ives composed the *Concord* piano sonata while visiting Elk Lake, and began the *Universe Symphony*, one of his last major works, while at his wife's family's summer home in Keene Valley. Bartók wrote the *Concerto for Orchestra* in Saranac Lake, where he was taking the "cure" for tuberculosis.

Women are notably absent from this list of resident and visiting artists, with one exception. Jeanne Robert Foster grew up in grinding poverty in Johnsburg, and went on to be an editor of the *Transatlantic Review*. Her circle of friends included Ezra Pound, T.S. Eliot, and John Butler Yeats, father of the Irish poet. Her poetry-and-prose memories of her youth were published in *Adirondack Portraits* (Syracuse University Press, 1989).

Folk arts from the 19th-century Adirondacks reflect the lumbering days, in songs and tall tales, and the Gilded Age, in rustic furniture and decorative items local carpenters created for the Great Camps. Traditional music can be heard at many of the arts centers listed elsewhere in this chapter; the best place to see rustic furniture in quantity and quality is at the Adirondack Museum, in Blue Mtn. Lake. Throughout the park the icons of North Country material culture are ubiquitous: the guideboat, pack basket, lean-to, and Adirondack chair. The art of storytelling is also alive and well in informal gathering places and on stage.

Today, the cultural scene in the Adirondacks is remarkably diverse, showcasing native skills and crafts, and honoring the fine artists who visited the region. There's real community pride in libraries, arts centers, theater companies, historic-preservation groups, museums, and musical ensembles. But beyond the good feelings and active schedules, there's also a level of excellence that rises above sometimes humble settings. The following descriptions will tell you where to go in search of history and the arts throughout the park, but you'll have to call or write to get a current schedule of events. Local radio stations and weekly papers offer calendars of events for communities within the park; the *Adirondack Daily Enterprise* has a weekly calendar that extends from Blue Mtn. Lake to Keene, and *The Chronicle*, based in Glens Falls, lists numerous southern Adirondack happenings. *Adirondack Life* has a bimonthly calendar in each issue, "Inside & Out," which does cover the entire Adirondack Park, but it's always a good idea to call ahead to confirm ticket availability or location of an event.

ARCHITECTURE

Compared to touring Vermont, with its many postcard-pretty villages, old-house hunting in the Adirondack Park may be disappointing to the historic-preservation buff. Bear in mind that settlements in the North Country, especially in the central Adirondacks, are considerably newer than New England towns, and that the communities which date back to the 1700s along

Sunset Cottage, given to the Adirondack Museum by Mrs. C.V. Whitney in 1995, is a gem of rustic embellishment.

Nancie Battaglia

Lakes George and Champlain were destroyed during the French and Indian and Revolutionary wars. Devastating fires before the turn of the century in towns such as Tupper Lake and Indian Lake obliterated hundreds of prosperous businesses and homes. However, along the eastern edge of the park, there are several lovely towns with fine buildings dating back to 1790.

The celebrated Adirondack rustic style of architecture, which borrowed designs from Swiss chalets, English half-timber buildings, pioneer cabins, and even Japanese pagodas, isn't easy to view from the comfort of an automobile. You'll find rustic lodges and boathouses in all their twiggy glory mainly on remote lakeshores: **Sagamore** (315-354-5311), the former Vanderbilt summer estate near *Raquette Lake*, and **White Pine Camp** (518-327-3030), the summer White House of Calvin Coolidge, on *Osgood Pond*, are two Great Camps you can easily see. Visiting **Santanoni Preserve**, near *Newcomb*, requires a 10-mile round trip, but it's well worth the effort. You can reach the impressive rustic complex by walking, cross-country skiing, biking, or riding a horse-drawn wagon, and you get a real sense of its woodland isolation.

Adirondack Architectural Heritage (518-834-9328; 1759 Main St., Keeseville) is a parkwide non-profit organization founded in 1990 devoted to historic preservation. Tours of public and private sites in summer and fall, lectures, workshops, and technical assistance to building owners are just a few of the programs and services offered by AARCH.

LAKE GEORGE AND SOUTHEASTERN ADIRONDACKS

For many travelers, *Warrensburg* is the gateway to the Adirondacks. Along Main Street (Rte. 9), there are stately 19th-century homes, from Greek Revival and Gothic cottages to Italianate villas and Queen Anne mansions. The oldest building in Warrensburg, near the stoplight for the Schroon River Road, is a modest stone structure; a former blacksmith shop, it dates back to 1814. Along the Schroon River (Rte. 418 west), you can see remnants of the village's

The United Presbyterian Church in Putnam was built in 1857.

B. Folwell

industrial center in several old mill buildings; the Grist Mill, now a restaurant, still has grindstones, chutes, grain-grinding apparatus, and a small exhibit that describes the building's past. Also on Rte. 9, *Chestertown* has a historic district with colorful Greek Revival houses and restored storefronts.

Lake Luzerne remains a community with quiet streets, well-kept Victorian homes, and nine churches. **St. Mary's Episcopal Church**, built about 1860, is an unusual mix of Gothic stone-and-stick work, with complex slate roof lines and stunning stained-glass windows (across from the Lamplight Inn).

In the rolling hills of Washington County, between Lake Champlain and Lake George, a few late 18th- and early 19th-century buildings can be seen along roads branching off Rte. 22. Near *Putnam*, follow the signs to the **United Presbyterian Church** and you'll be rewarded with a view of a stunning Greek Revival church. On Rte. 9L, which goes up the east side of Lake George, you'll see the quaint stone **Harrisena Community Church** and several early farmhouses near the southern end of the lake.

CHAMPLAIN VALLEY

Essex County is especially rich in architectural sights. Beginning in the south, the town of _Ticonderoga_ is a major destination for history lovers. **Fort Ticonderoga** is about 2.5 miles south of the village on Rte. 22, but you can find the tumbledown walls and rusting cannons of **Fort Mount Hope** by exploring near the old cemetery on Burgoyne St. At the head of Montcalm St. is a replica of John Hancock's Boston home, built by Horace Moses in 1926. Moses made his fortune with the Strathmore Paper Company and funded many town beautification projects, including the **Liberty Monument**, a bronze statue by Charles Keck. A walking tour that highlights Ticonderoga's bustling 19th-century industrial history is available (518-585-6366).

At _Crown Point_, there were several fortifications along the lake dating back to the French occupation of the Champlain Valley; near the bridge to Vermont, off Rte. 22, is **Fort Crown Point**. West of Crown Point is **Ironville**, a well-preserved gem of an early 19th-century community. On the way to Ironville, in **Factoryville**, you'll see the only octagonal house in the Adirondacks.

Historic markers erected by New York State abound along Rte. 22 as you approach _Port Henry_. The original settlement here supplied lumber for the forts at Crown Point and for Benedict Arnold's naval fleet. Later, the discovery of abundant iron ore shaped the town. Evidence of this prosperity shows up in an ornate downtown block, elaborate churches, and the exuberant high Victorian **Moriah Town Office** building, formerly the headquarters of the Witherbee-Sherman Iron Company, near the Amtrak station. In the carriage house next to the town offices the **Railroad and Mining Heritage Park** is being developed (518-546-3341).

Farther north along Champlain's shore is _Westport_, which was first settled in 1770. Buildings from that era have all disappeared, but a few homes near the lake on Washington St., off Rtes. 9N and 22, date back to the 1820s. Westport was a vital port shipping out iron, lumber, wool, and other farm products before the Civil War, and a thriving summer community afterwards. Following Rte. 22, you pass Gothic cottages and impressive stone houses overlooking the lake. Between Westport and Essex, on Rte. 22, is the tiny farm community of _Boquet_, with its odd little octagonal schoolhouse, recently restored and occasionally open to the public.

The Adirondack community richest in architectural treasures is undoubtedly _Essex_; it's as if the clock stopped here in 1856. There are wonderful Dutch Colonial, Georgian, Federal, and Greek Revival buildings in excellent repair throughout the town: check under "Historic Buildings and Districts" for more information. Continuing on Rte. 22, _Willsboro_ and _Keeseville_ contain many historic buildings. Keeseville has several homes made of buff-pink native sandstone which date back to the 1830s, and buildings in the full range of 19th-century styles from Dutch Colonial to Federal and Greek Revival to Gothic Revival and Romanesque. The **Stone Arch Bridge** over the Ausable River, built in 1842, is the largest single-span arch bridge in the country.

The monograph *Crossing the River*, published by the Friends of North Country (518-834-9606), highlights historic bridges in Essex County, and makes an excellent driving tour. Another interesting driving tour for the historic **Boquet River** is published by the Boquet River Association (518-962-8296); the loop begins just off the Northway and follows the river through Elizabethtown, Wadhams, Whallonsburg, Boquet, and Essex to its northernmost point, at Willsboro, and then goes south to Reber and Lewis. A map with interpretive signs along the route has been published by the Champlain Valley Heritage Network (518-597-4646; Rte. 1, Box 220, Crown Point) and highlights historic sites, farmsteads, local industries, and vistas from Keeseville to Ticonderoga.

HIGH PEAKS AND NORTHERN ADIRONDACKS

The Ausable River valley holds many historic buildings that are visible along roadways. South of Keene Valley, it's worth a quick detour off Rte. 73 at **_St. Hubert's_** to see the massive Victorian inn, the **Ausable Club**. It's "members only" inside the building, but you can get a rare glimpse of the kind of hostelry that visitors once enjoyed throughout the Adirondacks. North on Rte. 9, between **_Upper Jay_**, **_Jay_**, and **_Au Sable Forks_**, there are fine Federal-style stone and brick houses and churches; in Jay, the sole remaining covered bridge in the Adirondacks was dismantled in 1997. You can see its three sections (Mill Hill Rd., $^1/_4$ mi. off Rte. 9), but it's anyone's guess when the structure will once again span the Ausable River.

The Olympic Village — **_Lake Placid_**, that is — has only a few buildings left from its earliest days, when the settlement of **North Elba**, near the ski jumps, was a iron-mining center: one that's easy to spot on **Old Military Road** is the **Stagecoach Inn**.

In **_Saranac Lake_**, which was incorporated in 1892, the tuberculosis industry inspired its own architecture, manifested in "cure porches" and "cure cottages." The group **Historic Saranac Lake** sponsors lectures and tours from time to time highlighting buildings of note (518-891-0971); a current project is restoring a cure cottage used by Béla Bartók.

Tucked back in the woods at **_Loon Lake_**, partly visible from County Rd. 99, is a surprising collection of cottages and other elaborate buildings designed by Stanford White. The best way to see these haunting structures is by playing a round of golf at the Loon Lake course.

North of **_Newcomb_** on CR 25, en route to the Upper Works trailhead for the High Peaks, is the **Adirondac blast furnace**, an immense stone monolith built in 1854 that produced high-quality iron. Continuing on the road, you'll pass a faded white farmhouse that was the office of an early iron-mining concern. (The other deserted buildings nearby belonged to the Tahawus Club.)

On **_Upper Saranac Lake_**, which straddles the High Peaks and Northwest Lakes regions of this book, there are fine examples of rustic architecture, but you'll need a canoe to paddle by **Wenonah Lodge**, **Prospect Point** (now a Christian summer camp), **Camp Wonundra** (now "The Point," a sumptuous inn), **Pinebrook**, **Eagle Island** (now a Girl Scout camp), and **Sekon Lodge**. Don't expect more than a tantalizing peek at these places hidden by the trees, and for heaven's sake, don't go ashore on private lands. Another vehicle for touring the lake may be the summer mail boat; check at the Saranac Lake post office to learn if the mail-delivery person is taking passengers.

NORTHWEST LAKES

For boathouse fans, _Upper St. Regis Lake_, near Paul Smiths, has many lovely waterfront buildings, in high rustic, cobblestone, and shingle style. You'll need a boat to make this tour, and you'll have to paddle several miles from the public put-in on Keese Mill Rd., west of Paul Smith's College. Also, a reminder — respect landowners' privacy by staying away from docks and shore.

CENTRAL ADIRONDACKS

The heart of the Adirondacks has few buildings dating from before the Civil War, but it's home to a vernacular architectural style that honors French-Canadian and Yankee traditions in steep-roofed, simple homes. _Olmstedville_, off Rte. 28N, has a cluster of Greek Revival storefronts and houses from the 1840s. Farther south, on Rte. 30, _Wells_ has several nicely restored Victorian-era homes along the Sacandaga River. For rustic architecture, a boat tour of _Raquette Lake_, either on Bird's mail boat (315-354-4441), or the _W.W. Durant_, a replica of an old steamboat (315-354-5532), allows glimpses of the Great Camps like **Pine Knot** (the first rustic camp designed by William West Durant), **Camp Echo**, and **Bluff Point** (the former Collier estate). **Great Camp Sagamore** (315-354-5301) occasionally offers tours of nearby rustic estates.

ARTS CENTERS AND ARTS COUNCILS

The arts scene is surprisingly lively in this, New York's most rural area, thanks in part to the long-time leadership of the New York State Council on the Arts. Through grants from the state council to arts presenters, producers, and non-profit galleries, and a re-grant program to fledgling and volunteer organizations, all kinds of arts programs can be found in all kinds of towns.

ADIRONDACK ART ASSOCIATION
518-963-7270.
Schoolhouse Gallery, Essex.
Season: Spring–fall.
Open: Daily.

This 30-year-old community gallery showcases regional professional artists in solo and group exhibitions, from quilts to photography and water-color paintings to designer crafts.

ADIRONDACK LAKES CENTER FOR THE ARTS
518-352-7715.
Rte. 28, next to the post office, Blue Mtn. Lake.
Mail: Box 101, Blue Mtn. Lake NY 12812.
Season: Year-round.
Price: Concert, film, and theater tickets $5–$12. Discounts for seniors, children. Workshop fees vary.

Since 1967 this multi-arts center has brought a full palette of programs to Blue Mtn. Lake, population 150 (give or take). The Adirondack Lakes Center for the Arts, a former garage, has presented hundreds of concerts, including performances by the Tokyo String Quartet, Doc Watson, the Dixie Hummingbirds, Paul Taylor, the Seldom Scene, Odetta, Livingston Taylor, and more.

Exhibitions include contemporary paintings, sculpture, photography, and crafts; Adirondack furniture; children's art; and traveling shows. Complementing the shows are intensive workshops for adults, on weekends in fall and winter and weekdays in summer. Programs for kids range from crafts, dance, and music workshops to films and family presentations of storytelling, New Vaudeville, and magic.

The Arts Center/Old Forge presents fine arts exhibitions year-round.

Nancie Battaglia

ARTS CENTER/OLD FORGE
315-369-6411.
Rte. 28, Old Forge.
Season: Year-round.
Price: Concert & theater tickets $5–$12. Donations suggested for special exhibitions.
Gift Shop: Open 7 days in July & Aug.; during exhibitions rest of year.

The Arts Center/Old Forge is the oldest community-arts organization in the region, and the organization continues to grow, change, and pursue new directions. The facility is a former boat-storage barn, but it's truly transformed by annual events such as the Adirondacks National Exhibition of Watercolors (Aug.–Sept.) and the October quilt show. The same space hosts theater by Pendragon, a touring company from Saranac Lake, and children's performances. Classical concerts are often held in the Nichols Memorial Church, a few miles away, while bluegrass, folk, or jazz programs may be on stage at McCauley Mtn. Ski Area, at the Old Forge beach front, or in the center's black box theater.

In the summer, there are local history outings and lectures and presentations by artists and writers. Throughout the year, the arts center shows contemporary American and foreign films in different venues and offers crafts workshops for adults from boatbuilding to basketry. There are numerous kids' programs for ages 5 and up. The center also has a cooperative crafts shop on Main Street, one block past Old Forge Hardware.

ARTS COUNCIL FOR THE NORTHERN ADIRONDACKS
518-962-8778.
Rte. 22, Westport.
Season: Year-round.

Launched as an advocacy group for local artists and craftspeople, the Arts Council for the Northern Adirondacks publishes a comprehensive summer events calendar for exhibitions; lectures; fairs; music, theater, and dance performances; and children's programs. The organization also offers grants to working artists, presents traditional and contemporary musicians from the region in different towns, and sponsors traveling juried art shows.

LAKE GEORGE ARTS PROJECT
518-668-2616.
Canada St., Lake George.
Season: Year-round.
Price: Concerts are free.

Of all the Adirondack arts institutions, the Lake George Arts Project (LGAP) is decidedly the hippest. Over the years, LGAP has organized contemporary sculpture shows on the frozen lake, in tree-shaded Shepard Park, and alongside the scenic highway up Prospect Mtn. The offices and gallery are on the ground floor of the old courthouse in the center of town; special exhibitions featuring regional artists with national renown are scheduled monthly. Ongoing programs are fiction and poetry workshops, weekly summer concerts in the park, the hot Lake George Jazz Festival (Sept.), and the Black Velvet Art Party, a celebration of terminal tackiness, usually held on a Saturday after Halloween.

LAKE PLACID CENTER FOR THE ARTS
518-523-2512.
Saranac Ave., Lake Placid.
Season: Year-round.
Tickets: Concert & theater
  $6–$12. Discounts for
  seniors, students.

The Lake Placid Center for the Arts (LPCA) has metamorphosed through different identities, beginning as the Center for Music, Drama, and Art; then as an accredited two-year arts school; and next as the summer campus for the Parsons School of Design. Now a multi-arts center with a community-service focus, the facility is topnotch, with a beautiful theater that seats about 300, well-equipped studios, and a bright, airy gallery. Exhibitions are slated throughout the year, with two juried shows for regional artists and craftspeople, and solo and group works depicting the Adirondacks.

Presentations include visiting theater groups; contemporary American and foreign films; folk music; dance-company residencies; gala programs by soloists of the New York City Ballet; and excellent classical and chamber performances during the summer. The summer Lake Placid Chamber Music Festival highlights many acclaimed ensembles, including the Amadeus Trio.

The LPCA also is home to the Community Theater Players, who offer three or four shows annually. For kids, in July and August, there's the free "Young and Fun" performance series on weekday mornings and programs throughout the school year.

CINEMA

During the silent-film era, the Adirondacks provided a backdrop for popular films including *The Shooting of Dan McGrew*, *The Wilderness Woman*, *Glorious Youth*, and dozens more; the movie industry thrived for more than a decade in unlikely places such as Saranac Lake, Plattsburgh, and Port Henry. There were cowboy scenes at Ausable Chasm, "Alaskan" trapper cabins in Essex County farmyards, and adventures supposedly set in South America, Siberia, Switzerland. As the cameras rolled, Washington crossed the frozen Delaware — somewhere on the Saranac River.

In 1941, Alfred Hitchcock's only comedy, *Mr. and Mrs. Smith*, was set at the Lake Placid Club. A few years later, *Lake Placid Serenade*, which featured dizzying reels of figure skating and Roy Rogers as king of the Placid winter carnival, was a commercial success. In 1958, scenes of *Marjorie Morningstar* were shot in Schroon Lake; local extras were paid the princely sum of $125 per day. (*The Sweet Hereafter*, from the Adirondack novel by Russell Banks, was filmed in Canada, alas.) Today there are many places where you can catch foreign, classic, and first-run films.

LAKE GEORGE AND SOUTHEASTERN ADIRONDACKS

Carol Theater (518-494-0006; Main St., Chestertown) Open Memorial Day–fall. First-run films; children's matinees.

HIGH PEAKS AND NORTHERN ADIRONDACKS

Berkeley Theater (518-891-5470; Broadway & Berkeley Square, Saranac Lake) New theater, first-run films.
Lake Placid Center for the Arts (518-523-2512; Saranac Ave., Lake Placid) Foreign and contemporary American film series in fall, winter, and spring.

Palace Theater (518-523-9271; Main St., Lake Placid) Recently restored Art Deco stenciling in the lobby and displays of Lake Placid movie memorabilia. Current American releases, 3 screens, open daily year-round.

NORTHWEST LAKES
State Theater (518-359-3593; Park St., Tupper Lake) Recent releases.

CENTRAL ADIRONDACKS
Adirondack Picture Show (518-548-6199; Rte. 8, Speculator) A huge barn, probably the oldest movie theater in the park still operating. First-run films in the summer.

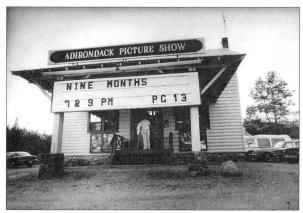

The Adirondack Picture Show, in Speculator, opened when the talkies came out.

Nancie Battaglia

Lake Theater (518-648-5950; Main St., Indian Lake) Recent films nightly from late May–fall; occasional foreign films on fall weekends in conjunction with the Adirondack Lakes Center for the Arts; films during Indian Lake's Winter Festival, in February.

Tamarack Moviehouse (315-357-2001; Rte. 28, Inlet) Recent films nightly Memorial Day–Labor Day; weekends in fall and winter. Check out the ice-cream parlor next door. Closed in winter.

Strand Theater (315-369-6703; Main St., Old Forge) Carefully restored vintage moviehouse. Two or three shows nightly; children's matinees; occasional foreign films in cooperation with the Arts Center/Old Forge.

CRAFTS INSTRUCTION

Weave a traditional Adirondack pack basket, spin a skein of wool, tie a dry fly, build a guideboat — you can learn these old-time skills, as well as contemporary crafts, in several centers across the park. Classes for adults range from one or two-day intensive programs to week-long sessions; prices vary. Always call ahead to register for these workshops.

HIGH PEAKS AND NORTHERN ADIRONDACKS

Adirondack Mountain Club (518-523-3441; Adirondak Loj Rd., Lake Placid) Painting, photography, and traditional craft classes that make use of a spectacular natural setting for both materials and inspiration.

Lake Placid Center for the Arts (518-523-2512; Saranac Ave., Lake Placid) Watercolor painting, photography, basketry, figure drawing, and other classes for adults, year-round.

Newcomb Visitor Interpretive Center (518-582-2000; Rte. 28N, Newcomb) Weekend classes year-round in Adirondack basketry, fly tying, watercolor painting, and nature photography. Also children's programs on Saturdays.

NORTHWEST LAKES

Paul Smiths Visitor Interpretive Center (518-327-3000; Rte. 30, Paul Smiths) Workshops similar to the Newcomb center, above.

CENTRAL ADIRONDACKS

The Adirondack Lakes Center for the Arts offers workshops in pottery, quilting, basketry, boatbuilding, and other crafts.

Nancie Battaglia

Adirondack Lakes Center for the Arts (518-352-7715; Rte. 28, Blue Mtn. Lake) Painting, photography, guideboat building, woodcarving, rustic furniture-making, basketry, and other crafts, year-round.

Arts Center/Old Forge (315-369-6411; Rte. 28, Old Forge) Watercolor painting, wooden boatbuilding, quilting, pottery, rug making, lampshade making, basketry, and more, year-round.

Sagamore (315-354-5311; Sagamore Rd., Raquette Lake) Weekend courses in traditional music and dance, basketry, woodcarving, rustic furniture building, quilting, nature illustration, papermaking and so forth. Fees include room and board.

DANCE

The **Lake Placid Center for the Arts** (518-523-2512) sponsors a modern dance company in residence each year: in 1997, Rebecca Kelly's group was in residence for two weeks. The program always includes classes for adults and children; usually several evening performances and a children's daytime program are scheduled. The LPCA also presents modern dance concerts throughout the year, and classes in traditional clogging.

North Country Dancing

Square, round, and altogether shapeless dancing to the fiddle and banjo is a North Country tradition. Neophytes are welcome at community square dances, and callers usually explain each dance. During the summer, there are weekly dances on the tennis courts in **Schroon Lake** (518-532-7650). In Stony Creek, **Stony Creek Mountain Days** (518-696-2332) also feature old-time dancing.

BEYOND THE BLUE LINE

You'll have to venture outside the Adirondack Park for a full calendar of professional dance, but by traveling not too far afield you can catch rehearsals and performances of the New York City Ballet at the **Saratoga Performing Arts Center** (518-587-3330; Saratoga Spa State Park) in *Saratoga Springs*. At rehearsals, seating is usually open so you can get up close, to really get a sense of the sheer physical strength of the dancers. At the other end of the spectrum, the annual ballet gala, in July, is an elegant, magical evening.

ELDERHOSTEL

The Adirondack Park is a favorite learning laboratory for Elderhostel, the international educational organization for people over age 60. Generally, these inexpensive, informal, non-credit courses last five or six days and cover history, nature, folklore, and even culinary arts, in sessions led by local experts. Some recent Elderhostel programs have included maple-sugar traditions, Lake George shipwrecks, canoeing, ethnic groups in the Adirondacks, historic preservation, and the region's role in the American Revolution.

Adirondack sites for Elderhostel programs include **Sagamore Lodge**, in *Raquette Lake* (315-354-5311); Adirondack Mountain Club, at **Adirondak Loj**, outside *Lake Placid* (518-523-3441); **Silver Bay Association**, on the northern end of Lake George (518-543-8833); and **Fort Ticonderoga** (518-585-2821). For more information write to Elderhostel, 75 Federal St., Boston MA 02110.

HISTORIC BUILDINGS AND DISTRICTS

More than two dozen sites in the Adirondack Park are on the National Register of Historic Places; oddly enough, all of the state land — the Adirondack Forest Preserve — is a historic district, although there are very few important buildings left on these lands for reasons too complicated to explain fully here. Suffice it to say that once private land becomes public property, the terrain is to be returned to a natural condition, and structures must be destroyed. At least, that's the usual scenario. **Santanoni Preserve**, a hundred-year-old rustic enclave described earlier in this chapter, is slowly being stabilized thanks in large part of the efforts of Adirondack Architectural Heritage and the Town of Newcomb.

Listed below is a selection of architecturally significant places, forts, interesting homes, and local preservation organizations.

LAKE GEORGE AND SOUTHEASTERN ADIRONDACKS

MARCELLA SEMBRICH MEMORIAL STUDIO
518-644-2492.
Lakeshore Dr./Rte. 9N, Bolton Landing.
Season: Mid-June–Labor Day; daily 10–5.
Small admission fee.

During this early decades of this century, Bolton Landing was a mecca for opera stars and composers, such as Samuel Barber and Gian Carlo Menotti. From 1921-1935, Marcella Sembrich, a Polish soprano, made her home here. Born Marcella Kochanska, she was a European sensation, and in 1898, she joined New York's Metropolitan Opera. Sembrich founded the vocal departments of the Juilliard School, in Manhattan, and the Curtis

The Marcella Sembrich Memorial Studio honors an operatic superstar.

Courtesy of the Marcella Sembrich Memorial Studio

Institute, in Philadelphia; during the summers, a select group of students came to her cottage studio under the pines. The charming little museum now houses a collection of music, furniture, costumes, and opera ephemera related to Sembrich's brilliant career, including tributes from the leading composers of the day; stroll around the lakeside trail for a peaceful moment. Music lectures and concerts by young composers are held on summer afternoons and evenings.

CHAMPLAIN VALLEY

Courtesy of Crown Point State Historic Site

Ruins of the soldiers' barracks at Crown Point.

CROWN POINT STATE HISTORIC SITE
518-597-3666.

Poking into Lake Champlain, there's a thumb-shaped point that parts the waters, with Bulwagga Bay to the west and the long reach of the

Rte. 17, off Rtes. 9N & 22,
Crown Point.
Season: May–Oct.;
Weds.–Sat. 10–5, Sun.
1–5.
Handicap Access: Yes.

lake on the east. The sweeping view to the north once provided an ideal spot for guarding the territory. The French built a gargantuan stone octagon here in 1734, Fort St. Frederic, which was attacked repeatedly by the British in 1755-58 and finally captured by them in 1759. Colonial forces launched their assault on the British ships in Lake Champlain from Crown Point in 1775.

In 1910, the ruins of the French, British, and colonial forts were given to the state of New York. There's an excellent visitor center that explains the archaeology and political history of this haunting promontory through exhibits and audiovisual programs, and several miles of interpretive trails winding around stone walls and redoubts.

ESSEX COMMUNITY HERITAGE ORGANIZATION

518-963-7088.
Rte. 22, Essex.

During the brief peaceful period between the French and Indian War and the American Revolution, William Gilliland, an Irish immigrant, bought up huge tracts of land along Lake Champlain. He envisioned a string of prosperous communities, and by 1770, had established Essex. Unfortunately the town lay smack in the path of General Burgoyne as British troops marched from Canada to Saratoga and, just a decade after the settlers arrived, the settlement was destroyed.

By 1800, Essex was again thriving thanks to iron mining, stone quarrying, shipbuilding, and other commerce. By 1850, the population of the town was 2,351, but when railroads came to eastern New York, in the 1870s, fortunes changed for Essex and other lakeside towns.

That era was the peak of the town's prosperity, and then the population dwindled steadily to its current level of about a thousand residents. Because of this decline, and the lack of economic opportunities, there was little need for new housing; old buildings were preserved out of necessity. Today Essex contains one of the most intact collections of pre-Civil War buildings in the Northeast. The Essex Community Heritage Organization has published an excellent booklet describing the dozens of fine homes, inns, and commercial buildings in town ($3), and a self-guided walk through town in summer or fall is a delightful way to spend a day.

PENFIELD HOMESTEAD MUSEUM

518-597-3804.
Old Furnace Rd., off Rte. 74, Ironville.
Season: Mid-May–Columbus Day, daily 9–4.

A sign in the front yard of the homestead makes an astonishing claim: the site is the birthplace of the Electrical Age. In 1831 Allen Penfield used a crude electromagnet to separate iron ore from its base rock, thus testing electricity in an industrial application for the first time.

Fee: Nominal.
Handicap Access: Partial.

Ironville today is a lovely, quiet spot so different from its heyday as the center of a major iron industry during 1830-80. The complex is an open-air museum dedicated to the local mines, forges, and old railroads, with an eclectic historical collection in the homestead itself, a white-clapboard Federal building circa 1826. The other buildings along the lane in town are mainly Greek Revival, in excellent condition; there's a self-guided walking tour of the 550-acre grounds that takes you for a nice hike in the woods to find remnants of the days of iron. In mid-August, Heritage Day is a festival of traditional crafts and skills, with wagon rides and a chicken barbecue, and there's a harvest festival in the fall.

HIGH PEAKS

**HISTORIC SARANAC
    LAKE**
518-891-0971.
132 River St., North Elba
    Town Hall, Saranac Lake.
Season: Year-round.

The healthcare-industry history of Saranac Lake is unique, and in 1980, Historic Saranac Lake was founded to commemorate the special architecture that evolved to help tuberculosis patients get more fresh air and sunlight. Numerous cure cottages and sanatorium-related buildings have now been recognized on the National Register of Historic Places. The group has published a walking tour of selected structures, presents lectures and conferences, and is a key player in restoring the village's railroad station.

John Brown's body lies in North Elba.

B. Folwell

JOHN BROWN FARM
518-523-3900.
John Brown Rd., off Old
    Military Rd., Lake Placid.

In 1849, abolitionist John Brown came to North Elba, near Lake Placid, to help Gerrit Smith launch a self-sufficient enclave for free blacks.

Season: Mid-May–Oct. (exc.
 Mon. & Tues.) 10–5.
Handicap Access: Yes.

Smith owned more than 100,000 acres across northern New York, and his plan was to give 40 acres to each would-be black homesteader. The idea may have been doomed from the start since the families — many of them from northern cities — were not prepared to farm in the harsh climate or work the rugged, unprepared ground. Most of the residents of "Timbuctoo," as it became known, left within a few years of their arrival. Brown himself lived only a few years at the farm, leaving his family for months at a time in order to pursue a failing wool business and antislavery concerns. After his final adventure in Harper's Ferry, Brown was executed on December 2, 1859, in Charlestown, Virginia.

In 1870 the property was acquired by a group of the abolitionist's admirers. Today the farmhouse and outbuildings, managed by New York as a state historic site, contain exhibits related to John Brown's life, and his "body lies a-mouldering in the grave" nearby.

**ROBERT LOUIS
 STEVENSON
 MEMORIAL COTTAGE**
518-891-4480.
11 Stevenson Ln., Saranac
 Lake.
Season: July 1–Sept. 15
 (exc. Mon.) 10–4.
Fee: Nominal.

In 1887–88, Robert Louis Stevenson took the "cure" for tuberculosis in Saranac Lake, sleeping in an unheated porch all winter, and taking in plenty of fresh air while hiking and skating. During his Adirondack stint, Stevenson wrote a dozen essays for *Scribners*, started *The Master of Ballantrae*, and worked on *The Wrong Box*, a collaborative effort with Lloyd Osbourne. In a letter to Henry James, the Scotsman described his tiny cottage: "Our house . . . is on a hill, and has sight of a stream turning a corner in the valley — bless the face of running water! — and sees some hills too, and the paganly prosaic roofs of Saranac itself; the Lake it does not see, nor do I regret that; I like water (fresh water, I mean) either running swiftly among stones, or else largely qualified with whiskey."

The Stevenson Society was founded in 1916 to commemorate the writer's life and works; one of the group's original projects was to interest Gutzon Borglum, the sculptor best known for creating Mt. Rushmore, in designing a bronze bas-relief depicting Stevenson — now next to the front door. The society still manages the cottage, which has displays of Stevenson letters, photographs, memorabilia, and first editions, and sponsors readings and lectures.

NORTHWEST LAKES

**BETH JOSEPH
 SYNAGOGUE**
518-359-7229.
Lake St., Tupper Lake.
Season: July–Aug.

Built in 1905, Tupper Lake's temple is a elegant, symmetrical structure made of simple pine boards and tall arched windows. Beth Joseph once served an active congregation, but after the 1930s, attendance declined. Scout troops met in the basement, and for a time, a group of Baptists even worshiped there as they didn't have a church of their own. In 1959, the synagogue closed, and stood vacant for 25 years.

Community interest in the historic building was rekindled by a summer resident, who encouraged former temple members to get the structure listed on the National Register of Historic Places and begin restoration work. Local residents of all religions pitched in with donated labor, materials, and funds; the ornate embroidered velvet Torah covers were painstakingly restored by a local weaver. In 1991, work was completed, and now the facility hosts art exhibitions, concerts, lectures, and other events.

WHITE PINE CAMP
518-327-3030.
White Pine Rd., Paul
  Smiths.
Season: Summer; guided
  tours only.
Fee: Nominal.

Calvin Coolidge's summer White House for 1926 was this lovely secluded cluster of 20 buildings nestled along the shores of Osgood Pond. Open to the public for its first season in 1995, White Pine Camp depicts the architecture and social history of an Adirondack Great Camp; there are interpretive exhibits, occasional activities for children, and woodland trails. Some cabins are available to rent by the week; see Chapter Three, *Lodging*.

CENTRAL ADIRONDACKS

**GREAT CAMP
  SAGAMORE**
315-354-5311.
Sagamore Rd., off Rte. 28,
  Raquette Lake.
Season: July 4–fall.
Tours: Call for schedule.
Fee: $6; $3 children.

Adirondack entrepreneur William West Durant built Sagamore, a massive rustic lodge, along the lines of a Swiss chalet, in 1897, and sold it to Alfred G. Vanderbilt, Sr., in 1901. Even though the Vanderbilts spent much of their time elsewhere, Sagamore was a self-sufficient village in the heart of the wilderness, with its own farm and a crew of craftsmen to supply furniture, hardware, and boats. Today, the millionaires' complex — main lodge, dining hall, rustic guest cottages, casino playhouse, open-air bowling alley, and boathouse — and the artisans' barns, carriage house, workshops, and blacksmith shop are open to the public. Two-hour tours are presented by college interns; a highlight is sending a vintage ball down the lane toward the pins in order to demonstrate the loop-de-loop ball return.

Sagamore is in a gorgeous setting on the shore of Sagamore Lake, four miles off the main road on a rough dirt road. Besides tours for the public, the Great Camp sponsors workshops and conferences, is available for overnight accommodations, has a small gift shop and cafe, and can be hired for special events like wedding receptions.

LECTURE SERIES

An Adirondack education is possible through numerous public lectures at libraries, museums, town halls and other sites. The **Atmospheric Science Research Center** (518-946-2142) on *Whiteface Mtn.* presents natural history and environmental science lectures on Tuesdays in July and August. At the **Visitor Interpretive Centers** in *Paul Smiths* (518-327-3000) and *Newcomb* (518-582-2000) there are nature, history, and arts presentations year-round. The **Huntington Lecture Series**, presented in July and August by the Adirondack Ecological Center (a major research facility associated with the State University of New York's College of Environmental Science and Forestry), at the Newcomb visitor center, is an excellent assortment of programs on current environmental topics.

Since 1978, **Adirondack Discovery,** based in *Inlet* (315-357-3598; mail: Box 545, Inlet NY 13360), has become a sort of mobile Chatauqua, offering guided canoe trips and hikes to historic sites and along old railroad routes, evening lectures ranging from aerial photography tips to old postcard collections, hands-on workshops by local craftspeople, and folk music performances in Inlet, Indian Lake, Raquette Lake, Speculator, Old Forge, Minerva, Silver Bay, North Creek, Ticonderoga, and Saranac Lake. In 1997, for example, Adirondack Discovery presented more than a hundred different programs during July and August.

LIBRARIES

There are 30-some public libraries inside the Adirondack Park, and visitors are always welcome, rain or shine. Several libraries have special collections of books of regional interest, classic and children's videos, and even mini-museums. Most libraries offer children's programs, readings by regional writers, films, travel lectures, how-to sessions, concerts and even Internet access; pick up a schedule locally for details. A brief sampling of libraries with noteworthy collections, exemplary programs, or fine buildings follows.

LAKE GEORGE AND SOUTHEASTERN ADIRONDACKS

Caldwell Lake George Library (518-668-2528; 340 Canada St., Lake George) Films, lectures, workshops. Catch a performance by Shirley McPherson, the librarian, if you can — she's an expert on local ghost stories.

Horicon Free Library (No phone; Rte. 8, Brant Lake) Tiny, picturesque cobblestone building perched over the lake.

A book-filled nook at the Keene Valley Library.

Nancie Battaglia

CHAMPLAIN VALLEY

Black Watch Library (518-585-7380; Montcalm St., Ticonderoga) Designed as a medieval-looking "shrine to literacy" in 1905, and named after the 42nd Highland Regiment, which fought at Ticonderoga in 1758.

Paine Memorial Free Library (518-963-4478; 1 School St., Willsboro) Lovely brick building overlooking the Boquet River. The Paine Jordan bird-skin collection is here for ornithologists to study; there's also a good local history selection. Numerous summer programs, from art exhibitions to traditional craft demonstrations.

Westport Library Association (518-962-8219; Washington St., Westport) Look for the clock tower. Great old building with fireplaces, antique woodwork, natural lighting, high ceilings, and comfy couches. Lecture series and occasional concerts on the library lawn.

HIGH PEAKS

Keene Valley Library (518-576-4335; Main St., Keene Valley) Excellent local history and mountaineering collection with monographs, maps, photographs, and rare books. Lectures, readings, special exhibitions on local history.

Lake Placid Library (518-523-3200; 67 Main St., Lake Placid) Story hours for children; good general collection.

Saranac Lake Free Library (518-891-4190; 100 Main St., Saranac Lake) Extensive Adirondack collection in the William Chapman White Room, open by appointment. Brown-bag luncheon lecture series, evening lectures; gallery featuring local artists; Charles Dickert Wildlife Museum open in July and August.

NORTHWEST LAKES

Cubley Library (518-327-6313; Paul Smith's College, Paul Smiths) College reference library, with fall and winter concert series open to the public.

Goff Nelson Memorial Library (518-359-9421; 41 Lake St., Tupper Lake) Good Adirondack collection available to readers whenever the library is open; crafts and local history exhibits; lectures.

CENTRAL ADIRONDACKS

Indian Lake Public Library (518-648-5444; Pelon Rd., Indian Lake) New facility. General collection, with lectures and special programs year-round.

Johnsburg Library (518-251-4343; Main St., North Creek) New town library with general collection and computer stations.

Old Forge Library (315-369-6008; Crosby Blvd., Old Forge) Adirondack collection, lecture series, writers' workshops, children's programs, performances by Adirondack storytellers.

Raquette Lake Library (315-354-4005; Dillon Rd., Raquette Lake) Charming turn-of-the-century building with window seats and fireplace; lectures and special programs.

MUSEUMS

The Adirondack Museum has a marvelous collection of rustic furniture.

Nancie Battaglia

THE ADIRONDACK MUSEUM
518-352-7311.
Rtes. 28 & 30, Blue Mtn. Lake.

Simply put, no visit to the Adirondacks is complete without a trip to the Adirondack Museum; even if you've been there within the last few years, you ought to go back again to see what's

Season: May 23–Oct. 15, daily 9:30–5:30.
Fee: $10 adults; discounts for children, seniors, groups.
Handicap Access: Yes.
Book and gift shop; snack bar.

new and improved. If you've never seen the complex, described by the *New York Times* as "the best museum of its kind in the world," you're in for a surprise. Perched on the side of Blue Mtn., and overlooking the island-studded lake, is a major outdoor museum that is user-friendly, scholarly, beautiful, amusing, and superlative in every way.

The museum's theme is interpreting man's relationship to the Adirondacks, and it does so in 23 exhibit buildings. Adjacent to the gatehouse is a theater showing "The Adirondacks: The Lives and Times of an American Wilderness," an award-winning film. In the galleries of the main building, there are changing exhibits; in 1998 the centerpiece show is hunting and fishing paintings by A.F. Tait, Winslow Homer, and others.

There are scores of wooden boats, including fine Adirondack guideboats and a Gold Cup racer; there are dozens of carriages, sleighs, and wagons. You can glide through August Belmont's private railroad car and imagine yourself en route to your very own Great Camp, or you can picture the other extreme of Adirondack life, in buildings on logging and mining. In "Woods and Waters: Outdoor Recreation in the Adirondacks," you'll find hunting and fishing paraphernalia and natural history exhibits. On Merwin Hill, Bull Cottage showcases rooms of rustic furniture. If all this seems like too much walking, there's even a building where you can sit down and let hundreds of old photographs parade by.

The museum is a great place for children who can read and understand historical ideas; there are audio- and videotape stations that add depth to the displays. One suggestion, though: parents should keep a close eye on young ones who may be tempted to touch fragile artifacts. The Marion River Carry locomotive, located in the center of the campus, is a good place to let active kids be themselves.

The museum comes alive with craft demonstrations, music, and storytelling on selected days. The Rustic Furniture Makers' Fair, in September, showcases 40 or so builders so that visitors can decide how to begin their own Adirondack collections. There are numerous other events from conferences to the No-Octane Regatta: A Wooden Boat Classic, held in Blue Mtn. Lake in June.

It's probably a natural response to plan a visit to the Adirondack Museum on a rainy day, but thousands of other folks think along the same lines, and the place can get crowded. Far better to pick a gorgeous day when you can savor the view and the many outdoor displays, and see the exhibits without having to jockey for position.

ADIRONDACK HISTORY CENTER
518-873-6466.
Court St./Rte. 9, Elizabethtown.

If all the military skirmishes along Lake Champlain have blurred into one confusing cloud of cannon smoke, the Essex County Historical Society's museum has a nifty sound-and-light show

Vintage Watercraft

In 1843 John Todd visited the lonely settlers in Long Lake and wrote, "Their little boats were their horses, and the lake their only path." Traditional wooden boats, especially the guideboat, performed a major role in 19th-century work and play. At several gatherings across the park, you can get a taste of this era, and enjoy beautifully restored guideboats, canoes, sailboats, and classic powerboats.

The **No-Octane Regatta** (518-352-7311) held in **_Blue Mtn. Lake_** in June attracts a glorious array of muscle- and wind-powered watercraft. There are builders' displays at the Adirondack Lakes Center for the Arts and lectures and toy-boat races at the Adirondack Museum, but the main attraction is on the waterfront, off Rte. 28, where boats are displayed. There are old-fashioned contests, including canoe jousting, where standing contestants try to knock each other out of canoes with long, padded poles, and the hurry-scurry race, where participants' boats are anchored out in the lake: the competitors run from the beach, swim to the boats, clamber in, then paddle or row to the finish line.

The **Maritime Festival** in **_Essex_** (518-963-7504) features antique boats on Lake Champlain, plus races, a parade, music, and house tours, in July.

The **Wooden Canoe Heritage Association Assembly** (no phone; Box 226, Blue Mtn. Lake) is a four-day canoe confabulation held at Paul Smith's College, in **_Paul Smiths_**, in late July. There are demonstrations and workshops by boatbuilders, lectures on historic voyages and techniques, and opportunities for the public to paddle and sail traditional canoes.

The **Adirondack Chapter of the Antique and Classic Boat Society** (315-369-3552) holds its annual show and rendezvous on the **_Fulton Chain of Lakes_** in July; visitors can get a good look at all that mahogany and brass when the boats are at the public docks, or watch the parade through the lakes in the afternoon. Woody cars are also displayed near the Old Forge beach.

Early August brings **Boats and Autos of Yesterday** to **_Bolton Landing_**, sponsored by the fledgling Lake George Antique Boat and Auto Museum (518-644-9821). The event coincides with the annual antique show held at the Bolton school.

In **_Cleverdale_**, on the eastern side of Lake George, Castaway Marina hosts its annual **Antique and Classic Boat Show** (518-585-6472) in late August. This is another place to see gleaming old Fay & Bowens, Chris-Crafts, HackerCrafts, and Garwoods.

Season: Mid-May–mid-Oct.; Mon.–Sat. 9–5, Sun. 1–5.
Fee: $3; $2 seniors, $1 children 6–16.
Handicap Access: Yes.

that puts the battles into a geographical and chronological context. That's not the only reason to visit: the Adirondack History Center interprets local pioneer life — mining, farming, trapping, logging — through its permanent exhibits, and showcases contemporary local artists during the summer.

There's a stagecoach that once carried passengers from Elizabethtown to Keene, a fire tower that you don't have to climb a mountain to enjoy, a roomful of dolls, and the wonderful Colonial Garden of perennials and herbs. For Adirondack and genealogical scholars, there's an excellent library open by appointment year-round.

1812 HOMESTEAD
518-963-4071.
Rte. 22, Willsboro.
Season: July–Oct. 15, daily 1–4:30.
Fee: Nominal.

History comes alive at this early farm complex, with an original homestead, barn, and schoolhouse. Families can try making candles, cooking in an open hearth, or gathering eggs, and meet the farm's resident oxen, sheep, and pigs. Demonstrations include blacksmithing, spinning, shingle-making, quilting, and other old-time skills. In season, the farm makes apple cider and maple sugar; call ahead to learn about special events.

Fort Ticonderoga commands a sweeping view of Lake Champlain.

Courtesy of Fort Ticonderoga Museum

FORT TICONDEROGA
518-585-2821.
Fort Rd., off Rte. 22, Ticonderoga.
Season: Mid-May–mid-Oct., daily 9–5.
Fee: $6; children 10–13 $5; under 10 free.
Handicap Access: Yes.
Museum shop; snack bar; picnic grove.

High above Lake Champlain is another must-see for Adirondack visitors: Fort Ticonderoga. In 1755, the French built a fort, *Carillon*, on the site, and for the next quarter century, the stone fortification was a key location in the struggle to claim North America. The Marquis de Montcalm defended the site against numerous British invaders until 1758, when Lord Jeffery Amherst captured the fort. Ticonderoga was British territory until Ethan Allen and the Green Mountain Boys took the fort "in the name of Jehovah and the great Continental Congress," during the American Revolution.

In the early 1800s, the Pell family acquired the ruins and fields where the soldiers once camped. Work was begun in 1908 to rebuild the barracks and parade grounds, making Fort Ticonderoga the nation's first restored historic site (in contrast, Colonial Williamsburg's restoration dates back to the 1930s).

Inside the barracks are exhibits on the French and Indian War and the American Revolution, from intricately inscribed powderhorns to blunderbusses, cannons, and swords. The grim side of winter warfare is clear, and there's little glorification of the ordeal of battle. Below the barracks is the subterranean kitchen, which once supplied thousands of loaves of bread every day to the standing army. Beneath the walls, on a broad plain facing the lake, is the King's Garden, a beautiful spot that's been cultivated for hundreds of years and is open for tours. The walled English-style garden dates back to the 1920s and is one of a handful of places recognized by the Garden Conservancy.

There's plenty of action at the fort in the summer, from demonstrations of black-powder shooting and cannon firing to fife-and-drum drills. On some weekends, there are encampments of regiments reenacting battles, or bagpipe-band concerts. There's also a boat tour every day in July and August, on the *Carillon*, which goes from Fort Ti to Crown Point and back, for an extra fee.

The fort is set in a spectacular spot with a magnificent view of the lake, but don't end your visit there. It's worth a side trip up Mt. Defiance, near town, to get an even higher perspective. From the top of that hill, a show of British cannons so intimidated the officers at Ticonderoga and Mt. Independence, a fort across the lake in Vermont, that colonial troops fled both strongholds. (Shots were never fired.) Bring a pair of binoculars and a picnic lunch.

SIX NATIONS INDIAN MUSEUM
518-891-0769.
Buck Pond Campsite Rd., Onchiota.
Season: July 1–Labor Day, daily 9:30–6; May–June, Sept.–Oct. by appointment.
Fee: $2; $1 children.

Native people did travel to the Adirondacks for spring fishing, summer gathering, and fall hunting: the mountains, forests, and lakes offered abundant resources. At many local institutions this information is overshadowed by all the other stories those museums have to tell, but at Six Nations, the kaleidoscopic collection of baskets, beadwork, quill work, tools, weapons, paintings, drums, cradle boards, hats, pottery, and clothing all celebrate the Iroquois tribes' lives and times. Artifacts fill cases, line the walls, hang from the ceilings; take the time to look closely and you'll be rewarded.

LAKE GEORGE AND SOUTHEASTERN ADIRONDACKS

In Warren County you'll find numerous small museums to visit. The **Bolton Historical Museum** in *Bolton Landing* (518-644-9960; Rte. 9N) is housed in a former Catholic church. Nineteenth-century photos of Lake George hotels by Seneca Ray Stoddard give a taste of the Gilded Age; more

The Bolton Historical Museum highlights the lakeshore community's heritage.

Nancie Battaglia

contemporary photos show sculptor David Smith at work in his Bolton Landing studio. There's an assortment of furniture, clothing, agricultural implements, and items relating to the town's days as a summer retreat for musical superstars.

In *Brant Lake*, the **Horicon Museum** (518-494-7286; Rte. 8) is a well-kept nine-room farmhouse full of antiques, agricultural implements, prints, photos, toys, and dolls open from Memorial Day through Labor Day. The **Frances Kinnear Museum**, open year-round in a historic *Lake Luzerne* home (518-696-4520; 2144 Main St.), is similarly chock-full of local memorabilia; the town is also home to two summer museums: the **Mill Museum**, set in a park near the lake (no phone; Mill St.), and the **Schoolhouse Museum** (518-696-3500; Main St., near the Norstar Bank). In *Chestertown*, local history comes alive from July to Aug. at the **Town of Chester Museum of Local History** (518-494-3758; Town Hall, Main St.), with neat displays on village life.

In *Lake George*, in the old courthouse, the **Lake George Historical Museum** (518-668-5044; Canada St.) is three floors of exhibits, from the 1845-vintage jail cells in the basement to "the church that cheated the hangman." The detailed folk-art model was carved in 1881 by a convicted murderer. He sold it, hired a new lawyer, appealed his conviction, and was acquitted. Also in Lake George is **Fort William Henry** (518-668-5471; Canada St.), a restored log fortress dedicated to French and Indian War history, with life-size dioramas, assorted armaments, and lots of action: military drills, musket and cannon firing, fife and drum bands. The fort is open daily spring–fall.

In *Schroon Lake*, the **Schroon–North Hudson Historical Society** (518-532-7798; Olden Dr.) is open Thurs.–Sun. in July and Aug.; in *Warrensburg*, the **Warrensburg Museum of Local History** (518-623-9826; 47 Main St.) highlights the town's early industries, from garment factories to sawmills.

CHAMPLAIN VALLEY

Ticonderoga has two local-history museums: the **Heritage Museum** (518-585-6366; Bicentennial Park), and the **Historical Society** (518-585-7868; Hancock House), located in a replica of John Hancock's Boston home. The Heritage Museum depicts local 19th-century industries including paper- and pencil-making, in a Victorian office building that's open daily in July and Aug. and on fall weekends. Hancock House was the first home of the New York State Historical Association (which is now based in Cooperstown), and the house has several period rooms illustrating social history from the 1700s to the turn of the century, including some fine antiques. There's an extensive research library open by appointment year-round.

HIGH PEAKS AND NORTHERN ADIRONDACKS

In *Lake Placid*, the train station for the Adirondack Division of the New York Central is home to the **Lake Placid–North Elba Historical Society Museum** (518-523-1608; Averyville Rd.). There's a nostalgic country store display, sporting gear and memorabilia from the 1932 Olympics, and a music room honoring residents Victor Herbert and Kate Smith; the place is pretty lively in the summer with lectures and concerts. Open June–Sept., Tues.–Sun. afternoons.

Brand-new in the Olympic Center is the **Lake Placid Winter Olympic Museum** (518-523-1655), which is open daily year-round. Photographs, vintage films, equipment, trophies, clothing, and memorabilia illustrate the two sets of Olympic competitions that have come to town.

In the *Saranac Lake* Free Library, the **Charles Dickert Memorial Wildlife Museum** (518-891-4190; 100 Main St.) is open July and Aug., with displays of hundreds of stuffed mammals, birds, and fish native to the Adirondacks.

CENTRAL ADIRONDACKS

Riley's Tavern in *Piseco* is home to the **Piseco Lake Historical Society** (518-548-6401; Piseco Lake Rd.), a local collection of antiques and ephemera open in the summer; in *Edinburg*, the **Nellie Tyrell Edinburg Museum** (no phone; RD 1) is an old schoolhouse with displays showing life before the creation of the Great Sacandaga Reservoir. *Northville* is home to two museums right on South Main Street: the **Gifford Valley Schoolhouse**, behind the municipal offices, and the **Paul Bradt Museum**, which is filled with North American wildlife and housed inside the village office complex. The outdoor museum complex near *Caroga Lake*, the **Caroga Historical Museum** (518-835-6335; London Bridge Rd.) recreates pioneer life in the southern Adirondacks in a farmstead, schoolhouse, and country store, and hosts changing exhibits.

In *Olmstedville*, the **Minerva Historical Society** (518-251-2229; Main St.) is open July and Aug.; displays honor artists who visited the area, such as Winslow Homer. In *Old Forge*, the **Town of Webb Historical Association** (315-369-3838; Main St.) has exhibits on railroads, resorts, rustic furniture, and early industries; the museum is open year-round. Just east of Old Forge is the **Forest Industries Exhibit Hall** (315-369-3078; Rte. 28), with displays on forest management, logging history, and dioramas open Memorial Day–Labor Day.

BEYOND THE BLUE LINE

In *Glens Falls*, the **Hyde Collection** (518-792-1761; 161 Warren St.) contains an exceptional private art collection including works by da Vinci, Botticelli, El Greco, Rembrandt, Rubens, Degas, Renoir, Cezanne, and Picasso, along with famous American artists, and 16th- through 19th-century antique furnishings, all in a handsomely restored villa. There's a new wing with changing exhibits, and many participatory programs. Also in Glens Falls, the **Chapman Historical Museum** (518-793-2826; 348 Glen St.) is a historic house with a modern gallery highlighting photographs by Seneca Ray Stoddard.

Southeast of the Adirondacks, in *Granville*, the **Pember Museum of Natural History** (518-642-1515; 33 W. Main St.) is a wonderfully preserved Victorian gentleman's collection of hundreds of birds, butterflies, and trophy heads in polished wood cases. Just opened in fall 1995 is the **Slate Valley Museum** (518-642-1717; 17 Water St.), also in Granville. It depicts the social history and folk art of the area's quarries. In *Saratoga Springs*, next door to Lincoln Baths, a public spa, is the **National Museum of Dance** (518-584-2225; Rte. 9). Open from Memorial Day through the fall, the museum's collection includes costumes, films, and sets, hundreds of photographs, and special exhibitions highlighting international dance history.

North of the park, in *Chazy*, is another private museum, the **Alice T. Miner Colonial Collection** (518-846-7336; Main St.), in a three-story mansion with a fine textile collection, china and glass, rare books, colonial furniture, and strange curiosities from around the world. In *Plattsburgh*, the **Kent-DeLord House Museum** (518-561-1035; 17 Cumberland Ave.) is a nicely restored late 18th-century home. Near *Malone* is the **Farmer Boy's Home** (518-483-1207; Stacy Rd., Burke), the setting for *Farmer Boy*, by Laura Ingalls Wilder. The farmstead, which is gradually being restored, was the home of Almanzo Wilder in the mid-19th century.

South of the park, in *Johnstown*, but pertinent to Adirondack studies is **Johnson Hall State Historic Site** (518-762-8712; Hall Ave.). The restored 1763 Georgian mansion was the home of Sir William Johnson, who served as superintendent of Indian affairs for the northern colonies; the Adirondack fur trade was a mainstay of his wealth. The Colonial Market Fair is a popular event, and the site hosts reenacted encampments of frontiersmen, Canadian fur traders, and native people.

The guidebook *Adirondack Odysseys* (Adirondack Museum and Berkshire House Publishers, 1997) details a hundred historic sites from the Mohawk Valley to the St. Lawrence River, with entertaining capsule histories of the region and information useful to traveling families.

MUSIC

Traditional North Country music is represented by dance and fiddle tunes that have roots in French-Canadian and Irish music, and by ballads of the lumber woods, like "Blue Mountain Lake," "The Jam on Gerry's Rocks," "The Wild Mustard River," and "Once More A-Lumbering Go."

To hear authentic old-time instrumental music, look for the occasional fiddle jamborees or square dances, sponsored by arts groups and towns: the **Forest, Field, and Stream Festival** in September at the **Adirondack History Center** (518-873-6466) features traditional music and the **Adirondack Museum** (518-352-7311), in Blue Mtn. Lake, occasionally presents music within exhibit settings, like songs about lumbering performed in the logging buildings.

Long Lake **Parks and Recreation** (518-624-3077) sponsors fiddlers' gatherings in spring and fall; you can dance like a wave of the sea at **Stony Creek Mountain Days** (518-696-2332) in August. The **Adirondack Fiddlers Association** meets once a month at the Schuylerville American Legion Hall (518-695-3011). To hear folk songs and ballads, check with music presenters listed below: the *Schroon Lake* **Arts Council** (518-532-7675) stages an annual Adirondack folk festival in August.

Besides traditional music, there are many excellent summer chamber-music series outlined in the following pages. Watch for events sponsored by a new organization, the **Lake Placid Institute** (518-523-1312), which brings world-class musicians to town for symposia and performances in different venues.

LAKE GEORGE AND SOUTHEASTERN ADIRONDACKS

LAKE GEORGE ARTS PROJECT
518-668-2616.
Canada St., Lake George.

During the second weekend in September, the Lake George Jazz Festival, in Shepard Park, is the place to be. The bands — often Latin or Afro-Caribbean stars — are topnotch, the vibe is cool, and the price is free. The arts project also sponsors music in the village park on summer nights, from reggae to new blues.

LUZERNE CHAMBER MUSIC FESTIVAL
518-696-2771.
Luzerne Music Center,
    Lake Tour Rd., 1.3 mi. off
    Rte. 9N, Lake Luzerne.
Season: July–Aug.
Tickets: $10.

Members of the Philadelphia Orchestra (who also perform at the Saratoga Performing Arts Center in July and Aug.) present a superb chamber-music concert series on Monday nights. Artistic directors of the center are Toby Blumenthal, piano, and Bert Phillips, cello, and they pride themselves on bringing internationally acclaimed soloists to join the resident ensembles. The music center is also a summer camp for gifted young musicians, and the free student/faculty recitals held Fridays, Saturdays, and Sundays are definitely worth a listen.

SCHROON LAKE ARTS COUNCIL
518-532-7675.
Boat House Theater, Schroon Lake.
Mail: Box 668, Schroon Lake NY 12870.
Season: July–Aug.
Tickets: $5; $3 children.

On the lakeshore, yet within walking distance of downtown Schroon Lake, the Boat House Theater is a fitting spot to hear traditional Adirondack music. The arts council presents evening concerts and dance performances in summer in the historic building, and a festival of folk music, storytelling, and rustic crafts each August. Featured regional folk artists have included Chris Shaw, Peggy Eyres, Dan Berggren, Roy Hurd, and storyteller Bill Smith.

SEAGLE COLONY
518-532-7875.
Charley Hill Rd., Schroon Lake.
Season: July–Aug.
Tickets: Prices vary.

Oscar Seagle, famed tenor and voice teacher, established this country retreat in 1915. Vocal music is still the primary program, with coaching and master classes in opera and musical theater for conservatory students and aspiring performers. Every Sunday evening in the summer, the nondenominational Vespers concerts feature exceptional choral singing; public concerts featuring scenes from opera and musical theater are held in July.

CHAMPLAIN VALLEY

MEADOWMOUNT SCHOOL OF MUSIC
518-873-2063.
Lewis-Wadhams Rd., Lewis.
Mail: RFD 2, Westport NY 12993.
Season: July–Aug.
Tickets: Prices vary.

A short list of Meadowmount's alumni gives a hint of the talent that has rusticated in the hills of the Boquet Valley: Yo-Yo Ma, Itzhak Perlman, Pinchas Zukerman, Michael Rabin, Lynn Harrell. Distinguished faculty and promising student members give free concerts at the camp on Wednesdays and Sundays, while the annual scholarship-benefit concert features world-famous string players in a cozy, informal setting. Meadowmount student groups also play in free outdoor concerts in nearby towns, so check locally for scheduling; several performances are held at the Kent-DeLord House in Plattsburgh.

TICONDEROGA FESTIVAL GUILD
518-585-6716.
Montcalm St., Ticonderoga.
Mail: Box 125, Ticonderoga NY 12883.
Season: July–Aug.
Tickets: Prices vary.

An enormous striped tent in the center of town is the festival guild's summer home; under the big top there are weekly performances of music, dance, and theater, with concerts on Tuesday nights, and "Arts Trek" kids' shows on Wednesday mornings. Guests in past seasons were the Syracuse Symphony Baroque Ensemble, folk group

Woods Tea Company, Ko-Motion Movement Theater, and the Hudson Vagabond Puppets.

HIGH PEAKS AND NORTHERN ADIRONDACKS

ADIRONDACK FESTIVAL OF AMERICAN MUSIC
518-891-1057.
Various locations, Saranac Lake.
Mail: Box 562, Saranac Lake NY 12983.
Season: July.
Tickets: Prices vary.

Since 1973, Gregg Smith, one of the country's leading choral directors, and the Grammy-award-winning Gregg Smith Singers have called Saranac Lake their summer home. Their gift to the community is music, music, music. The month-long festival includes workshops for music teachers, composers, and schoolkids, and there are dozens of choral, chamber, jazz, cabaret, and pops concerts sprinkled throughout Saranac Lake in churches, parks, and the town hall. Resident ensembles are the Adirondack Festival Chorus, the Adirondack Chamber Orchestra, among others; guest artists have included the Dave Brubeck Quintet.

The Lake Placid Sinfonietta performs in a park overlooking Mirror Lake on summer evenings.

Nancie Battaglia

LAKE PLACID SINFONIETTA
518-523-2051.
Various locations, Lake Placid.
Mail: Box 1303, Lake Placid NY 12946.
Season: July–Aug.
Tickets: Prices vary.

In 1917, the Sinfonietta was established to be the house orchestra at the Lake Placid Club, playing for the guests at the exclusive resort. Now the 18-member chamber orchestra is a valued community resource, presenting free Wednesday night concerts in the band shell overlooking Mirror Lake in the center of town (7pm; bring a cushion), children's programs at the Lake Placid Center for the

Arts, the Pops and Picnic at the Horseshoe Grounds on Old Military Rd., and the annual Train Station Concert at the Lake Placid–North Elba Historical Society in August. On Sunday nights, the Sinfonietta performs in the art center's theater with selected guest artists; the programs range from newly commissioned works by American composers to Mozart, Haydn, Bach, and Schubert. Vienna Night is a Strauss celebration usually held in early August; the gala features dinner, dancing, and music through the night.

BEYOND THE BLUE LINE

It's confusing, but the **Lake George Opera Festival** (518-793-3866; Box 2172, Glens Falls), isn't in Lake George. From its original home in a tin-roofed barn in Diamond Point, the summer opera festival has moved (to *Glens Falls*, a few miles down the road), and matured to become one of the country's most prestigious series. Performances — always in English — are staged at the Queensbury High School Auditorium, and the organization is actively seeking a permanent home.

Saratoga Springs isn't too far beyond the Adirondack Park, and the **Saratoga Performing Arts Center** (518-587-3300; Saratoga Springs) is a wonderful outdoor setting for the New York City Opera, the Philadelphia Orchestra, the Newport Jazz Festival-Saratoga, and the new Saratoga Chamber Music Festival. From mid-June through Labor Day, SPAC is busy practically every night.

Washington County, east of Lake George and just this side of the Vermont border, is home to two fine chamber groups in *Cambridge*: **Music from Salem** (518-677-2495; Hubbard Hall, Cambridge NY 12816), with the Lydian String Quartet in residence, and **L'Ensemble** (518-677-5455; Content Farm Rd., Cambridge).

NATURE CENTERS

The Adirondack Park has two new facilities that explain the region's natural history through permanent exhibits, public programs, workshops for children and adults, and extensive trails for hiking, snowshoeing, and cross-country skiing. In the lobbies, interactive computer stations allow visitors to get detailed information about specific towns, great canoeing and hiking destinations, and services for tourists. Works by regional artists are featured in rotating exhibitions.

The **Visitor Interpretive Center** in *Paul Smiths* (518-327-3000) has a wonderful butterfly house with flowers, plants, and indigenous insects, and also sponsors a wildflower festival in July. The VIC in *Newcomb* (518-582-2000) is home to the Huntington Lecture Series, with talks by ecological experts; you can also try snowshoeing for free on their trails through old-growth forest. Both centers are active year-round.

Children can explore nature in workshops and guided hikes at the Adirondack Park Visitor Interpretive Centers.

Nancie Battaglia

Up Yonda Farm (518-644-9767; Rte. 9N, Bolton Landing) is a lovely lake-view property that opened in 1997 as an environmental education center. The site, operated by Warren County, is busiest during warm weather, with guided trail walks, after-dark tours, and programs on birds, bats, butterflies, and other beasts.

NIGHTLIFE

Compared to a half century ago, when Duke Ellington's and Count Basie's bands played in local hotels, nightlife here in the nineties is pretty sedate. For live music, check out the offerings at arts centers listed above, and more than a dozen free concerts on Thursday and Friday nights in *Saranac Lake* sponsored by the **Saranac Lake Chamber of Commerce** (518-891-1990). Most of the tour boats described in Chapter 6, *Recreation*, schedule moonlight cruises with live music.

Stony Creek Inn (518-696-2394), across from Floyd's Mall in *Stony Creek*, has rock, country, and blues every weekend from spring through fall. In *Lake George*, **John Barleycorn's Pub** (518-668-9348; Canada St.) books good local bands for dancing into the wee hours. **Kindred Spirits** in *Olmstedville* (518-251-5131; at the Four Corners) is an outfitter's shop that presents Adirondack singers and songwriters in summer and fall in a coffeehouse setting. **Water-hole #3** in *Saranac Lake* (518-891-9502/6215, Main St.) is the liveliest source for music in the High Peaks, presenting big names like Leon Russell and local rockers on Fridays and Saturdays.

SEASONAL EVENTS

Throughout the Adirondack Park, special occasions celebrate local traditions and old-time North Country culture. The events listed below (in chronological order by region) emphasize history, music, storytelling, crafts and skills, or a combination of the arts. You'll also find annual athletic contests, such as the White Water Derby and the Whiteface Mtn. Uphill Footrace listed in Chapter Six, *Recreation*; craft fairs and antique shows are noted in Chapter Seven, *Shopping*, while affairs with a gustatory focus, like the Newcomb Steak Roast, are outlined in Chapter Five, *Restaurants and Food Purveyors*.

LAKE GEORGE AND SOUTHEASTERN ADIRONDACKS

Lake George Winter Carnival spans several weekends beginning in February, with kid-oriented activities, fireworks, races, and contests (518-668-2233).

Lake Luzerne Winter Extravaganza is usually the first weekend in February, with a particular highlight being the outhouse races. There are snow-sculpture contests, sleigh rides, snowshoe races, and a craft fair (518-696-2713).

Hague Winter Carnival is slated for the second full weekend in February, starting off with a torch-light parade on Friday evening. Daytime action includes the National Ice Auger and Chisel Contest, which involves boring through frozen Lake George, and plenty of other competitions for adults and children, from broom hockey to ice fishing and cross-country skiing (518-543-6161).

Americade is reportedly the world's largest motorcycle-touring rally. Held in and around Lake George in early June, there are guided rides on Adirondack back roads, seminars, swap meets, and banquets. Bikes range from tasteful special-edition Harleys worth tens of thousands of dollars, to rusty "rat bikes" that look like found-object sculptures. The participants aren't scary; they're just ordinary folks who love motorcycles (518-656-9367).

Summerfest features music, arts and crafts, and games for kids in Shepard Park in Lake George, on the last weekend in June (518-668-5755).

Stony Creek Mountain Days highlight Adirondack skills and pastimes in lumberjack contests, craft demonstrations, square dancing, and wagon rides, followed by fireworks, held the first weekend in August (518-696-2332).

Adirondack Folk Music Festival is an all-day affair in Schroon Lake that also includes rustic furniture and crafts, in mid-August (518-532-9259).

Warren County Country Fair is a family-oriented fair, with the usual 4-H and agricultural exhibits, a horse show, historical displays, traditional music, a pony pull, carnival rides, and fish-and-wildlife exhibits, held in mid-August at the fairground on Horicon Ave. outside Warrensburg (518-623-3291).

Barbershop Quartet and Chorus Festival in Bolton Landing features singers from around the country, on Labor Day Weekend (518-644-3831).

CHAMPLAIN VALLEY

Celebrate Essex marks the beginning of the summer season in this lakefront community, with walking tours and other activities, in late May (518-963-7452).

Marigold Festival in Westport includes a street fair, programs for children, and crafts, on Memorial Day weekend (518-962-8383).

Grand Encampment of the French and Indian War at Fort Ticonderoga features hundreds of make-believe French, Scottish, and colonial troops, Native American scouts, and camp followers in authentic costumes, in late June (518-585-2821).

Essex Maritime Festival highlights the town's lakefront heritage through an antique boat show, music performances, parades, rowing races, and other events, in Essex, in mid-July (518-963-7501).

Old-Time Folkcraft Fair, on the lawn of the Paine Memorial Library in Willsboro, is a showcase for local artisans and a chance to learn traditional North Country skills in late July (518-963-4478).

Essex County Fair, in Westport, features harness racing, livestock and agricultural displays, a midway, educational programs by Cooperative Extension, and lots of cotton candy. The fair runs for five days in mid-August (518-962-4810).

Forest, Field and Stream Festival, at the Adirondack History Center in Elizabethtown, happens during the height of fall color, in September, with a full slate of storytelling, old-time music, craft demonstrations, black-powder shooting, and participatory programs for children (518-873-6466).

Apple Folkfest at the Penfield Museum, Ironville, features traditional crafts, music, animals, and activities for children, in early October (518-597-3804).

Haunted Fort at Fort Ticonderoga, in late October, turns the historic site into a gallery of ghoulish mysteries (518-585-2821).

HIGH PEAKS

Saranac Lake Winter Carnival, in February, is reputedly the oldest winter carnival in the country. On the shore of Lake Flower, there's an awesome ice

Saranac Lake's winter carnival always has an ice palace as its centerpiece.

Courtesy of the Adirondack Collection,
Saranac Lake Free Library

palace, dramatically lit by colored spotlights each evening; events include ski races, a parade, concerts, and special activities for kids (518-891-1990).

Round the Mountain Festival in Saranac Lake is a spring celebration with an afternoon of bluegrass bands, a barbecue, and a canoe race, all on the second Saturday in May (518-891-1990).

Native American Festival at Whiteface Mtn., in Wilmington, celebrates music, dance, crafts, and skills of Northeastern tribes, on the first weekend of August (518-946-2233).

Teddy Roosevelt Days in Newcomb celebrate T.R.'s wild ride to the presidency with historical programs and sports contests, in mid-September (518-582-2811).

NORTHWEST LAKES

Woodsmen's Field Days in Tupper Lake highlight old-time lumber skills and underline the importance of logging in the Adirondack economy today. There's a parade with sparkling log trucks hauling the year's biggest, best logs; contests for man (ax-throwing, log-rolling, and speed-chopping), beast (skidding logs with draft horses), and heavy equipment (precision drills for skidders and loaders); clowns and games for kids. It's all on the second weekend in July, in the municipal park on the lakefront in Tupper Lake (518-359-3328).

Adirondack Wildflower Festival at the Visitor Interpretive Center in Paul Smiths offers guided wildflower walks, wildflower craft workshops, wildflower cooking demonstrations, and art programs for kids, in late July (518-327-3000).

CENTRAL ADIRONDACKS

Indian Lake Winter Festival on Presidents' Weekend in February mixes local history programs with outdoor events such as cross-country ski treks, downhill races at the town ski area, snowmobile poker runs, and snowshoe events throughout Indian Lake and Blue Mtn. Lake. There's music and sometimes square dancing in the evenings, plus community suppers (518-648-5112).

Neighbor Day opens the summer season in Old Forge, with music, crafts, kids' performances, and special art exhibitions across town, in early June (315-369-6411).

Minerva Day at the town beach on Minerva Lake and in downtown Olmstedville, features a parade, craft demonstrations, and activities for kids on the last Saturday in June (518-251-2869).

Old Home Days in Wells are held the first full weekend in August, with a parade featuring horse-drawn wagons, antique cars, floats, and marching bands. There's all kinds of music, plus a carnival and a craft fair (518-924-7912).

Fox Family Bluegrass Festival at Old Forge's McCauley Mtn. presents the town's own bluegrass stars plus other national bands, in early August (410-267-0432).

Bluegrass Festival in Long Lake's Sabattis Park brings top upstate bands and dancers for an outdoor show on the third Saturday in August (518-624-3077).

Gore Mountain Oktoberfest is the last weekend in September in North Creek, with plenty of oom-pah-pah and *gemütlichkeit*. There's live music and German-style dancing, a crafts fair, ethnic food and beer booths, children's activities, and rides on the ski area's chairlift to view the fall foliage (518-251-2612).

Apple Festival, also in Sabattis Park, is family fun with performances and games for kids, apple-cider making, a craft show, and apple pies galore, usually on the Saturday before Columbus Day (518-624-3077).

THEATER

LAKE GEORGE AND SOUTHEASTERN ADIRONDACKS

ADIRONDACK THEATRE FESTIVAL
518-798-7479.
French Mountain Playhouse, Lake George.
Season: Summer; occasional winter shows in other venues.

The Adirondack Theatre Festival, a young, ambitious new professional group, was launched in June 1995 to present innovative comedy, solo performers, and children's workshops. Founders of the company were involved with the production of the Broadway hit *Rent*, and bring real sophistication to their shows.

LAKE GEORGE DINNER THEATER
518-761-1092, year-round information.
518-668-5781, summer reservations.
Holiday Inn, Lake George.
Season: Mid-June–mid-Oct.
Tickets: Dinner & play $39; lunch & matinee $29; theater $24.
Handicap Access: Yes.

This Actors Equity company presents one show a season in a semi-proscenium setting; a sample from past playbills includes *Oil City Symphony*, *Dames at Sea*, *Little Mary Sunshine*, *Mixed Emotions*, and *On Golden Pond*. Productions are thoroughly competent, as is the food at the Holiday Inn's banquet room.

CHAMPLAIN VALLEY

DEPOT THEATER
518-962-4449.
Delaware & Hudson Depot,
Rte. 9N, Westport.
Mail: Box 414, Westport NY
12993.
Season: June–Sept.
Tickets: $15–18; $13–14
students, seniors.
Handicap Access: Yes.

Westport's D&H depot has found a surprising new life as home to a fine professional equity acting company directed by Westport native Shami McCormick. The former freight room comes alive with four or five plays each summer: 1997's smash hit was *Damn Yankees* by Richard Adler and Jerry Ross, performed on an elaborate revolving stage. Each year, a new musical debuts, and performance-art pieces by visiting artists are scheduled midweek. Depot Theater offers matinees for each of its shows — a nice option on a rainy day — but be sure to call ahead for tickets.

The region is also home to two new community theater organizations. The **Essex Theatre Company** (518-963-7442; Box 295, Essex) was formed in 1993 to showcase local talent. Productions in recent summers were held at the Masonic Lodge and included *The Fantasticks*, *On Golden Pond*, and musical cabarets. The **Boquet River Theatre Festival** (no phone; Box 701, Willsboro) performs in the Whallonsburg Church, on Rte. 22; programs are geared toward young audiences and performers.

HIGH PEAKS AND NORTHERN ADIRONDACKS

COMMUNITY THEATRE PLAYERS, INC.
Mail: Box 12, Lake Placid
NY 12946.

An amateur group founded in 1972, CTP usually mounts four shows a year at the Lake Placid Center for the Arts and other venues. Productions — consistently good — have included such mainstays as *Peter Pan*, *Brigadoon*, *Babes in Toyland*, *Li'l Abner*, and so forth.

PENDRAGON THEATRE
518-891-1854.
148 River St., Saranac Lake.
Season: Year-round.
Tickets: $12; $10 students, seniors.
Handicap Access: Yes.

This highly successful local troupe was awarded the prestigious Governor's Art Award in spring 1995, and has received acclaim for performances at the Edinburgh International Arts Festival, the Dublin Theatre Festival, and in Stockholm at the English-Speaking Theater. During the summer, Pendragon puts on three or four shows in repertory format; in 1997 shows included *Six Degrees of Separation* by John Guare and *The Importance of Being Earnest* by Oscar Wilde. In the fall, there's a classic show, and during the school year, actors form the Prop Trunk Players and tour local classrooms.

Pendragon, anchored by husband-and-wife team Bob Pettee and Susan Neal, was founded in 1981. The group's performances are worth a special trip.

CENTRAL ADIRONDACKS

ACT, INC.
315-369-6411.
Arts Center, Rte. 28, Old
 Forge.
Season: Spring & winter.
Tickets: Prices vary.
Handicap Access: Yes.

Musicals are on the menu for this spirited local group; past shows included *Annie, Oklahoma!*, and *Hello, Dolly.* Folks — with surprisingly rich voices — come from miles around to be on stage at the Arts Center in Old Forge during mud and snow season. In wintertime, there's usually a special children's show beside the Broadway plays.

WRITERS' PROGRAMS

The **Writer's Voice**, a nationwide program of the YMCA, has a center at Silver Bay Association (518-543-8833), on the northern end of Lake George. Workshops and readings by nationally known poets, travel writers, novelists, and essayists are slated for spring and summer. The **Lake George Arts Project** (518-668-2616) offers fall and spring workshops in poetry, creative nonfiction, and fiction led by regional writers with national reputations; a literary collection is published each year to present student and faculty work.

The **Old Forge Library** (315-369-6008) offers summer writing workshops, readings, and a regional authors' fair with dozens of Adirondack writers.

CHAPTER FIVE
Always in Good Taste
RESTAURANTS & FOOD PURVEYORS

Until the late twentieth century, Adirondack cuisine was not something to get excited about. Early taverns and hostelries offered travelers what grew grudging from the ground (beans, cabbage, onions, turnips, and potatoes), along with a bit of salt pork, perhaps a haunch of venison, or maybe, if the guests were particularly blessed, a freshly caught speckled trout. Food was food; you ate it because you were hungry, and that was that.

Courtesy of the Adirondack Museum

In the 1930s, roadside tourist stops like this one in Port Henry offered "regular meals" at all hours.

The arrival of railroad service to many North Country towns enlivened dining options considerably by bringing in fresh seafood, warm-weather fruits, and exotic vegetables. By the 1880s, as humble woodsmen's lodges gave way to grand hotels, there was an elite clientele to please. Menus evolved into elaborate affairs listing *quenelles*, *duxelles*, and *mirepois*, alongside the caviar, fresh figs, sweetbreads, and lobster.

The grand hotels and their elaborate style fell out of favor by the 1920s. Vacations became family car trips, and a new kind of restaurant specializing in unadorned, hearty, eat-and-run chow sprang up along the highways. Diners proliferated at the crossroads. Resorts with individual sleeping cabins and dining buildings where guests could gather for breakfast and supper became the standard for lodgings.

Today many towns still have a diner, where local news is discussed and the coffee's always hot. The original screen-door, roadside places are rarer: Tail O' the Pup, on Route 86 in Ray Brook, which hasn't changed much from when it began in 1946, and Burke-Towne, a breakfast-and-lunch place in Raquette Lake, come to mind as examples. (Listed under *Lodging*, Chapter 3, are those resorts which still offer meals to guests under full or modified American plans.)

In the 1990s the restaurant scene in the Adirondack Park underwent a revival. Competition created a number of four-star establishments that could hold their own anywhere in the country, with clusters of exceptional restaurants in Lake Placid and elsewhere. Nowadays, there's a surprising variety of eateries for what remains basically a rural area. Across the park there are old-timey ice cream parlors, a couple of barbecue joints, lots of decent family restaurants, plus many places with spotless linen tablecloths, fresh flowers, and color-coordinated candles on the tables, staffed by waiters and waitresses who can adroitly pronounce the names of foreign foods. A couple of options are literally moving experiences: the cruise-and-dine ship *William West Durant* (315-354-5532; Raquette Lake), which delivers an excellent lunch, dinner, and Sunday brunch from May through Columbus Day during its Raquette Lake excursions, and the *Norridgewock III* (315-376-6200), which features a 10-mile water-taxi ride into Beaver River, the most remote community in New York State, for meals at a rustic lodge.

In preparation for this chapter, the author and 10 other Adirondack residents took to the byways, looking for restaurants that operate with a clear sense of what they were trying to do and that demonstrate their purpose through good service, quality food, and fair prices. So, you'll find listed here some very cheap places as well as some fancy places, and all kinds of choices in between. We hope that the descriptions give you an impression of what to expect once you walk in the door of any given restaurant, or lead you to explore a new part of the region. Near the end of the chapter is a selection of informal places (taverns, diners, and similar joints) that are worth a quick stop.

The list that follows is long, but it's by no means exhaustive. The Lake George area alone has scores of restaurants, including nearly two dozen eateries that tout home-cooked Italian food. Thus, in these pages, if you're a veteran Adirondack eater, you may not find your favorite place. Maybe we didn't get a chance to eat there during the months this research was going on, or maybe we did try the place and felt that other places were more noteworthy.

We present here everything from neighborhood joints where five bucks gets you a satisfying bellyful, and the company's good to boot, to thoroughly elegant restaurants with well-deserved renown. Each restaurant is designated with a price code that summarizes the cost of one meal (appetizer, entrée, and dessert), but does not include wine, cocktails, sales tax, and tip. (Nouvelle cuisine — tiny portions marooned on enormous plates — never really got a foothold in the Adirondacks. If you're not prepared for a large serving, order an appetizer for your main course.)

The restaurants are grouped by region, starting with Lake George and the southeastern portion of the Adirondack Park. Within the regions you'll find the towns in alphabetical order, with restaurants described alphabetically under each town. At the end of the chapter, you'll find a sampling of bakeries, brewpubs, candy makers, delicatessens, farmstands, maple-syrup makers, and so on. You'll also find a short calendar of community suppers that offer great chow at low prices. All these places are listed in the index, too.

Dining Price Codes   Inexpensive: Up to $15
                         Moderate: $15–$20
                         Expensive: $20–$35
                         Very Expensive: Over $35

Credit Cards   AE: American Express
                         CB: Carte Blanche
                         D: Discover
                         DC: Diners Club
                         MC: MasterCard
                         V: Visa

Meals   B: Breakfast
                         L: Lunch
                         SB: Sunday Brunch
                         D: Dinner

ADIRONDACK RESTAURANTS

LAKE GEORGE AND SOUTHEASTERN ADIRONDACKS

Bolton Landing

HOUSE OF SCOTTS
7034 Lakeshore Dr.
518-644-9955.
Open: Daily mid-May–Oct.
Serving: L, D.
Price: Moderate to
   Expensive.
Cuisine: American.
Credit Cards: AE, DC, MC,
   V.
Reservations: Yes.
Handicap Access: Yes.

A huge wraparound porch offering tables set with floral linens and fresh flowers provides the best setting for a meal at this good family-run restaurant; the dark-paneled dining room seems a bit gloomy. The menu is extensive and imaginative, with coquille of sea scallops provençal on fettuccine a best bet for an appetizer or even a light entrée. House of Scotts is one of the few places in the Adirondacks that you can get an authentic Caesar or Greek salad prepared at your table.

There's an extensive wine list with reasonably priced choices from California, Washington State, France, and Australia. Entrée options range from abundant cioppino served over angel-hair pasta to tournedos topped with crabmeat and béarnaise sauce to ginger-glazed boneless roast duckling. Simpler dishes like poached salmon, grilled filet mignon, and broiled sea scallops are also available. Desserts — rich, gooey, dense with chocolate and plopped with real whipped cream — are right out of the Precholesterol Epoch.

At Pumpernickel's, an enormous cuckoo clock hangs above the fireplace.

Nancie Battaglia

PUMPERNICKEL'S
518-644-2106.
Lake Shore Dr.
Closed: Mar.; Mon.–Weds.
   in winter
Serving: L, D summer; D
   winter.
Cuisine: German.
Price: Moderate.
Credit Cards: AE, MC, V.
Reservations: Yes.
Handicap Access: Yes.

It's almost too bad that Pumpernickel's boasts America's largest cuckoo clock, an eleven-foot tall timepiece that hung for many years in Times Square. It makes the place appear like a German theme park, and it might distract you from the food, which is very special indeed.

German cooking has a bad reputation — heavy, greasy, inert. But in the capable hands of chef Hans Winter, the wursts and the schnitzels and virtually everything on Pumpernickel's menu tastes vivid, intense, almost light. Don't miss the potato pancakes with applesauce; they're deftly fried, a crisp treat. Dinner comes with hearty soup and a decent salad bar as well as plenty of side dishes, plus a fresh loaf of pumpernickel on every table.

It's a great place to take children, of course. And it's a great place to come *without* children, because families with kids have been neatly corralled into a loft where they can watch the cuckoo clock without bothering other diners. The service is swift and pleasant. And it's the only place in the southern Adirondacks with a wide selection of the finest German beers on draft.

**SAGAMORE DINING
   ROOM**
518-644-9400.
At the Sagamore Hotel,
   Sagamore Rd.
Serving: B, D.
Cuisine: New American.
Price: Expensive.
Credit Cards: All major.
Reservations: Suggested.
Handicap Access: Yes.

In the great pantheon of restaurants at the posh Sagamore Resort, the Sagamore Dining Room sits a notch or two below the pricey, jackets-only Trillium and the Club Grill, at the Sagamore golf course. A cozy, romantic getaway the cavernous hall is not, but try a window table with a glittering view of Lake George and make the mood your own. The wait staff is informed and gracious, the wine steward makes your every choice sound inspired, and the decor is all cool tones of sage, celadon, and pale rose — a merciful change after the down-home look of so many Adirondack inns.

All of which would be beside the point if the food itself didn't live up to the promise of its cost. Happily, it does. While you *can* order just an entrée at $20 or for the same price enjoy free run of the appetizer-and-salad buffet, we recommend going for broke and for the entrée-buffet combination, which at $32 for four or five courses is a steal. Somehow the good chefs at the Sagamore have mastered the impossible: how to keep a long-lived buffet selection looking good and tasting better. Appetizers include smoked-chicken-and-five-cheese quesadillas, seared corn-and-wild-rice cakes, an orzo salad with new-cut dill, a Southwestern vegetable soup, and a vaguely Asian-herbed beef-and-cellophane-noodle salad.

And that's just for starters. Now comes the main event: your choice of pan-seared, morel-sauced salmon with saffron couscous, or a thick barbecued veal chop with plum puree, or grilled Cornish game hen gussied up with sprigs of thyme and fat, ripe raspberries. The only trouble after all this gourmandizing is finding room for dessert.

Incidentally, a 17-percent service charge is automatically added to every bill, along with the 7-percent state service tax.

Chestertown

Sharon and Greg Taylor in the dining room of their Friends Lake Inn.

Nancie Battaglia

FRIENDS LAKE INN
518-494-4751.
Friends Lake Rd.
Open: Year-round.
Serving: B, L (winter only), D.
Cuisine: Contemporary American.

This rambling, handsomely restored inn began serving the public before the Civil War, when it was built as a boardinghouse for tannery workers, and became a local hot spot during Prohibition. Friends Lake Inn today is a rewarding destination for a romantic weekend getaway or a fine meal.

Price: Expensive.
Credit Cards: AE, DC, MC, V.
Reservations: Recommended.
Handicap Access: Yes.

The wine list is longer than the local phone book, and there's a fabulous selection of American craft and imported beers. If the choices have you confused, innkeepers Sharon and Greg Taylor sponsor occasional beer- and wine-tasting events that pair imaginative cuisine with interesting beverages.

For appetizers try straw-and-hay pasta or sautéed shrimp in hazelnut butter; salmon strudel is heavenly as an entrée. Desserts are all made on the premises and match the seasons admirably, from fresh fruit tarts in summer to grand chocolate concoctions for the holidays.

MAIN STREET ICE CREAM PARLOR
518-494-7940.
Main St.
Open: Daily.
Serving: L, D.
Cuisine: Deli, ice cream parlor.
Price: Inexpensive.
Handicap Access: Yes.

Antiques, advertising art, old photographs, farm implements, and the telephone switchboard that once served all of the southern Adirondacks fill the walls charmingly here, and the food's fun, too. Sandwiches, soups, and chili are excellent; go for the thick, complicated sandwiches layered on rye and stuffed with bacon, tomatoes, Russian dressing, cheese, and meat. The ice cream concoctions are definitely worth saving room for, whether it's a sundae topped with local maple syrup or a coffee or chocolate malted made with lots of real malt powder.

O.P. FREDERICK'S
518-494-4141.
Junction Rtes. 8 & 9, at Loon Lake.
Closed: Mon., Apr.
Serving: L, D summer; D only winter.
Cuisine: American.
Price: Moderate.
Credit Cards: MC, V.
Reservations: No.
Handicap Access: No.

A few years back, O.P. Frederick's closed for a thorough renovation; if you stopped there in the old days and found it a boring establishment where everything tasted of microwaves, you might want to give it another try.

The food is uneven — the fish in particular tends to be dry — but this place's failings now stem from too much ambition, not too little. Some of the food is truly delicious: a crab-cake-with-shrimp-sauce appetizer, for instance. Desserts are uniformly good, especially the apple crisp. Along with a short, standard wine list, O.P. Frederick's offers a nice assortment of microbrewed beers, something that's becoming more common in the Adirondacks, especially with the local popularity of F.X. Matt's crisp Saranac Pale Ale.

For evenings when a dinner at the nearby Friends Lake Inn seems like a little too much bother and a little too much money, this is a low-key substitute. The help and many of the customers are local, and especially on weekends, O.P. Frederick's is a humming, happy place.

**RENE'S MOUNTAIN
VIEW HOUSE**
518-494-2904.
White Schoolhouse Rd., 1
mi. E. of Rte. 8.
Open: Year-round.
Serving: D.
Cuisine: Swiss, Continental.
Price: Expensive.
Credit Cards: AE, DC, MC,
V.
Reservations: Recom-
mended.
Handicap Access: Yes.

Swiss-born chef Rene Plattner and his wife, Barbara, came to Chestertown in the 1980s to revitalize an old inn and have run the Mountain View
House since 1989. Their attention to detail is evi-
dent everywhere in the restaurant, from the vintage china with its leaping-deer motif (made in the
1930s for a another resort in town), to the tangy
vinaigrette on the house salad, to the plump spaetzel beneath several of the meat entrées, to an
award-winning creation called Chocolate Trilogy, a
zillion-calorie affair that proceeds from a dense,
rich torte to a heavenly mousse.

The Swiss potato soup alone is worth the drive.
Other signature dishes include lobster ravioli in
basil cream sauce, and a civet of venison, featuring farm-raised venison with
onions, white grapes, and croutons. Fresh fish is well prepared in simple
sauces that allow the fish's true flavor to shine. Think ahead when ordering so
you'll be sure to have room for dessert. Even the ice cream is made in Rene
and Barbara's kitchen, and you can get it in a cookie basket festooned with
fresh berries.

Hadley

**SARATOGA ROSE INN
AND RESTAURANT**
518-696-2861,
1-800-942-5025.
Closed: Mon.–Weds. fall &
spring; open daily in
summer.
Serving: L, D.
Cuisine: Italian, Continental.
Price: Moderate to Expen-
sive.
Credit Cards: D, MC, V.
Reservations: Recom-
mended.
Handicap Access: Ramp in
rear.

High above town like a great pink wedding
cake is this lovingly restored Victorian inn.
Owners Nancy and Anthony Merlino have pulled
out all the stops in their effort to invoke the high-
living yet homey Gilded Age, with chandeliers,
mock-faded wallpaper, hardwood floors, and marble hearths. Dining rooms occupy what used to be
the parlor, library, and living room of the old mansion, and the picture lacks only a player piano in
the corner cranking out a ghostly tune.

Semi-formal Italian and European cuisine perhaps best describes Tony Merlino's ambitious
efforts in the kitchen. His selection of classic continental fare — richly sauced, comfortably seasoned,
and often generously stuffed — includes shrimp
scampi, veal marsala, ravioli, tortelloni, rolled sole, pork tenderloin, salmon,
and duckling in orange sauce. Small but tasty salads come with the meal, and
desserts range from homemade rice pudding to old-time ice cream parfait.

If all this serious eating makes a full bottle of wine too much to manage, the
restaurant offers a welcome array of wines by the glass. Also, check local
papers for off-season promotions, like half-price entrées.

Lake George

THE BARNSIDER
518-668-5268.
Rte. 9.
Closed: Columbus
  Day–May 1.
Serving: L, D.
Cuisine: American,
  barbecue.
Price: Inexpensive to
  Moderate.
Credit Cards: All major.
Handicap Access: Yes.

The Adirondack Park is not what anyone would call ribs country, but as folks keep on discovering the family-run Barnsider, this could change. Owner-chef Ed Pagnotta's rack of pork "Q" is as flat-out scrumptious as it gets, real ribs nirvana. Pagnotta's parents ran a produce market and deli on this roadside spot, so he comes by his food savvy naturally. The method, says the chef, is called "Memphis style," and involves "a process using dry rub which kind of marinates the ribs, then I throw 'em in a water smoker, and use hickory and oak for wood, which filters up through the oven and heats up the water, which I think keeps a moister flavor."

The only trouble with the Barnsider is the on-site competition. Generous halves of barbecue chicken are every bit as tender and savory with smoke as the ribs, and now there's smoked baked beans and brisket, too. What's an omnivore to do? Our suggestion: get the chicken 'n' ribs combo. It comes with good corn on the cob and onion rings as stiff and round as hula hoops.

The Barnsider also offers build-your-own burgers, grilled swordfish, a children's menu, and beer in mock fruit jars that go neatly with the country-and-western decor. Prompt, cheerful service and outdoor decks make a summer dinner at this congenial spot a real Adirondack find.

EAST COVE
518-668-5265.
Rte. 9L & Beach Rd.
Open: Daily May–Oct.;
  Weds.–Sat. Nov.–Apr.
Serving: D, SB.
Cuisine: American,
  seafood.
Price: Moderate to
  Expensive.
Credit Cards: AE, DC, MC,
  V.
Handicap Access: Ramp in
  rear.

Just a city block or so from Lake George's Million Dollar Beach, but psychologically miles away from the t-shirts and souvenir jive of Canada St., is this cozy, overgrown log cabin decked out with ship's-wheel chandeliers, old hand-colored engravings, and flags. East Cove is a spot that locals cherish, and they come early — the place opens for dinner at 5pm — to unwind after a long day.

The moment you sit down, your server arrives with a bowl of tasty homemade cole slaw, some carrot and celery sticks, and a basket of rolls. There's a good selection of American wines available by the glass; you might want to sample some as you decide what to order from the extensive menu, which includes usually half a dozen specials. Shrimp scampi is what regulars rave about. The generous entrée of jumbo crustaceans is perfectly cooked and finished off with a velvety garlic-and-cream sauce. Occasionally sautéed soft-shell crab is offered, and it, too, comes with a rich garlicky sauce.

Meat eaters can choose from herb-crusted rack of lamb finished with

Madeira demi-glace (also a large portion), pork tenderloin, veal with artichokes and mushrooms, and big steaks. Chicken comes Santa Fe style, with sun-dried tomatoes, broccoli, and feta cheese, or à la Louise, with tarragon-cream sauce. Salads are forgettable iceberg lettuce and a cherry tomato or two, but desserts are delicious, over-the-top creations like raspberry rumble (raspberry-laced cheesecake with Oreo-cookie crust) and cappuccino silk pie.

RIDGE TERRACE
518-656-9274.
Rte. 9l.
Open: May–Oct.
Serving: D.
Cuisine: American.
Price: Moderate to
    Expensive.
Credit Cards: MC, V.
Handicap Access: Yes.

Chef Raymond Rios and his wife, Norma, have a winning place here on the east side of Lake George. A big rustic chalet set among tall evergreens, Ridge Terrace is quiet and comfortable, with a very extensive menu.

Folks come from as far away as Vermont for the succulent olive-oil-braised veal chop and seafood au gratin; an appetizer-size portion of the latter makes a lovely light meal. Among the more intriguing main courses are planked salmon served on wilted greens, real chateaubriand with duchess potatoes piped around the platter, and chicken wrapped in spinach and phyllo with a cognac cream sauce. If you're traveling with children, this is a good choice; while the atmosphere is mellow, kids are made welcome, and there's a menu just for them.

TAMARACK INN
518-668-5400.
440 Canada St.
Open: Daily.
Serving: B, L, D.
Cuisine: Regional
    American.
Price: Moderate.
Credit Cards: AE, DC, MC,
    V.
Reservations: Recom-
    mended in summer.
Handicap Access: Yes.

The Tamarack Inn is on the northern end of Lake George's main drag — the Adirondack end. And the mood and decor reflect the location: the handsome cabinlike building is chock-a-block with Adirondack boats, trophy deer, stuffed mallards, and North Country prints. It prepares you for the drive north up into the mountains, or eases you back into the real world after a weekend at camp.

Like most Lake George restaurants, the Tamarack is usually crowded on summer nights, as vacationers sample the seafood dishes that make up much of the menu, or drink the daiquiris and other specialty drinks from the full-service bar. Among the entrées are low-cal specials for those worried about fitting into their bathing suits on nearby Million Dollar Beach. The breakfast menu focuses on flapjacks. Dinner includes country favorites like Yankee pot roast, twin beef filets, and grilled honey chicken breast.

"I can remember when we were building this place, back when I was a boy," says Peter Ferrone, who runs the Tamarack with his brother John. "We hauled the fieldstone up, we did it all." They built well — the Tamarack seems a solid place likely to remain for many seasons to come.

Lake Luzerne

**DEFINO'S HERITAGE
RESTAURANT**
518-696-3733.
Northwoods Rd., off
Rte. 9N.
Open: Mid-May–mid-Oct.;
Weds.–Sun.
Serving: D.
Cuisine: Italian.
Price: Moderate.
Credit Cards: MC, V.
Reservations: Suggested for
summer weekends.
Handicap Access: Yes.

Everything — from the creamy garlic salad dressing to the crusty, hot bread to carrot cake — is made from scratch in the kitchen here, and the ambiance at DeFino's is as warm and comfortable as the food. The place used to be a dude ranch in the thirties, but the overgrown log cabin is a welcoming restaurant under quiet pines today. Linguine with white clam sauce is a good pick, a huge serving with plenty of shellfish, and chicken cacciatore is authentic and hearty. For real home cooking, you can't go wrong with the baked chicken or stuffed cabbage. When you finally push your chair back from the table, you'll feel like you're one of the family — happily stuffed, but maybe you can find room for a smidgen of dessert.

PAPA'S
518-696-3667.
Main St.
Closed: Oct.–late May.
Serving: B, L (until 8pm; ice
cream until 10pm).
Cuisine: Ice cream parlor.
Price: Inexpensive.
Credit Cards: None.
Handicap Access: No.

Don't miss this landmark if you're anywhere in the vicinity. Papa's is the real thing — an ice cream parlor with roots stretching back to the thirties. The decor here proves it, with old postcards and photographs of the Hudson Valley mill towns and glass milk bottles from the dairies that once thrived in this valley. You can certainly order a wonderful breakfast or a great burger or a peanut-butter-and-bacon sandwich, but really, you're here for the ice cream concoctions: floats, malts, sundaes, splits, shakes, and cones. They're all served in the right kind of tulip glass or boat; even the cones come in little twisted-wire holders. You can dine in one of the little booths or take your treat out on the deck overlooking the river. On Thursday nights in the summer, barbershop singers serenade you.

THE WATERHOUSE
518-696-3115.
Rte. 9.
Closed: Mon. in winter.
Serving: L, D.
Cuisine: American.
Price: Moderate.
Credit Cards: MC, V.
Handicap Access: Yes.

After a day in the saddle at a dude ranch or a hot afternoon tubing on the Hudson River, try the Waterhouse as a reward for sampling the rigors of the southeastern Adirondacks. If you're weary and hungry enough to eat a cow, this is the place.

Locals know the score. Meat, *big* meat, is what to come here for, notwithstanding exotic teasers like Cajun shrimp and clams casino. Steaks, pork chops, lamb chops, prime rib, sirloin tip, or prime rib with lobster tail . . . go ahead, order up. There's nothing particularly cutting edge about the preparation, and who cares? Sometimes nothing else will do but a bowl of homemade cabbage soup, a whopping sirloin à la bordelaise (saucy, with lots of peppercorns), and a wedge of real pie to top it off.

Hosts Tom and Betty McCutcheon work hard to maintain a friendly atmosphere in the long-lived Waterhouse. Knotty-pine walls are festooned with American collectibles — spinning wheel, weathervane, mixing bowls, and the like. The mood is twinkly with the starry glow of tiny Christmas lights, and the prompt service is as direct and forthcoming as the chow.

Schroon Lake

CHESAPEAKE'S
518-532-7042.
Rte. 9.
Closed: Mar.
Serving: L, D, summer;
 D winter.
Cuisine: Continental.
Price: Expensive.
Credit Cards: AE, MC, V.
Reservations: Recommended for summer.
Handicap Access: Yes.

On a warm summer afternoon, you can dine on the spacious porch overlooking the Pharaoh Lake Wilderness Area, or on a chilly winter night, you can curl up on a sofa by the fire in the cozy barroom with a glass of excellent merlot. Chesapeake's manages to be elegant and comfortable at the same time.

Chef Gerard Moser's creations are delicious from start to finish. At lunch, try stuffed eggplant dressed with balsamic vinaigrette or grilled chicken and peanut salad. A few recommended dinner selections: pork Robert, with a whole-grain mustard white-wine sauce; chicken Rita, which is a chicken breast stuffed with artichokes, prosciutto, and Boursin cheese; and the mixed grill, which includes a sweet fillet of mahimahi along with a lamb chop and a pork tenderloin. If you're a prime rib lover, big slabs of juicy beef are a bargain on Mondays in July and August.

PITKIN'S
518-532-7918.
Main St.
Open: Year-round.
Serving: B, L, D.
Cuisine: American.
Price: Inexpensive.
Credit Cards: None.
Handicap Access: Street-
 level entry.

If only every town had a spot as good as Pitkin's — where the homemade soups are thick with real stuff (not cornstarch), pies are heavenly, service is brisk — why, we'd never leave. The cole slaw and potato salad are the best around, and then there's the barbecue. Sure, Pitkin's looks like your average North Country diner with giant lake trout and panoramic color photos on the walls, but there's authentic Texas-style barbecue, beef brisket, pork ribs, and chicken. On Thursday nights in the summer, the lines of ribs fans snake down Main Street, and the wait for a table can be long. Happily, the restaurant is open all year, and you can get barbecue at lunch. Even in mud season.

TERRIO'S CARRIAGE HOUSE

518-532-7700.
Rte. 9.
Closed: Mon.–Weds. in fall–winter.
Serving: D.
Cuisine: American.
Price: Moderate.
Credit Cards: AE, D, MC.
Reservations: Recommended for summer weekends.
Handicap Access: Dining room but not bar.

This place really *was* a carriage house, once part of a stately Schroon Lake manor, and it's decorated with antiques. Eclectic antiques: a suit of armor in one corner, a brace of brass fondue pots in another, a luge, license plates, baskets. The menu is a little the same way, covering the waterfront of American resort cuisine with no special Adirondack emphasis: Alaskan king crab, Long Island roast duckling, fried calamari, Cajun chicken.

The cooking is straightforward and solid, with an emphasis on calories. The house special is the Crabarooney, two small pieces of filet mignon topped with Alaskan crabmeat and béarnaise sauce. Everything comes with soup or salad, the baked potatoes are good, and if you remember to ask the waitress, they even have Saranac Pale Ale with which to wash it all down. Desserts are unmemorable, but novelty coffees are fun.

The main room and the porch with a wood stove are usually bustling, and kids are welcome. The children's menu is a junior version of the abundant adult fare. On Tuesdays, the restaurant offers a twin-lobster special, and on Thursdays they grill steaks in different ways and offer them at special prices. All in all, this is the place to eat if you've just emerged from a long backpack in the Pharaoh Lakes and want some serious food!

Stony Creek

STONY CREEK INN

518-696-2394.
Corner Branch Rd. & Hadley Rd.
Closed: Mon. & Tues. Dec.–Mar.
Serving: L on weekends, D.
Cuisine: American.
Price: Inexpensive to Moderate.
Credit Cards: No.
Reservations: Accepted, but not necessary.
Handicap Access: Yes, but not restrooms.
Special Features: Live music on Fri. & Sun.

The Inn is a southern Adirondack institution, one of the funkiest spots between Saratoga and Montreal. You can get a good solid dinner here during the week (the fish is especially good), but it's on Sunday night that the joint really jumps, when there's great Mexican food and local bands.

Long a mecca for square dancers, and known as the home stage for the regionally renowned Stony Creek Band, the Inn now presents everything from straight country to rhythm and blues, old-time fiddle to salsa. All this music — a rarity in the area — attracts crowds from far and wide; owner Dot Bartel says her mailing list of 600 names includes regulars from New Jersey and Vermont. Along with hot tunes, the Stony Creek Inn offers some unbeatable specials: steamed clams and roast beef for ten bucks on Wednesdays and two prime rib or two steak dinners for $20 on Fridays.

During summertime, there's acoustic music on Friday nights, and for those who indulge themselves a tad too enthusiastically at the long and well-stocked bar, the rooms upstairs are 15 bucks a night.

Warrensburg

BRUNETTO'S
518-623-1041.
Rte. 9, just south of Northway Exit 23.
Open: Tues.–Sun.
Serving: D.
Cuisine: Italian.
Price: Moderate to Expensive.
Credit Cards: MC, V.
Handicap Access: Yes.
Special Features: Bring your own wine or beer.

Granted, the setting isn't exactly inspiring: exterior repairs on this roadside restaurant and cabins never seem to be quite completed, but the full parking lot night after night is a sure tip-off. Brunetto's serves great food, and plenty of it.

As soon as you're seated, a waiter comes around with a corkscrew for the wine that you've remembered to bring and a thick slice of paté and crackers. The temptation is to fill up on the freebies, but show some restraint. Salads are served family-style with homemade dressings, another challenge to hold back for better things to come.

Seafood takes center stage here, in appetizers such as steamed mussels or clams casino (highly recommended), and lovely entrées like salmon in dill caper sauce or seared tuna loin. Brunetto's regulars, though, cheerfully put on their plastic bibs and plow through the awesome zuppa di mussels, which comes in a vast bowl containing about two pounds of pasta, five dozen mussels, and maybe a whole head of garlic. It's enough for a couple of meals.

If you're not in the mood for fish, the rack of lamb is very good, as are the chicken picatta and chicken marsala. If you're a devoted dessert eater, ask the wait staff for suggestions. In all our trips to this landmark, we've never even nibbled the sweets.

THE GRIST MILL
518-623-3949.
River Rd. (Rte. 418 just beyond the iron bridge).
Open: Weds.–Sun. year-round; daily Memorial Day–Labor Day.
Serving: D.
Cuisine: Contemporary American.
Price: Expensive.
Credit Cards: AE, DC, MC, V.
Reservations: Recommended.
Handicap Access: Yes.

This restaurant — which had a reputation for pretentious priciness in the past — has gotten markedly better. In fact, the Grist Mill comes as close to being a destination restaurant as any dining room in the southern Adirondacks.

Part of its appeal is assuredly the food. Meals begin with a generous green salad studded with artichoke hearts and a bread tray with slices from half a dozen different loaves from the ovens of Rock Hill, a superb bakery south of Glens Falls. There's usually at least one interesting appetizer on the seasonal menu, and the entrées show off chef Shane Newell's Culinary Institute of American training: salmon filet with a basil-pesto-and-molasses glaze, for instance, or thyme-roasted lamb with fresh-

Nancie Battaglia

The Grist Mill in Warrensburg was once a working mill on the Schroon River.

Special Features: Mill museum, screen porch overlooking the river.

mint-and-mustard-seed sauce. There's a solid wine list, but the real joy is the beer selection — not only some of America's best microbrews, but from time to time the restaurant's own wheat ale, crafted under contract at a nearby brewhouse.

The real star of the Grist Mill, though, is probably the mill itself. The 1824-vintage structure has been impeccably restored over the last few years, and soon a working waterwheel will spin next to the screened-in cocktail deck. The wide planks and wooden chutes, the old grindstones, even the charcoal-scrawled graffiti from a bygone era make this as much as museum as an eatery; tours can be arranged, in fact, if you call ahead. You should call ahead in any event, because the joy of eating here is greatly amplified if you reserve a table by the long window that overlooks the Schroon River.

MERRILL MAGEE HOUSE
518-623-2449.
2 Hudson St.
Closed: Mar.
Serving: L Tues.–Sat. May–Oct.; D daily.
Cuisine: Continental.
Price: Expensive.
Credit Cards: AE, DC, MC, V.
Handicap Access: Yes.

Behind a prim white picket fence and across the street from Warrensburg's pocket-size bandshell is the Merrill Magee House, a historic inn with charming dining rooms and a cozy wood-paneled pub. Meals begin with a basket of excellent homemade breads and proceed to good salads; entrées range from traditional rack of lamb to wiener schnitzel to Maryland crabcakes with basil tartar sauce, tournedos béarnaise, and fresh fish.

Authentic English ales and stouts are available in the pub, and the wine list is quite complete. Special dinner evenings are scheduled from time to time, with the annual nouvelle Beaujolais celebration a highlight of the fall. It features an array of unusual salads, tables laden with wild game appetizers and entrées, and a roomful of heavenly desserts.

CHAMPLAIN VALLEY

Crown Point

**FRENCHMAN'S
    RESTAURANT**
518-597-3545.
Main St.
Open: Year-round.
Serving: B, L, D.
Cuisine: American.
Price: Inexpensive.
Credit Cards: MC, V.
Handicap Access: Yes.

Even if it weren't the only sit-down restaurant in town, the Frenchman's would be a good place to stop. The place is spotless, the service is quick, the portions are generous. Breakfast is busy here, since the place is a magnet for catching up on Champlain Valley chitchat.

The menu has a good selection of thick sandwiches, homemade soups, and salads, and daily specials are often successful attempts at ethnic cuisines, like Cajun-spiced grilled chicken on a hard roll. Save room for dessert, especially homemade fruit pie or chocolate cake.

Elizabethtown

DEER'S HEAD INN
518-873-9903.
Court St.
Open: Year-round.
Serving: L, D.
Cuisine: American,
    Continental.
Price: Inexpensive to
    Moderate.
Credit Cards: AE, MC, V.
Handicap Access: Yes.

This rambling inn, built in 1808, has been recently repaired and repainted outside. Inside, the low-key owners, Mark Ormiston and John De La Rue, have created a pleasant ambiance in the inn's three adjoining dining rooms. The two front rooms — one outfitted with a stone fireplace — are decorated in blue and white, and the walls are hung with landscapes by a well-known Adirondack artist, Ruth Rumney. The cozy dining room in the back is wood-paneled and lined with shelves of old books.

Dinners at the Deer's Head include porterhouse and sirloin steak; chicken provençal; pork tenderloin prepared with apricots, currants and pine nuts; and seafood dishes including scampi and broiled trout. There are always evening specials and you can count on prime rib on Saturdays. The dinner menu also offers simpler dishes like steak sandwiches, pasta with marinara sauce, and burgers. Lunches include cold and grilled sandwiches, soups and salads, all reasonably priced.

The service is friendly and efficient, the chef's creations are satisfying, and the surroundings are peaceful.

Essex

THE ESSEX INN
518-963-8821.
16 Main St.
Open: Year-round.
Serving: B, L, D, SB.
Cuisine: American.

The owners of this landmark establishment, Trish and John Walker, have created bright, welcoming surroundings in the 1810 inn in the center of the small, historic village of Essex. Tables are placed by the windows in the two front dining

Price: Moderate to Expensive.
Credit Cards: AE, MC, V.
Handicap Access: Through the rear courtyard.

rooms, and meals are also served on the columned veranda, a great place to sip a glass of wine and watch the summer people amble by.

On a recent June evening, the soup was a flavorful, velvety cheddar cheese, and the house salad was an outstanding combination of assorted greens, tomatoes, and cucumbers. An entrée special was succulent boneless pork chops stuffed with Brie and scallions, served with mashed potatoes and green beans; a strip steak was accompanied by a crisp potato cake. The menu also includes pan-roasted chicken, poached salmon with dill sauce, and pasta, although the pasta wasn't quite up to the standards set by the preliminaries. The most memorable dessert was a juicy, delicious apple crisp topped with whipped cream, served in a fat brown crock.

Lunches are simpler, but quite good: turkey club sandwich, Reuben, grilled cheese, burger. On Sundays, the champagne brunch offers hearty selections such as lasagna, baked ziti, and chicken, along with the usual eggs and pancakes.

JAMES FOX'S SHIPYARD RESTAURANT
518-963-4200.
Rte. 22 at Essex Shipyard.
Closed: Mid-Oct.–Memorial Day weekend.
Serving: L, D daily.
Cuisine: American, Continental.
Price: Moderate–Expensive.
Credit Cards: MC, V.
Reservations: Recommended in July & Aug., especially for lake-view tables.
Handicap Access: Yes.

A white clapboard house with a porch and intimate dining rooms overlooking Lake Champlain, this new restaurant is an appealing addition to the Essex dining scene. Chef-owner James Fox, who moved to town from Connecticut, has devised a selection of mostly chicken and seafood dishes with light, delectable sauces. The lunch menu offers grilled chicken and Greek salads, plus sandwiches, pasta, and a daily soup, along with good New England clam chowder.

Dinner starts with appetizers like vegetable spring rolls, mussels in Pernod and saffron broth, and Cajun shrimp. The impeccable house salad is tossed with a dill vinaigrette. Only two meat dishes are presented as entrées: strip steak and boneless loin pork chops with black onion gravy, braised red cabbage, and garlic mashed potatoes. Poached salmon is sublime, as are the golden brown crabcakes and curried chicken breast with chutney, coconut, and almonds. For dessert, try the lemon souffle, blueberry walnut crisp, or a silken dark chocolate eclair — all simply divine.

OLD DOCK RESTAURANT
518-963-4232.
Lake Shore Rd.
Open: Mid-May–Columbus Day.
Serving: L, D.

Relaxing in the sun at an outdoor table at the Old Dock, watching a loon ride the rippling waves of Lake Champlain, can be a sublime experience. If only the food were as heavenly. The Old Dock's menu (seafood chowder, coconut shrimp, jerk chicken, to name a few choices) certainly looks

Cuisine: American.
Price: Moderate to
  Expensive.
Credit Cards: AE, D, MC,
  V.
Handicap Access: Inside
  dining room only.

tempting, but the execution is often disappointing. Along with the chef, the servers, too, need a little more direction from the restaurant's owners — like being advised not to present a large glass of a weak warm liquid in lieu of iced coffee.

Back to the ambiance. Three stone steps at the side of the historic red-painted building lead down to a wooden deck surrounded by lawn, trees, and a little garden. Gulls wheel in the blue sky, sailboats drift past, and the Essex ferry heads majestically toward the adjacent landing on its way from Charlotte, Vermont. So sip your glass of fruity merlot or chilled chardonnay and soak up the atmosphere.

At the Sunburst Tea Garden, you can savor scones with real clotted cream.

Nancie Battaglia

**SUNBURST TEA
  GARDEN**
618-963-7482.
Main St.
Open: Mid-June–mid-Sept.
Serving: Weds.–Sun.
  2–5pm.
Cuisine: English cream
  teas.
Price: Inexpensive.
Credit Cards: No.
Handicap Access: Yes; park
  in adjacent lot.

True bliss on a summer afternoon is sitting at a shady table set on the rolling green lawn at the Sunburst Tea Garden, nibbling on a cucumber sandwich, and gazing at Lake Champlain and the Green Mountains beyond. You enter this bit of heaven through a flower-covered trellis next to a white-painted cottage. The grass is dotted with tables and chairs, some with umbrellas and some set under a broad maple tree. A small fountain burbles pleasantly and fat robins splash in a nearby birdbath. Elsa Sorley, the charming woman who runs this lovely place, hands you a small menu that, along with the offerings, contains a quote from Henry James: "There are few hours in life more agreeable than the hour dedicated to the ceremony known as afternoon tea." A visit to Sunburst proves this sentiment.

For tea, you can order scones with clotted cream and jam, cucumber sandwiches, a plate of assorted tea sandwiches and cookies, or a slice of sponge cake with strawberries or chocolate mud pie. Hot teas include orange pekoe, Darjeeling, Earl Grey, or caffeine-free herb tea. Lemonade and iced tea are available, too.

If you truly love it here, you can spend the night. Sunburst is also a bed and breakfast with a couple of sweet little rooms.

Mineville

GLORIA'S COUNTRY INN
518-942-3065.
50 Fisher Hill Rd.Open:
 Weds.–Sun.
Serving: D.
Cuisine: American.
Price: Inexpensive to
 Moderate.
Credit Cards: MC, V.
Handicap Access: Yes.

Mineville used to be a rugged, bustling iron-mining town, but by the 1960s, Republic Steel had deserted its operations. A bright spot in this now-quiet community is Gloria's, where the food is the epitome of country fare. Everything — except the booze in the bar — is homemade.

Friday buffets are outstanding, with roast turkey (go ahead, ask for a drumstick), roast beef, meatballs, and seafood, plus all kinds of salads and sides. The dessert array contains dozens of pies and cakes; it's impossible to choose just one, so try two. On other nights, the food is just as tasty, but you have to make your selection off the menu.

Port Henry

The wheels still spin at the Miss Port Henry, a carefully restored diner that's open all day, every day.

Lohr McKinstry

MISS PORT HENRY DINER
518-546-3663.
3 Church St.

At any hour, day or night, the liveliest scene in this settlement is undoubtedly the Miss Port Henry, which began its working life as a horse-

Open: 24 hours, year-round.
Serving: B, L, D.
Cuisine: American.
Price: Inexpensive.
Credit Cards: No.
Handicap Access: Yes.

drawn lunch wagon. The diner has been a permanent fixture in downtown Port Henry since the Depression. For many years, though, it lingered doomed and decrepit, but energetic new owners brought the eatery back to life in 1996. Today, decked out in shades of green and cream, it's nostalgic but not gimmicky, and the chow is dandy.

Chicken and biscuits are a hit, as is meatloaf and gravy. Italian night, with lasagna, spaghetti, manicotti, and more, is every Wednesday. Be sure to save room for pie — or have it for breakfast.

Ticonderoga

THE CARILLON
518-585-7657.
61 Hague Rd.
Closed: Weds.
Serving: L, D.
Cuisine: Seafood.
Price: Expensive.
Credit Cards: AE, MC, V.
Handicap Access: No.

Carillon is the original French name of Fort Ticonderoga, the historic site three miles from this restaurant, which is a modest red-painted wooden building close by Rte. 9, on a hill.

Seafood is always very fresh, and the catch of the day lives up to its name. Soups, especially the creamy seafood bisque, are excellent. Lean fish fillets, shrimp, and bay scallops are competently prepared without fuss and their succulent flavor shines through; the seafood potpie is delicious. Homemade desserts are a cut above the usual.

EDDIE'S RESTAURANT
518-585-7030.
Rte. 9N, 5 mi. S. of Ticonderoga village.
Open: Year-round.
Serving: L, D.
Cuisine: American, Italian.
Price: Moderate.
Credit Cards: AE, MC, V.
Handicap Access: Yes.

New at Eddie's are an outside deck overlooking the lake and all-you-can-eat Italian nights, but this handsome, friendly little place already had plenty going for it. Stuffed shells, homemade spaghetti, and linguine are all quite fine, plus there's a full salad bar and good desserts like peach cobbler. If you're not in the mood for pasta, there's standard American fare like steaks and prime rib — which is the special on Saturday nights and comes with any of the pastas on the menu.

The restaurant is halfway between Ticonderoga and Hague, only a mile from Rogers Rock State Campground. The dramatic cliff high above the lake is where Major Robert Rogers — without his fabled Rangers — escaped the French and Indians in 1758 by making them think he'd jumped to the frozen lake from a great height. By sliding down the mountain he survived and went on to lead his crack troops on successful raids.

HOT BISCUIT DINER
518-585-3483.
Wicker St.
Open: Year-round.
Serving: B, L, D.
Cuisine: American.
Price: Inexpensive.
Credit Cards: None.
Handicap Access: Yes.

A few years back, a fire nearly destroyed this cheery, checked-tablecloth place, but thank heavens the owners decided to build up from the ashes. The Hot Biscuit's worth a stop for any meal or if you've got a sudden hankering for hot made-from-scratch gingerbread dolloped with whipped cream or genuine slow-cooked tapioca pudding. Everything's homemade, from blueberry muffins to the trademark biscuits; chili and soup are tasty and a real bargain.

The country dinner plates — less than five bucks and one special per day — feature stuffed peppers, knockwurst and kraut, pot roast, meatloaf, or chicken and biscuits, and come with real cornbread, vegetables, and potatoes. It's true comfort food at a reasonable price. Besides the chow, the place is a mini-museum, decorated with old photos, sheet music, tools, advertising art, and local mementos.

SCHOOLHOUSE RESTAURANT
518-585-4044.
Rte. 9N, Streetroad, 3 mi.
N. of Ticonderoga.
Open: Year-round.
Serving: D.
Cuisine: American.
Price: Moderate.
Credit Cards: AE, MC, V.
Handicap Access: No.

The Schoolhouse — not surprisingly — used to be a grade school, and it's just across the road from the cemetery in which Guy Baldwin, the inventor of the lead pencil, is buried.

The restaurant is downstairs in this restored building, with a dining room on one side and a pub on the other. Daily specials are written on the old chalkboards, and pull-down maps showing countries that no longer exist complete the scholastic motif. Dinners are moderately priced. Try steak or seafood, with scallops and juicy prime rib worthy choices. Pizza is also available.

WAGON WHEEL RESTAURANT
518-585-7755.
Wicker St. at Old Chilson Rd.
Open: Year-round.
Serving: B, L, D.
Cuisine: American.
Price: Inexpensive.
Credit Cards: MC, V.
Handicap Access: Yes.

A wooden wagon wheel in the parking lot creates the atmosphere for this rustic restaurant. The specialty here is breakfast, a never-heard-of-cholesterol kind of morning meal, with eggs, sausage, toast, pancakes, and home fries dished up in awesome portions. Club sandwiches and burgers are the lunch fare here, and dinner ranges from pasta to steaks.

The Wagon Wheel has very good service, with a pleasant staff; eat here more than once and they'll start calling you by name. Think of Ti restaurants in this way: Benedict Arnold and his officers would have eaten at the Carillon, decked out in full regalia; Ethan Allen and the Green Mountain Boys would be stoking their engines at the Wagon Wheel.

Westport

*Le Bistro at the Yacht Club
serves lovely meals indoors
and out.*

Nancie Battaglia

**LE BISTRO AT THE
  YACHT CLUB**
518-962-8777.
On Lake Champlain, off
  Rte. 22.
Open: Mid-June–mid-Sept.
Serving: L, D.
Cuisine: French.
Price: Expensive.
Credit Cards: AE, MC, V.
Handicap Access: Yes.

Bernard Perillat, former chef-owner of Le Bistro in Essex, has moved his signature French flair to one of the finest waterfront settings on either side of Lake Champlain. Guests arrive by car or they sail right up to the concrete dock that forms the front of the outdoor dining area.

Lunch offers an excellent way to sample the menu and enjoy an alfresco meal in the sun. (The restaurant faces east, so you won't see the sunset in the evening.) Choices include half a lobster with tarragon mayonnaise, sea bass with capers and white wine, or a subtle fish soup.

At dinner, start with garlicky escargot with mushrooms, and proceed to veal with shiitake cream sauce or an aged filet of beef. Fish entrées are always fresh, always nicely seasoned; chicken is prepared in a different way each day. The wine list is excellent, and Continental desserts feature seasonal fruits and top-quality chocolate.

**WESTPORT COUNTRY
  CLUB**
518-962-8283.
Liberty St.
Open: Mar.–Dec.
Serving: B Weds.–Sun.; L,
  D, SB.
Cuisine: American.
Price: Moderate to
  Expensive.

The owner of this beautifully situated country club is Arthur Pepin, and he calls his excellent restaurant "Peppy's on the Green." The windows in the wood-paneled dining room and the terrace overlook the lush, rolling 18-hole golf course, which is dotted with towering pine trees.

After taking your orders, the capable servers deliver a basket of homemade muffins to your table followed by the crisp house salad. Appetizer choices

Credit Cards: D, MC, V.
Handicap Access: Yes.

include wild-mushroom-and-goat-cheese strudel and scallops with beet vinaigrette. Among the tempting array of entrées are quail wrapped in prosciutto, pork loin Tuscany — prepared with caramelized garlic, sautéed mushrooms, roasted peppers, honey, and demi-glace — and tenderloin of beef with a blue-cheese-and-herb crust. Fish dishes such as baked swordfish and haddock were less elaborate and more successful. Note that the early dinner specials, offered from 5 to 6:30, are good values.

The lunch menu offers various salads, interesting cold and grilled sandwiches, and light entrées. Every Sunday there's an extravagant brunch, the perfect end to playing a round on the course.

WESTPORT HOTEL
518-962-4501.
Rte. 9N.
Open: Year-round.
Serving: B, L, D.
Cuisine: American.
Price: Moderate to
  Expensive.
Reservations: Yes.
Handicap Access: Yes.

The Westport Hotel has been in business since the first trains rolled into the station next door more than a century ago. Rather than linger as a relic of bygone days, though, this inn keeps up with the times in a carefully maintained set of cozy dining rooms and a menu that includes interesting contemporary touches as well as the tried and true.

Appetizers include seafood crêpes with garlic butter, clams casino, and shrimp served with chips and fresh salsa. Entrées range from vegetarian dishes to ginger-peanut chicken (recommended), seafood au gratin, pork loin, and grilled steaks. Desserts are homemade, and the wine list contains a useful selection of domestic and imported wines. On a warm night, try to dine on the porch; breezy and protected from the road, it's a pleasant place to recount the activities of the day and savor a well-made meal.

WESTPORT PIZZA
  AND PASTA
518-962-4878.
Pleasant St., at the intersection of Rtes. 9N/22.
Open: Year-round.
Serving: B, L, D in summer;
  D in winter.
Cuisine: Italian.
Price: Inexpensive to
  Moderate.
Credit Cards: None.
Handicap Access: Yes.

Pizza without peer is the prime pick at this old firehouse; it's made with an excellent sourdough crust and topped with everything from sausage and cheese to artichoke hearts and eggplant. Calzone, available with any or all of the toppings liberally stuffed inside, is also delicious.

The pasta is fine, too, such as linguine with clam sauce, or you can order excellent eggplant parmigiana. In the summer, eat at a table in the brick courtyard, leisurely sip a cold beer, then stroll down to the waterfront.

Willsboro

UPPER DECK AT WILLS-
  BORO BAY MARINA

The Upper Deck's two airy dining rooms — with walls of windows that are kept open in

518-963-8271.
Klein Dr., on Lake Champlain, off Point Rd.
Open: Mid-June–Labor Day.
Serving: L, D.
Cuisine: American, Continental.
Price: Moderate to Expensive.
Credit Cards: MC, V.
Handicap Access: Yes.

warm weather — overlook Willsboro Bay and the wooded cliffs beyond. To complement the ambiance, chef Darlene Robare has created menus that meld American dishes with world flavors. For example, enticing lunch selections include sun-dried-tomato tortillas rolled around grilled onion, zucchini, and shrimp or a grilled ham, cheese, and artichoke sandwich on a crusty roll. Soups are very good, especially the gazpacho.

For dinner, appetizers range from Caribbean chicken kabobs to shrimp rémoulade, which make nice transitions to robust cioppino, spicy tandoori salmon, or herb-crusted pork tenderloin served with plum chutney and butternut squash ravioli. There's a scaled-down menu for children, and if you'd prefer something not so fancy, reasonably priced burgers and flatbread pizza are available at lunch and dinner.

HIGH PEAKS AND NORTHERN ADIRONDACKS

A chain-saw-carved bear greets diners at the Elm Tree Inn.

Nancie Battaglia

Keene

ELM TREE INN
518-576-9769.
Rtes. 9N & 73.
Closed: Tues.
Serving: L, D.
Cuisine: American.
Price: Inexpensive to Moderate.

In 1995 renovations on this 19th-century landmark tavern were completed, and Purdy's — as it's locally known — looks terrific. There are now tables on the spacious porch (although this intersection is noisy during the summer months), and the two indoor dining rooms are nicely finished off with gleaming wainscoting.

Credit Cards: None.
Handicap Access: Yes.

The food is absolutely no-nonsense, reasonably priced, and delivered to your table with cheerful efficiency. Soups, like cream of mushroom or cream of spinach, are delicious; the cole slaw is probably the best in Essex County. Sandwiches and hand-patted hamburgers are huge, juicy, and worth, say, a half-hour drive. Dinners are fairly simple, like steak sandwiches or pork chops, and you can always fall back on the classic Purdy burger, topped with a thick slice of Bermuda onion and melted cheese. There's a full bar and a small selection of American wines.

Keene Valley

AUSABLE INN
518-576-9986.
Rte. 73/Main St.
Closed: Mon.
Serving: D.
Cuisine: American.
Price: Moderate.
Credit Cards: MC, V.
Handicap Access: Yes.

With its big stone fireplace and pine-paneled walls, the dining room at the Ausable Inn is as cozy as an Adirondack camp. The menu offers burgers, chicken in a basket, and other vacation fare, plus pasta, steak, and chicken in home-cooked sauces. Recommended are the pasta Ausable — shrimp and scallops in marinara sauce over linguine, and hunter's chicken, which has a tomato-based sauce with tarragon, shallots, and mushrooms. On Wednesdays, not-too-flamboyant Mexican fare is featured, and occasionally, fresh whole lobster is available at a great price.

Enjoying a cone at the counter of the Noon Mark Diner.

Nancie Battaglia

NOON MARK DINER
518-576-4499.
Rte. 73/Main St.
Open: Year-round.
Serving: B, L, D.

Everybody from High Peaks backpackers to investment bankers to local kids on bikes converges at the Noon Mark at some point during a typical week, to stoke up on great homemade doughnuts, cinnamon buns, pies, muffins, bread, soups,

Cuisine: Diner.
Price: Inexpensive.
Credit Cards: None.
Handicap Access: Yes.

French fries, and whatever else is on the menu. You can order breakfast any time, if you're not up for excellent chili made with chunks of beef round, or the trail blazer, a steak sandwich with sautéed mushrooms, onions, and peppers on a hard roll.

Dinners lean toward frozen things popped into the deep fryer, like clams or shrimp, but soup, salad, potatoes or rice comes with any choice, and nothing on the menu is more than $8. After a long day in the outdoors, try turkey or lasagna, and then order some heavenly pie to have for breakfast the next day.

Lake Placid

ALPINE CELLAR
518-523-2180.
Rte. 86, at the Alpine Motor
  Inn.
Closed: Mon. in summer;
  Mon.–Weds. in winter.
Serving: D.
Cuisine: German.
Price: Moderate.
Credit Cards: AE, DC, MC,
  V.
Reservations: Recom-
  mended for weekends.
Handicap Access: No.

Wolfgang Brandenburg's Alpine Cellar is a jolly rathskeller indeed, with scores of northern European brews on hand and accordion music ringing from the rafters. The bar is a cozy cavern where you're likely to run into former Olympic skiers and other characters, and the dining room has a blazing fireplace at its center.

The menu has authentic schnitzels, wursts, goulash, venison, and smoked pork chops, all of which come with the house salad plate of marinated beans and cucumbers in sour cream, plus red cabbage, spaetzel or potato pancakes, and homemade bread. The food is great, the service is quick, and the atmosphere is *gemütlichkeit*, for sure. On winter Wednesday nights, you can get bratwurst, sauerkraut, mashed potatoes — all you can eat — for about four bucks. Such a deal!

ARTIST'S CAFÉ
518-523-9493.
1 Main St.
Open: Year-round.
Serving: B, L, D, SB.
Cuisine: American.
Price: Inexpensive to
  Moderate.
Credit Cards: All major.
Reservations: Recom-
  mended for large parties.
Handicap Access: No.

One of a handful of downtown eateries with a view of Mirror Lake, the Artist's Café has a gallery of tables that seem to be perched right over the water. It's a snug spot ideal for a leisurely breakfast — try the Café Waffle, a Belgian waffle topped with fresh strawberries and maple syrup. Or it's a good place to meet friends for a quiet lunch or fuss-free dinner.

The menu includes sesame grilled chicken, pasta, beef, and lots of shrimp combinations, with midweek bargain prices for platters of steamed shellfish and big, tender steaks. Salads are quite good, with excellent creamy dill or homemade bleucheese dressing; desserts — although not made on the premises — range from peanut-butter chocolate pie to a crunchy, creamy caramel apple granny.

Alfresco dining overlooking Mirror Lake at the Boathouse.

Nancie Battaglia

THE BOATHOUSE
518-523-4822.
Mirror Lake Dr.
Open: Memorial
    Day–Columbus Day.
Serving: L, D.
Cuisine: American.
Price: Moderate to Expen-
    sive.
Credit Cards: MC, V.
Handicap Access: Yes.

This handsome restaurant was taken over by new owners in 1997. Although the lakeside location can't be beat, the service could be more professional and the menu could stand some expansion. Offerings are limited: for dinner, there are five pasta dishes, grilled chicken, seafood kabobs, and salmon, plus nightly specials. Appetizers include fried calamari or artichoke dip with pita; salads include fresh mozzarella, Caesar, and a basic mixed green number. Good imported and California wines are available by the glass or carafe.

On a recent visit, sea scallops in red pepper pesto over capellini and chocolate walnut strudel were very good, but the rest of the meal was just so-so for the price. Our verdict: keep your fingers crossed for some inspiration in the kitchen. The setting deserves it.

LAKE PLACID LODGE
518-523-2700.
Whiteface Inn Rd.
Open: Daily.
Serving: B, L, D.
Cuisine: Continental.
Price: Expensive to Very
  Expensive.
Credit Cards: AE, DC, MC,
  V.
Reservations: Suggested.
Handicap Access: No.

Fabulously restored and reconfigured in summer 1994, the Lake Placid Lodge is a genuine destination resort. The building is a wonderful old Adirondack camp, with a sweet little bar decorated with deep green walls and yellow-birch-log trim, wraparound porches with sweeping lake views, and a sitting room with a huge cobblestone fireplace. The dining room deftly combines austere elegance with rustic twig-work, in dark walls and delicate peeled branches extending from the floor to the ceiling.

The dinner menu is fantastic, with a long list of appetizers that reflect what's in season, such as sautéed sweetbreads, homemade tortellini, lobster risotto, and terrine of smoked salmon. Green salads are very good, and can be ordered as an entrée in the summer. Main courses run from whole Dover sole to grilled tuna Basquaise to beef tenderloin, prepared with imaginative sauces and presented beautifully; each meat or fish is combined with its own trademark potato, rice, or grain pilaf, and vegetable. Desserts are all made on the premises; the outstanding Ménage à Trois is three different crème brûlées.

The wine list contains thoughtfully chosen domestic, French, and Australian wines. The service is consummately professional and well informed.

If you'd like to try the Lodge, but with a more modest budget, breakfast and lunch are wonderful, and there's a bistro menu (soups, salads, appetizers) available in the bar. Sunday brunch costs more than lunch but less than dinner; for the holidays, the prix fixe dinners are divine.

Le Bistro Laliberté offers great dining in the heart of downtown Lake Placid.

Nancie Battaglia

LE BISTRO LALIBERTÉ
518-523-3680.
51 Main St., underneath
  Eastern Mountain Sports.

Two lovely, small dining rooms in shades of almond, peach, and forest green offer an intimate atmosphere at this upscale bistro that opened

Open: Year-round.
Serving: D.
Cuisine: Contemporary American, Continental.
Price: Expensive to Very Expensive.
Credit Cards: MC, V.
Reservations: Recommended in summer.
Handicap Access: No.

in July 1995, but the best place to eat in summer or fall is on the deck overlooking Mirror Lake. From several tables, you get a clear view of Whiteface, and trees screen the setting beautifully from the adjacent park. On Wednesdays in the summer, you can listen to the Lake Placid Sinfonietta as you dine.

Chef Robert Borden learned about pastries during a stint at Le Cirq, but the entire menu is as imaginative as you'll find anywhere in northern New York. For starters, try the mussels steamed in vermouth, salmon with Thai peanut sauce, or shrimp and andouille sausage brochette. Although the list of entrées is brief, the choices are intriguing and delicious: real cassoulet, with smoked duck, lamb sausage, and white beans; crisp lemon-rosemary chicken with potato-celery root puree; or shrimp and scallops provençal. Desserts are presented with a flourish. The Napoleon *pallaison* — an over-the-top creation — comes with polka dots of fruit puree, layers of shredded phyllo, fresh berries, and crème fraîche, while La Grand Opera is deep chocolate cake with the kind of sumptuous butter cream that few dare to make anymore. The chocolate soufflé is pure heaven.

The Averill Conwell dining room at the Mirror Lake Inn.

Nancie Battaglia

MIRROR LAKE INN
518-523-2544.
5 Mirror Lake Dr.
Open: Daily.
Serving: B, D, afternoon tea.
Cuisine: American, Continental.
Price: Expensive to Very Expensive.
Credit Cards: AE, CB, DC, MC, V.

The Mirror Lake Inn is a rarity these days: an elegant, modern, full-service hotel that's not part of any national chain. There's an aura of gracious comfort about the place, from the tiny, well-stocked bar to the airy Averill Conwell dining room, which, though it seats well more than 200, seems relaxed and intimate. It's the kind of restaurant that local folks flock to for special occasions, like anniversaries and Mother's Day.

Reservations: Suggested.
Handicap Access: Yes.

The extensive menu has been recently revamped, with somewhat bland spa cuisine selections as well as more robust offerings. Good appetizers include house-smoked jumbo shrimp, grilled duck and mango sausage, and venison paté. Beef is succulent here, especially the tournedos with shallots in a rosemary demi-glace; salmon au poivre is a fine choice for non-meat eaters. The wine list is lengthy, with numerous options in a full range of prices. Soups and breads are delicious; the overall impression of a meal here is very pleasant but not always memorable.

Just across Mirror Lake Drive is the **Cottage**, a breezy little bar right on the lake. It's a fine spot for enjoying a glass of wine or a draft beer; in the summer, the tame ducks paddle by, and in the winter, there's a tiny skating rink shoveled off in front.

NICOLA'S OVER MAIN
518-523-4430.
90 Main St., upstairs.
Open: Daily.
Serving: D.
Cuisine: Mediterranean.
Price: Moderate to Very
  Expensive.
Credit Cards: MC, V.
Reservations: Recom-
  mended in summer or
  for large parties.
Handicap Access: Yes.

Lake Placid natives remember this site as the former NAPA store, but under the assiduous care of Mike and Nia Nicola, the place has been transformed into one of the Olympic Village's top restaurants. (The Nicolas also own Mr. Mike's Pizza, Mr. Mike's Pizza Express, and the Main Street Diner; success at those restaurants has contributed to the polished presentation and wonderful menu here.)

The list of appetizers is long and tempting, with two calamari dishes, fritto misto, basilla torta (a layer cake of basil, soft cheese, and garlic to spread on bruschetta), and pikilia (assorted Greek dishes including tiropetes) at the top of the list. Salad lovers have plenty of great options, including niçoise, Caesar, spinach, and unique combinations of greens, fruits, and nuts, available in small and large sizes. Entrées range from a dozen kinds of excellent wood-fired pizza (try the gorgonzola, rosemary, and black olive) and fresh pasta dishes to grilled seafood, veal, pork, and chicken served with crusty hearth-baked bread. The dessert list often includes homemade tiramisu; there's a small wine list with appropriate selections and full-service bar.

TASTE OF INDIA
518-523-8298.
97 Saranac Ave.
Open: Year-round.
Serving: L, D, SB.
Cuisine: Indian.
Price: Inexpensive to
  Moderate.

Ethnic food in Lake Placid, a town that prides itself on international sports, has been pedestrian (Mexican, German, Italian) at best — until Taste of India opened in summer 1997. Planted next door to a mini-mart (convenient if you want to pick up a couple of cold beers to go with your vindaloo), it's a surprisingly attractive, friendly place.

Credit Cards: AE, MC, V.
Reservations: No.
Handicap Access: Yes.
Special Features: Take-out
and catering available;
bring your own wine or
beer.

There are scores of provocative choices for vegetarians and carnivores alike, in a full range of spiciness; if anything, the kitchen could turn up the heat just a little. Start your meal with vegetable pakoras, some poppadums, or shrimp pakoras. Take your next cue from the menu, which firmly states "AN INDIAN MEAL, WITHOUT BREAD, IS NOT COMPLETE," and order naan with garlic or the house special bread, stuffed with cauliflower, cheese, morsels of chicken tikka, and spices.

Tandoor items, especially the mixed grill Bombay, tend to be too dry; better choices are saagwala curries (garlicky, creamy spinach sauce for lamb, chicken, or shrimp), delectable chicken Jalferezi, bhuna lamb, shrimp masala, or the house vegetarian thali, with dal, chana masala (gingery chickpeas), roti bread, mattar paneer (yogurt cheese with peas), and rice. The house special biryani, packed with vegetables, lamb, and shrimp, is also quite good, and take-out portions are positively enormous. For dessert, the mango ice cream can't be beat.

TAVERNA MYKONOS
518-523-1164.
38 Saranac Ave.
Open: Year-round.
Serving: L, D.
Cuisine: Greek.
Price: Moderate.
Credit Cards: AE, DC, MC, V.
Reservations: No.
Handicap Access: Yes.

A bit off the Main Street circuit is this handsome Greek restaurant. Taverna Mykonos opened in winter 1995 in a former fur salon; renovations upstairs and down have created two clean, simple wood-paneled dining rooms.

The menu contains what you'd expect in an urban Greek restaurant: appetizers like saganaki (not too many Placidians yell "Opaa!" when the cheese flames, though), spanakopita, taramasalata, coriander mushrooms, and the like. The sandwich platters — souvlaki, gyros, lamb kebab — are the best value and come with thick home-fried potatoes and tzatziki (yogurt and cucumber salad). Dinner entrées include red snapper, shrimp, calamari, and other sea creatures served with Mediterranean flavors, plus moussaka, lamb kabobs, and such. The dessert list is quite extensive: ek-mek (shredded dough, almonds, custard, and cream), kataifi (walnuts, honey, and shredded dough), rice pudding, and even chocolate baklava.

THE THIRSTY MOOSE
518-523-3222.
Main St., across from the Olympic Arena.
Open: Year-round.
Serving: L, D.
Cuisine: American.

Family dining in Lake Placid can be a challenge: at one end of the spectrum is McDonald's, and at the other, places that cost $40 per person. Thankfully, the Thirsty Moose rises to the occasion with a menu that has plenty for kids to enjoy (burgers, chicken fingers, spaghetti), plus good options for the grown-ups. The dining room — booths ringing

Price: Inexpensive to
  Moderate.
Credit Cards: MC, V.
Reservations: No.
Handicap Access: Yes.

a big open space with a fireplace in the center — is child-friendly, but not generic looking. The beer selection is a treat, featuring Red Hook, Sam Adams, Saranac Pale Ale, and other quality brews, and the homemade nachos with chunky salsa offer the perfect starting point.

For entrées, try shrimp tequila served over pasta, excellent beef or turkey potpies, roast pork loin, or Mount Whitney chicken, with raspberry sauce.

VERANDA
518-523-2556.
1 Olympic Dr. (across from
  the Holiday Inn).
Closed: Mon. in summer;
  weekdays in winter.
Serving: L, D in summer;
  D in winter.
Cuisine: French.
Price: Expensive to Very
  Expensive.
Credit Cards: AE, CB, DC,
  MC, V.
Reservations: Recom-
  mended.
Handicap Access: Yes.

A marvelous view, lovely dining rooms in a stately old home, and a wonderful menu — our only complaint with the Veranda is that we wish it were open more in the winter. This place is worth a special trip, and eating on the deck is heavenly. A stunning panorama of the Sentinel Range marches across your field of view, with a bit of Mirror Lake showing in the foreground.

Downstairs are two dining rooms of comfortable size, each with cobblestone fireplaces; upstairs are three private dining rooms accommodating from six to 40 or so guests. All are finished with handsome woodwork and fine wallpapers and drapes.

Appetizers are all delectable, with the escargot, jumbo shrimp amandine, and vegetable terrine at the top of our list. The house salad (note that everything is à la carte) covers a dinner plate with artfully arranged shredded vegetables and greens; the Caesar salad is also good.

The entrée options are many, from duck breast with a duet of sauces (green peppercorn and raspberry), salmon quenelles, grilled rosemary lamb, aged steaks, and superb bouillabaisse. Desserts, all made in the Veranda's kitchen, show true French finesse, such as apple tart, peach Melba, and a delectable pastry filled with almond paste. The wine list is extensive, although house wines available by the glass are limited.

THE WOODSHED
518-523-9470.
237 Main St.
Open: Year-round.
Serving: D.
Cuisine: Contemporary
  American.
Price: Moderate.

Directly across from the 400-meter speed-skating oval, the wood-paneled, wood-floored Woodshed has been an Olympic Village landmark for years. New management took over in winter 1995, launching a menu that is imaginative and reasonably priced.

A pair of appetizers warrant special mention:

Credit Cards: AE, CB, DC, MC, V.
Reservations: Not required.
Handicap Access: Street-level entry.

baba ghanoush with pita and honey-mustard grilled shrimp. All dinners come with a nice salad and a boule of crusty homemade bread. Entrées change with the seasons: in winter, apple-sage stuffed pork chops or veal Marengo, with roasted garlic and sun-dried tomatoes, are good picks. In summer, try southwestern chicken with spicy black bean relish or shrimp salatta with fresh basil, pine nuts, and tangy cheese. The Woodshed's trademark dessert is white-chocolate mousse served in a cookie shell; if you don't have room to eat it by yourself, order one to share. Beer and wine-tasting events are popular affairs in fall and spring.

Ray Brook

Ray Brook's own king of the barbecue, Eddie Yanchitis, in front of his restaurant.

Nancie Battaglia

TAIL O' THE PUP
518-891-5092.
Rte. 86, next to the Evergreens cabins.
Closed: Mid-Oct.–mid-May.
Serving: L, D.
Cuisine: Barbecue.
Price: Inexpensive.
Credit Cards: None.
Handicap Access: Yes.

For more than half a century, Tail O' the Pup has served happy travelers with its winning combination of great, cheap food and come-as-you-are atmosphere. You can eat at a picnic table under the stars or beneath a huge tent, inside at a booth, or even beep for a carhop. Bring the kids: they'll love the place, especially on the nights when "Dr. Y," the owner, is dressed up and dancing around in his lobster outfit.

The ribs and chicken are terrific, smoked and smothered with tangy, not-too-sweet sauce, and come with waffle fries, corn on the cob, and a minuscule dab of pretty good cole slaw. On Wednesday, Thursday, and Friday nights, you can also get steamed clams or whole lobster for bargain prices. Onion rings are just the way the should be, crunchy and sweet; better order a couple of portions for the table. About half a dozen good imported and domestic beers are on tap; eat here more than once and you'll get coupons good for free drafts.

Saranac Lake

THE BELVEDERE RESTAURANT
518-891-9873.
57 Bloomingdale Ave.
Open: Year-round.
Serving: D.
Cuisine: American, Italian.
Price: Moderate.
Credit Cards: None.
Handicap Access: Yes.

Since 1933, there's been a member of the Cavallo family in the Belvedere's kitchen, and the restaurant is known for consistently good Italian home cooking. If you've been to a Midwestern supper club, you'll recognize the ambiance: the rambling dining room, a dark and smoky bar, a crew of regulars who have their own special tables. The staff is competent and treats you like a member of the community; if you don't want to feel like a tourist, this is the place. The drinks are reasonably priced, including a good selection of Italian and California wines.

Hot sausage is made right here, and provides zip to thick tomato sauces; recommended entrées include veal and peppers, chicken cacciatore, and lasagna with homemade noodles. Appetizers are few and downright quaint — celery and olives, for instance. For dessert, try spumoni or save room for cheesecake.

CASA DEL SOL
518-891-0977.
154 Lake Flower Ave.
Open: Year-round.
Serving: L, D.
Cuisine: Mexican.
Price: Inexpensive to
  Moderate.
Credit Cards: None.
Reservations: No.
Handicap Access: Yes, but
  restrooms are not
  accessible.

Suspicious about just how good Mexican food could be this far from the border? Cast those doubts aside: Casa del Sol offers ample fire and spice in its authentic dishes. The place has been wildly successful since it began in the late seventies, so much so that sometimes the staff forgets the necessary niceties in dealing with the public. Leave your credit cards at home; don't ask about reservations (Tom Brokaw tried and failed); and you won't be seated — even if there are empty places — if your party isn't complete. Expect to wait for a table in the summer and on weekends, but you can certainly spend a little time on the patio sipping an outstanding margarita made with designer tequila.

In 1997, the menu underwent a long overdue update, and low-fat black bean selections were added to offset the heavier *frijoles refritos*. Chimichangas (shrimp, beef, or chicken), flautas (chili verde, chorizo, or beef), enchiladas with red or green sauce, tostadas, tacos, quesadillas, burritos, and combination plates are all consistent and as good as you might find in the Southwest. Salads and soups, especially the tortilla soup, are delicious. Desserts — well, who lusts for dessert in a Mexican restaurant? Have a cup of steaming hot chocolate with a shot of Kahlua.

THE FOOTE-REST CAFÉ
518-891-6867.
138 Broadway.
Open: Year-round.Serving: L, D.
Cuisine: American, vegetarian.
Price: Inexpensive.
Credit Cards: None.
Handicap Access: No.

Friendly, funky, and no frills describe this college-town joint that takes up a storefront in a not-yet-gentrified section of downtown. Bookshelves packed with the classics and well-thumbed magazines line the walls; tables and chairs are a hodgepodge of styles. You place your order at the counter and a server brings it to you. There's an earnest hippie aura to the place that's disarming.

The food is quite good, especially homemade soup or chili served in a crusty boule of homemade bread. (Slurp the soup, then eat the bowl — what a concept!) Dinner entrées like eggplant parmesan or pasta are filling and tasty. Save room for dessert, or come for just dessert and coffee after a Pendragon Theatre performance. Chocolate earthquake cake is like, wow, man.

LA BELLA RISTORANTE
518-891-1551.
175 Lake Flower Ave.
Open: Year-round.
Serving: D.
Cuisine: Italian.
Price: Moderate to Expensive.
Credit Cards: MC, V.
Handicap Access: Yes.

Walls made of peeled cedar logs, white tablecloths, and fresh flowers make this new Saranac Lake eatery a appealing spot, and the unending sounds of Frank Sinatra on the CD player hammer home the fact this is an Italian restaurant. Well, actually, the owners escaped from war-torn Bosnia, but they've definitely got panache with Mediterranean cooking.

Hot antipasto, which includes clams casino, eggplant parmesan, and calamari, is a great starter for two to share or a nice light meal. You can order sauces with your choice of pasta (ziti, linguine, fettuccini, or cappelini), or try more elaborate presentations, like gnocchi bolognese, mussels fra diavolo, or seafood neapolitan over tortellini. Pasta à la guesta, with scallops, shrimp, and half a lobster, occasionally offered as a special, is definitely recommended. For dessert, spumoni.

The same extended family operates **Jimmy's**, in downtown Lake Placid. The menu is similar, and the dining room is smaller (but with a view of Mirror Lake). Parking nearby can be a problem, though, on summer nights.

A.P. SMITH'S
Hotel Saranac of Paul Smith's College.
518-891-2200.
101 Main St.

This comfortable, spacious dining room has at least two important roles: to offer reliable fare to travelers and to train future restaurateurs who are students of nearby Paul Smith's College. The

A Paul Smith's College culinary arts student shows offerings for an international buffet at the Hotel Saranac.

Nancie Battaglia

Open: Year-round.
Serving: B, L, D.
Cuisine: American, Continental.
Price: Moderate.
Credit Cards: AE, DC, MC, V.
Reservations: Required for theme buffet.
Handicap Access: Yes.
Special Features: Bakery in lobby.

hosts, bartenders, wait staff, bakers, and "cheffies" are all anxious to please.

The regular menu includes simple char-broiled steaks and salmon fillets and adventuresome entrées like pork tenderloin in black currant-Zinfandel sauce and sautéed shrimp in cilantro sauce. Dinners come with a basic green salad, fresh vegetables, house-baked rolls; good spinach and Caesar salads are also available. Daily specials — bargain priced — often feature a vegetarian dish. On Thursday nights during the school year, the culinary arts students prepare multi-course buffets on ethnic themes (Cajun, Polynesian, German), which are served in the lovely second-floor lobby.

Wilmington

THE HUNGRY TROUT
518-946-2217.
Rte. 86, at the Ausable River bridge.
Closed: Mid-Mar.–mid-May, Nov.
Serving: D.
Cuisine: Continental.
Price: Expensive.
Credit Cards: AE, MC, V.
Handicap Access: Yes.

A mile-long section of the legendary West Branch of the Ausable River wraps around this motel/restaurant/fly shop complex, and fine views of Whiteface Mountain and a foaming waterfall can be seen from the dining room. Arrive before dark, as the setting sun puts a golden glow on the hillside; the scenery is awesome, and upstages the food.

The menu is extensive, with numerous trout (farm-raised) dishes, plus quality lamb, steaks, chicken, and excellent Norwegian salmon. The house salad, dressed with balsamic vinaigrette, is quite good, and desserts range from premium ice creams to fruit pies. If you'd like to sample this spot, but prefer not to spend a bundle, try the little tavern on the ground floor, R.F. (as in Rat Face McDougall, a trout fly) McDougall's. It's casual, with a lighter menu and lots of good beers on hand.

WILDERNESS INN II
518-946-2391.
Rte. 86.
Open: Year-round.
Serving: L, D summer;
  D only in winter.
Cuisine: American.
Price: Moderate.
Credit Cards: DC, MC, V.
Handicap Access: Yes.

The Wilderness Inn is an amusing jumble of chatchkes and Christmas decorations and auto-graphed photos of long-gone Hollywood stars like Desi Arnaz, Abbott and Costello, and Peter Lorre. In warm weather, if you want to escape the rampant nostalgia and concentrate on the food, you can dine alfresco on a wooden deck or in a gazebo. To be sure, there's no particular view, just cars and trucks passing by on the Lake Placid road.

Lunch includes nice, big Caesar salads with grilled chicken or deli-style roast beef, turkey, or ham sandwiches. For dinner, start with the salad bar (nothing out of the ordinary — cold pasta, baked beans, pickled peppers, lettuce, and crudités), and proceed to meat-eater's nirvana, reflected in slabs of steak and giant stuffed pork chops. Desserts, like cheesecake and strawberry shortcake, are all homemade, and there's a full bar.

NORTHWEST LAKES

Cranberry Lake

CRANBERRY LAKE INN
315-848-3301.
Rte. 3.
Closed: Apr.
Serving: B, L, D.
Cuisine: American.
Price: Moderate.
Credit Cards: MC, V.
Handicap Access: Inquire.

Snowshoes, antique tools, vintage photographs, pack baskets, and stuffed wildlife adorn the rustic walls of this full-service family restaurant overlooking the third largest lake in the Adirondacks. For lunch, there are good burgers, Philly cheese steaks, club sandwiches, homemade soup, and chili. Dinner entrées include steaks, chops, chicken, seafood; if you're at the inn on a weekend, definitely order the prime rib. It's a big, juicy slab that brings in crowds for miles around.

WINDFALL HOUSE
315-848-2078.
Tooley Pond Rd., 4 mi. S. of
  Rte. 3.
Closed: Mon., Tues.
Serving: L, D.
Cuisine: American.
Price: Moderate.
Credit Cards: None.
Handicap Access: Call ahead.

Named for a massive storm that swept over the region before the Civil War, the Windfall House is a nice family restaurant offering a complete menu of steaks, chicken, chops, and nightly specials. Homemade Italian dishes add interest; the salad bar and dessert list are distinct delights.

Lake Clear

A bull moose watches over the dining room at the Lodge at Lake Clear.

Nancie Battaglia

THE LODGE AT LAKE CLEAR
518-891-1489.
Rtes. 30 & 186.
Closed: Tues. Mar.–Apr.
Serving: D.
Cuisine: German.
Price: Expensive to Very Expensive.
Credit Cards: MC, V.
Reservations: Recommended.
Handicap Access: No.

Bring a small group of friends to this charming old-time Adirondack inn for dinner. That way you can sample many of the interesting appetizers (marinated herring, smoked oysters, and pâté, for example) and desserts (Black Forest cake, homemade ice cream, and apple strudel). Soups, especially oxtail, are wonderful.

Entrée choices — usually four to eight options each night — are heirloom German recipes that feature farm-raised venison, rabbit, duckling, pork, and veal in traditional sauces, plus sauerbraten, rouladen, and schnitzels. After dinner, take your party down to the rathskeller to sit by the fire and digest.

Tupper Lake

THE PINE GROVE
518-359-6669.
166 Main St., just past Leroy's Auto Sales.
Open: Year-round.
Serving: L, D.
Cuisine: American, Italian.
Price: Moderate.

A nice unassuming place on the north end of town, the Pine Grove makes you feel at home. Italian food (the owners are the Philippi family) is authentic and flavorful, but the menu includes a surprising array of choices, from Cajun shrimp to chicken fajitas, served in little skillets and prepared with a bit of zest. Portions are ample but not over-

Credit Cards: MC, V.
Handicap Access: Inquire.

whelming; don't skip the homemade soup and desserts.

At the Wawbeek, a table by the fire is cozy.

Nancie Battaglia

THE WAWBEEK
518-359-2656.
Panther Mtn. Rd., off Rte. 30.
Closed: Nov.; Mon. & Tues. in off season.
Serving: D, year-round; B, L July–Aug.
Cuisine: Contemporary American, Continental.
Price: Expensive to Very Expensive.
Credit Cards: AE, DC, MC, V.
Reservations: Recommended for weekends.
Handicap Access: Side door.

On a summer visit to the Wawbeek, head to the second-story deck to enjoy a cocktail overlooking gorgeous Upper Saranac Lake. You'll see sailboats and canoes gliding down the waters and pretty little islands. Under new ownership these last few years, the Wawbeek remains one of the most delightful dining destinations around. The building — with two magnificent fireplaces and two screen porches — is worth the trip, and the setting is simply wonderful. Arrive before dark!

Appetizers include seviche, pâté, and scampi. In summer, the garlic-and-cilantro-spiked gazpacho is an excellent choice for a low-fat starter; on the other end of the spectrum is the rich, creamy shellfish bisque. The house salad dressings, especially the honey-dijon vinaigrette, are exceptionally good. The wine list is uncomplicated, offering an array of suitable Californian, Australian, and French wines.

Entrées include Jamaican-style prawns in jerk sauce (a very generous serving with bold — but not overwhelming — spices), rack of lamb, scallops à la Wawbeek (sauced with garlic, lemon, and parmesan), simple but elegant penne with kalamata olives and oregano. Poached salmon with fresh dill is usually on the menu, as are high-quality aged steaks. Desserts include tarts, elaborate chocolate creations, and ice creams; try the homemade strawberry shortcake if it's available.

Wanakena

THE PINE CONE
315-848-2121.
Ranger School Rd.
Closed: Mon.
Serving: L, D.
Cuisine: American.
Price: Moderate.
Credit Cards: None.
Handicap Access: Street-
level entry.

A classic north woods tavern with respectable fare, the Pine Cone is worth a visit just to check out the ceiling — it's plastered with caps of all descriptions, somewhere in the vicinity of a thousand chapeaux. Come by boat from Cranberry Lake for one of the pig roasts or barbecues; there's plenty of dock space.

The Friday fish fry (beer-batter haddock) is fine, and try the prime rib, which is quite popular. You'll find the service to be quick and friendly.

CENTRAL ADIRONDACKS

Big Moose

BIG MOOSE INN
315-357-2042.
Big Moose Rd., 6 mi. N. of
Rte. 28.
Closed: Apr. & Nov.
Serving: L, D.
Cuisine: American,
Continental.
Price: Moderate to
Expensive.
Credit Cards: AE, MC, V.
Reservations: Recom-
mended.
Handicap Access: Yes.

Overlooking Big Moose Lake is this old-time lodge, a favorite destination for year-round residents who want to go someplace special on birthdays, anniversaries, and other occasions; some people even come by seaplane for dinner. In the summer, eating on the lakeside deck is a treat; ask for a table by the windows in the winter.

The menu was revamped in 1997, with some great new ideas. When you sit down at the table, your server brings a loaf of the homemade parsley-romano bread and herb-infused olive oil for dipping. Appetizers include blackened scallops with basil garlic mayonnaise, ravioli of the day, and focaccia with feta cheese and sun-dried tomatoes. Regarding entrées, the inn is known far and wide for aged steaks, but chicken chasseur, with bordelaise sauce and a hint of gorgonzola cheese; grilled portabella mushrooms with pasta; or shrimp with artichoke hearts are all nice picks. Desserts are homemade, with pie at the top of the list.

BIG MOOSE STATION
315-357-3525.
Big Moose Rd.
Closed: Mon.–Weds. in
winter.
Serving: B, L, D.
Cuisine: American.
Price: Moderate.

This attractively restored depot for the Adirondack Railroad hasn't seen regular passenger service for years, but it's still a fine destination for hungry travelers. The down-home fare is tasty, presented in ample portions, and the setting is charming. For breakfast, try waffles or thick French toast; at lunch, hearty soups and a grilled burger or

Credit Cards: No.
Handicap Access: Yes.

club sandwich. At dinner, go for the nightly specials, like Friday fish fry.

Blue Mountain Lake

FOREST HOUSE
518-352-7776.
Rtes. 28/30.
Open: Year-round.
Serving: L, D daily in
    summer; D Fri.–Sun.
    in winter
Cuisine: Italian.
Price: Moderate.
Credit Cards: MC, V.
Handicap Access: Yes.

For more than a hundred years, between Indian Lake and Blue Mountain Lake, there's been a place by the side of the road named the Forest House. The latest incarnation is a nice little Italian restaurant with a Culinary Institute of America grad as the chef.

Soups are delicious, and can be as exotic as eggplant or traditional as minestrone. Recommended entrées include chicken saltimbocca, balsamic shrimp and scallops, and veal dishes. A small but complete wine list offers chianti, merlot, and suitable dry white wines.

Caroga Lake

THE OUTLET
518-835-3991.
Rte. 10 S. of Caroga Lake.
Open: Daily.
Serving: D, SB.
Cuisine: American.
Price: Inexpensive to
    Moderate.
Credit Cards: MC, V.
Reservations: Yes.
Handicap Access: Yes.

This eatery takes its name from the outlet of the Caroga lakes, which narrow down to marsh-lined shores, right beside the new outdoor deck. Numerous windows in the dining room make you feel if you were outdoors even if the weather isn't inviting. The Outlet is a casual place with friendly service and good, home-cooked fare; specials are often inexpensive. For those reasons it's popular with large groups, but still comfortable for dinner for two.

**PINNACLE
    RESTAURANT**
518-835-4121.
Rtes. 10 & 29A N. of
    Canada Lake.
Open: Tues.–Sun.,
    May–Oct.
Serving: D.
Cuisine: American.
Price: Moderate.
Credit Cards: All major.
Reservations: Yes.
Handicap Access: No.

This handsome rustic building perched high above Canada Lake has one of the loveliest views of any Adirondack restaurant; its long-windowed facade offers a panorama stretching to West Lake filtered through tall oak trees. There's a small open deck with tables — perfect for watching spectacular sunsets, but looking out through storm clouds and mist can be captivating as well. The food is good, but not exceptional. It's the scenery that's the star here.

UNGER HOUSE
RESTAURANT
518-835-8005.
NY 10 & 29A.
Open: Year-round.
Serving: D.
Cuisine: American.
Price: Moderate.
Credit Cards: AE, DC, MC,
V.
Reservations: Yes.
Handicap Access: Yes.

A warm, comfortable atmosphere provides a good setting for the Unger House's varied menu of steaks, chops, and seafood, and a range of specials that are usually imaginatively seasoned and quite good. There's a soup-and-salad bar: the fresh homemade bread is tasty, but avoid the temptation to fill up before dinner. In a recent visit, our only complaint involved the water — the not-so-good well water should be replaced by bottled water.

Eagle Bay

THE ECKERSONS
315-357-4641.
Rte. 28.
Open: Year-round.
Serving: L, D in summer;
D in winter.
Cuisine: American.
Price: Moderate.
Credit Cards: All major.
Handicap Access: Yes.

Every day of the week offers a different dinner special at Eckersons. On Friday, it's fried or broiled fresh haddock; thick-cut prime rib is Saturday; and on Sunday, the feature is honest-to-goodness roast turkey with savory stuffing, homemade mashed potatoes, and gravy. The menu also includes pork chops, chicken dishes, shrimp, and steaks; near the bar is a medium-size salad bar.

Eckersons is right on a major snowmobile trail connecting Old Forge and Big Moose, and can be quite busy on winter weekends. The service here is fast and friendly. If you're a martini drinker, they mix a first-rate one here and plop in their very own pickled green cherry tomato instead of an olive.

Forestport Station

BUFFALO HEAD
315-392-2632.
Off Rte. 28 in Forestport
Station on North Lake
Rd.
Open: Year-round.
Serving: L, D.
Cuisine: American.
Price: Moderate.
Credit Cards: AE, DC, MC,
V.
Reservations: Yes.
Handicap Access: Yes.

As you drive north on Rtes. 8, 12, and 28 from Utica you pass billboards emblazoned with a huge buffalo head, proclaiming that this restaurant is "famous for fine food." This statement isn't merely advertising hype, it's the Buffalo Head's well-earned reputation. Large dining rooms accommodate crowds easily, the service is excellent, the menu has a varied list of steaks and fish, and the place is deservedly popular in all seasons.

The Buffalo Head name traces back to logging days, when immigrant work crews came by train to Forestport Station. For some reason now lost in the mists of time, a worker brought a buffalo head along with him, which the loggers nailed to the side of the railroad depot. The nickname stuck for that particular stop on the old Adirondack Division of the

New York Central, and the restaurant, across the street from the station, carries on the bison motif.

Garoga

ROYAL MOUNTAIN INN
518-762-1079.
Rtes. 10 & 29, south of Caroga lakes.
Closed: Mon.–Thurs.
Serving: D.
Cuisine: German.
Price: Moderate.
Credit Cards: No.
Reservations: Recommended.
Handicap Access: No.

There is no better place in the southern Adirondacks for German cooking than the Royal Mountain Inn, a small roadhouse just a bit south of the park boundary. Its unpretentiousness contrasts with the great food: wiener schnitzel is mouthwatering, bratwurst and beef rouladen typically Teutonic. Condiments like applesauce and pickles come with all meals, but best of all are the potato pancakes. Order a plate or two for your table. A good selection of German beers and wines complements the entrées. The restaurant is small, so reservations are a must.

Gloversville

DICK AND PEG'S NORTHWARD INN RESTAURANT
518-725-6440.
Route 29A, N.W. of Gloversville.
Closed: Sun.–Mon.
Serving: D.
Cuisine: American.
Price: Moderate to Expensive.
Credit Cards: AE, DC, MC, V.
Reservations: No.
Handicap Access: Yes.

Near the southern border of the Adirondack Park, Dick and Peg's has long been known for its fine food and huge barroom. The dining areas are cozy, comfortable, and packed with collectibles (owls predominate), which conceal the building's handsome architecture.

The restaurant can be quite crowded on weekends, so regulars allow enough time to enjoy the bar while waiting for a table. Shrimp and steak dinners are recommended; the house specialty — potatoes au gratin — is a must. The service is excellent, and there's no doubt this is a family business run with pride.

Indian Lake

CHILI NIGHTS
518-648-5832.
Main St., at Marty's Tavern.
Closed: Mon.–Weds.
Serving: L, D.
Cuisine: Mexican.
Price: Moderate.
Credit Cards: MC, V.

In 1997 an unlikely place took over the front room of a local watering hole and surprised everyone by offering authentic Mexican food and even real south-of-the-border crooners on the jukebox. There's Mexican beer on draft, fried ice cream for dessert, and an upbeat, earnest ambiance that's hard to resist.

Appetizers include the usual suspects — nachos,

Reservations: Suggested for parties of six or more.
Handicap Access: Yes.

guacamole, and such — but the entrée list is every bit as complete and tasty as any of the other Mexican eateries in the Adirondacks. If a chimichanga or chiles rellenos isn't for you, then try the steaming chili served in a bowl made of bread, or perhaps a mildly hot vegetarian fajita. Specials often include delicious fresh seafood enchiladas.

Inlet

SEVENTH LAKE HOUSE
315-357-6028.
Rte. 28.
Closed: Nov.
Serving: D.
Cuisine: Contemporary American.
Price: Expensive.
Credit Cards: MC, V.
Reservations: Suggested.
Handicap Access: Yes.

Hamilton County, which stretches from Long Lake to Hope Falls, covers nearly as much territory as Rhode Island, and without a doubt, Seventh Lake House is the best restaurant in the whole county. Chef/owner Jim Holt has presided here since 1989, and his varied seasonal menus continue to offer innovative new dishes made from the best ingredients.

The place is elegantly simple, with white tablecloths, an imposing fireplace, and lots of picture windows facing toward the lake. There's a comfortable bar off to one side, and a big canopied deck stretching across the back trimmed with tiny Christmas lights.

Appetizers are very tasty, ranging from smoked venison ravioli or smoked trout with Dijon-horseradish sauce to "turkey toes," spicy deep-fried morsels. Soups are heavenly, especially the black bean. Try the Caesar salad. Entrées run the gamut of fresh seafood on angel-hair pasta to triple meatloaf made with beef, veal, and pork — a combination that relegates all other recipes to shame. Steak, lamb, chicken, and fresh fish are excellent, every one. Desserts are scrumptious and made on the premises, with signature creations being a flourless chocolate gateau and the Adirondack, a pastry made with fresh apples, walnuts, and maple syrup.

For mud season, Seventh Lake House sponsors a day of goofy races and a Bavarian buffet, and just before the blackflies hatch, in May, is the Fire and Spice competition for amateur and professional chefs. That event is definitely worth a trip so that you can savor Indian, Tex-Mex, Caribbean, and Thai dishes from dozens of amateur and professional kitchens.

Long Lake

LONG LAKE DINER
518-624-3941.
Rte. 30.
Closed: Holidays.
Serving: B, L.

Under new management and totally refurbished since December 1996, this spotless, bright restaurant is hard to beat. The staff is friendly and fast, and it's impossible to find a clunker on the

Cuisine: American.
Price: Inexpensive.
Credit Cards: MC, V.
Handicap Access: Yes.

menu. In the morning, go for the eggs benedict or Belgian waffles with real maple syrup; at lunch, homemade soups, char-grilled burgers, club sandwiches, and huge Caesar salads are all good. Whatever you choose, save room for one of Chuck Frost's scrumptious sticky buns.

The attractive pine-paneled tavern at the Long View Lodge looks over Long Lake.

Nancie Battaglia

LONG VIEW LODGE
518-624-2862.
Rte. 28/30.
Open: Year-round.
Serving: B, L, D.
Cuisine: American.
Price: Moderate to
 Expensive.
Credit Cards: MC, V.
Reservations: Not neces-
 sary.
Handicap Access: Yes.

Extensive renovations completed in 1995 have made the Long View Lodge into one of the area's most attractive restaurants. The main dining room is cozy and bright, with a huge fireplace; the airy pine-paneled bar offers nearly every table a view toward the lake, and you can catch summer breezes from a sheltered deck that's well away from the road.

Breakfasts are hearty stuff like pancakes and bacon and eggs. The lunch menu includes burgers, club and grilled sandwiches, and excellent homemade quiche. For dinner, try the shrimp-and-scallop kebab or cheese ravioli as an appetizer or a light meal. Entrées include meatless pastas, old-fashioned roast turkey with all the trimmings, chicken breast with white zinfandel sauce, pork loin with applesauce, and swordfish with ginger-leek butter. (Simpler dishes are more successful, though.) For dessert, there's tiramisu, homemade pies, good fruit crisps (in season), and ice cream sundaes.

Mayfield

LANZI'S ON THE LAKE
518-661-7711.
Rte. 30.
Open: Daily Memorial
　Day–Columbus Day.
Serving: L, D.
Cuisine: American.
Price: Moderate to
　Expensive.
Credit Cards: All major.
Reservations: Yes.
Handicap Access: Yes.

On the western shore of Great Sacandaga Lake, this spacious, attractive modern restaurant is deservedly popular. Ample docks and a long outdoor deck invite boaters. No need to dress up — the mood here is vacation casual.

Dinner portions are quite large and often provide leftovers for meals the next day. Fresh fish and quality steaks are carefully prepared; vegetables, salads, and desserts are tasty, too. Lanzi's can become crowded on weekends, so reservations are recommended. Try to avoid nights when big parties are scheduled.

North Creek

GARDENS
518-251-2500.
Main St., at the Copperfield
　Inn.
Open: Jan.–Mar., May–Oct.
Serving: B, L, D.
Cuisine: Contemporary
　American.
Price: Moderate to
　Expensive.
Credit Cards: All major.
Reservations: Recom-
　mended for weekends.
Handicap Access: Yes.

With its marble foyer, sparkling chandeliers, and opulent decor, the Copperfield Inn offers a distinctly out-of-the-Adirondacks dining experience: the place seems to have been conjured out of a pattern book for 18th-century reproductions, which would be unsettling if the fare weren't in keeping with the illusion. Thankfully, the food at Gardens, the inn's elegant dining room, is good.

The whole complex — less than ten years old — underwent another round of building and renovations that were completed in summer 1997. Gardens is tucked away from the lobby, in a series of horseshoe-shaped raised platforms with floral carpet, swooping drapes, and arched windows overlooking a patio. Lunch is a fine way to get acquainted with this spot, and salads really shine: an excellent offering is the grilled seafood salad, with scallops and shrimp over greens dressed with citrus vinaigrette. The prime rib sandwich is a first-rate slab of choice beef, and the plump, sweet steamed clams can be out of this world. Other lunch dishes include shrimp and pesto and chicken rosemary.

For dinner, you can start with some of those grand steamers or a creamy lobster puff. Entrées range from chicken Montana (grilled chicken breast with mushrooms, sun-dried tomatoes, and capers in a white wine sauce), veal marsala, scallops Theodore (broiled with sherry), or rack of lamb. Pies are all made on the premises, with mud pie — a vast slab of coffee ice cream with fudgy layers — a specialty of the house.

If you'd like casual dining at the Copperfield, there's **Trapper's Tavern**, which serves thin-crust pizza, chili, and sandwiches. A sports bar that is the liveliest place in town during rafting and ski season, Trapper's can be very noisy.

SMITH'S RESTAURANT
518-251-9965.
Main St., across from the
Copperfield Inn.
Open: Year-round.
Serving: B, L, D.
Cuisine: American,
German.
Price: Inexpensive.
Credit Cards: AE, MC, V.
Handicap Access: Yes.

Not to be outdone by its glamorous across-the-street neighbor, Smith's had a makeover in 1997 too. But the knotty-pine walls and Naugahyde booths still give an authentic feel to this reliable family restaurant. Several offerings really stand out: chunky New England clam chowder; roast pork or turkey dinners (served with a mountain of stuffing, real mashed potatoes, and excellent gravy); sauerbraten or knockwurst plates (with buttery spaetzel). Don't miss a piece of pie; although we'd place the coconut cream at the head of the class, all are good. Beer and wine are available.

North River

GARNET HILL LODGE
518-251-2444.
Thirteenth Lake Rd. (5 mi.
off Rte. 28.)
Open: Year-round.
Serving: B, L, D.
Cuisine: Country.
Price: Moderate to
Expensive.
Credit Cards: MC, V.
Handicap Access: Portable
ramp.

On a Saturday night in midwinter, this is one of the busiest places around. Crowds of red-cheeked, wool-clad patrons, hungry after a day of skiing on 50 kilometers of exemplary Nordic trails, line up for the once-a-week gourmet brunch. Others chat — or nap — in the huge couches flanking the fireplace, which was made with rocks from the garnet mines down the road.

And if it's quieter much of the rest of the year, Garnet Hill is no less agreeable. The view from the glassed-in porch commands Thirteenth Lake and the mountains to the west in the Siamese Ponds Wilderness Area. The atmosphere is homey: there's a ping-pong table and board games — this is a good spot for families. For the best dining experience, order a simple dish like baked chicken over something that promises elaborate sauces. Most everything is freshly prepared, including the wonderful breads and pies made by baker Mary Jane Freebern. Portions are generous to a fault; the kitchen clearly doesn't want any skiers running out of carbohydrates.

HIGHWINDS INN
518-251-3760.
Top of Barton Mines Rd.,
off Rte. 28.
Closed: Nov.–Dec.,
Mar.–May.
Serving: D daily in
summer; Fri.–Sun. fall &
winter.
Cuisine: Regional
American.

Restaurants with terrific views are surprisingly rare in the Adirondacks, and Highwinds is a contender for featuring the best, a panorama of the magnificent Siamese Ponds Wilderness Area, with Puffer and Bullhead mountains and Botheration Pond framing the vista. And it offers food and service that are just as special.

Be sure to make reservations — there are just eight tables at the restaurant (and four rooms in the inn; see Chapter Three, *Lodging*). Make sure to stop

From the glassed-in dining room of Highwinds Inn, the view goes on for miles and miles.

Nancie Battaglia

Price: Moderate to
    Expensive.
Credit Cards: D, MC, V.
Reservations: Recommended.
Special Features: BYOB,
    fireplace.

in North Creek or Indian Lake for a bottle of wine. And, make sure you've checked the almanac before you book your table: what you want is to be here at sunset, which means right at the opening hour in midwinter.

The friendly, low-key staff will take care of everything else, often pointing you to a particularly delicious special, salmon-and-mushrooms in phyllo, perhaps. The salads — straight from nearby gardens in summer — are impeccable; the soups are rich and filling; come winter, there's a fire in the garnet-boulder fireplace to warm you up after a trip around the cross-country ski trails that they reserve for their guests. Highwinds defines an Adirondack approach to elegance: not fussy, just perfect.

Old Forge

THE FARM RESTAURANT
315-369-6199.
Rte. 28.
Closed: Spring & late fall.
Serving: B, L.
Cuisine: American.
Price: Inexpensive.
Credit Cards: None.
Handicap Access: Yes.

This big, fun eatery, packed with fascinating antiques from floor to ceiling, runs like clockwork, presenting great service and very good food. For breakfast — which is available all day — try blueberry pancakes, omelettes, or cinnamon French toast. For lunch, homemade chili (topped with sharp cheddar cheese) and soups are tasty; also recommended are bacon cheeseburgers and Reubens. There's a children's menu, and beer and wine can be ordered with lunch.

THE FERNS PASTA HOUSE
315-369-2582.
Main St.

Walt and Lesa Parent, who had a great thing going at the Maple Diner for many years, took over the former Pinocchio's Kitchen in late

Open: Year-round.
Serving: B, L, D.
Price: Inexpensive.
Cuisine: Italian, American.
Credit Cards: None.
Reservations: No.
Handicap Access: No.

1997. Now they're offering good home-cooked family fare three meals a day and decent Italian dishes in the evening. The prices are down-to-earth (less than ten bucks for dinner entrées), and the place is cozy no matter what the season. It's a good spot if you've got picky eaters in tow and want a restaurant with some grown-up choices for the rest of the crew.

THE KNOTTY PINE
315-369-6859.
Rte. 28, Thendara.
Open: Year-round.
Serving: D.
Cuisine: American.
Price: Moderate.
Credit Cards: AE, MC, V.
Handicap Access: Yes.

A treasured local place, especially for the Friday fish fry, the Knotty Pine is known for its friendly atmosphere. The restaurant has been attractively converted from a house into a spacious eatery, with a bar as you enter and a large dining room to the right.

The menu includes prime rib, sirloin, beef fillets, chicken marsala, and tender beef en brochette; Cajun shrimp on angel-hair pasta is listed as an appetizer but makes a nice light meal. Children are welcome, and there's a special menu for them.

A working waterwheel graces the exterior of the Old Mill.

Nancie Battaglia

THE OLD MILL
315-369-3662.
Rte. 28.
Open: Year-round.
Serving: D.
Cuisine: American.
Price: Moderate to
  Expensive.

Come early to the Old Mill to relax in the new bar, which is a bright, soaring space with exposed beams, couches clustered by the fireplace, and lots of windows. There's also a porch for alfresco dining, but unfortunately it faces the highway rather than the Moose River, which is just beyond the parking lot.

Credit Cards: MC, V.
Handicap Access: Yes.

Meals start off with a big tureen of delicious homemade soup, to be dished out family-style. Salads are reliably good and similarly generous. Entrées include steaks, chops, roast duckling, and chicken; some recommended dishes include the steamed-shrimp-in-the-rough platter, char-grilled rack of lamb (nicely marinated with red wine and rosemary), and stuffed pork chops. The service is competent and congenial.

VAN AUKEN'S INNE
315-369-3033.
Rte. 28, Thendara, behind
   the Adirondack Railroad
   depot.
Open: Year-round.
Serving: L, D.
Price: Moderate.
Cuisine: American.
Credit Cards: MC, V.
Reservations: Suggested for
   dinner on weekends.
Handicap Access: Yes.

Since June 1996, Kathy and Paul Rivet have taken loving care of this century-old inn, renovating guest rooms and public areas and compiling one of the most innovative menus around. For the perfect summer lunch, sample a steak salad, with slivers of rare sirloin, kalamata olives, blue cheese, and red onions over greens, or order the shrimp and andouille sausage sandwich, served on a crusty French roll. Turkey hash with zingy mustard sauce occasionally surfaces as a special; it's wonderful.

For dinner, start with almond-crusted goat cheese or satay-style beef skewers with peanut sauce. Main course selections include grilled veal chop in blood orange sauce, scallops with lime cilantro mayonnaise, grilled vegetables with polenta, and pasta puttanesca. Aged beef and pork medallions with apple ginger chutney are also very good, and desserts are all homemade.

Speculator

HIGGINS HOUSE
518-548-6445.
Rte. 8.
Open: Year-round.
Serving: L, D.
Cuisine: American,
   Mexican, seafood.
Price: Moderate.
Credit Cards: MC, V.
Handicap Access: No.

Higgins House is in one of the friendliest of North Country villages: Speculator, population 500. The old-time Adirondack hermit French Louie hung out in Kunjamuk Cave, which is an easy walk from Elm Lake Road; if Higgins House had been around at the turn of the century, Louie would definitely have hiked in to mooch a hot meal on a cold day.

Stop here for Mexican food on Fridays or spicy chicken wings anytime. The Mexican pizza, a flour tortilla covered with cheese, salsa, beans, and peppers, is huge and delicious. The seafood is fresh and well prepared; Higgins House also offers a variety of juicy, thick burgers served on kaiser rolls.

The service is excellent and attentive. Pecan pie with whipped cream is just one of their homemade desserts; save room or take a slice home.

THE INN AT SPECULATOR
518-548-3811.
Rte. 8, 2 mi. E. of the 4
Corners.
Open: Year-round.Serving:
B (some days), L, D.
Cuisine: American,
seafood.
Price: Moderate.
Credit Cards: AE, MC, V.
Handicap Access: No.

The inn is nestled in the trees between Speculator and Lake Pleasant and has been serving meals since the forties. Get a table in the back dining room for nice views of Lake Pleasant, or on Thursdays, when the county board is in session, hang out by the bar for eavesdropping on the movers and shakers of New York's least-populated county.

The inn has a new chef and his market specials are great. Appetizers include shrimp scampi and sautéed artichoke hearts, along with stuffed clams and shrimp cocktail. Steaks, veal, and seafood are carefully prepared, with a tenderloin/scampi combination a favorite offering. The beef burgundy is hearty and generous. Desserts include homemade pies and cakes.

KING OF THE FROSTIES
518-548-3881.
Rte. 8.
Closed: Tues.
Serving: B, L; D summer
only.
Cuisine: American, some
Filipino specials.
Price: Inexpensive.
Credit Cards: None.
Handicap Access: Yes.

King of the Frosties has always had one of the all-time great names for a roadside ice cream stand and diner, and now, with new management and remodeling, it's worth a stop for more than just dessert. Try the Filipino noodle soup for a real treat; burgers, chicken, and salads are also fine if you want something quick and simple.

Look for the ice cream line outside on hot summer days. This is a rustic counterpart to Martha's, the noteworthy Lake George destination, and just as good for soft ice cream.

MELODY LODGE
518-548-6562.
Rte. 30.
Closed: Mon.–Tues. in
winter.
Serving: L, D.
Cuisine: American.
Price: Moderate to
Expensive.
Credit Cards: AE, MC, V.
Handicap Access: Yes.

Melody Lodge feels almost like an Adirondack Great Camp, with its assorted antiques and lovely view down Page Hill toward Lake Pleasant. The rambling inn (there are 10 guest rooms with shared baths upstairs) was built in 1912 as a singing school for young girls, and first opened to the public as a restaurant and hotel in 1937.

Try the well-seasoned Steak by George or savory haddock. A dessert tray features lots of homemade goodies, from good chocolate cake to fruit pies.

ZEISER'S RESTAURANT
518-548-7021.
Rte. 30, at the 4 Corners.
Open: Call for days.
Serving: L, D.
Cuisine: Continental.

Aged premium beef and exceptional lamb chops, plus some German specialties like sauerbraten, are the offerings here. Zeiser's is a gracious restaurant, tinged with the quiet aura of an old-fashioned club; prints of famous race horses decorate one of the dining rooms and bottles of

Price: Expensive to Very
  Expensive.
Credit Cards: MC, V.
Handicap Access: Yes.

antique single-malt Scotch fill large glass cases. Genevieve Zeiser, the owner, wait staff, and chef, makes it all work — without shortcuts — but be prepared to linger a couple of hours over dinner.

John D. McDonald, the mystery writer and originator of Travis McGee, was a regular here. There's a dining room dedicated to his memory, displaying autographed copies of his books.

Stillwater

STILLWATER
315-376-6470.
Stillwater Rd.
Closed: Apr.
Serving: B, L, D.
Cuisine: American.
Price: Moderate to
  Expensive.
Credit Cards: AE, D, MC,
  V.
Handicap Access: Yes.

You'll find this hotel at end of a long gravel road, overlooking a wilderness reservoir that has more resident loons than any other water body in the Northeast. Guests come in all seasons, by snowmobile, canoe, motorboat, or car.

Breakfasts are good, featuring the usual eggs, bacon, home fries, and so forth. At lunch, the choices are many, from good homemade soups to fried calamari or barbecued beef to sausage-and-pepper heroes or the monster burger, a 14-ounce patty with cheese, lettuce, tomato, and fries. Dinner entrées include pastas, veal dishes, prime beef, chicken, and fish; there's a children's menu, too.

ROAD FOOD AND QUICK BITES

LAKE GEORGE AND SOUTHEASTERN ADIRONDACKS

In *Bolton Landing*, **Jule's Service Diner** (no phone; Main St.) is a cute old-time diner that was formerly in Attleboro, Massachusetts; soups, baked goods, and sandwiches are definitely a cut above the usual. In *Chestertown*, **The Place** (518-494-3390; Rte. 8) has inexpensive, homemade Italian food and a pleasant atmosphere. In *Lake George*, **S.J. Garcia's** (518-668-2190; 192 Canada St.) offers a fair mix of reasonably good Mexican food and wicked margaritas. In *Warrensburg*, **Bill's Restaurant** (518-623-2669; 190 Main St.) makes a fine roast-turkey sandwich and serves breakfast all day. **Dragon Lee** (518-623-3796; 35 Main St., next to Stewart's) has a huge menu with great carry-out options; sauces tend to be on the syrupy side, so ask for spicy, not sweet.

CHAMPLAIN VALLEY

In *Elizabethtown*, **Connell's Country Kitchen** (518-873-9920; Rte. 9) has plain, satisfying fare like baked scrod and homemade spaghetti plus a great apple crisp. In _Ticonderoga_, **Doc's Restaurant** (518-585-6474; Montcalm St. & Champlain Ave.) offers good club sandwiches, meatball subs, tasty pizza, and calzone. The **General's Gate** (518-585-2730; 136 N. Champlain Ave.) has a full salad bar and offers good ground-sirloin burgers, baked ziti, and a full range of entrées. The **North Country Pub** (518-585-4024; 155 Montcalm St.) serves tasty soups, hearty sandwiches with homemade French fries and excellent cole slaw.

HIGH PEAKS AND NORTHERN ADIRONDACKS

In _Ausable Forks_, the **D&H Freighthouse** (518-647-8800; Rte. 9N) is open from late spring through fall, serving decent pizza, good sandwiches and burgers, and homemade pies, cakes, and muffins in the front office of an old-time railroad warehouse. In _Lake Placid_, **Desperadoes** (518-523-1507; Cold Brook Plaza, near the Grand Union) is open for dinner every night and lunch Thurs–Sat., serving fajitas, quesadillas, flautas, and chiles rellenos, along with good margaritas. Likewise, the **Down Hill Grill** (518-523-9510; 434 Main St.) is a good choice for lunch or a no-jive dinner; burgers, sandwiches (try the chipotle chicken sandwich), and Mexican food; start off with the Mexican layer dip, with black beans, sour cream, guacamole, tomatoes, jalapenos, and cheese, if you've got a hungry crew in tow. **Mama Lena's** (518-523-1531; 245 Main St.) makes reasonable Italian food like lasagna in big portions; order one meal, take it back to your cabin, and share it. **Mr. Mike's Pizza** (518-523-9770; 332 Main St.) has great pizza with all kinds of exotic toppings, good eggplant parmesan, and big, delicious salads for eat-in or carry-out; they deliver, too. In _Wilmington_, the **Country Bear** (518-946-2691; Rte. 86) bakes good homemade bread for its sandwiches and dishes out really fine chili, with or without meat. At **Steinhoff's Inn** (518-946-2220; Rte. 86), check out the dioramas of skiing and fly fishing above the bar as you devour a big, fat burger and exceptional fries.

NORTHWEST LAKES

In _Cranberry Lake_, the **Stone Diner** (315-848-2678; Rte. 3) is cheerful place with good chow and ice cream.In _Tupper Lake_, **The Rose** (518-523-9621; Cliff Ave., behind the bank) is a family restaurant with thick burgers, occasional fresh seafood specials, and heavenly pies. In _Star Lake_, **Mountain Gate Inn** (315-848-9992; Rte. 3) has a complete and reasonably priced menu for breakfast, lunch, and dinner, plus ice cream.

CENTRAL ADIRONDACKS

If you're entering the Adirondacks from Amsterdam or Gloversville, here are a couple of options for inexpensive food: in _Bleecker_, at **Hap's Tavern** (518-725-1652; County Rte. 125), don't let the parking lot — which may be bumper to bumper with pickups and motorcycles — dissuade you from stopping, especially if you're in the mood for good bar food. The restaurant itself is a quiet pink oasis offering tasty, well-prepared specials.

In _Caroga Lake_, go to **Lake's Log Cabin** (518-835-4009; Rte. 10) for simple, homemade food like soups and sandwiches for lunch and dinner; the **Talk of the Town** (518-835-8918; Rtes. 10/29A) has pizza, grinders, fried chicken and shrimp, sandwiches, and occasional specials like baked seafood on tap. If you're staying nearby, there's free delivery to cottages within three miles, and a modest charge for further afield. In _Rockwood_, at the very southern tip of the Adirondack Park, try the **Rockwood Tavern** (518-762-9602; Rtes. 29 & 10) for inexpensive lunches and dinners. Pizza, served all day, is the best around.

In _Wells_, stop at the **Country Kitchen** (518-924-3771; Rte. 30) for simple, low-priced fare brought to you with speedy service. The menu's long on fried foods, and desserts are huge. In _Speculator_, the **Café** (518-548-3020; Rte. 8, behind Speculator Department Store) offers good, homemade breakfasts and lunches and bakes terrific pies every day.

In _Long Lake_, the **Island Snack Bar** (518-624-2160; Rtes. 28/30, by the bridge) is a tidy little diner serving hearty breakfasts and good homemade soups and sandwiches for lunch. It's open well before the crack of dawn if you need a hot meal before fishing or hiking. Although it doesn't look like much from the outside, the **Cellar** (518-624-5539; Walker Rd.) serves great pizza and has a friendly atmosphere.

In _Old Forge_, the **Muffin Patch** (315-369-6376; Rte. 28) serves breakfast, lunch, and dinner in July and August and breakfast and lunch the rest of the year. Some top picks there are Belgian waffles with pecans and strawberries, the roast-pork club sandwich, spinach salad, and ice cream specialties like the pecan turtle sundae. For carry-out, don't miss the **Pied Piper** (315-369-6582; Rte. 28, near the Tourist Information Center); their broasted chicken is out of this world, and the roasted potatoes are pretty good too. The best burger in Old Forge can be found at **Slickers** (315-369-3002; Rte. 28, near the covered bridge); we also like the nachos with guacamole and salsa.

ADIRONDACK FOOD PURVEYORS

BAKERIES

Albo's Just Desserts (315-369-6505; Main St., Old Forge) Rich cheesecake, down-home pies and cookies, and breads, year-round.

Bluebird Bakery (518-623-3301; 200 Main St., Warrensburg) Chocolate-mousse cake, cinnamon rolls, cheese fans, almond pockets, eclairs, crullers, brownies, doughnuts. . . . The Bluebird has all that a pastry lover can ask for, and less — for those of us who crave sugary buns yet feel guilty about gobbling them down, there are Mini Meltaways, petite sweets in a small yet satisfying size. Open year-round; closed Mon.

Crown Point Bread Company (518-597-4466; 90 Buck Mountain Rd., Crown Point) True French country bread made in a wood-fired oven; available at the gas station in Crown Point or at the source, baker Yannig Tanguy's cabin in the forest.

The Donut Shop (315-357-6421; Rte. 28, Eagle Bay) A giant doughnut-shaped sign looms high above this drive-in on the edge of Eagle Bay, home of the best doughnuts in the central Adirondacks. A couple of hot cinnamon-and-sugar-dipped sinkers and a steaming cup of black coffee makes a terrific cheap breakfast. Open May–Oct.; closed Tues.

Evelyn's Bakery and Delicatessen (518-873-9256; Court St., behind the hardware store, Elizabethtown) A wonderful source for fresh breads, cookies, cupcakes, scones, muffins, and strudels, and a great place for a light meal. Sandwiches, quiches, soups, and cold salads (rice-and-bean and angel-hair pasta, for example) are excellent. Evelyn's is open for breakfast and lunch daily, and until 8pm Thurs.–Sat.

Great American Bagel Factory (518-523-1874; 9 Main St., Lake Placid) Big, fat, delicious bagels (though more expensive than you're likely to find elsewhere), deli sandwiches (stuffed with anything from mortadella to avocado slices), good salads, and occasional ethnic specials like chicken satay or baba ghanoush make this place an interesting stop for lunch or a take-out picnic. Allow plenty of time; unfortunately, the service can be inept.

Lake Flour Bakery (518-891-7194; 14 River St., Saranac Lake) Authentic, crusty baguettes; chewy semolina bread; strawberry-cheese, chocolate, and plain croissants; bagels; homemade ice-cream sandwiches. Open Mon.–Sat. winter; daily in summer.

On Lake Placid's Main Street, Leslie's has the most appetizing window displays.

Nancie Battaglia

Leslie's Placid Baked Goods (518-523-4279; 99 Main St., Lake Placid) With the most interesting window on Lake Placid's Main Street, Leslie's is a treat for the eyes, nose, and tastebuds: the display changes often, showcasing vintage clothing and antique toys interspersed with the cookies, cakes, and pies; intriguing smells are broadcast outdoors by a fan; the giant snickerdoodles, molasses crinkles, and chocolate-chip cookies are great to munch on when you're strolling. Closed Apr.

Lilly's Place (518-623-3194; 84 Main St., Warrensburg, at the Pillars) A tiny patisserie in two spotless former motel rooms, Lilly's has a couple of tables for lunch, or you can take out your chicken or spinach crêpe, ham-and-cheese croissant, Caesar salad, or fettuccine. The pastries are heavenly, with apple strudel and Linzer torte stand-out selections. If you'd like something with an Adirondack flavor, try the warm bread pudding smothered with raspberry sauce or maple syrup. Open daily year-round.

Nathan's Adirondack Bakery (315-369-3933; Crosby Blvd., Old Forge, around the corner from Old Forge Hardware) Nathan's is *the* place for wonderful, chewy bagels and bialys; the dense, crusty 8-grain bread is good, too. Cinnamon buns, sour-cream doughnuts (heaven!), bran muffins, pizza slices, and special-occasion cakes are highly recommended. Open weekends during the school year; daily in July & Aug.

A Piece of Cake (518-576-9943; Rte. 73, Keene, next to Evergreen Trading) Only a couple of years old and anxious to please. A Piece of Cake has a full range of deli items and makes very good sandwiches on unusual, chewy homemade veggie or whole-wheat rolls. Rockhill bread is available, along with elaborate cakes, tortes, and pies.

Spruce Mountain Bakery and Pizza (518-623-2911; Rte. 9, bet. Chestertown & Warrensburg) Seen from the highway, Spruce Mountain Bakery might not look too inviting, but do check it out. The Danishes and other gooey, sweet offerings are very good, and the light, buttery onion rolls are excellent. Real, crusty Italian bread is made every morning.

BREWPUBS AND MICROBREWERIES

Adirondack Trail Brewing Company (315-392-4008; Rte. 28, Alder Creek) Good light ales are made on the premises and likable food: barbecue ribs on Thurs. and fish fry on Fri.

Lake Placid Pub & Brewery (518-523-3813; 14 Shore Dr., across from the Mirror Lake beach) New in 1997, with a half dozen ales and beers, including very strong Ubu ale and a sweet amber brew. Lunch and light suppers are available; there's a deck overlooking Mirror Lake for summer sipping.

Lake Titus Brewery (518-483-2337; Rte. 30, Lake Titus) North of Paul Smith's College, on a deserted stretch of highway, is an old convenience mart that makes the tastiest beer in the Adirondacks. The setting is funky — you can sample a cold one at a picnic table in the parking lot — but the brew is worth a stop if you're in Saranac Lake or thereabouts. Try the pale ale or amber. Lake Titus beers are also sold at the Lake Flower Deli in Saranac Lake.

CANDY

The Candy Man (518-946-7270; Rte. 9, Jay; & Alpine Mini-Mall, Lake Placid) There are no shortcuts here, no high-tech approaches; the Candy Man even makes all the fillings in the Jay shop and covers them with a generous layer of chocolate. Dark chocolate, especially with coffee cream filling, is quite good. The sugar-free candies get high marks for tasting remarkably like the real thing. Open year-round; mail orders available.

Wagar's Confectionary (1-800-292-4277, 518-668-2693; 327 Canada St., Lake George) Don't miss this landmark if you're anywhere near Lake George. Wagar's has a wonderful old-time soda fountain and excellent chocolates. Adirondack Bear Claws — oblong hunks of dark or milk-chocolate-covered caramel spiked with giant cashews, almonds, or pecans — might be the best Adirondack invention of the 20th century. Almond-butter crunch and chocolate-dipped apricots are also good.

The Yum Yum Tree (518-891-1310; 46 Main St., Saranac Lake) Home of the Spirited Truffles, rich, buttery candies that come in Irish Coffee, Amaretto, Grand Marnier, Raspberry Schnapps, White Russian, and other flavors. The Yum Yum Tree also has a bakery counter offering croissants, breads, strudel, and rolls. For the truly chocoholic, there are chocolate-dipped chocolate chip cookies made on the premises. Open year-round; truffles can be shipped.

DELICATESSENS AND GOURMET SHOPS

Adirondack General Store (518-494-4408; 108 East Shore Dr., Adirondack) Some stores have little niches for reserved newspapers; the Adirondack General Store has slots for reserved pies. The pies are definitely worth asking for in advance, and they're practically no more expensive than the cardboard-box numbers at the Grand Union. Baker Joan Lomnitzer also makes dozens of different soups including tangy Reuben soup, excellent corn chowder, and spicy chili; the deli sandwiches are inexpensive and generous. Open year-round.

The Country Gourmet (518-576-2009; Rte. 73, Keene Valley) Tracy Whitney and Jane Martin have developed a unique and successful shop in the shadow of the High Peaks where they sell frozen homemade entrées like Orange Curry Chicken, Beef Bundles, and various casseroles. Meals are designed to feed three or four adults, need to be heated in a conventional oven, and cost about $3 per serving, depending on the ingredients. The Country Gourmet also has a full range of baked goods from tasty muffins and cookies to celebration cakes, plus frozen pizza dough, gourmet coffee beans, unusual pastas and sauces, and condiments. Closed Apr.

Kalil's Grocery (315-357-3603; Rte. 28, Inlet) This independent grocery makes splendid tabouli, hummus, cole slaw, and potato salad in its deli, and has authentic pita bread sent up from a Lebanese bakery in Utica. You can buy

The Country Gourmet puts together interesting gift baskets.

Nancie Battaglia

other great local products here, too: Garlic Burst Salsa made by Seventh Lake House and some truly incendiary hot sauce from the Red Dog Tavern.

Lakeview Deli (518-891-2101; 102 River St., Saranac Lake) Exceptional sandwiches, fresh salads, gourmet treats like spinach-artichoke dip, Lake Titus beer, Green Mountain coffees, sourdough bread, and exotic sodas are on tap at the Lakeview, just across the street from Lake Flower. Open year-round.

Village Meat Market (518-963-8612; Rte. 22, Willsboro) Great sandwiches; homemade breads, rolls, and doughnuts. Open year-round.

FARM MARKETS AND ORCHARDS

The **Lake Placid–Essex County Visitors Bureau** (518-597-4646; Bridge Rd., Crown Point) has published a brochure that lists dozens of farmstands, including a place in North Hudson where you can buy buffalo meat (Adirondack Buffalo Company; 518-532-9466; Blue Ridge Rd.). Most of the roadside stands are near Crown Point and Ticonderoga, in the temperate Champlain Valley.

The **Adirondack Farmers Market Cooperative** (518-298-3755; Box 136, Chazy) organizes several Adirondack Park locations for farmers' markets, which feature native-grown fruits and vegetables, honey, maple syrup, jams and jellies, herbs and herbal teas, and all kinds of flowers. In *Elizabethtown* the market is under a huge tent on the lawn in front of the Essex County Courthouse on Friday mornings, late May–late Sept. In *Lake Placid*, at the Horse Show Grounds on Rte. 73, the market is Sat. from 3–6pm, late June–late Sept. In *Port Henry*, the market is on Friday afternoons beginning the last week in June, on Main St. In *Ticonderoga*, look for the striped tent next to the Heritage Museum on Sat. mornings late June–late Sept. In *Westport*, market day is Thurs., starting at 10am, near the Inn on the Library Lawn, July–Sept.

Bessboro Orchards (518-962-8609; Rtes. 9N & 22, Westport) Lou Gibbs has worked hard to establish his small, high-quality orchard and offers many varieties of eating apples that he sells as they're picked. Open in fall.

Gunnison's Orchards (518-597-3363; Rte. 9N & 22, Crown Point) Honey from the bees that pollinate the trees, and all kinds of apples, including Spencer, Gala, Empire, Jonagold, and MacIntosh, are available right up until springtime at this impressive roadside orchard. Of course, October is the best time for a visit, but even if you're traveling the highway in the winter, stop in. Gunnison's will ship gift packs to anywhere in the country, in late fall. Open Mon.–Sat. year-round.

King's Apple Orchard (518-834-7943; Mace Chasm Rd., off Rte. 9, Keeseville) This orchard opens in August, offering Tydemans and other early apples; later on in the fall and through December, you can get Paula Red, MacIntosh, Cortland, Empire, and Red Delicious apples.

Ledgetop Orchards (518-597-3420; Lake Rd., off Rte. 22, Crown Point) Not too far from the Crown Point bridge, you pick your own sour pie cherries in July, gather drops from the apple orchard in the late September, and select the perfect jack-o-lantern at the farm stand in October. The stand offers Cortland, Empire, Red Delicious, MacIntosh, and Kendall (think of a crunchier Mac) apples beginning in early September.

Pray's Family Farms (518-834-9130; Rte. 9N, Keeseville) People come from miles around when the strawberries ripen at Pray's, usually in mid-June. Besides the berries (there are blackberries and raspberries, too), the roadside stand sells home-grown vegetables of all kinds, right up to pumpkin season. Check out the jack-o-lantern display around Halloween.

Rivermede (518-576-4386; Beede Rd., Keene Valley) Brown eggs, maple syrup from the farm's sugarbush, and fresh beans, broccoli, herbs, leaf lettuce, new potatoes, scallions, squash, tomatoes, carrots, and more come from this High Peaks area farm. Valley Grocery, in Keene Valley, often has Rivermede produce in its cooler.

Valley View Farms (518-585-9974/6502; Rte. 9N, Ticonderoga) Just south of the Ticonderoga Country Club you can enjoy another aspect of the country: pick-your-own strawberries mid- to late June, red raspberries in late July, and blueberries spanning both seasons. (Note that fruit ripening always depends on the weather; if spring is late and cold, it's best to call ahead to be sure the berries are ready for you.) There's also a farm stand with fresh vegetables open about June 20–late September.

HEALTH FOODS

Nori's Natural Foods (518-891-6079; 70 Broadway, Saranac Lake, near the post office) Recently expanded to encompass two storefronts, Nori's has a natural-food deli with daily lunch specials and excellent salads, plus all you'd expect from a good health-food store: bins of grains and flours; jugs of oil, honey, and maple syrup; and canisters of herbs line the walls. There's a selection of Kiss My Face lotions and insect repellents, plus a cooler full of North Country cheeses and organically grown vegetables. The bulletin board is a good source for checking out local alternative-lifestyle happenings. Open year-round.

MAPLE SYRUP

Upstate New York is a leading producer of high-quality maple syrup, and Adirondack syrup tastes no different from the Vermont stuff, which seems to get all the glory. Across the park, you can buy local syrup in craft shops, general stores, and farm stands; listed below you'll find a sampling of a few syrup processors who sell directly from their homes and sugarbushes. There are many more folks who make syrup, and they advertise that fact with a large lithographed tin sign showing a maple leaf.

If you'd like to learn about sap, taps, and boiling off, the *Uihlein-Cornell Maple Sugar Project* (518-523-9137; Bear Cub Rd., Lake Placid), a joint project of the New York State College of Agriculture at Cornell University and Henry Uihlein, is open most weekday afternoons from spring through fall. Admission is free; in Mar. & Apr., you can observe the entire process from the tree to the finished product. The Visitor Interpretive Center in Paul Smiths also has special maple-sugar season demonstrations.

Alstead Farms (Patrick Whitney; 518-576-4793; Alstead Hill Rd., Keene) Wholesale and retail Adirondack maple syrup, $1/2$ pint to 5-gallon drums.
Frog Alley Farm (518-576-9835, Rte. 73, Keene Valley) Retail maple syrup.
Leadley's Adirondack Sugar Bush (Jack Leadley, Sr.; 518-548-7093; Rte. 30, Speculator) Retail maple syrup.
Morningside Farm (Sandy and Frank Labar; 518-251-2694; Minerva) Retail maple syrup.
Toad Hill Maple Products (Randy Galusha; 518-623-2272; Athol) Syrup, sugar, and a complete line of maple-syrup-making supplies.

MEAT MARKETS

Doty's Country Road Beef House (518-891-3200; Lake Colby Dr., Saranac Lake) The folks at Doty's make excellent breakfast and Italian sausages, and offer a full variety of aged beef cuts, lamb, pork, and deli meats. Open year-round.
Jacobs & Toney (518-623-3850; 157 Main St., Warrensburg) The front of the building proclaims "Meat Store of the North," and the folks here pride themselves on prime beef cut to order, fresh pork, chicken, lamb, and home-made fresh sausage. Open year-round.

Oscar's smokes ham, sausage, turkey, fish, and cheese in its Warrensburg shop.

Nancie Battaglia

Oscar's Adirondack Mountain Smoke House (1-800-627-3431; 22 Raymond Lane, Warrensburg) For half a century, the Quintal family has been smoking up a storm — wonderful hams, sausages, cheese: in all, about 200 different smokehouse products — in a shop just off Warrensburg's main street. You can get smoked trout, boneless smoked chicken breast, smoked lamb, and eight kinds of bacon. Oscar's blends a variety of flavored cheese spreads, and the shop has gourmet crackers, condiments, and mixes. It's also a terrific butcher shop for fresh meat and bratwurst, weisswurst, knockwurst, all kinds of wieners and wursts. Open year-round; mail-order catalog available.

Shaheen's Super Market (518-359-9320; 252 Park St., Tupper Lake) A family-run store staffed by genuinely friendly folks who still carry grocery bags out to your car, Shaheen's is known for quality meats cut to order. Occasionally, homemade Lebanese specialties appear in the cooler; the kibbe is very popular and sells out within hours. Open year-round.

SPECIAL EVENTS: BARBECUES AND COMMUNITY SUPPERS

Throughout the Adirondacks, civic organizations, fire departments, historical societies, and church groups put on a variety of public suppers. Don't be shy! Visitors are welcome at these affairs, and furthermore, the food is generally cheap and delicious.

A North Country favorite is the chicken barbecue, with half chickens marinated in a tangy lemon-based sauce cooked outdoors over the coals. The trimmings are usually an ear of roasted sweet corn, potato salad, cole slaw or tossed salad, roll, watermelon wedge, and coffee; the price hovers around the $7 mark, less for kids' portions. There are also steak roasts, clambakes, pig roasts, and buffets. Listed below in chronological order are some of the annual feasts found in the Adirondacks; check local newspapers for more.

Newcomb Lions Club Chicken Barbecue (518-582-3211; Newcomb) At the Newcomb Town Beach, on Lake Harris, off Rte. 28N, first Sat. in July.

North Creek Fire Department Chicken Barbecue (518-251-2612; North Creek) At the North Creek Ski Bowl, off Rte. 28, first Sat. in July.

Keene Valley Fire Department Open House and Chicken Barbecue (518-576-4444; Keene Valley) At the firehall, on Market St., Keene Valley, fourth Sun. in July.

Newcomb Fire Department Steak Roast and Parade (518-582-3211; Newcomb) Rib-eye steaks, burgers, corn, hot dogs, and salads, at the Newcomb Town Beach, last Sun. in July.

Hague Fish & Game Club Barbecue (518-543-6353; Hague) At the fish and game club, off Rte. 9N, first Sat. in Aug.

Inlet Volunteer Hose Co. Chicken Barbecue (315-357-5501; Inlet) At the Fern Park pavilion, second Sat. in Aug.

Chilson Volunteer Fire Department Chicken Barbecue (518-585-6619; Ticonderoga) At Elks Field, Rte. 22, Ticonderoga, second Sun. in Aug.

Penfield Museum Heritage Day Chicken Barbecue (518-597-3804; Penfield Homestead Museum, Ironville) On the museum grounds, third Sat. in Aug.

Keene Fire Department Open House and Chicken Barbecue (518-576-4444; Keene) At the firehall, on East Hill Rd., last Sat. in Aug.

Plump Chicken Inn (518-251-2229; Minerva Historical Society, Olmstedville) Chicken and biscuits, homemade pickles and salads, real mashed potatoes, plus live music and costumed serving wenches, at Minerva Central School, in Olmstedville, last Sat. in Aug.

Lewis Volunteer Fire Co. Ox Roast (518-873-6777; Lewis) At the firehall on the last Sun. in Aug.

Indian Lake Pig Roast (518-648-5112; Indian Lake Volunteer Fire Dept., Indian Lake) Succulent roast pork and stuffing, steamed clams, homemade clam chowder, corn, and burgers, held at the Indian Lake firehall, on Rte. 28, Sat. before Labor Day.

Fire department barbecues offer inexpensive and satisfying family fare.

B. Folwell

Secret Recipe Chicken

Chances are if you asked a local grillmeister for the chicken barbecue sauce recipe, you'd be told it was a family heirloom not to be shared with casual visitors. Actually most of the Adirondack barbecues rely on variations of the Cornell University recipe; since 1949, the Poultry Science Department of the school has distributed close to a million copies of it. Below you'll find that secret marinade so that you can replicate smoky, lemony chicken at home.

> 1 cup good cooking oil
> 1 pint cider vinegar (some folks use lemon juice and vinegar)
> 3 TB salt (or less, to taste)
> 1 TB Bell's poultry seasoning
> $1/2$ tsp black pepper (or more, to taste)
> 1 egg

Beat the egg vigorously. Then add the oil and beat again to emulsify the sauce. Add other ingredients. Dunk chicken halves in the sauce and let marinate in the refrigerator for a few hours. While grilling over hot coals, baste each side.

The sauce will keep in the refrigerator for about a week. Enough for 8 to 10 half chickens. Leftover barbecued chicken makes superb chicken salad.

Bloomingdale Fire Department Field Day (518-891-3189; Bloomingdale) Chicken barbecue and games, held at the firehall, off Rte. 3, Sun. before Labor Day.

Westport Marina Labor Day Lobsterfest (518-962-4356; Washington St., Westport) Lakeside feeding frenzy at the Westport Marina, on the Sun. before Labor Day. Advance tickets are necessary.

Fish & Game Club Lobster and Clam Bake (518-532-7675; Schroon Lake). At the Fish and Game Club headquarters, second Sun. in Sept.

Raquette Lake Fire Department Clambake (315-354-4228; Raquette Lake) Ever wonder how to remove grit and sand from steamers? At the Raquette Lake Fire Department's annual bash, they run the clams through a commercial dishwasher. Advance tickets necessary; held on the second Sun. in Sept.

WINE AND LIQUOR STORES

You can purchase wine and liquor in numerous shops throughout the park. Some of the smaller places are adjacent to taverns, or even the owners' homes; you may have to ring a buzzer to have them open up for you. Note that New York State liquor stores are closed on Sundays; beer and wine coolers are available in grocery stores, although you can't buy either until after noon on Sunday.

A handful of shops stand out for their good selection of domestic and imported wines and knowledgeable staff. In *Lake Placid*, **Terry Robards Wines and Spirits** (518-523-9072; 243 Main St.) is worth a visit; Robards was a columnist for the *Wine Spectator*, and occasionally sponsors amusing dinners with wine tasting. If you're looking for a summery wine to go with a picnic, or a particular pressing from an obscure vineyard, he's the one to ask. Further south in the Adirondacks, in *Speculator*, Elizabeth Gillespie at **Speculator Spirits** (518-548-7361; Rte. 30) knows her grapes, and her tiny shop offers an astonishing variety of wines. In *Inlet*, talk to Walter Schmid at the **Wine Shop** (315-357-6961; Rte. 28, near the hardware store), for advice about great German, French, Australian, and domestic wines.

CHAPTER SIX

A Land for All Seasons
RECREATION

Adirondack woods and waters beckoned to 19th-century visitors with promises of a primeval wilderness overflowing with fish and game. City "sports" relied on the Adirondack guides to row them down lakes, lead them through forests in pursuit of deer or moose, cook them hearty meals, and finally tuck them into balsam-bough beds at night. The popular press swelled with accounts of these manly Adirondack adventures, and by the 1870s, the North Country was a great destination for thousands.

Nancie Battaglia

Fishing from an Adirondack guideboat is a classic way to spend a misty morning.

In those rough-and-tumble days, hunting and fishing were the prime recreational pursuits. Hiking through the woods was something done as a last resort: "[I]f there is one kind of work which I detest more than another, it is *tramping*; . . . How the thorns lacerate you! How the brambles tear your clothes and pierce your flesh!" wrote William H.H. Murray in his 1869 best seller, *Adventures in the Wilderness*. Boating was simply a method of transportation, to row from one campsite to the next or a necessary component of a hunting or fishing trip. Near the turn of the century, recreational canoeing swept the nation (the idea of using Native American watercraft for fun came over from England), and the Queen of American Lakes, Lake George, was the scene of jolly American Canoe Association meetings.

Hiking or mountain climbing for pleasure was a 19th-century notion that coincided with the growth of grand hotels across the Adirondacks. Walking in the woods — dressed in long skirts, shirtwaists, high boots, wool stockings, gloves, hats, and veils — was fine for ladies; they could hire their own guides, too, to take them up High Peaks or into pristine scenes. Hiking was healthful: breathing in pine-scented, ozone-laden air was regarded as a tonic for frail, dyspeptic, or consumptive patients.

With the advent of the automobile, recreation in the Adirondack Park changed. No longer were the lake country and High Peaks inaccessible to the masses; no longer did the exodus north take long days and large sums. Vacations were within reach of almost every working person, and with the help of a reliable Ford or Chevy, so were the Adirondacks. In the wake of this new, more democratic summer vacation approach, the huge hotels closed one by one, to be replaced by motels and housekeeping cabins. The New York State Conservation Department responded by creating car-camping havens under the pines.

Today in the Adirondack Park, whether you come for health, adventure, solitude, or just plain fun, you'll find that outdoor recreation opportunities are limited only by your imagination. Nowhere else east of the Mississippi is there such a variety of sport: wilderness canoeing, backcountry hiking, rock climbing, downhill and cross-country skiing, fishing, big-game hunting . . . the list goes on. If you want to get away from civilization, this is indeed the place; there are nearly three million acres of public lands to explore. In that regard, the Adirondack Park compares favorably to the national parks, and there's an added bonus: there's no entry fee when you cross the Blue Line. You may hike, bird watch, canoe, ski tour, or snowshoe in the forest preserve without having to buy a special permit.

If your taste runs to a round of golf, or watching a chukker of polo, you'll find those here, too. There are tour boats to ferry you around scenic lakes, and pilots to hire for flying high above the mountaintops. The park might also be regarded as the birthplace of two of the cornerstones of American popular culture: theme parks and miniature golf.

In this chapter you'll find descriptions of myriad diversions, along with suggestions on how to find the requisite gear, who to call for further details. What you won't find in this chapter are specific instructions on where to begin or end a particular hike, climb, or canoe trip; it's important that you take the responsibility to read guidebooks and study maps. Each season a few unprepared outdoors-folk become unfortunate statistics due to errors in judgment. The Blue Line encircles a wonderful park, but if you get lost, we can't "just turn the lights on" (as one urban dweller suggested to forest rangers involved in a search) to find you.

ADIRONDACK GUIDES

A n Adirondack woodsman "falls so to speak out of his log cradle into a pair of top boots, discards the bottle for a pipe, possesses himself of a boat and a jackknife and becomes forthwith a full-fledged experienced guide," wrote an observer in 1879. William H.H. Murray described guides thusly: "A more honest, cheerful, and patient class of men cannot be found the world over. Born and bred, as many were, in this wilderness, skilled in all the lore of woodcraft, handy with the rod, superb at the paddle, modest in demeanor and speech, honest to a proverb, they deserve and admire the admiration of all who make their acquaintance." Of course, not everyone agreed with him — one 19th-century writer declared "a more impudent, lazy, extortionate, and generally offensive class . . . would be hard to find" — but Murray's view became the popular ideal.

The Adirondack Guides' Association was established in 1891 as a backwoods trade union to adopt uniform pay for a day's work (then about a dollar a day), and follow the state's new game-protection laws. Nowadays, the Department of Environmental Conservation (DEC) licenses hundreds of men and women as guides for rock climbing, hunting, fishing, and whitewater rafting. Guides pass a written exam that tests woods wisdom and responses to weather and safety situations; they must also know first-aid and CPR.

There are several hundred guides who are members of a select group within the DEC-licensees: the New York State Outdoor Guides Association (NYSOGA). These folks make a point of preserving wild resources as well as helping clients find the right places for hunting, fishing, camping, and climbing; many guides practice low-impact camping and offer outdoor education.

Under the separate sports headings in this chapter, you'll find a sampling of licensed guides for different outdoor activities, but for a complete listing of all the NYSOGA guides and their specialties, you can contact Doris Herwig (PO Box 4704, Queensbury NY 12804).

BICYCLING

As the twentieth century draws to a close, bicycling is undergoing a true renaissance in the region. New publications and maps plus new trail systems provide the information that visitors have been waiting for. Highways, byways, and skidways offer challenges, variety, and great scenery for road and mountain bikers; May through October are the best months. In April, road bikers might find that the snowbanks are gone, but a slippery residue of sand remains on the road shoulders. Likewise, springtime backcountry cyclists might discover patches of snow in shady stretches of woods or stretches of muddy soup on sunnier trails. At the other end of the year, note that big-game season begins in October, and some of the best mountain-biking destinations are also popular hunting spots.

The most comprehensive book for cyclists is *25 Bicycle Tours in the Adirondacks: Road Adventures in the East's Largest Wilderness* by Bill McKibben, Sue Halpern, Barbara Lemmel, and Mitchell Hay (Countryman Press). It describes

Woods roads across the park make great mountain-bike trails.

Nancie Battaglia

loop trips in wonderful detail, with an eye toward scenic and historic destinations. Three free guides offer more riding options: **Historic Boquet River Bike Trails** (518-873-6301; Boquet River Association, Elizabethtown NY 12932) outlines excellent road trips with interesting historical stops; **Essex County Visitors Bureau** (518-523-2445; Olympic Center, Lake Placid NY 12946) has a selection of 25 backcountry bike trips of varying difficulty; and **Franklin County Tourism** (518-483-6788; Box 6, Malone NY 12953) publishes a brochure describing 15 off-the-beaten-path treks. Also, **Lake Champlain Bikeways** (518-597-4646; Visitor Center, Bridge Rd., Crown Point NY 12928) has identified a network of interconnected routes around the lake, with a map in progress. The Annual Guides published by *Adirondack Life* have listed dozens of bike trips; back issues are available (518-946-2191; Box 410, Jay NY 12941). For still more trip ideas, ask at regional bike shops.

If you'd like to join a group on a van-supported trip, **John and Jackie Mallery** (518-624-2056; Box 366, Long Lake) offer guided bike tours of selected North Country destinations. Also, **Sagamore Great Camp** (315-354-5411; Sagamore Rd., Raquette Lake) sponsors occasional mountain-bike weekends.

As mountain biking has become increasingly popular, the Inlet–Old Forge area has emerged as a center for the sport. Old Forge opened its extensive snowmobile trails to pedalers in 1996; call the **Central Adirondack Association** (315-369-6983, Main St., Old Forge NY 13420) for a map. Inlet is perched on the edge of the Moose River Recreation Area, which is laced with old logging roads, and in May and September there are mountain-bike weekends that attract hundreds of cyclists sponsored in part by **Mountain Man Outdoor Supply** (315-357-6672; Rte. 28, Inlet NY 13360). Also, lift-serviced biking is available at both of the New York State–owned ski areas, **Gore Mtn.** (518-251-2441; Peaceful Valley Rd., North Creek NY 12853) and **Whiteface Mtn.** (518-946-2233; Rte. 86, Wilmington NY 12997).

All-terrain bicycles are barred from wilderness and primitive areas in the Adirondack Park, but many wilderness hiking trails are inappropriate for bikes anyhow: too steep, too narrow, too wet, too rocky. In the state-land areas designated as wild forest, you'll find old logging roads that make excellent bike routes, and in most of these places, you'll find far fewer people.

Road cyclists will discover that many state highways have wide, smooth shoulders. You won't have to contend with much traffic in May and June or September and October except on weekends, but be aware that main roads become quite busy with all kinds of vehicles from log trucks to sight-seeing buses to RVs throughout the summer. Also, be prepared for any long trips: check topographical as well as highway maps for significant hills on your proposed route. Always carry plenty of water and a good tool kit. *Wear a helmet!*

BICYCLE DEALERS AND OUTFITTERS.

CHAMPLAIN VALLEY

Westport Cycle and Sport (518-962-8988; 125 Pleasant St., Westport) New and used bikes and repairs.

HIGH PEAKS AND NORTHERN ADIRONDACKS

Adirondack Adventure Tours (518-523-1475; 126 Main St., Lake Placid) Mountain bike rentals; guided bike trips; trip planning.
Barkeater Bicycles (518-891-5207; 15 Broadway, Saranac Lake) New and used bikes; repairs.

Rules of the Trail

- **Ride on open trails only.** Respect trail and road closures and avoid trespassing on private lands. Wilderness areas are closed to cycling.
- **Leave no trace.** Even on open trails, you should not ride under conditions where you will leave evidence of your passing. Practice low-impact cycling by staying on the trail and not creating any new ones. Pack out at least as much as you pack in.
- **Control your bicycle.** There is no excuse for excessive speed.
- **Always yield the trail** to hikers and others. Make your approach known well in advance; a friendly greeting or a bell works well.
- **Never spook animals**. Give them extra room and time to adjust to your presence; use special care when passing horseback riders.
- **Plan ahead**. Know your equipment, your ability and the area in which you are riding, and prepare accordingly. Be self-sufficient; carry the necessary supplies and tools you may need.

From the *International Mountain Bicycling Association*

Bear Cub Adventure Tours (518-523-4339; 30 Bear Cub Rd., Lake Placid) Guided mountain-bike trips.

High Peaks Cyclery (518-523-3764; Saranac Ave., Lake Placid) Road and mountain bike sales, repairs, and rentals.

Placid Planet (518-523-4128; Saranac Ave., Lake Placid) New and used bikes and repairs. Recommended.

NORTHWEST LAKES

World Cup Ski & Bike (518-359-9481; 58 Park St., Tupper Lake) Mountain and road bikes for sale and to rent; repairs.

CENTRAL ADIRONDACKS

Beaver Brook Outfitters (518-251-3394; Rte. 28, Wevertown) Mountain bike rentals.

Garnet Hill Lodge (518-251-2821; Thirteenth Lake Rd., North River) Mountain bike rentals for use on their trails only.

Mountainman Outdoor Supply Company (315-357-6672; Rte. 28, Inlet) Mountain bikes and gear for sale and rent; maps, guidebooks, outdoor clothing. Sponsors mountain-bike weekend in early fall.

Pedals & Pedals (315-357-3281; Rte. 28, Inlet) Bikes for sale and rent; repairs.

Sporting Propositions (315-369-6188; Rte. 28, Old Forge) Bikes for sale and rent; group rates available.

BEYOND THE BLUE LINE

There are two excellent bike shops in *Glens Falls*: **Inside Edge** (518-793-5676; 624 Upper Glen St.) and the **Bike Shop** (518-793-8986; Quaker Rd.). Just south of the park's boundary, in the Million Dollar Half Mile in *Lake George*, is **Syd and Dusty's Outfitters**, which rents mountain bikes (518-792-0260; Rte. 149, Lake George NY 12845). In *Plattsburgh*, **Wooden Ski and Wheel** (518-561-2790; Rte. 9, Plattsburgh NY 12901) is a professional shop for new bikes, tune-ups, and equipment.

BOATING

Scores of lovely Adirondack lakes have public launches for motor- and sailboats, operated by the New York State Department of Environmental Conservation, villages, or individual businesses; you'll find these clearly marked on regional road maps. Many state campgrounds (listed under "Camping" later in this chapter) have boat ramps. If you have a reserved campsite, there's no extra charge to launch a boat, and if you'd like to visit Lake Eaton, Buck Pond, or Eighth Lake, for example, you pay the day-use fee. Note also that

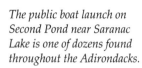

The public boat launch on Second Pond near Saranac Lake is one of dozens found throughout the Adirondacks.

Nancie Battaglia

motorboats (over 10 hp) and sailboats (longer than 18 feet) used on Lake George must have a permit, available from local marinas or the Lake George Park Commission (518-668-9347; Box 749, Lake George).

Marinas and boat liveries offer yet another chance for folks with trailers to get their boats in the water. Many more options are open to canoeists and kayakers who can portage their boats a short distance, so look under "Canoeing" for further information.

The *New York State Boater's Guide* contains the rules and regulations for inland waters, and is available from offices of the Department of Transportation. Some statewide laws for pleasure craft:

- You must carry one personal-flotation device for every passenger in your boat. Children under 12 are *required* to wear life jackets while on board.
- Any boat powered by a motor (even canoes with auxiliary small motors) and operated mainly in New York State must be registered with the Department of Motor Vehicles.
- When traveling within 100 feet of shore, dock, pier, raft, float, or an anchored boat, the speed limit is 5 mph. (Maximum daytime speed limits are 45 mph, and night time, 25 mph, although on many lakes with rocky shoals, or on water bodies which are also popular with non-motorized craft, lower speeds are prudent).
- Powerboats give way to canoes, sailboats, rowboats, kayaks, and anchored boats.
- The boat on your right has the right-of-way when being passed.
- Running lights *must* be used after dark.
- Boaters under 16 must be accompanied by an adult, or, if between 10–16 and unaccompanied, they must have a safety certificate from a NYS course.
- Boating under the influence of alcohol carries heavy fines and/or jail sentences.
- Littering and discharging marine-toilet wastes into waterways is prohibited.

Zebra Mussels

A tiny, striped mollusk from the Caspian Sea was accidentally introduced into Michigan's Lake St. Clair in the 1980s when a European freighter discharged its ocean-water ballast. From there, zebra mussels (*Dreissena polymorpha*) have been spread by recreational boaters to Lake Erie, Lake Ontario, and recently, Lake Champlain. Zebra mussels can clog water-intake pipes, attach themselves to navigational markers in such quantity that the buoys sink, and damage boat hulls. Beside affecting manmade objects, the non-native mussels have the potential to irrevocably change a lake's ecology. The mussels' free-swimming larvae are so small that thousands can be found in a boat's live well or cooling system and even bait buckets, and if these contaminated waters are released into lakes and rivers, the mussels may spread into new territory.

Canoes and car-top boats usually don't harbor the mussels because they're not left at anchor long enough for mussels to attach and because they don't carry water when transported from one lake to the next. Trailerable boats, especially inboards, pose a greater risk, but boat owners can minimize that by flushing the cooling system on land thoroughly before launching in a new lake, and rinsing the boat hull and trailer. To be doubly safe, you can use a mild bleach solution for the rinse, or let the boat and trailer dry out completely on a hot, sunny day.

BOAT LIVERIES AND MARINAS

Privately owned marinas and boat liveries offer a variety of services; complete listings are available from tourist-information booklets published by Warren, Essex, Clinton, Franklin, Fulton, Herkimer, and Hamilton counties (see Chapter Eight, *Information*). Listed below you'll find a sampling of places that may rent motorboats, sailboats, or canoes; offer gas, parts, and service for boat engines; or have deep-water launch ramps and overnight dockage.

LAKE GEORGE AND SOUTHEASTERN ADIRONDACKS

Lake George

Lake George Boat Rental (518-668-4828; Christie Lane, Lake George)
Castaway Marina (518-656-3636; Rte. 9L, Warner Bay)
Chic's Marina (518-644-2170; Rte. 9N, Bolton Landing)
Norowal Marina (518-644-3741; Sagamore Rd., Bolton Landing)
F.R. Smith & Sons (518-644-51811 Sagamore Rd., Bolton Landing)
Ward's Marina and Dockside Restaurant (518-543-8888; Rte. 9N, Hague)
Werner's Boat Rentals (518-543-8866; Rte. 9N, Silver Bay)

Loon Lake

Loon Lake Marina (518-494-3410; jct. Rtes. 8 & 9, Chestertown)

Schroon Lake

Maypine Marina (518-532-7884; off Rte. 9, Schroon Lake)

CHAMPLAIN VALLEY

Lake Champlain

Essex Marine Base (518-963-8698; off Rte. 22, Essex)
Essex Shipyard Point (518-963-7700; off Rte. 22, Essex)
Indian Bay Marina (518-963-7858; East Bay Rd., off County Rd. 27, Willsboro)
Snug Harbor Marina (518-585-2628; off Rte. 22, Ticonderoga)
Van Slooten Harbour Marina (518-546-7400; 140 S. Main St., Port Henry)
Westport Marina (518-962-4356; Washington St., Westport)
Willsboro Bay Marina (518-963-4472; Point Rd., off Rte. 22, Willsboro)

HIGH PEAKS AND NORTHERN ADIRONDACKS

Lake Placid

Lake Placid Marina (518-523-9704; Mirror Lake Dr., Lake Placid)
Captain Marney's Boat Rentals (518-523-9746; 3 Victor Herbert Rd.)

Saranac Lakes

Ampersand Bay Resort (518-891-3001; Ampersand Bay Rd., off Rte. 3, Saranac Lake)
Crescent Bay (518-891-2060; off Rte. 3, Saranac Lake)
Swiss Marine (518-891-2130; 7 Duprey St., Saranac Lake)

NORTHWEST LAKES

Big Tupper Lake

Blue Jay Campsite (518-359-3720; Rte. 30, Tupper Lake)
McDonald's Boat Livery (518-359-9060; Moody Bridge, Rte. 30, Tupper Lake)

Cranberry Lake

Cranberry Lake Boat Livery (315-848-2501; Rte. 3, at Robinson's IGA, Cranberry Lake)
The Emporium (315-848-2140; Rte. 3, Cranberry Lake)
Woods Adventure Rentals (315-848-5005) Water taxi service; motorboats to rent.

Fish Creek Ponds

Hickok's Boat Livery (518-891-0480; Rte. 30, Tupper Lake) Fish Creek Ponds and Upper Saranac Lake.

CENTRAL ADIRONDACKS

Big Moose Lake

Dunn's Boat Service (315-357-3532; Big Moose Rd., Big Moose)

Blue Mountain Lake

Blue Mtn. Lake Boat Livery (518-352-7351; Rte. 28)

Fulton Chain of Lakes (First through Eighth lakes)

Clark's Marine Service (315-357-3231; Rte. 28, Eagle Bay) On Fourth Lake.
Inlet Marina (315-357-4896; South Shore Rd., off Rte. 28, Inlet) On Fourth Lake.
Palmer Point (315-357-5594; off Rte. 28, Old Forge) On Fourth Lake.
Rivett's Marine Recreation & Service (315-369-3123; off Rte. 28, Old Forge) On First Lake.

Great Sacandaga Lake

Bobilin's Marina (518-661-5713; Lakeside Dr., Mayfield)
Edinburg Marina (518-863-8398; County Rte. 4, Edinburg)
Northampton Marine (518-863-8127; Rte. 30, Northville)
Park Marine Base (518-863-8112; Sacandaga Park, off Rte. 30, Northville)

Lake Pleasant

Lake Pleasant Marine (518-548-7711; Rte. 8, Lake Pleasant)
Lemon Tree (518-548-6231; Rte. 30, Speculator)

Indian Lake

Lakeside Marina (518-648-5459; off Rte. 30, Indian Lake)

Long Lake

Coddington's Boat House (518-624-2090; Rte. 30, Long Lake)
Deerland Marina (518-624-3371; Rte. 30, Long Lake)
Long Lake Marina (518-624-2266; Rte. 30)

Piseco Lake

Piseco Lake Lodge (518-548-8552; Old Piseco Rd., Piseco)

Raquette Lake

Burke's Boat Livery (315-354-4623; Rte. 28, Raquette Lake)
Raquette Lake Marina (315-354-4361; off Rte. 28, Raquette Lake)
South Bay Marina (315-354-4500; Rte. 28, Raquette Lake)

Stillwater Reservoir
Stillwater Shop and Boat Launch (315-376-2110; Stillwater Rd.)

BOAT TOURS

There are nearly 3,000 Adirondack lakes, ponds, and reservoirs to explore, but if you'd prefer not to be your own helmsman, practically every water body of significant size has a cruise vessel. Prices vary widely depending on the length of the tour, and what kind of frills come with it — music, dancing, and champagne, for example. The season generally runs from early May through October. Note that many of the boats are enclosed, so this is an activity you can try on a drizzly day. Regardless of whether you choose sunshine, clouds, or moonlight for your cruise, call ahead for a reservation.

LAKE GEORGE AND SOUTHEASTERN ADIRONDACKS
Lake George Shoreline Cruises (518-668-4644; Kurosaka La., Lake George) Several boats to choose from, including the adorable *Horicon*; narrated daytime and dinner cruises.

Lake George Steamboat Cruises (518-668-5777; Beach Rd., Lake George) Three enclosed boats, including the paddlewheeler *Minne-ha-ha*; narrated cruises; cocktail lounge; dinner cruises.

CHAMPLAIN VALLEY
Fort Ticonderoga Ferry (802-897-7999; Rte. 74, Ticonderoga) Inexpensive scenic trip across Lake Champlain.

The stern-wheeler Minne-ha-ha *heads out on a Lake George cruise.*

Nancie Battaglia

Lake Champlain Scenic & Historic Cruises (802-897-5331; Fort Ticonderoga, Ticonderoga) Operates the *Carillon*, which offers narrated tours near Fort Ticonderoga and longer cruises to Whitehall, NY, and Vergennes, VT.

Lake Champlain Ferries (518-963-7010; Rte. 22, Essex) Car ferry between Essex, NY, and Charlotte, VT, with hourly trips. Also, car ferry between Port Kent and Burlington with hourly trips. Passengers without cars are welcome (518-834-7960; Rte. 22, Port Kent).

HIGH PEAKS AND NORTHERN ADIRONDACKS

Lake Placid Marina Boat Tours (518-523-9704; Lake Dr., Lake Placid) Scenic trips on Lake Placid aboard the enclosed, classic wooden boats *Doris* (1950) and *Lady of the Lake* (ca. 1929).

CENTRAL ADIRONDACKS

Bird's Marina (315-354-4441; Rte. 28, Raquette Lake) Daily (except Sunday) rides on the mail-delivery boat.

Blue Mountain Lake Boat Livery (518-352-7351; Rte. 28, Blue Mtn. Lake) Cruises through the Eckford Chain of Lakes aboard two restored wooden launches, the *Neenykin* and the *Osprey*.

Dunn's Boat Service (315-357-3532; Big Moose Rd., Big Moose Lake) Tours of the setting of *An American Tragedy* aboard *Grace*, a beautiful inboard.

Norridgewock II (315-376-6200; Number Four Rd., Stillwater Reservoir) Tours on Stillwater Reservoir; access to Beaver River, the most isolated community in the park.

Old Forge Lake Cruises (315-369-6473; Rte. 28, Old Forge) Narrated 28-mile cruise on the Fulton Chain of Lakes aboard the *Uncas* or the *Clearwater*. Also offers weekend shuttles to Inlet from Old Forge for lunch or exploring town.

Raquette Lake Navigation Co. (315-354-5532; Pier I, Raquette Lake) Lunch, brunch, and dinner cruises — by reservation only — aboard the posh *W.W. Durant*.

BOWLING

Many of the Great Camps and swank 19th-century hotels featured open-air bowling; at Sagamore in Raquette Lake you can check out a truly rustic alley adorned with bark and twigs. Why not commemorate this continuing tradition with a gutter ball or two at a regional keglers' hall? Bowling isn't a bad option for a gloomy day, and most places offer drinks and snacks.

In *Lake George and Southeastern Adirondacks*, choices include **Lake George Bowl**, 518-668-5741; Rte. 9, Lake George, and the **Lake Luzerne Com-**

munity Center, 518-696-4545; 2505 Lake Ave., Lake Luzerne. For *Champlain Valley* towns, try **Adirondack Lanes**, 518-585-6077; Hague Rd., Ticonderoga or **Keeseville Bowling Center**, 518-834-7777; 4 Main St., Keeseville. Around the *High Peaks and Northern Adirondacks* lanes are found at the high-tech **Bowl Winkles** (518-523-7868; 340 Main St., Lake Placid); **Saranac Lake Bowling Alley**, 518-891-1860; 8 Bloomingdale Ave., Saranac Lake; and **Riverside Hotel and Bowling Alley**, 518-647-9905; Rte. 9N, Au Sable Forks. Rain or shine, in the *Northwest Lakes*, you can try the **Tupper Bowl**, 518-359-2234; Moody Rd., Tupper Lake.

CAMPS

Famous folks spent their summers at Adirondack camps: Vincent Price was a counselor at Camp Riverdale, on Long Lake; Bonnie Raitt is an alum of Camp Regis, on Upper St. Regis Lake; G. Gordon Liddy went to Brant Lake Camp; Arlo Guthrie and his mother, a dance instructor, enjoyed many seasons at a Raquette Lake camp.

Throughout the Adirondacks summer camps offer a wide range of programs. There are high-adventure canoeing, backpacking and rock-climbing camps, with emphasis on self-reliance in the wilderness. There are also very comfortable camps that offer nice cabins, good food, and fine-arts or technology programs. Some camps are truly Great Camps — in the architectural sense — housed in impressive vintage estates. And several camps offer family sessions so that everyone can share in the fun.

The following list is a sampling of summer camps with winter and summer addresses and phone numbers. Note that camps owned by the Boy Scouts of America are generally open only to members of certain troops; Girl Scout camps are usually open to all girls, with a modest fee to join as a scout (for insurance coverage). Likewise, YMCA camps are open to youngsters once they pay their dues.

If you're in the Adirondacks during July or August, and would like to visit a particular camp with your prospective happy camper, you should call ahead; also, many camps will send videos to give you a taste of the action.

LAKE GEORGE AND SOUTHEASTERN ADIRONDACKS

Adirondack Camp: Director Matthew Basinet; 518-547-8261; www.adirondackcamp.com; Box 97, Putnam Station NY 12861. Coed. Established in 1904 on the east side of Lake George. Wilderness trips, team sports, culinary arts, crafts, drama. Ages 7–15; 4-week session.

Brant Lake Camp: (Boys). Directors, Karen G. Meltzer, Robert Gersten, Richard Gersten; summer phone: 518-494-2406; Brant Lake NY 12815. Winter office: 212-734-6216; 1202 Lexington Ave., New York NY 10028. Established in 1917 and still run by the same family. Programs include a full range of team sports; water sports (canoeing, waterskiing, fishing, swimming, sailing); computers; crafts, music, photography, theater. Ages 7–15 in different divisions; 8-week session. Also, **Brant Lake Dance and Tennis Center for Teenage Girls** for ages 12–16; 4 weeks; and **Brant Lake Sports Center for Teenage Girls** highlighting basketball, soccer, softball, volleyball and tennis for ages 12–16; 2 weeks.

Camp Somerhill: Director, Lawrence Singer; summer phone: 518-623-9914; High St., Athol NY 12810. Winter office: 914-793-1303; 20 Huntley Rd., Box 295, Eastchester NY 10709. Coed; on private lake. Programs in athletics, science, horseback riding, creative arts, water sports; overnight backpack and canoe trips; flying lessons; trips to Boston, Montreal, and museums. Ages 7–17; 2–8 weeks.

Chingachgook on Lake George: Director, George W. Painter; summer phone: 518-656-9462; Pilot Knob Rd., Pilot Knob NY 12844. Winter office: 518-373-0160. Established in 1913 on the east side of Lake George; affiliated with the Capital District YMCA. Coed; program includes sailing, waterskiing, canoeing, hiking, arts, drama, team sports, ropes course. Ages 7–adult; 1–2 weeks. Also operates the **Lake George Family Sailing School**.

Double "H" Hole in the Woods Ranch: Executive Director, Max Yurenda; 518-696-5676; RR 2, Box 288, Lake Luzerne NY 12846. Established in 1993 on Lake Vanare. Coed; for children with cancer or blood-related diseases and/or neuromuscular impairments that preclude attending other camps. Horseback riding, ropes course, water sports; creative arts; children's farm; winter sessions with downhill skiing. Ages 6–16; 7–10 days.

Forest Lake Camp: Director, Garry Confer; 518-623-4771; Box 67, Warrensburg NY 12885; winter office: 908-534-9809; Box 648, Oldwick NJ 08858. Established in 1926. Horseback riding, water and team sports, theater, creative arts, wilderness trips. Sessions for boys and girls. Ages 8–16; 4 weeks.

Luzerne Music Center: Directors, Bert Phillips and Toby Blumenthal; 518-696-2771; Lake Tour Rd., Lake Luzerne NY 12846. Winter office: 1-800-874-3202; 7648 Ponte Verde Way, Naples FL 33942. Established in 1980. Coed; excellent chamber music program led by members of the Philadelphia Orchestra; recreation includes canoeing, whitewater rafting, team sports. Ages 10–18; 4 weeks. Also 1-week session for adults.

Point O' Pines Girls Camp: Directors, Sue and Jim Himoff; 518-494-3213; RR 1, Box 191A, Brant Lake NY 12815. Girls; on Brant Lake; 8-week session; team sports, gymnastics; dance, horseback riding, drama, fine arts. Ages 7–15; 8 weeks.

Skye Farm Camp and Retreat Center: Director, Debi Paterson; 518-494-3432; Sherman Lake, Bolton Landing NY 12814. Winter office: 518-494-7170; HCR 2, Box 103, Warrensburg NY 12885. Boys; girls; adults. Operated by United Methodist Church; full summer program for children; special fall hiking and canoeing weekends for adults; winter cross-country skiing and snowshoeing days. Ages 6–adult; 1 week.

Sonrise: Directors, Larry and Ruth McReynolds; 518-494-2620; PO Box 51, Pottersville NY 12860. Boys; girls; coed; adults. Lutheran; affiliated with Atlantic District Missouri Synod. On Schroon Lake; full program; conference center open year-round; Elderhostel sessions.

Word of Life: Director, Mike Calhoun and John Page; 518-532-7111; PO Box 600, Schroon Lake NY 12870. Sessions for girls; boys; coed; adults on an island and at a ranch. Non-denominational Christian camps and full-service conference center. Wide range of indoor, outdoor and team sports; horseback riding. Ages 6–13 at the ranch; 13–18 on the island; 1 week.

CHAMPLAIN VALLEY

Camp Dudley: Director, Wheaton Griffin; 518-962-4720; Camp Dudley Rd., Westport NY 12993. Established in 1885; the oldest boys' camp in the country. Affiliated with the YMCA but operated independently. On Lake Champlain; activities include water sports, hiking, backpacking, golf, soccer, arts, drama, photography, tennis. Ages 10–15; 4 weeks and 8 weeks.

Normandie: Director, Waldemar Kasriels; 518-962-4750; Furnace Point Rd., Westport NY 12993. Established in 1966; coed. Emphasis on water sports: water skiing, windsurfing, kayaking, canoeing, plus land sports and field trips. Ages 9–17; 2, 4, 6, and 8 weeks.

North Country Camps: Lincoln (Boys) and **Whippoorwill** (Girls). Directors, Peter Gucker and Nancy Gucker Birdsall; 518-834-5527; 395 Frontage Rd., Keeseville NY 12944. Established by the Gucker family in 1920. Strong wilderness program with backpacking, canoeing, sailing, horseback riding; in-camp programs in swimming, windsurfing, kayaking, soccer, science, crafts, dance, music, crafts. Ages 8–15; 5 and 7 $^1/2$ weeks.

Pok-O-MacCready Camps: Pok-O-Moonshine (Boys); **MacCready** (Girls); and **Pok-O-MacCready Outdoor Education Center** (Sept.–June). Director, Jack Swan; 518-963-8366 (summer camps); 518-963-7967 (outdoor center); Mountain Rd., Willsboro NY 12996. Winter office: 203-775-9865; Box 5016, Brookfield CT 06804. Established in 1905; on Long Pond. Summer sessions highlight horseback riding, sailing, backpacking, gymnastics, lacrosse, tennis, canoeing, rock climbing, archery, crafts, dance, drama. 6 weeks. During fall, winter, and spring, the campus is an outdoor education center for school groups, featuring traditional skills and crafts and earth studies. Nearby is the **1812 Homestead**, a hands-on historical site.

HIGH PEAKS AND NORTHERN ADIRONDACKS

Camp Colby: Director, Dan Capuano; 518-891-3373; Rte. 86, Saranac Lake NY 12983; winter: Department of Environmental Conservation, Room 505, 50

Taking the plunge at Camp Treetops, Lake Placid.

Nancie Battaglia

Wolf Rd., Albany NY 12233. Coed environmental-education camp for New York State teens. Hiking, canoeing, wildlife ecology, arts and crafts. 1 week.

Camp Treetops: Director, Brad Konkler; 518-523-9329; North Country School, PO Box 187, Lake Placid NY 12946. Established 1920; coed. Besides horseback riding, llama trekking, canoe-camping trips, rock climbing, sailing, and a full range of nature and arts programs, the camp is also a working farm, where kids take care of the animals and gardens. Ages 7–13; 7 weeks.

Eagle Island: Director, Amy Erickson; 518-891-0928; Eagle Island, Boat Rte. 863, Saranac Lake NY 12983. Winter office: Girl Scout Council of Greater Essex County, NJ, 201-746-8200; 120 Valley Rd., Montclair NJ 07042. Established in 1937. Sessions for girls, families, and women. Located on an island in a rustic Great Camp; strong program in water sports; open to non-Girl Scouts, too. Ages 8–17; 2 weeks.

Young Life Saranac Village: Director C. L. Robertson, 518-891-3010; HCR 1, Box 88, Saranac Lake NY 12983. Established in 1970; coed, non-denominational Christian camp for teens. Located in the rustic Great Camp Prospect Point. Programs include all water sports, team sports, Bible studies. 1 week.

NORTHWEST LAKES

Camp Regis-Applejack: Directors, Michael and Pauline Humes; 518-327-3117; PO Box 245, Paul Smiths NY 12970. Winter office: 914-997-7039; 107 Robinhood Rd., White Plains NY 10605. Coed; established 1946; Quaker philosophy. Based at a former estate on the shore of Upper St. Regis Lake; canoeing, kayaking, sailing, waterskiing; hiking; team sports; arts and crafts; photography; wilderness overnight trips for senior campers; excursions to Montreal, Cape Cod, and Maine. Ages 7–17; 4 weeks and 8 weeks.

Star Lake Computer Camp: Director, Dick Leroux; Star Lake SUNY Campus, Star Lake NY 13690. Winter office: 315-267-2167; Raymond Hall, SUNY,

Potsdam NY 13676. Coed. Campers explore the natural world around Star Lake, then create databases to develop a guidebook and map; outdoor activities include canoeing, hiking, camping. Ages 9–14; 1 week.

CENTRAL ADIRONDACKS

Camp Baco (Boys) and **Camp Che-Na-Wah** (Girls). Director, Robert Wortman; Lake Balfour, Minerva NY 12851. Winter office: 516-374-7757; 80 Neptune Ave., Woodmere NY 11598. Camp Baco established in 1923; on private lake. Activities include swimming, canoeing, sailing, waterskiing, tennis, lacrosse, mountain biking, photography, drama, music, crafts. Ages 6–16; 8 weeks.

Camp Mark Seven: Director, Fr. Thomas Coughlin; 315-357-6089; Fourth Lake, Old Forge. Winter: 301-933-1126; 306 Fallsworth Pl., Walkersville MD 21793. Coed; for deaf children, teens, and adults. Canoeing, camping, swimming, water skiing, team sports, arts and crafts. Emphasis on deaf culture and self images; session for children of deaf adults. Ages 10–20, adults and senior citizens; 1 and 2 weeks.

Camp Russell: 315-392-3290; Woodgate NY 13494. Winter office: 315-866-1540; Box 128, Herkimer NY 13350. Boys. Established in 1918; affiliated with General Herkimer Council Boy Scouts. Programs include water sports, forestry, riflery, overnight canoeing and camping trips. 1 week.

Cedarlands Scout Reservation: Director, Richard W. Bashant; 518-624-4371; Walker Rd., Long Lake NY 12847. Winter office: 315-735-4437; Oneida Council BSA, 1400 Genesee St., Utica NY 13501. Boy Scouts only. Water sports, crafts, overnight wilderness trips, outdoor skills, rock climbing, conservation. Ages 10–17; 1 week.

Deerfoot Lodge: Director, Charles Gieser; 518-548-5277; Whitaker Lake, Speculator NY 12164. Winter office: 518-966-4115; RD 2 Box 159B, Greenville NY 12083. Boys; non-denominational Christian camp. Activities include water sports, hiking, wildlife study, survival skills, overnight canoeing and camping trips. Ages 8–16; 2 weeks. Also **Tapawingo**, for girls, at Camp of the Woods; 518-548-5091; Rte. 30, Speculator.

4-H Camp Sacandaga: Director, James Tavares; 518-548-7993; Cornell Cooperative Extension; Page St., Speculator NY 12164. Winter office: 518-853-3471; Cooperative Extension, PO Box 1500, Fonda NY 12068. Coed; established in 1945; originally a Civilian Conservation Corps camp. Programs include environmental education, creative arts, horseback riding, sailing, water sports. Campers need not be current 4-H members. Ages 8–19; 1 week.

Fowler Camp and Conference Center: Director, Kent Busman; 518-548-6524; Sacandaga Lake, Speculator NY 12164. Winter office: 518-374-4573; 1790 Grand Blvd., Schenectady NY 12309. Coed; established 1954. Affiliated with the Reformed Church in America. Water sports, hiking, crafts, nature study, overnight canoeing and camping trips. Late summer and fall sessions for adults in Adirondack history and environment. Ages 9–18; 1 week.

CAMPING

Sleeping under the stars on a remote island, in the bugless confines of a recreational vehicle, or nestled within the cozy comfort of a backpacking tent deep in the forest — camping possibilities in the Adirondacks cater to all tastes. The Department of Environmental Conservation (DEC) operates 40-some public campgrounds, most of which are on beautiful lakes or peaceful ponds, and all of which are open from Memorial Day through Labor Day. Many campgrounds open earlier, and some stay in operation late into the fall. Most state campgrounds now have informative brochures showing individual sites and local services, which can be found in nearby towns or by contacting the publisher (315-768-7137; Box 1, New York Mills NY 13417).

The smaller places (those with 100 sites or fewer) tend to be quieter; some campgrounds accommodate upwards of 400 groups and can resemble little cities in the woods. However, camping in the North Country is still very much a family experience. The only hassles you may encounter might be from persistent chipmunks and red squirrels who regard your cooler as their lunch counter.

Facilities at state campgrounds include a picnic table and grill at each site, water spigots for every 10 sites or so, and lavatories. Not every campground has showers. Many facilities have sites for mobility-impaired campers, with hard-surface areas, water spigots at wheelchair height, and ramps to restrooms.

Camping is also permitted year-round on state land, but you need a permit to stay more than three days in one backcountry spot or if you are camping in a group with more than 10 people. These permits are available from local forest rangers. Some locations such as Stillwater Reservoir, Lows Lake, or Lake Lila have designated primitive camping spots with fire rings and/or privies,

Canoeing is a great way to explore the Adirondacks, and many state campsites are located on quiet lakes or ponds.

Nancie Battaglia

but you may camp elsewhere provided you pitch your tent at least 150 feet from any trail, stream, lake, or other water body. (Check the information on low-impact camping, below.) Also, along the Northville–Lake Placid Trail and on popular canoe routes you'll find lean-tos for camping. These three-sided log structures are a trademark of the Adirondack wilds. A handy guide with useful tips for family trips as well as destinations is Barbara McMartin's book *Adventures in Backpacking* (North Country Books, 1996).

Reservations can be made for a site in the state campgrounds by calling **Park.Net** (1-800-456-CAMP), a computerized reservation service, but by all means check out their Worldwide Web page (www.Park-Net.com). It shows amazing detail for every state campground, so you can see for yourself if site #4 at Lake Durant is on the water. (It is.) You can reserve a place for a single night or as long as three weeks and charge it to your credit card. DEC campgrounds will cheerfully take you on a first-come, first-served basis if space is available; before July 4 and after September 1, it's usually easy to find a nice site without a reservation. Campsites cost about $10-$15 per night in 1997; the reservation fee is $7.50.

DEC public campgrounds do not supply water, electric, or sewer hook-ups for recreational vehicles; for these amenities, there are privately owned campgrounds in many communities. Check Chapter Five, *Lodging*, for these facilities. Also, some towns offer public camping; check with local tourist-information offices, listed in Chapter Eight, *Information*.

PUBLIC CAMPGROUNDS

LAKE GEORGE AND SOUTHEASTERN ADIRONDACKS

Eagle Point (518-494-2220; U.S. Rte. 9, 2 mi. N. of Pottersville) 3-day minimum stay for reserved sites; boat launch; showers; swimming.

Hearthstone Point (518-668-5193; Rte. 9N, 2 mi. N. of Lake George Village) On Lake George. 3-day minimum for reserved sites; showers; swimming.

Lake George Battleground (518-668-3348; Rte. 9, $^1/_4$ mi. S. of Lake George Village) Historic site. 3-day minimum for reserved sites; showers. Easy walk to downtown and tour boat docks.

Lake George Islands (518-644-9696; numerous sites on Narrows Islands, Glen Islands, Long Islands) Access by boat; tents only; swimming. No dogs allowed.

Luzerne (518-696-2031; off Rte. 9N, Lake Luzerne) On Fourth Lake. 3-day minimum for reserved sites; showers; swimming; canoe and rowboat launch; no powerboats allowed.

Rogers Rock (518-585-6746; Rte. 9N, 3 mi. N. of Hague) On Lake George. Historic site. 3-day minimum for reserved sites; boat launch.

A peaceful tent site under the pines near Long Lake.

Nancie Battaglia

CHAMPLAIN VALLEY

Ausable Point (518-561-7080; Rte. 9, N. of Port Kent) On Lake Champlain. 3-day minimum for reserved sites; showers; swimming; boat launch. Near wildlife refuge; good place to explore by canoe.

Crown Point Reservation (518-597-3603; off Rte. 9N, near the bridge to Vermont) On Lake Champlain. Showers; boat launch. Across from fort.

Lincoln Pond (518-942-5292; County Rte. 7, 6 mi. S. of Elizabethtown) 3-day minimum for reserved sites; swimming; showers; canoe or rowboat rentals; no powerboats allowed.

Paradox Lake (518-532-7451; Rte. 74, 2 mi. E. of Severance) Swimming; showers; canoe or rowboat rentals; boat launch.

Poke-O-Moonshine (518-834-9045; Rte. 9, 6 mi. S. of Keeseville) Showers; access to hiking and rock climbing on Poke-O-Moonshine Mountain.

Putnam Pond (518-585-7280; off Rte. 74, 6 mi. W. of Ticonderoga) Swimming; showers; canoe or rowboat rentals; boat launch.

Sharp Bridge (518-532-7538; Rte. 9, 15 mi. N. of Schroon Lake) Showers; access to Hammond Pond Wild Forest.

HIGH PEAKS AND NORTHERN ADIRONDACKS

Buck Pond (518-891-3449; off Rte. 30 near Onchiota) Swimming; showers; canoe or rowboat rental; boat launch.

Lake Harris (518-582-2503; Rte. 28N, Newcomb) Swimming; showers; boat launch.

Meacham Lake (518-483-5116; Rte 30, 9 mi. N. of Paul Smiths) Swimming;

The Bear Truth

As humans have become enamored of sleeping out in the wilds, some wild animals have learned to recognize coolers, packs, and tents as potential food sources. Hungry black bears or pesky raccoons may not be in evidence when you set up camp, but it's best to take all precautions. If your site has a metal locker for food storage, use it. Otherwise, stash your supplies and cooking gear well away from your tent: put it in a pack or strong plastic bags and suspend it between two trees with a sturdy rope at least 20 feet off the ground. Tie it off by wrapping several times around one tree and tie a complicated knot; bears have been known to swat down food stashes within their reach, climb saplings, and even bite through ropes. Don't try to outsmart bruin by putting your food in an anchored boat away from shore; bears swim well. The campsite caretaker can give you an update on the bear situation.

If a bear does visit your camp, loud noises (yelling, banging on pots, loud whistles) usually discourage it. Attacks are extremely rare in the Adirondacks; do keep your dog under control in the event of a close encounter of the ursine kind.

---

showers; horse trails and barn; some primitive sites accessible by foot only; boat launch.

Meadowbrook (518-891-4351; Rte. 86 near Ray Brook) Showers, no swimming. Closest campground to downtown Lake Placid.

Saranac Lake Islands (518-891-3170; off Rte. 3 S.W. of Saranac Lake Village) Access by boat; tents only.

Taylor Pond (518-647-5250; Silver Lake Rd., 9 mi. N.W. of Au Sable Forks) Boat launch.

Wilmington Notch (518-946-7172; Rte. 86, Wilmington) On the West Branch of the Ausable River. Great area for fly fishing.

NORTHWEST LAKES

Cranberry Lake (315-848-2315; off Rte. 3, 1 mi. S. of Cranberry Lake Village) 2-day minimum stay for reserved sites. Swimming; showers; rowboat or canoe rentals.

Fish Creek Pond (518-891-4560; Rte. 30, 12 mi. E. of Tupper Lake) 3-day minimum for reserved sites. Swimming; showers; canoe or rowboat rentals; boat launch; nature and Beginner Camper programs.

Rollins Pond (518-891-3239; Rte. 30, near Fish Creek Pond campsite) 3-day minimum for reserved sites. Showers; canoe/rowboat rentals; boat launch.

CENTRAL ADIRONDACKS

Alger Island (315-369-3224; off South Shore Rd., W. of Inlet) 2-day minimum stay for reserved sites; on Fourth Lake; access by boat; tents only.

Browns Tract Ponds (315-354-4412; Uncas Rd. W. of Raquette Lake) 2-day minimum for reserved sites. Swimming; canoe or rowboat rentals; no powerboats allowed.

Caroga Lake (518-835-4241; Rte. 29A S. of Caroga Lake) 2-day minimum for reserved sites. Swimming; showers; boat launch.

Eighth Lake (315-354-4120; Rte. 28, between Raquette Lake and Inlet) 3-day minimum for reserved sites. Swimming; showers; canoe or rowboat rentals; boat launch.

Forked Lake (518-624-6646; North Point Rd., off Rte. 30 near Long Lake) 2-day minimum. Primitive walk-in or canoe-in sites; launch for cartop boats.

Golden Beach (315-354-4230; Rte. 28, 3 mi. E. of Raquette Lake) On Raquette Lake; swimming; showers; boat or canoe rentals; boat launch.

Indian Lake Islands (518-648-5300; off Rte. 30, 11 mi. S. of Indian Lake hamlet) 3-day minimum for reserved sites; access by boat; tents only; boat launch.

Lake Durant (518-352-7797; Rte. 28/30, 3 mi. E. of Blue Mtn. Lake) 3-day minimum for reserved sites. Swimming; showers; canoe rentals; boat launch; handicap-access campsite.

Lake Eaton (518-624-2641; Rte. 30, 2 mi. N. of Long Lake bridge) 2-day minimum for reserved sites. Swimming; showers; canoe or rowboat rentals; boat launch.

Lewey Lake (518-648-5266; Rte. 30, across from Indian Lake Islands access) 2-day minimum for reserved sites. Swimming; showers; canoe or rowboat rentals; boat launch.

Limekiln Lake (315-357-4401; Limekiln Lake Rd., off Rte. 28 E. of Inlet) 2-day minimum stay for reserved sites. Swimming; showers; canoe or rowboat rentals; boat launch.

Little Sand Point (518-548-7585; Piseco Lake Rd., off Rte. 30, Piseco) 2-day minimum for reserved sites. On Piseco Lake; swimming; canoe or rowboat rentals; boat launch.

Moffit Beach (518-548-7102; off Rte. 8, 4 mi. W. of Speculator) 3-day minimum for reserved sites. On Sacandaga Lake; swimming; showers; canoe or rowboat rentals; boat launch.

Northampton Beach (518-863-6000; Rte. 30, 2 mi. S. of Northville) 3-day minimum for reserved sites. On Great Sacandaga Lake; swimming; showers; canoe or rowboat rentals; boat launch.

Point Comfort (518-548-7586; Piseco Lake Rd., Piseco) 2-day minimum for reserved sites. On Piseco Lake; swimming; showers; canoe or rowboat rentals; boat launch.

Poplar Point (518-548-8031; Piseco Lake Rd.) 2-day minimum for reserved sites. On Piseco Lake; swimming; canoe or rowboat rental; boat launch.

Sacandaga (518-924-4121; Rte. 30, 4 mi. S. of Wells) 2-day minimum for reserved sites. On Sacandaga River; swimming; showers; no powerboats.

Tioga Point (315-354-4230; Raquette Lake) 2-day minimum for reserved sites. On Raquette Lake; access by boat; some lean-tos, although it's best to bring a tent.

CANOEING AND KAYAKING

Paddlers agree: the Adirondack Park offers some of the best canoeing and kayaking in the Northeast. Some might argue that the region rivals the Boundary Waters Canoe Area in Minnesota for excellent backcountry tripping. For thrill seekers, there's *serious* whitewater (up to Class V) on the Upper Hudson, the Moose, portions of the Schroon, and other rivers; for flatwater fans, there are long trips linking lakes, such as the 44-mile route from Long Lake to Tupper Lake, the 35-mile trip from Old Forge to Blue Mtn. Lake, or the 25-mile trip from Osgood Pond to Lake Kushaqua. In the St. Regis Canoe Area it's possible to paddle for weeks on end and visit a different pond or lake each day. There's even a 3-day race, the Adirondack Canoe Classic, that covers 90 miles of water in a long diagonal from the Fulton Chain of Lakes to Saranac Lake village (see the listing under "Annual Events" in this chapter).

Given that the possibilities seem unlimited, you may wonder how a newcomer chooses where to go. Three guidebooks cover Adirondack destinations for human-powered watercraft: *Adirondack Canoe Waters: North Flow* by Paul Jamieson and Donald Morris (Adirondack Mountain Club); *Adirondack Canoe Waters: South and West Flow* by Alec Proskine (Adirondack Mountain Club); and *Fun on Flatwater: Family Adventures in Canoeing* by Barbara McMartin (North Country Books). Both *Adirondac* and *Adirondack Life* magazines frequently publish articles describing canoe trips; check a local library for back

Peaceful, island-studded lakes are ideal for paddling.

Nancie Battaglia

issues or contact the publications (listed in Chapter Eight, *Information*). There's also a fine topo sheet, *Adirondack Canoe Waters*, published by Adirondack Maps, in Keene Valley, that shows several routes; it's available in regional bookstores and sporting goods stores.

The Department of Environmental Conservation (518-891-1200; Rte. 86, Ray Brook NY 12970) has recently revised its series of pamphlets that describe various canoe routes including the Bog River area near Tupper Lake, Stillwater Reservoir, and many others; ask for *Adirondack Canoe Routes* or the "official map and guide" of the area you wish to paddle. The excellent 24-page booklet *Guide to Paddling Adirondack Waterways* is available by calling 1-800-487-6867. Canoeing on Niagara Mohawk Power Company's impoundments on the Beaver, Raquette, Sacandaga, and Oswegatchie rivers is outlined in a free brochure available at information booths or by calling NiMo (315-474-1511). Some tourist information offices, such as the Saranac Lake Chamber of Commerce (518-891-1990), offer useful brochures and maps, too; ask for *Canoe Franklin County*. Note that these brochures and simplified maps are not suitable for navigating; always consult U.S. Geological Service topographic maps for the area you're traveling through.

When you're planning for any trip, allow an extra day in case the weather doesn't cooperate. Remember that you're required to carry a life jacket for each paddler; lash an extra paddle in your canoe, too. Bring plenty of food and fuel, a backpacker stove, and rain gear. A poncho makes a good coverall for hiking, but you're far better off with rain jacket and pants in a canoe, since a poncho can become tangled if you should dump the canoe. Do sign in at the trailhead registers when you begin your trip.

If you're still overwhelmed by making a decision about where to go, consult one of the outfitters or guides listed below. (These are folks specializing in canoeing or kayaking and offer good-quality equipment; many boat liveries and marinas also rent aluminum or Coleman canoes.) And if you're anxious to try canoeing, but just aren't sure of your abilities, there are plenty of places where you can get lessons in flatwater or whitewater techniques. Your local Red Cross office may schedule water safety courses and basic canoe instruc-

---

Don't Drink the Water

The cool, clear water may seem like the ideal thirst quencher, but please resist the temptation to drink freely from Adirondack lakes, rivers, ponds, and streams. Sadly, due to careless campers and occasional animal pollution, these wild waters may harbor a microscopic parasite known as *Giardia lamblia*, which can cause bloating, diarrhea, cramping, and vomiting. Giardiasis — also known as Beaver Fever — is easily diagnosed (with a stool sample) and treated (with quinicrine or Flagyl), but it's better to avoid the ailment in the first place. Practice good campsite sanitation. Treat all drinking water by boiling 10 minutes, by using a specially designed giardia-proof filter, or with chlorine or iodine tablets.

tion, or you can contact the Tri-Lakes office of the American Red Cross (518-891-3280; 52 Broadway, Saranac Lake NY 12983) for workshop dates.

CANOE OUTFITTERS AND TRIP GUIDES

LAKE GEORGE AND SOUTHEASTERN ADIRONDACKS

Adirondack Mountain Club (518-668-4447; Luzerne Rd., Lake George) Spring, summer, and fall canoe workshops in different locations; guided canoe tours for women, youth, and Elderhostel groups.

W.I.L.D./W.A.T.E.R.S. (518-494-7478; Rte. 28, The Glen) Canoe and kayak instruction for youth and adults; whitewater clinics; kayak camp for youth; lodging available.

HIGH PEAKS AND NORTHERN ADIRONDACKS

Adirondack Rock and River Guide Service (518-576-2041; Alstead Hill Rd., Keene) Whitewater kayaking instruction; guided trips; lodging.

All Seasons Outfitters (518-891-3548; 168 Lake Flower Ave., Saranac Lake) Guided day and overnight canoe trips; flatwater canoe lessons; complete trip outfitter.

Bear Cub Adventure Tours (518-523-4339; 30 Bear Cub Rd., Lake Placid) Whitewater canoe and kayak instruction; guided trips.

Birchbark Tours (518-891-5704; 32 Glenwood, Saranac Lake) Guided canoe trips.

Jones Outfitters Ltd. (518-523-3468; 37 Main St., Lake Placid) Canoe rentals and sales.

Middle Earth Expeditions (518-523-9572; Rte. 73, Lake Placid) Guided wilderness trips.

Tahawus Guide Service; 518-891-4334; Box 424, Lake Placid) Guided canoe and traditional guideboat trips.

Young's Foothills (518-891-1221; Box 345, Saranac Lake) Guided canoe trips.

NORTHWEST LAKES

Adirondack Canoes and Kayaks (518-359-2174, 1-800-499-2174; Rte. 3, Tupper Lake) Rentals, tours, paddling instruction.

McDonnell's Adirondack Challenges (518-891-1176; Rte. 30, Lake Clear) Complete year-round outfitter and guide service.

Northern Pathfinders (1-800-882-PATH; Box 214, Lake Clear) Guided canoe trips; shuttle service.

Raquette River Outfitters (518-359-3228; Rte. 30, Tupper Lake) Complete trip outfitter; guided trips; car shuttles.

St. Regis Canoe Outfitters (518-891-1838; Floodwood Rd., Lake Clear) Trip outfitter; guided trips; canoe instruction; car shuttles.

CENTRAL ADIRONDACKS

Blue Mountain Outfitters (518-352-7306/352-7675; Box 144, Blue Mtn. Lake) Complete trip outfitter; guided trips; car shuttles; sporting goods shop; canoe rental and sales.

Free Spirit Adventures (518-924-9275; Rte. 30, Wells) Kayaks, canoes, and outdoor gear. Guided paddling trips — even in winter!

Moose River Company (315-369-3682; Main St., Old Forge) Guided trips.

Mountainman Outdoor Supply Company (315-357-6672; Rte. 28, Inlet) Kayaks, canoes, camping gear, books, maps.

Old Forge Outfitters (315-369-6699; at Whitewater Challengers, Rte. 28, Old Forge) Whitewater and touring kayaks; lessons; rentals.

Stillwater Shop (315-376-2110; Stillwater Rd., Stillwater Reservoir) Canoe rentals; camping supplies for sale.

Tickner's Moose River Canoe Outfitters (315-369-6286; off Rte. 28, Old Forge) Complete trip outfitter; canoe instruction; canoe rentals and sales; special River and Rail excursion with Moose River paddle and return via the Adirondack Scenic Railroad.

DIVING

No amount of wishful thinking could turn the chilly Adirondack depths into crystal-clear Caribbean seas, but there is plenty to discover beneath the waves in Lake George. In fact, it's the site of New York's first underwater heritage preserve and home to numerous 18th- and 19th-century shipwrecks; request the guide for *The Sunken Fleet of 1758* from local tourism offices or the conservation department (518-897-1200) to learn more. **Batteaux Below**, a maritime historic preservation group (518-587-7638) sponsors an annual underwater weekend in the fall; past speakers have included Clive Cussler, author of *Raise the Titanic*.

Rentals, instruction, and air service are available at **Divers' World** (518-644-2094; Rte. 9N, Bolton Landing), **Lake George SCUBA Center** (518-798-4486, Bay Rd., Lake George), **Northern Lake George Resort** (518-543-6528; Rte. 9N, Silver Bay), and **Ward's Dockside Marina** (518-543-8888, Rte. 9N, Hague).

FAMILY FUN

Besides countless pristine natural attractions, the Adirondack Park offers plenty of manmade amusements and privately owned curiosities. Ausable Chasm, a spectacular gorge of carved sandstone cliffs near the park's northeastern corner, is one of the country's oldest tourist meccas, dating back to 1870. Since the 1930s, visitors have filled their pockets with glittering garnets at the Barton Mines tour. Santa's Workshop, near Whiteface Mountain, is the oldest theme park in the world, dating back to 1946, and it is *the* place to mail your Christmas cards from since the postmark reads "North Pole, NY." Frontier Town, near North Hudson, combines Adirondack historic sites, like a working iron forge and a gristmill, with Wild West zest. On the other end of the spectrum, there are new-wave fun parks with towering water slides and pools that generate their own whitecaps.

You'll find miniature-golf courses listed under a separate heading, Olympic spectator events outlined under "Olympic Sports," and annual races and competitions later in this chapter. Described below is a potpourri of places to go and things to do.

Price Code

Adult Admission:	Inexpensive	Moderate	Expensive
(Children's tickets are less.)	**under $8**	**$9-$15**	**over $15**

LAKE GEORGE AND SOUTHWESTERN ADIRONDACKS

Natural Stone Bridge & Caves (518-494-2283; Stone Bridge Rd., Pottersville) 5 caves; stone archway; mineral shop. Open daily Memorial Day–Columbus Day. Inexpensive.

Water Slide World (518-668-4407; Rtes. 9 & 9L, Lake George) Wave pool; water slides; bumper boats. Daily mid-June–Labor Day. Expensive.

House of Frankenstein Wax Museum (518-668-3377; Canada St., Lake George) From the Phantom of the Opera to modern horrors. Open daily Memorial Day–Columbus Day. Inexpensive.

Magic Forest (518-668-2448; Rte. 9, Lake George) Rides and games, entertainment, Santa's Hideaway. Open Memorial Day–Labor Day. Moderate.

Movieworld Wax Museum (518-668-3077; Canada St., Lake George) Elvis and Batman in the lobby; lots of other wax figures and movie memorabilia. Open Memorial Day–Labor Day. Inexpensive.

CHAMPLAIN VALLEY

Ausable Chasm (518-834-7454; Rte. 9, Ausable Chasm) Deep gorge, known as a tourist attraction since the 1870s; boat ride. Daily mid-May–mid-Oct. Moderate.

Frontier Town (518-532-7181; off exit 29 of I-87; North Hudson) Wild West theme park; historic exhibits. Daily Memorial Day–Labor Day. Moderate to Expensive.

At North Pole, New York,
Santa is always in season.

Nancie Battaglia

HIGH PEAKS AND NORTHERN ADIRONDACKS

High Falls Gorge (518-946-2278; Rte. 86; Wilmington) Waterfalls on the Ausable River. July–Aug. Moderate.

Santa's Workshop (518-946-2212; Rte. 431, Wilmington) Reindeer; craft demonstrations; Santa; rides. Daily Memorial Day–Columbus Day; some winter weekends. This is the only place in the Adirondacks where you can buy a personalized magic wand. Moderate.

Whiteface Mountain Chairlift Ride (518-946-2223; Rte. 86, Wilmington) Recommended for fall foliage. Late June–Columbus Day. Inexpensive.

CENTRAL ADIRONDACKS

Adirondack Scenic Railroad (315-369-6290; Rte. 28, Thendara) Excursions from Thendara to Minnehaha or Carter Station, about 4 and 6 miles, respectively. Train robberies, Halloween ride, other special events. May–Nov. Inexpensive.

On a hot day, nothing's cooler than the water slide at Enchanted Forest.

Nancie Battaglia

Barton Garnet Mine Tours (518-251-2706; Barton Mines Rd., North River) Tours of open-pit mines; rock collecting; mineral shop. July–Aug. Inexpensive.

Calypso's Cove (315-369-2777; Rte. 28, Old Forge) Bumper boats, batting cages, driving range, go-karts. Memorial Day–Columbus Day. Moderate.

Easy Rolling Skate Park (315-369-6924; North St., Old Forge) Rink for roller and in-line skaters. Year-round. Inexpensive.

Enchanted Forest/Water Safari (315-369-6145; Rte. 28, Old Forge) New York's largest water theme park. Daily Memorial Day–Labor Day. Expensive.

Gore Mountain Gondola Rides (518-251-2411; Peaceful Valley Rd., North Creek) Fall weekends. Inexpensive.

McCauley Mountain Chairlift Ride (315-369-3225; McCauley Mtn. Rd., Old Forge) Chairlift ride; tame deer. Daily June 25–Labor Day; weekends Memorial Day–June 24; Labor Day–Columbus Day. Inexpensive.

Sherman's Carousel (518-835-4110; off Rte. 10, Caroga Lake) Wonderful old merry-go-round; Ferris wheel, beach, and picnic grounds. Open daily July–Aug. Inexpensive.

BEYOND THE BLUE LINE

New York's largest theme park — **Great Escape Fun Park** (518-792-6568; Rte. 9, Lake George) — is just south of Lake George village. It's an awesome complex with 100 rides, shows, and attractions; the newly restored Comet roller coaster is regarded as one of the world's classic thrills. Open daily June–Labor Day, plus some spring and fall weekends. Expensive. In Vail Mills, south of Mayfield, is **Adirondack Animal Land** (518-883-5748: Rte. 30), a game park with a herd of miniature horses, emus, fainting goats, kangaroos, zebras, camels, llamas, donkeys, and other friendly creatures. Inexpensive.

FISHING

Brook trout, lake trout, landlocked salmon, muskellunge, great northern pike, pickerel, walleye, smallmouth bass, largemouth bass, bullhead, whitefish, and assorted panfish are all native to Adirondack waters; toss in the exotics like brown trout, rainbow trout, splake, tiger musky, and kokanee, and an angler's alternatives approach Neptune's harvest. Of course, we offer no guarantees that you'll actually catch anything. But with preparation — like reading a guidebook or calling one of the hotlines or spending a day with a guide on remote waters — you may be able to tell the story about the big one that *didn't* get away.

Begin your fishing education with the *New York State Fishing Regulations Guide* published by the Department of Environmental Conservation and available at DEC offices, sporting-goods stores, tourist information centers, or by mail (DEC, 50 Wolf Rd., Albany NY 12233). The free booklet details all the seasons and limits for various species. Everyone over age 16 who fishes in the Adirondacks must have a New York fishing license, which can be purchased at sporting-goods stores and town offices. Nonresidents can get special 5-day licenses; state residents over 70 are eligible for free licenses.

In general, trout season runs from Apr. 1–Sept. 30; bass season from the third Saturday in June–Nov. 30; northern, walleye, and pickerel from the first Saturday in May–Mar. 15. There are helpful hotlines for fishing tips describing what's hitting where on which kind of bait. For the southern part of DEC Region 5, including Lake George, lower Lake Champlain, Schroon Lake, and the Central Adirondacks, call 518-623-3682; for the High Peaks and Northwest Lakes area, call 518-891-5413.

Lakes, ponds, rivers, and streams give anglers plenty of options.

Nancie Battaglia

If you'd like to read about fishing, county and town tourism offices listed in Chapter Eight have the lowdown on local angling. There are a couple of books that you can find in book stores: *Good Fishing in the Adirondacks* (Backcountry Books) by Dennis Aprill and *Fishing in the Adirondacks* (Adirondack Sports Publications) by Francis Betters.

To get in the proper frame of mind for fishing, nothing beats a trip to a local fish hatchery. In *Lake George and Southeastern Adirondacks*, the **Warren County Fish Hatchery** (518-623-4141; Hudson St., Warrensburg) is open daily. In the *Champlain Valley*, the **Essex County Fish Hatchery** (518-597-3844; Creek Rd., Crown Point) is also open every day. The only fish ladder in the park is on the Boquet River (518-963-7266; School St., Willsboro); if you time it just right in the fall, you can watch big salmon ascend the watery staircase. In the *Northwest Lakes* the **Adirondack Fish Hatchery** (518-891-3358; Rte. 30, Saranac Inn) specializes in raising landlocked salmon for stocking lakes.

Acid rain has had an effect on fishing in the southwestern quadrant of the Adirondack Park, where there's more precipitation and thinner soils. About 200 lakes and ponds that once supported fish are now dead; research has shown it's not the direct effects of low pH levels, but acidic waters leaching toxic minerals from the soil that are to blame. Efforts to combat acidification by applying lime have shown some effect on small ponds. Biologists are also breeding trout that can survive in more acidic waters, but as yet these creatures have not been widely stocked. The good news is that more than two thousand lakes and ponds and countless miles of rivers and streams have stabilized at pH levels that support fish and all kinds of wildlife. For more information about acid rain, its effects, and what you can do to offset its spread, contact your local chapter of Trout Unlimited, or the DEC.

FISHING GUIDES AND OUTFITTERS

LAKE GEORGE AND SOUTHEASTERN ADIRONDACKS

Ann's Bait & Tackle Shop (518-644-9989; Norowal Rd., Bolton Landing)

The Crossroads (518-494-3821; Dixon Rd., Chestertown) Large selection of bait and tackle.

Ellsworth Sport Shop (518-668-4624; Rte. 9, Lake George)

Gibaldi Guide Service (518-494-7059; Schroon River Rd., Warrensburg) Guided trips on Lake George, Lake Champlain, or to wilderness waters.

Lake George Camping Equipment (518-644-9941; Rte. 9N, Bolton Landing) Charter boat for salmon, trout, or bass on Lake George.

Lockhart Charter Fishing & Guide Services (518-623-2236; 70 Library Ave., Warrensburg) Ice-fishing and regular season trips on Lake George for salmon, lake trout, and northern pike; backcountry trips.

The Outdoorsman Sport Shop (518-668-3910; Rte. 9N, Diamond Point) Bait and tackle.

Remington's Garage and Sport Shop (518-494-3260; Rte. 8, Brant Lake) Bait and tackle; guided trips.

Sand n' Surf Charter Service (518-668-4622; Rte. 9N, Diamond Point) Charter boat for salmon, lake trout, bass on southern Lake George; 1 night free lodging with half-day off-season charter.

Ted's Charter Fishing Service (518-668-5334; Rte. 9N, Diamond Point) Charter boat for salmon, lake trout, bass on southern Lake George; 1 night free lodging with half-day off-season charter.

CHAMPLAIN VALLEY

Adirondack-Champlain Guide Service (518-963-7351; RR 297, Willsboro) Guided trips on Lake Champlain and backcountry lakes.

HIGH PEAKS AND NORTHERN ADIRONDACKS

Adirondack Mountain Club (518-523-3441; Adirondak Loj, Lake Placid) Fly-fishing workshops.

Adirondack Tri-Lakes Sportfishing (518-891-3893; HC1, Box 25, Saranac Lake) Guided trips.

No-Kill Fishing

Angling for fun rather than for the frypan is catching on across the country, especially in trout waters. If you'd like to match wits with a wild piscine, and then send it back for another day, here are some tips for catch-and-release fishing.

Use a barbless hook or take a barbed hook and bend down the barb with a pair of pliers. Be gentle landing your fish; some anglers line their nets with a soft cotton bag. When removing the hook, it's best not to handle the fish at all, since you can disturb the protective coating on the skin. If you have to touch the fish, wet your hands first, don't squeeze the body and don't touch the gills. If you can, extract the hook without touching the fish by holding the hook's shank upside down and removing it. Usually, the creature will swim happily away. If your fish is tired, you can cradle it gently facing upstream so that water flows through the gills, or if you're in a lake, move it back and forth slowly as a kind of artificial respiration.

With the opening of trout season in April 1995, a five-mile-long section of the West Branch of the Ausable River between Lake Placid and Wilmington was designated for catch and release only. The action here can be terrific on late spring days; with the new no-kill rules, it's bound to remain excellent for years to come.

Blue Line Sport Shop (518-891-4680; 82 Main St., Saranac Lake) Tackle and camping gear.

Francis Betters Guide Service (518-946-2605; Rte. 86, Wilmington) Fly fishing on the Ausable River; fly-fishing and fly-tying instruction; tackle shop.

Pat Gallagher Guide Service (518-523-9727; Box 306, Lake Placid) Wilderness fishing trips.

Hungry Trout (518-946-2217; Rte. 86, Wilmington) Fly shop; fly-fishing instruction; access to private section of the Ausable River.

Jones Outfitters (518-523-3468; 37 Main St., Lake Placid) Fly-fishing instruction; guide service; rod and reel repairs; Orvis shop.

Light Line Adventures (518-523-1186; 24 Cherry St., Lake Placid) Fly-fishing trips for bass and pike.

Placid Bay Ventures Guide & Charter Service (518-523-1744; 70 1/2 Saranac Ave., Lake Placid) Charter boat on Lake Placid; wilderness fishing trips.

River Road Bait & Tackle (518-891-2128; off Rte 3, Bloomingdale) Trout flies; rods and reels.

Tahawus Guide Service (518-891-4334; Rte. 86, Ray Brook) Fishing trips to remote streams; corporate retreats.

Young's Foothills (518-891-1221; Box 345, Saranac Lake) Guided trips for trout, bass, and pike; ice fishing.

NORTHWEST LAKES

Tip Top Sport Shop (518-359-9222; 40 Park St., Tupper Lake)

CENTRAL ADIRONDACKS

Adirondack Mountain & Stream Guide Service (518-251-3762; Hardscrabble Rd., Olmstedville) Wilderness fishing trips.

Thomas Akstens (518-251-2217; Bartman Rd., Bakers Mills) Fly-fishing instruction; Adirondack patterns for bass and trout flies.

Beaver Brook Outfitters (518-251-3394; Rtes. 8 & 28, Wevertown) Guided trips, Orvis equipment, fly-tying and fly-fishing lessons.

Ed's Fly Shop (518-863-4223; Rte. 30, Northville)

Hodel's Pro Hardware (315-357-2341; Rte. 28, Inlet) Tackle and camping gear.

Moose River Company (315-369-3682; Main St., Old Forge) Fishing tackle and fly-fishing gear; outdoor equipment.

Mountainaire Adventures (518-251-2194; Rte. 28, Wevertown) Guided fishing trips; lodging.

North Country Sports (518-251-4299; Thirteenth Lake Rd., North River) Wilderness fishing trips; tackle; books and videos; hand-tied flies.

Wharton's Adirondack Adventures (518-548-3195; Box 544, Lake Pleasant) Guided wilderness fishing trips.

GOLF

Savor the green rolling hills, craggy peaks, deep blue lakes, bracing air, and the Adirondacks do recall Scotland's landscape just a wee bit. Perhaps then it's no surprise that there are dozens of courses tucked in mountain valleys throughout the park. Once upon a time, there were even more golf clubs than are open today, links that were attached to grand hotels and exclusive private clubs. The book *Adirondack Golf Courses . . . Past and Present* (Adirondack Golf, 1987), compiled by Peter Martin, outlines the history of regional golf with dozens of old photographs and anecdotes. New in 1997 is the *I Love NY Golfer's Guide* (1-800-ILOVENY), which describes dozens of courses across the state; a new annual magazine, *New York Golf* (Divot Communications) is available at selected pro shops in the region.

Adirondack golf courses today range from informal, inexpensive, converted cow pastures to challenging, busy, championship links. At most places, you don't have to reserve a tee time, and at only a few are golfers required to rent carts. An added benefit: many of the golf courses have decent restaurants where you can enjoy a sandwich or a beer after the round.

Duffers at Loon Lake, an 18-hole course that dates back to the turn of the century.

Nancie Battaglia

Price Code

Greens Fees:	Inexpensive	Moderate	Expensive	Very Expensive
(9 holes)	under $15	$15-$25	Over $25	Over $40

LAKE GEORGE AND SOUTHWESTERN ADIRONDACKS

Bend of the River Golf Course (518-696-3415; Rte. 9N, Hadley) 9 holes; par 35; 2,700 yards. Inexpensive. One of the first courses to open in the spring.

Cronin's Golf Resort (518-623-9336; Golf Course Rd., Warrensburg) 18 holes; par 70; 6121 yards. Inexpensive.

Green Mansions (518-494-7222; Darrowsville Rd., Chestertown) 9 holes; par 36; 2700 yards. Moderate.

Sagamore Resort & Golf Club (518-644-9400; Federal Hill Rd., Bolton Landing) 18 holes; par 70; 6900 yards. Very Expensive. Designed by Donald Ross; challenging.

Schroon Lake Municipal Golf Course (518-532-9359; Hoffman Rd., Schroon Lake) 9 holes; par 36; 2958 yards. Inexpensive.

1000 Acres Golf Club (518-696-5246; Rte. 418, Stony Creek) 9 holes; par 35; 3900 yards. Inexpensive.

Top of the World (518-668-2062; Lockhart Mtn. Rd., Lake George) 9 holes; par 36; 2900 yards. Inexpensive to moderate.

CHAMPLAIN VALLEY

Cobble Hill Golf Course (518-873-9974; Rte. 9, Elizabethtown) 9 holes; par 34; 3000 yards. Inexpensive. Completed in 1897; great views of the High Peaks.

Moriah Country Club (518-546-9979; Broad St., Port Henry) 9 holes; par 32; 3000 yards. Inexpensive.

Port Kent Golf Course (518-834-9785; Rte. 373, Port Kent) 9 holes; par 30; 2047 yards. Inexpensive.

Ticonderoga Country Club (518-585-2801; Hague Rd. Ticonderoga) 18 holes; par 71; 6300 yards. Moderate.

Westport Country Club (518-962-4470; Liberty Rd., Westport) 18 holes; par 72; 6200 yards. Moderate. Challenging; beautiful views.

Willsboro Golf Club (518-963-8989; Point Rd., Willsboro) 9 holes; par 35; 3100 yards. Moderate.

HIGH PEAKS AND NORTHERN ADIRONDACKS

Ausable Club (518-576-4411; Ausable Club Rd., St. Huberts) 9 holes; Scottish links-type course. Inexpensive. Open to non-members in Sept. only, Mon.–Thurs.

Ausable Valley Country Club (518-647-8666; Golf Course Rd., Au Sable Forks) 9 holes; par 34; 2700 yards. Inexpensive.

Craig Wood Country Club (518-523-9811; Cascade Rd., Lake Placid) 18 holes; par 72; 6544 yards. Moderate. Named after Lake Placid native Craig Wood, who won both the U.S. Open and Masters in 1941.

Lake Placid Club Resort (518-523-4460; Mirror Lake Dr., Lake Placid) 2 18-hole courses; 1 9-hole course. Expensive.

Loon Lake Golf Club (518-891-3249; Rte. 99, Loon Lake) 18 holes; par 70; 5600 yards. Inexpensive. Completed in 1895, one of the oldest courses in the Adirondacks.

Saranac Inn Golf & Country Club (518-891-1402; Rte. 30, Saranac Inn) 18 holes; par 70; 6500 yards. Moderate. Beautifully maintained course.

Saranac Lake Golf Club (518-891-2675; Rte. 86, Saranac Lake) 9 holes; par 36; 6100 yards. Moderate.

Whiteface Club Golf Course (518-523-2551; Whiteface Inn Rd., Lake Placid) 18 holes; par 72; 6500 yards. Moderate. Designed by Walter Hagen and John VanKleek; beautiful views.

NORTHWEST LAKES

Clifton-Fine Golf Course (315-848-3570; Rte. 3, Star Lake) 9 holes; par 36; 2854 yards. Inexpensive.

Buzz Off

Springtime in the Adirondacks can be lovely, but this earthly paradise has a squadron of tiny, persistent insects to keep humans from overwhelming the countryside. We speak here of blackflies. Bug season is usually late May through June, although its duration depends on the weather. If you are planning an extended hike, golf outing, streamside fishing trip, horseback ride, or similar activity, you'll want to apply insect repellent, wear light-colored clothing (blue, especially dark blue, seems to attract blackflies), and tuck in your pantlegs and shirt: the Adirondack red badge of courage is a bracelet of bites around the ankles or waist. Avoid using perfume, shampoo, or scented hairspray — these products broadcast "free lunch!" to hungry little buggers.

There's a pharmacy of lotions and sprays that use varying amounts of DEET (diethyl-meta-toluamide) as the active ingredient, but note that products containing more than 25% DEET should not be applied to children's skin. DEET should not be used on infants. Avon's Skin-So-Soft bath oil has remarkable powers of insect repellency without mysterious chemical additives. Fabric softener sheets, like Bounce, can be tucked into your hatband to keep flies away from your face. Some Adirondackers prefer pine-tar based bug dopes, like Ole Woodsman, that also have the lasting aroma of authenticity; after a good dose of Ole Woodsman, your pillows and sheets will be scented, too.

Tupper Lake Golf & Country Club (518-359-3701; Country Club Rd., Tupper Lake) 18 holes; par 71; 6250 yards. Inexpensive.

CENTRAL ADIRONDACKS

Brantingham Golf Course (315-348-8861; Brantingham Rd., Brantingham Lake) 18 holes; par 71; 5300 yards. Inexpensive.

Cedar River Golf Course (518-648-5906; Rtes. 28/30, Indian Lake) 9 holes; par 36; 2700 yards. Inexpensive.

Inlet Golf Course and Country Club (315-357-3503; Rte. 28, Inlet) 18 holes; par 72; 6000 yards. Moderate.

Lake Pleasant Golf Course (518-548-7071; Rte. 8, Lake Pleasant) 9 holes; par 35; 2900 yards. Inexpensive.

Sacandaga Golf Club (518-863-4887; Rte. 30, Sacandaga Park, Northville) 9 holes; par 36; 3000 yards. Inexpensive.

Nick Stoner Golf Course (518-835-4211; Rte. 10, Caroga Lake) 18 holes; par 70; 5800 yards. Moderate.

Thendara Golf Club, Inc. (315-369-3136; off Rte. 28, Thendara) 18 holes; par 72; 6000 yards. Moderate. Designed by Donald Ross.

Wakely Lodge & Golf Course (518-648-5011; Cedar River Rd., Indian Lake) 9 holes; par 34; 2600 yards. Inexpensive.

HIKING AND BACKPACKING

Walk on the wild side. The Adirondack Park has more than 2,000 miles of marked hiking trails that lead to pristine ponds, roaring waterfalls, spectacular peaks, ice caves, and hidden gorges; perhaps the toughest choice for an Adirondack visitor is selecting where to go. There are dozens of guidebooks to help you make that decision. The *Discover the Adirondacks* series (Lakeview Press and Backcountry Publications) by hiker-historian Barbara McMartin divides the park into 11 geographical regions and describes the natural and human histories of dozens of different destinations; besides marked trails, she suggests some basic bushwhacks to reach great views. The guidebooks published by the Adirondack Mountain Club (ADK) slice the Adirondacks into six regions; there's also a volume dedicated to 132-mile Northville–Lake Placid Trail. These publishers offer a couple of volumes that sample trips from all corners of the park. McMartin has recently compiled a children's guide, *Adventures in Hiking*, that's a useful source of numerous family outings. For details on these books, check the bibliography in Chapter Eight, *Information*, and for local sources, consult the bookstore section in Chapter Seven, *Shopping*.

For even more reading on tramps and treks, there's *Adirondac* magazine,

*Taking a coffee break during a
High Peaks hike, 1890.*

Courtesy of *Adirondack Life* magazine

published by ADK; *Adirondack Life,* especially the Annual Guide, outlines
plenty of good long walks; and the Department of Environmental Conserva-
tion has free guides to trails in the various wilderness and wild forest areas.
Some towns offer hiking maps; for example, if you're in the Blue Mountain
Lake vicinity, ask for the trail map at the post office, or at the Tupper Lake
Chamber of Commerce, ask for their sheet on nearby mountains to hike.

The Adirondack woods are free of many of the natural hazards that you
need to worry about in other locales. There's some poison ivy in the Champlain Valley, but very little in the High Peaks, Northwest Lakes, and Central
Adirondacks. Rattlesnakes are found only in isolated parts of the Tongue
Mountain range near Lake George, and rarely in the Champlain Valley; keep
your eyes open when crossing rock outcrops on warm, sunny days. These
Eastern timber rattlers are quite shy and nonaggressive, but do take care not to
surprise one.

In some parts of the park, you can leave the trailhead and not see another
person until you return to your car and look in the rearview mirror. The Five
Ponds Wilderness Area, between Stillwater Reservoir and Cranberry Lake, is
especially remote. Parts of the Northville-Placid trail are many miles from the
nearest road; passing through the West Canada Lakes or Cold River areas, you
might go several days with just the cry of the loon or howl of the coyote for
company. Going end-to-end on this long trail requires a minimum of 10 days,
and a solid amount of backcountry knowledge, but you can pick shorter sections of the trail for three-day junkets. Parts of the High Peaks — especially
from southern access points — offer similar overnights. It's possible to find solitude even in the middle of the busy summer season if you select the right destination. Lest we make it sound too daunting, there are plenty of easy hikes in
the 2- to 5-mile length that traverse beautiful terrain in all sections of the park.

Wherever you choose to go, be prepared. Your pack should contain a flashlight, matches, extra food and water, map, compass, and extra clothes. At many trailheads, there's a register for signing in. Forest rangers use this data to estimate how much use a particular area receives; and, in the unlikely event that you get lost, the information about when you started, where you were planning to go, and who you were with would be helpful to the search team.

For neophyte hikers, the trails at the Visitor Interpretive Centers at Newcomb and Paul Smiths are ingeniously designed to offer a wide range of nature in a relatively short distance, and you won't be too far from the building no matter how long you travel. You can join a guided trip to learn about wildflowers, mushrooms, trees, or birds. There are also wheelchair-accessible trails at both centers.

Several organizations and guide services lead trips and offer map-and-compass, woodcraft, and low-impact-camping workshops.

HIKING GUIDES AND ORGANIZATIONS

Adirondack Discovery (315-357-3598; Box 545, Inlet) Guided day hikes to places of historical and geological interest in July and Aug.

Adirondack Mountain Club (518-668-4447; Luzerne Rd., Lake George) Hikes with naturalists; fall foliage hikes; wilderness overnights; weekends for women, youth, and senior citizens. Many programs in the High Peaks at Adirondak Loj (518-523-3441).

Adirondack Park Visitor Interpretive Centers (518-327-3000; Rte. 30, Paul Smiths; 518-582-2000; Rte. 28, Newcomb) Guided hikes; nature trails; ecology programs for adults and children.

On the summit of Pitchoff Mountain, near Keene.

Nancie Battaglia

Tick, Tick, Tick

A few cases of Lyme Disease have been recorded in the Adirondacks in recent years, and hikers should take precautions against exposing themselves to deer ticks (*Ixodes dammini*). The ticks can be found in deep woods although they prefer to stay on their host animals, whitetail deer and deermice. Dogs — especially exuberant ones that go crashing through the brush — are more at risk than humans; have your pet inoculated against Lyme Disease.

New York State has approved the sale of Permanone, a tick repellent that can be applied to clothing. Be careful! It's a very strong material that should not be placed on your skin or pets. You can minimize your exposure to ticks by wearing long pants (with cuffs tucked into your boots) and long-sleeve shirts, using a good insect repellent, and staying on the trail. If you wear light-colored clothing, the ticks are easier to spot, and you can check yourself and your kids for the vermin while you're in the woods.

Deer ticks are very tiny, no bigger than a sesame seed. They don't fly. If you find an eight-legged crawling creature on your body, it could be a spider, a wood tick (not a carrier of Lyme), or an arachnid locally called a "ked," which, despite its scary-looking crablike pincers, is harmless.

Humans face the highest risk of tick contact in June and July. If you find a tick attached to your skin, pull it out steadily with a pair of tweezers or your fingers, grasping as close to the tick's mouth as you can. Save the creature in a jar — your doctor will probably want to see it. Apply a topical antiseptic to the bite. A tick must feed for several hours before the disease is transmitted.

If you see on your skin a clear area encircled by a red rash and are feeling flu-like symptoms, you may have been exposed to Lyme Disease. Visit your doctor or a medical center for a Lyme test, but be aware that it takes several weeks after exposure for your body to show antibodies. Lyme symptoms mimic many other ailments so it's difficult to get an accurate diagnosis; most medical practitioners will begin a course of antibiotics if they believe you've been exposed.

Birchbark Tours (518-891-5704; 32 Glenwood, Saranac Lake) Wildflower and bird hikes; special-needs backpack trips; historical trips.

McDonnell's Adirondack Challenges (518-891-1176; Rte. 30, Lake Clear) Backpack trips.

Middle Earth Expeditions (518-523-9572; HCR 01 Box 37, Lake Placid) Backpack and day trips.

Sagamore Great Camp (315-354-5301; Sagamore Rd., Raquette Lake) Nature weekends with lodging.

Wilderness Education Association (518-891-2915; North Country Community College, Saranac Lake) Excellent workshops and seminars in wilderness issues and techniques for trip leaders.

Low-Impact Camping

Wilderness camping in the not-too-distant past relied on techniques like digging deep trenches around tents, cutting balsam boughs for backwoods beds, sawing armloads of firewood, and burying garbage and cans. For camp clean-up, we used to think nothing of washing dishes in the lake, and scrubbing ourselves vigorously with soap as we cavorted in the shallows. All of these activities left a lasting mark on the woods and waters; today it's important to leave no trace of your visit.

Low-impact camping is perhaps easier than old-fashioned methods once you know a few of the basics. Most of the skills are simply common sense: think of the cumulative effects of your actions when you set up camp and you're on your way to becoming a responsible wilderness trekker.

Choose a site at least 150 feet away from the nearest hiking trail or water source, and try to select a place that will recover quickly after you leave. Separate your tent from your cooking area to avoid attracting animals to your bedside and to distribute the impact of your stay. When you leave, tidy up. Be sure the spot is absolutely clean of any trash — even stuff we commonly regard as biodegradable — and spread dirt or dead leaves around any trampled areas.

Use a portable stove for backcountry cooking rather than a campfire. (You can use only dead and down wood in the forest preserve; cutting trees on state land is prohibited.) Plan your meals ahead so that you don't have extra cooked food; if no one in the party can assume the role of "master of the clean plate club," then pack out all your leftovers. Wash your dishes and your body well away from streams and lakes using a mild vegetable-based soap.

How to s—t in the woods is something to consider; nothing kills that "gee, isn't it terrific out here in the wilderness" feeling more than finding unmistakable evidence of other humans. Bring a shovel or trowel and bury that hazardous waste at least six inches down and 150 feet from the nearest water. Lean-tos and some designated backcountry campsites have privies; use them.

HORSEBACK RIDING, POLO, AND WAGON TRIPS

New York's North Country may not have the wide, open spaces of the Wild West, but there are hundreds of miles of wilderness horse trails to explore, and plenty of outfitters to put you on a suitable mount. The possibilities range from hour-long rides to three-day guided backcountry forays; if you have your own horse, the Department of Environmental Conservation (DEC) has trail networks across the park, and even operates campgrounds that accommodate man and beast. For a handy booklet describing these trails, contact the DEC, 518-897-1200; Ray Brook NY 12977. One rule applies for bringing in out-of-state horses: proof of a negative Coggins test is necessary. If you plan

Riding through a meadow in the High Peaks.

Nancie Battaglia

to camp more than three nights in the forest preserve, or in a group of 10 or more, you'll need a permit from the local forest ranger.

Hay rides, sleigh rides, and wagon trips are available in many communities. You can ride a carriage through Lake George Village, or around Mirror Lake in Lake Placid; there's no need to make a reservation. Listed below are outfitters and teamsters who offer wagon trips and places to ride. In general, local stables are open only during warm weather.

If you enjoy just watching horses, there are two excellent annual horse shows in Lake Placid, located a canter away from the Olympic ski jumps: the **Lake Placid Horse Show** in late June, and the **I Love NY Horse Show** (518-523-9625; North Elba Town Hall, Lake Placid) in early July. At both, the emphasis is on Olympic-level competition for hunters, jumpers, and riders. There are weekend polo games at the Bark Eater Inn (518-576-2221; Alstead Hill Rd., Keene) starting in late June. Admission is free; the Adirondackers play against teams from Saratoga Springs and Vermont. If you're an accomplished rider, you may even be able to join in a pick-up game.

A legacy of the dude-ranch days in the southeastern Adirondacks, **Painted Pony** (518-696-2421; Howe Rd., Lake Luzerne) presents professional rodeo competitions Wednesday, Friday, and Saturday nights in July and August, rain or shine. This is the home of the country's oldest weekly rodeo, complete with trick riding and roping, clowns and novelty acts, and there's more rodeo action at **1000 Acres** (518-696-2444; Rte. 418, Stony Creek).

OUTFITTERS AND STABLES

LAKE GEORGE AND SOUTHEASTERN ADIRONDACKS

Bailey's Horses (518-696-4541; Rte. 9N, Lake Luzerne) Western trail rides; lessons; hay wagon or carriage rides around Lake Vanare; winter trail rides; trips to Lake George horse trails by reservation.

Bennett Stables (518-696-4444; Rte. 9N, Lake Luzerne) Trail rides.

Circle B Ranch (518-494-4074; Atateka Rd., Chestertown) Wagon, sleigh, and hay rides.

Circle L Ranch (518-623-9967; High St., Athol) Horse-pack outfitter; 1/2 and full-day trips.

Saddle Up (518-668-4801; Rte. 9N, Lake George) Trail rides.

1000 Acres (518-696-2444; Rte. 418, Stony Creek) Guided trail rides.

HIGH PEAKS AND NORTHERN ADIRONDACKS

Circle 7 (518-582-4011; Rte. 28N, Newcomb) Wagon trips to Santanoni Preserve by reservation only; hunting and fishing pack trips.

Tom Dillon (518-582-2414; Rte. 28N, Newcomb) Wagon trips to Santanoni.

Sentinel View Stables (518-891-3008; Harrietstown Rd., Saranac Lake) English and Western lessons; jumping instruction; bridle trails.

XTC Ranch (518-891-5684; Forest Home Rd., Saranac Lake) Wilderness trail rides; sleigh rides; special holiday trips and meals in a backwoods cabin.

Wilson's Livery Stable (518-576-2221; Alstead Hill Rd., Keene) Western or English trail rides by the hour or day; wagon and sleigh rides; open year-round.

NORTHWEST LAKES

Cold River Ranch (518-359-7559; Rte. 3, Tupper Lake) All-day rides by reservation only; pack-horse trips for fishing, hunting, and camping; no children under 14. Lodging.

CENTRAL ADIRONDACKS

Adirondack Saddle Tours (315-357-4499; Uncas Rd., Inlet) Trail rides; pack-horse trips into Moose River Recreation Area.

Adirondack Wilderness Stables (518-548-5454; Rte. 8, Lake Pleasant) Hourly, half- or full-day rides, English or Western; lessons.

Brookside Stables (518-251-3058; Trout Brook Rd., Olmstedville) Trail rides.

T & M Equestrian Center (315-357-3594; Rte. 28, Inlet) Guided trail rides, Western only; hay and sleigh rides by reservation; overnights to Moose River Recreation Area.

PUBLIC HORSE TRAILS

LAKE GEORGE AND SOUTHEASTERN ADIRONDACKS

Lake George Trail System: E. side of Lake George, off Pilot Knob Rd.; 41 mi. of carriage roads on an old estate; lean-tos.

Lake Luzerne: Off Rte. 9N near Lake Luzerne hamlet; on Fourth Lake; campsite (518-696-2031), with corral; 5 mi. of trails on state land that connect with many miles of privately owned trails.

Pharoah Lake Horse Trails: Pharoah Lake Wilderness Area, E. of Schroon Lake. 12 mi. of sandy woods roads; lean-tos.

HIGH PEAKS AND NORTHERN ADIRONDACKS

Cold River Horse Trails: 6 mi. E. of Tupper Lake off Rte. 3; 13- and 32-mile-loop dirt trails; lean-tos and corral. Connects with Moose Pond Trail and Santanoni trails.

Meacham Lake: 3.5 mi. N. of Paul Smiths, off Rte. 30; 10 miles of trails; lean-tos and barn.

Moose Pond Trail: Starts at Santanoni trailhead just N. of Newcomb off Rte. 28N; 10 miles.

Raquette Falls Horse Trail: Branches off Cold River Trail; 2 miles.

Santanoni Trail: N. of Newcomb off Rte. 28N; 10-mile round-trip.

NORTHWEST LAKES

Saranac Inn Horse Trail System: Off Rte. 30 near Saranac Inn; several short trails to ponds in the St. Regis Canoe Area; 11-mile round-trip on the Fish Pond Truck Trail.

CENTRAL ADIRONDACKS

Moose River Recreation Area: Between Indian Lake and Inlet off Rte. 28; 28-mile dirt road plus many miles of old logging roads; campsites.

Independence River Wild Forest: Off Number Four Rd. near Stillwater Reservoir; assembly area at Chases Lake Rd., off Rte. 12, Greig. 28 miles of sand roads; connects with Otter Creek; barn.

Otter Creek Trails: Near Greig, off Rte. 12; nearly 50 miles of sandy roads; connects with Independence River. Recommended.

HUNTING

Native Americans, colonial scouts, and 19th-century travelers regarded the Adirondacks as happy hunting grounds. Early accounts describe shooting deer year-round for cooking at camp and for swank Manhattan restaurants. Old pictures show small groups of men displaying dozens of bucks; the moose — never truly abundant in the Adirondacks — probably disappeared in part due to overhunting. (Other factors were loss of habitat and diseases transmitted by deer.) Market hunting has been outlawed for a century. The Adirondack Guides Association was a major force in pushing to state to enact hunting laws that would ensure that deer would not face the same fate as the moose.

Many Adirondack counties now hold more resident whitetail deer than

A successful Adirondack hunt in the 1890s.

Nancie Battaglia

year-round humans, and hunting is a popular, regulated pursuit each fall. Beside deer, there are seasons for black bear (the 1997 bear take for the Adirondack Park was more than 400), snowshoe hare, coyote, bobcat, and other small mammals, plus ruffed grouse, woodcock, wild turkey, and waterfowl. The booklets outlining game seasons are available from Department of Environmental Conservation offices, or by writing to DEC, 50 Wolf Rd., Albany NY 12233; licenses can be purchased from sporting goods stores, town offices, or DEC. Non-residents may purchase special 5-day licenses. If you have never had a New York State hunting license, you must show proof that you have attended a hunter education course. Turkey hunting requires a special stamp from DEC; waterfowl hunters must possess a Federal Migratory Bird Hunting Stamp.

In general, big-game seasons begin with early bear (mid-Sept.–mid-Oct.); archery for deer or bear (late Sept.–mid-Oct.); muzzleloading for deer or bear (one week in mid-Oct.); and regular big-game season (third Saturday in Oct. through the first Sunday after Thanksgiving.) Bow and black-powder hunters may take antlerless deer; during regular season, it's bucks only in the Adirondack Park.

Wilderness, primitive, and wild-forest areas of the forest preserve are all open to hunting. Hunters — even if they have a brand-new, state-of-the-art GPS unit — should be proficient with map and compass. Global-positioning units don't always work well in thick forest, and batteries do wear out.

Paper companies, which own about a million acres, also offer memberships and leases for hunting and fishing privileges; contact Finch Pruyn & Co. (518-793-2541; 1 Glen St., Glens Falls) or the Empire State Forest Products Association (518-463-1297; 123 State St., Albany) for information. While hunting, please respect the boundaries of private posted lands.

Listed below are some shops and licensed guides specializing in hunting.

GUN SHOPS

LAKE GEORGE AND SOUTHEASTERN ADIRONDACKS
Adirondack Gun and Tackle (518-532-7089; Main St., Schroon Lake)
The Crossroads (518-494-3821; Dixon Rd., Chestertown) Full range of sporting goods.
Ellsworth's Sport Shop (518-668-4624; Rte. 9, Lake George)
Nemec's Sport Shop (518-623-2049; 263 Main St., Warrensburg)

HIGH PEAKS AND NORTHERN ADIRONDACKS
Blue Line Sport Shop (518-891-4680; 82 Main St., Saranac Lake)
Jones Outfitters (518-523-3468; 37 Main St., Lake Placid)

NORTHWEST LAKES
Fortune's Hardware (518-359-9471; 61 Main St., Tupper Lake)
Tip Top Sport Shop (518-359-9222; 40 Park St., Tupper Lake)

CENTRAL ADIRONDACKS
Adirondack Sportsmen (518-863-4525; 221 Bridge St., Northville)
Hodel's Pro Hardware (315-357-2341; Rte. 28, Inlet)
Moose River Company (315-369-3682; Main St. Old Forge)
Pumpkin Mountain Gun Shop (518-352-7772; Rte. 28, Blue Mtn. Lake)

HUNTING GUIDES

LAKE GEORGE AND SOUTHEASTERN ADIRONDACKS
Lake Luzerne Guide Service (518-696-4646; 2101 Lake Ave., Lake Luzerne) Big game.
Trout Brook Guide Service (518-532-7089; Main St., Schroon Lake) Big and small game.

CHAMPLAIN VALLEY
Adirondack–Champlain Guide Service (518-963-7351; Long Pond, Willsboro) Big game, grouse, and snowshoe hare.

HIGH PEAKS AND NORTHERN ADIRONDACKS
Middle Earth Expeditions (518-523-9572; Cascade Rd., Lake Placid) Big game; lodging.
Placid Bay Ventures (518-523-2001; 70 Saranac Ave., Lake Placid) Big game; lodging.

Smith's Taxidermy & Guide Service (518-891-6289; 41 Broadway, Saranac Lake) Big game.

Stillwaters Guide Service (518-523-2280; Cascade Rd., Lake Placid) Big game; bow hunting; snowshoe hare with beagles.

Young's Foothills (518-891-1221; Box 345, Saranac Lake) Black-powder and bow hunting.

NORTHWEST LAKES

Cold River Ranch (518-359-7559; Rte. 3, Tupper Lake) Pack-horse hunting trips.

CENTRAL ADIRONDACKS

Adirondack Mountain & Stream Guide Service (518-251-3762; Hardscrabble Rd., Olmstedville) Big game; snowshoe hare with hounds.

Adirondack Saddle Tours (315-357-4499; Uncas Rd., Inlet NY 13360) Pack-horse hunting trips.

Wharton's Adirondack Outfitters (518-548-3195; Box 544; Lake Pleasant) Big game.

ICE SKATING

Considering that Adirondack waters exist more months of the year in a solid rather than liquid state, it's no wonder that ice skating is a popular pastime here. The modern sport of speed skating was launched in Saranac Lake and Lake Placid: in the early 1900s, more world records were set — and broken — by local bladesmen than at any other wintry place. Nowadays, there's backcountry skating on remote lakes and ponds or skating on plowed rinks in the towns and even indoor figure skating or hockey on Zamboni-maintained ice sheets.

If you'd like to try wilderness skating, wait until January. Cold, clear, still weather produces the most consistent ice. Ice that's two inches thick will support one person on skates, but it's better to wait for at least three inches to form, since currents and springs can create weak spots. Ice is thinner near shore, and steer clear of inlets, outlets, and other tributaries. In the _Champlain Valley_, Webb-Royce Swamp near Westport is a terrific place to skate. Ponds in the _High Peaks_ are often good for skating by New Year's Day, especially if there's been little snow. You can scout Chapel Pond, off Rte. 73 south of Keene Valley, or the Cascade lakes, on the same road, north of Keene, or Heart Lake, at the end of the Adirondak Loj Road. Ask locally for more favorite places.

Many towns offer lighted rinks with warming huts; check with tourist offices for hours. _Long Lake_'s public rink is one of the better ones, and it's conveniently located on Rte. 30 between a diner and a hotel. There's free skating under the lights in Fern Park, in _Inlet_ (315-357-5501), and in _Old Forge_, on North Street (315-369-6983). Lake Champlain towns such as _Ticonderoga_ and _Westport_ often have good (or not so good, depending on the weather) skating. In _Lake Placid_, you can enjoy terrific ice outdoors most evenings at the **Olympic Speed Skating Oval**, on Main St., or you can skate in the Olympic Arena (518-523-1655) at scheduled times for a small charge. If you want to try speed skating, you can get rental skates, a lesson, and ice time in Lake Placid for about five bucks. _Tupper Lake_ (518-359-2531; McLaughlin St.) maintains rinks for hockey and skating; **Saranac Lake's Civic Center** (518-891-3800) has good ice indoors.

A few local shops specialize in hockey and figure skates, outfits, and equipment: **Ice Time** (518-523-9626; next to the Hilton Hotel, Lake Placid); **Skater's Patch Pro Shop** (518-523-4369; inside the Olympic Arena, Lake Placid); the **Cobbler's Shop** (518-523-3679; Main St., Lake Placid); and **The Edge in Sports** (518-523-9430; in front of the Olympic Arena, on Main St.). You can rent skates from the latter two for gliding around the speed oval, and from **High Peaks Cyclery** (518-523-3764; Saranac Ave., Lake Placid). Many of the sporting-goods stores throughout the region stock skates for children and adults.

Nancie Battaglia

Short-track speed skating is an exciting event to watch at the Olympic Center.

MINIATURE GOLF

If the thought of all that howling wilderness makes your kids scream for more familiar entertainment, perhaps one of the many mini-golf links can fill the bill. Throughout the park, there are countless opportunities to sink little bitty putts after avoiding windmills, Vikings, and loop-de-loops; several are listed below, but you may want to call ahead for hours. Historians take note: miniature golf was launched in downtown Lake George at the intersection of Beach Rd. and Rte. 9 in the early years of this century (but the course was recently dismantled). *Lake George* remains the Pebble Beach of Adirondack minis, and half a dozen courses are nearby. You can try **Around the World in 18 Holes** (518-668-2531; Rte. 9); **Fort Mini Golf** (518-668-5471; Fort William Henry Commons); **Gooney Golf/Haunted Castle** (518-668-2589; Rtes. 9/9N); **Magic Castle Indoor Golf** (518-668-3777; Canada St.). Further up the road, it's the **Narrows Pizza Miniature Golf Course** (518-532-7591; Rte. 9, Schroon Lake), and you won't have to worry about what's for dinner after the round.

For the *High Peaks and Northern Adirondacks* area, mini golf is an international affair at **Around the World in 18 Holes** (518-523-9065; Saranac Ave., Lake Placid). In Old Forge you can choose from **Magic Mountain** (315-369-6602; Main St.), **Nutty Putty Miniature Golf** (315-369-6636; Main St.), or **Over the Rainbow** (Rte. 28).

OLYMPIC SPORTS

Lake Placid is the only place in North America that has hosted two Winter Olympic Games, in 1932 and 1980. During the '32 games, the American team won the bobsledding events, took silver and bronze medals in speed skating, hockey, figure skating, and bobsledding, and thus was regarded as the unofficial Olympic champion. In 1980, Eric Heiden garnered five gold medals in speed skating, and the U.S. hockey team won the tournament following a stunning upset over the Russians in the semifinal round. The legacy of Olympic glory lives on here, at the training center on the Old Military Road, where hundreds of athletes eat, sleep, and work out in a high-tech setting, and in several specialized sports facilities in and around Lake Placid. In every season competitors come to town for coaching and practice.

There's just one place in the Northeast where you, too, can ride a real bobsled on an Olympic run: Mount Van Hoevenberg, just a few miles from downtown Lake Placid. This thrill does not come cheap; it's $25 for the longest minute you'll ever spend. (Note that the sleds are piloted by experienced professional drivers.) Rides are available Tues.–Sun. afternoons from Christmas through early March depending on the track conditions, and it's a good idea to call ahead. For $15 you can navigate a luge through some wicked curves, even

Nancie Battaglia

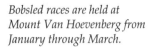

Bobsled races are held at Mount Van Hoevenberg from January through March.

in summer. In winter 1998, Cresta sleds arrived in the Olympic Village, for hair-raising races down the Whiteface Memorial Highway. The Olympic Regional Development Authority (ORDA) is the place to call for details on all of the Olympic venues and winter sports schedules (518-523-1655; Olympic Center, Lake Placid).

Watching international luge, skeleton, and bobsled competitions is almost as exciting as trying it yourself, and perhaps easier on the cardiovascular system. Races are held nearly every winter weekend. Dress warmly for spectating; you'll want to walk up and down the mile-long courses in order to see and hear the sleds zoom through Shady Corner, or spiral down Omega Curve. At some vantage points, the sleds fly by nearly upside-down, and the racket of the runners is a lesson in the Doppler effect. You'll definitely want to see several starts, too, where track stars have a decided advantage.

In the Olympic Arena, at the center of Lake Placid, you can watch Can/Am ice hockey tournaments, professional exhibition games, figure-skating competitions, and skating exhibitions, year-round. Since 1993, stars such as Kristy Yamaguchi and Scott Hamilton have come to Lake Placid in November and December to practice for national touring shows; ask at the arena about watching rehearsals. An annual highlight is the **Gus Lussi International Figure Skating Championships** in mid-February. There are speed-skating races next door at the outdoor oval, and you can usually watch Olympic hopefuls training on winter afternoons.

Ski jumping on the 70- and 90-meter jumps is thrilling to see; watching people fly through the air is far more impressive in person than the sport appears on television. The annual **New Year's and Master's Ski Jump** is the last weekend in December, and world-team trials and meets are later in the winter; contact ORDA for a schedule. Dress warmly for spectating here too, since the bleachers are exposed to the elements. Surprisingly, this is one winter event that you can also enjoy in the summer: you can ride a chairlift to the base of the 90-meter jump, then go up the elevator to the top, for a small fee. The jump tower is open mid-May to early October, and the view is great. An annual favorite is the **Independence Day Ski Jump** sponsored by ORDA (518-523-1655); this is one Lake Placid spectator event you *don't* have to dress warmly for. Also, at the jumping complex (known as Kodak Sports Park), you can watch the U.S. freestyle skiers training in summer and fall. The skiers go off jumps, tumble through the air, and land in a huge tank of water with their skis still attached.

At Whiteface Mountain, you can see the ballet and mogul portions of the **Freestyle World Cup** in late January, and occasional international downhill and slalom races. Or you can try the Olympic Mountain for yourself — look further in this chapter for skiing inspiration.

RACES AND SEASONAL SPORTS EVENTS

Events are listed in chronological order within each region.

LAKE GEORGE AND SOUTHEASTERN ADIRONDACKS

New Year's Day Polar Bear Swim (518-668-5755; Shepard Park, Lake George) No experience necessary!

Prospect Mountain Road Race (518-668-2195; Prospect Mtn. Memorial Highway, Lake George) 5.5 miles uphill all the way, in early May.

N.Y.S. Bass Federation Tournament (518-543-6353; Hague) On Lake George in late June.

Adirondack Distance Run (518-793-9848) 10-mile road race from Lake George to Bolton Landing in early July.

Summerun (518-532-7675; Box 741, Schroon Lake) 5- and 10-km run through downtown Schroon Lake and kids' fun run, on the first Saturday in Aug.

Adirondack Marathon (518-532-7676) Sanctioned qualifier for the big marathons on a beautiful course that circles Schroon Lake in late Sept.

CHAMPLAIN VALLEY

Rotary International Fishing Classic (518-561-5030) Sponsored by Plattsburgh Rotary Club, covering all of Lake Champlain; weigh stations at Port Henry, Westport, and Willsboro; in late May.

Montcalm Mile Run (518-585-6619; Ticonderoga) Footrace down Ticonderoga's main street on July 4th.

24-hour Marathon (518-962-4446; Westport) 10-person relay teams, with each member running a mile every hour; ultramarathon for solo runners. Noon Saturday to noon Sunday at the Essex County Fairgrounds, in Westport in late July.

HIGH PEAKS AND NORTHERN ADIRONDACKS

Crack of Noon Race (518-891-1990) 10-km cross-country fun races at Dewey Mtn., Saranac Lake, on Jan. 1.

Bobcat Snowshoe Race (518-327-6389; Paul Smith's College Sports Annex, Paul Smiths) Sprint and distance snowshoe races in mid-Jan.

Adirondack International Mountaineering Festival (518-576-2281; the Mountaineer, Keene Valley) Clinics and lectures by renowned ice and rock climbers in mid-Jan.

Woodchuck Shuffle (518-327-6389; Paul Smith's College) 20-km snowshoe race in early Feb.

Lake Placid Loppet (518-523-1655; Olympic Regional Development Authority, Lake Placid) 25- and 50-km citizens' races at Mount Van Hoevenberg in early Feb.

Empire State Winter Games (518-523-1655; ORDA, Lake Placid) Figure skating, luge, bobsled, speed skating, ski jumping, cross-country skiing and other events, in Lake Placid in early Mar.

Dewey Mountain Slip 'n' Slide (518-891-2697; Dewey Mtn., Saranac Lake) Races on snow, slush, or mud, using skis, snowshoes, whatever. Early Mar.

Lake Colby Ice Fishing Derby (518-891-2197; Saranac Lake Fish & Game Club, Saranac Lake) Early Mar.

Whiteface Mountain Cocoa Butter Open (518-523-1655; Whiteface Mtn. Ski Area, Wilmington) Citizens' downhill, slalom, and fun races in late Mar.

Ice Breaker Canoe Race (518-891-1990; Saranac Lake Chamber of Commerce, Saranac Lake) 5-mile race on the Saranac River in late Mar.

Ausable River Whitewater Derby (518-946-7200) Sponsored by the Ausable Valley Jaycees. 6-mile downriver canoe race on the East Branch of the Ausable River from Keene to Upper Jay on the last Sunday in Apr.

'Round the Mountain Canoe Race (518-891-1990; Saranac Lake Chamber of Commerce, Saranac Lake) 10-mile canoe race on Lower Saranac Lake and the Saranac River in early May.

Whiteface Mountain Uphill Footrace (518-946-2255; Wilmington) 8.3-mile race up the Whiteface Mountain Veterans' Memorial Highway on the second Sunday in June.

Willard Hanmer Guideboat and Canoe Races (518-891-1990; Saranac Lake Chamber of Commerce, Saranac Lake) Races on Lake Flower for guideboats, canoes, rowing shells, war canoes, and kayaks in early July.

Casio Mountain-Bike Series (518-523-1655; ORDA, Lake Placid) Cross-country races at Mount Van Hoevenberg in July and Aug.

Can-Am Rugby Tournament (518-891-1990; Saranac Lake Chamber of Commerce, Saranac Lake) North America's largest rugby meet, with more than 100 teams competing in fields throughout Lake Placid and Saranac Lake in early Aug.

Mike Flanagan Cycling Classic (518-523-3764; High Peaks Cyclery, Saranac Ave., Lake Placid) Loop race and tour near Lake Placid in late July.

International Lacrosse Tournament (518-523-2591; North Elba Park District, Lake Placid) At the North Elba Horse Show Grounds in mid-Aug.

Adirondack Century Ride (518-523-3764; High Peaks Cyclery, Saranac Ave., Lake Placid) 100-mile 1-day bike tour from Lake Placid to different destinations. Fall.

Flatwater Canoe and Guideboat Races (518-582-3211) Races for adults and children on Lake Harris, near Newcomb, mid-Sept.

NORTHWEST LAKES

Genesee Flatwater Weekend (518-359-3328) Sponsored by Tupper Lake Chamber of Commerce. 11-mile canoe race on the Raquette River near Tupper Lake on Saturday; 44-mile canoe race from Long Lake to Tupper Lake village on Sunday, on the second weekend in June.

St. Regis Invitational (518-189-1990) Sponsored by the Saranac Lake Chamber of Commerce. 7-mile race for canoes, kayaks, and guideboats starting and ending at Paul Smith's College. June.

Tin Man Triathlon (518-359-3328) Sponsored by Tupper Lake Chamber of Commerce. 1.2-mile swim, 56-mile bike, 13.1-mile run beginning at the Tupper Lake Municipal Park; third weekend in July.

24-Hour Marathon (518-359-3328) Tupper Lake Chamber of Commerce. 10-person relay teams each run 1-mile laps at the Tupper Lake High School track on the second weekend in Aug.

Mini Triathlon (518-359-3328) Tupper Lake Chamber of Commerce. Road bike, canoe, and foot races at the Tupper Lake Rod & Gun Club; in Sept.

Fall Foliage Canoe and Kayak Race (518-359-3328) 11-mile race on the Raquette River and Piercefield Flow, Tupper Lake. Late Sept.

Boo Bash & Dash (518-891-1900) Mountain-bike races at Big Tupper Ski Area , Tupper Lake and Dewey Mtn., Saranac Lake. Late Oct.

CENTRAL ADIRONDACKS

Jeff Meneilly Memorial Cross-Country Ski Race (315-357-5501) Sponsored by Inlet Chamber of Commerce. 5-km citizens' cross-country ski race; Empire State Games qualifier; late Jan.

Piseco Airport Race (518-548-4521) Sponsored by Speculator Chamber of Commerce. 10-km citizens' cross-country-ski race in Piseco on the first Saturday in Feb.

Trappers Traverse and **Blue Mtn. Summit Dash** (518-648-5112) Snowshoe races during the Indian Lake Winter Festival in Feb.

Kunjamuck Kick (518-548-4521) 10-km citizens' cross-country-ski race near Speculator, sponsored by the International Paper Company and the Speculator Chamber of Commerce in late Feb.

Sisu Cross Country Ski Race (518-863-4974; Lapland Lake Cross Country Ski Center, Storer Rd., Benson) 25-km citizens' ski race in late Feb.

Snowflake Derby (315-369-3225; McCauley Mtn. Ski Area, Old Forge) Community downhill races in early Mar.

Whitewater Derby (518-251-2612) Sponsored by North Creek Chamber of Commerce. Slalom race for canoes and kayaks on the Hudson River near North River on Saturday; downriver canoe race from North Creek to Riparius on the Hudson on Sunday; first weekend in May.

Piseco Triathlon (518-548-4521) Sponsored by Speculator Chamber of Commerce. Swim, road bike, and run circumnavigating Piseco Lake on the third Sat. in July.

Lane Lake Run (518-548-4521) Sponsored by the Speculator Chamber of Commerce. 10-km footrace around Lake Pleasant on the second Sun. in Aug.

Great Sacandaga Lake Triathlon (1-800-676-FULT) Sponsored by Fulton County Tourism. 10-km run, 23-mile bike, and 4-mile canoe race on Great Sacandaga Lake on the third Sun. in Aug.

Adirondack Canoe Classic (518-891-1990) Sponsored by the Saranac Lake Chamber of Commerce. 90-mile 3-day canoe race from Old Forge to Saranac Lake village in early Sept.

Mountain Bike Festival (315-357-6672; Inlet) Bike polo, distance races in the Moose River Recreation Area, other NORBA-sanctioned events in late Sept.

Moose River Festival (315-369-6983) Extreme race for kayaks and closed canoes through Class IV and V rapids. Sponsored by American Whitewater and the Central Adirondack Association in mid-Oct.

Reindeer Roundup (518-863-4974; Lapland Lake Cross Country Ski Center, Benson) 10-km citizens' cross-country-ski race; Empire State Games qualifier, before Christmas.

Preparing for the last leg of the 90-mile Adirondack Classic.

Nancie Battaglia

ROCK AND ICE CLIMBING

Learning the ropes of Adirondack rock climbing.

Nancie Battaglia

Plenty of steep, challenging rock walls can be found in the ***High Peaks***, and scattered cliff faces are hidden in the ***Central Adirondacks***. Possibilities for rock and ice climbers abound, from non-technical scrambles up broad, smooth slides to gnarly 700-foot pitches in the 5.11+ difficulty range. Adirondack climbers — from wannabes to folks with permanently chalky palms — all depend on a thick green guidebook, *Climbing in the Adirondacks: A Guide to Rock and Ice Routes in the Adirondacks* (Adirondack Mountain Club) by Don Mellor. This book is indispensable since the approaches to many of the best climbs involve a hike or bushwhack to the base. It also outlines hundreds of climbs and explains the local ethic on clean wilderness climbing: leave as little trace as possible and place a minimum of bolts.

The High Peaks

Dozens of mountaintops rise 4,000 feet or more above sea level in the Adirondack Park. You don't need to be a technical climber to enjoy the views, but you should be an experienced, well-prepared hiker capable of putting in at least a twelve-mile round trip. For trail descriptions and access points, consult the *Guide to Adirondack Trails: High Peaks Region* (Adirondack Mountain Club) or *Discover the Adirondack High Peaks* (Backcountry Publications). The following "Forty-Six" are in the area bounded by Newcomb on the south, Elizabethtown on the east, Wilmington on the north, and the Franklin County line on the west.

Peak	Elevation	Peak	Elevation
1. Mount Marcy	5344 feet	24. Mount Marshall	4380
2. Algonquin Peak	5115	25. Seward Mountain	4347
3. Mount Haystack	4961	26. Allen Mountain	4347
4. Mount Skylight	4924	27. Big Slide Mountain	4249
5. Whiteface Mountain	4866	28. Esther Mountain	4239
6. Dix Mountain	4839	29. Upper Wolf Jaw	4185
7. Gray Peak	4830	30. Lower Wolf Jaw	4173
8. Iroquois Peak	4830	31. Phelps Mountain	4161
9. Basin Mountain	4826	32. Street Mountain	4150
10. Gothics Mountain	4734	33. Sawteeth Mountain	4150
11. Mount Colden	4734	34. Mount Donaldson	4140
12. Giant Mountain	4626	35. Cascade Mountain	4098
13. Nippletop Mountain	4610	36. Seymour Mountain	4091
14. Santanoni Peak	4606	37. Porter Mountain	4085
15. Mount Redfield	4606	38. Mount Colvin	4085
16. Wright Peak	4580	39. South Dix Mountain	4060
17. Saddleback Mountain	4528	40. Mount Emmons	4040
18. Panther Peak	4442	41. Dial Mountain	4020
19. Table Top Mountain	4413	42. East Dix Mountain	4006
20. Rocky Peak Ridge	4410	43. Blake Peak	3986
21. Hough Peak	4409	44. Cliff Mountain	3944
22. Macomb Mountain	4390	45. Nye Mountain	3944
23. Armstrong Mountain	4390	46. Cousachraga Peak	3820

(Elevations from *Of the Summits, Of the Forests*, Adirondack Forty-Sixers, 1991)

The **Adirondack Forty-Sixers** is an organization dedicated to these High Peaks. To earn the members' patch, you must have climbed all of the mountains listed above. The group performs trail work and education projects; for information, write to Adirondack Forty-Sixers, RFD 1 Box 390, Morrisonville NY 12962.

Climbers can get tips in a few places. The **Mountaineer** (518-576-2281; Rte. 73, Keene Valley) sells climbing gear, topo maps, and guidebooks; advice is free, but don't monopolize the sales staff with time-consuming questions. Anyway, many of your answers can be found at the **International Mountaineering Festival** each January, sponsored by the Mountaineer. Hardware and software for climbing can also be found in Lake Placid at **Eastern Mountain Sports** (518-523-2505; 51 Main St.) and **High Peaks Cyclery** (518-523-3764; Saranac Ave.), which has an indoor climbing wall. In North Creek, **The Mountain** (518-251-3111; Main St.) opened with a bang in December 1997, with a huge selection of equipment and a state-of-the-art indoor cliff.

To learn the basics of climbing or to polish your skills if you've had some experience, a handful of guide services specialize in helping you climb higher:

Adirondack Alpine Adventures (518-576-9881; Rte. 73, Keene) Rock- and ice-climbing guide service; instruction for women, small groups, or individuals.

Adirondack Mountain Club (518-523-3441; Adirondak Loj, Lake Placid) Weekend workshops for beginners and intermediates; lodging.

Adirondack Rock and River (518-576-2041; Alstead Hill Rd., Keene) Rock- and ice-climbing guide service; instruction for beginners to experts; natural indoor climbing wall; lodging.

And More Peaks

In other parts of the park there are mountains nearly as high, with sweeping vistas of forests and lakes. A short list of pinnacles with marked trails and open summits or fire towers follows. Note that there are plenty more mountains in the park; ask locally for favorite vantage points.

Peak	Elevation	Closest Town
Snowy Mountain	3899 feet	Indian Lake
McKenzie Mountain	3832	Lake Placid
Lyon Mountain	3830	Chazy Lake
Wakely Mountain	3770	Indian Lake
Blue Mountain	3759	Blue Mtn. Lake
Hurricane Mountain	3678	Elizabethtown
Pillsbury Mountain	3597	Speculator
Ampersand Mountain	3552	Saranac Lake
Vanderwhacker Mountain	3386	Minerva
Crane Mountain	3254	Johnsburg
Pharoah Mountain	2557	Schroon Lake

ROWING

The Adirondack guideboat is the preeminent rowing machine for the region, and you'll find a selection of boatbuilders in Chapter Six, *Shopping*. **Adirondack Rowing** (518-585-7870; 306 Lake George Ave., Ticonderoga) sells all kinds of modern shells and offers lessons.

Most of the small-to-medium-size Adirondack lakes are especially suitable for rowing. Quiet lakes — Indian, Paradox, Forked, Star, Long, Lake Pleasant, and others — offer several miles of open water, yet have less powerboat traffic than say, Lake George or Schroon Lake. You'll also find that early morning or early evening, when the winds are relatively calm, are the best times to row. Do carry a flashlight if you go out at dusk. Mirror Lake, on the backside of downtown Lake Placid, is not open to motorboats, so there's another fine possibility for rowers. You might even be able to match a few strokes with Olympic athletes as they train; the U.S. Canoe and Kayak Team moved to town in 1997.

SAILING

The big lakes — George, Champlain, and Great Sacandaga — offer good sailing in the midst of beautiful scenery and have marinas for an evening's dockage or equipment repairs. In fact, any lake with a public launch is open to sailboats; the most suitable craft for bouldery-bottomed Adirondack lakes are those with centerboards you can pull up readily. Even then, remember to keep an eye out for unmarked rocks! Sailing on these island-studded waters can be tricky, since in the lee of an island you stand a good chance of being becalmed. Wind can whip shallow lakes into whitecapped mini-oceans, too. A portable weather radio should be included in your basic kit; Adirondack forecasts (out of Burlington, Vermont) can be found at 162.40 megahertz.

You can purchase Coast Guard charts for Lakes George and Champlain, but not for most of the small interior lakes. Some USGS topographical maps have troughs and shoals marked, but these maps are of limited use to sailors. Your best bet is to ask at boat liveries for lake maps, or at least find out how to avoid the worst rocks.

For hardware, lines, and other equipment you may need, check in the beginning portion of this chapter for a list of marinas. In the *Lake George* area, **Yankee Yacht Sales** (518-668-2862; Rte. 9N, Diamond Point), is well stocked with everything from the essentials to brand-new boats. They also offer sailing instruction and rent day-sailers and cruisers. On *Lake Champlain*, **Westport Marina** (518-962-4356; Washington St., Westport) has a good selection of sailing supplies. In the *Central Adirondacks* region, **Palmer Point** (315-357-5594; Fourth Lake, Inlet) sells sailboats and sailboards and offers lessons.

SCENIC FLIGHTS

*A chartered plane cruises
above the mountaintops.*

Nancie Battaglia

If climbing a mountain isn't for you, yet you still seek a bird's-eye view of the territory, why not charter a small plane to soar above the wilds? Several pilots offer sightseeing flights at a reasonable cost: a 15- to 20-minute flight covering about 50 miles of territory costs less than the average evening out. You can make special arrangements for longer flights, but a typical short trip costs about $50 for a family of four. Seaplane services are also equipped to take canoeists, fishermen, and hunters into ponds and lakes.

Listed below are a few fixed-wheel and seaplane services for private charters; you *must* call ahead for a reservation. Just beyond the border of the park, you can arrange for floating on air with **Adirondack Balloon Flights** (518-793-6342; Glens Falls).

Adirondack Flying Service (518-523-2473; Cascade Rd., Lake Placid) Scenic flights over the High Peaks; glider rides; air taxi.
Bird's Seaplane Service (315-357-3631; Sixth Lake, Inlet) Scenic flights; hunting and fishing charters.
Helms Aero Service (518-624-3931; Town Beach, Long Lake) Scenic seaplane flights; hunting and fishing charters.
Payne's Air Service (315-357-3971; Seventh Lake, Inlet) Scenic flights; hunting and fishing charters.

SCENIC HIGHWAYS

We may be biased, but we think that most Adirondack byways are pretty darn scenic: even Interstate 87 — the Northway — won an award as

"America's Most Beautiful Highway" the year it was completed. Specifically, we're talking here about roads up mountains so that everyone can enjoy the view. In the _Lake George_ area, **Prospect Mountain Memorial Highway** (518-668-5198; off Rte. 9 near Lake George village) snakes up a small peak to offer a terrific 100-mile view stretching from the High Peaks to Vermont and the Catskills. Not too far from _Lake Placid,_ **Whiteface Mountain Veterans Memorial Highway** (518-946-7175; off Rte. 431, Wilmington) has a great view, too, looking down on other summits and silvery lakes. Both are state-operated toll roads open daily from late May through the fall.

SKIING: CROSS COUNTRY AND SNOWSHOEING

Challenging backcountry routes can be found in the High Peaks and other wilderness areas.

Nancie Battaglia

The Adirondack Park is paradise for cross-country skiers. Most winters there's plenty of snow, especially in the higher elevations or west of the Champlain Valley. A wide range of destinations entices skiers, from rugged expeditions in the High Peaks to gentle groomed paths suitable for novices, plus hundreds of miles of intermediate trails in between. Many of the marked hiking trails on state land are not only suitable for cross-country skiing or snowshoeing, they're actually better for winter recreation since swampy areas are frozen, and ice-bound ponds and lakes can be easily crossed.

For suggestions on backcountry ski trails, consult _Classic Adirondack Ski Tours_ by Tony Goodwin (Adirondack Mountain Club), _Cross Country Skiing in the Adirondacks_ by Dennis Conroy (Countryman Press) or any of the books in the _Discover the Adirondacks_ series (Backcountry Publications and Lakeview Press) by Barbara McMartin. Both _Adirondack Life_ and _Adirondac_ magazines outline ski treks in their winter issues; if your local library has back issues, a treasure trove of potential ski trips is at your fingertips.

Many of the designated wilderness and wild-forest areas (described below) offer great ski touring on marked but ungroomed trails. The **Adirondack**

Challenge, a hiking-canoeing-skiing program sponsored by the Visitor Interpretive Centers (518-327-3000) describes several trips in a handy brochure. Another option for exploring the wild wintry woods is to hire a licensed guide; check under "Hiking and Backpacking" earlier in this chapter for backcountry trip leaders.

Before setting out on any of these wilderness excursions, prepare your pack with quick-energy food; a thermos filled with hot tea or cocoa; extra hat, socks, and gloves; topo map and compass; matches; flashlight; and space blanket. Dress in layers of wool, polypropylene, or synthetic pile. Don't travel alone. Sign in at the trailhead register. Let friends know your destination and when you plan to return.

Many towns maintain cross-country ski trails, and the **Visitor Interpretive Center** at Paul Smiths (518-327-3000) has many miles of easy trails. At the **Newcomb VIC** (518-528-2000), the trails are not quite so great for skiing, but you can try snowshoeing at no charge; the Tubbs company has donated 50 pairs of new snowshoes for the public to enjoy. Throughout the park, snowshoeing is enjoying a burst of popularity, as witnessed by a series of citizen races in Paul Smiths, Indian Lake, and Blue Mtn. Lake.

The **Jackrabbit Trail** (518-523-1365; Lake Placid) is a superb local resource, some 35 miles of groomed trails connecting Keene with Lake Placid, Saranac Lake, and Paul Smiths; eventually the route will extend to Tupper Lake. The trail combines old logging roads and trails and is named for Herman "Jack Rabbit" Johannsen, who laid out many of the routes in the 1920s. From some of the hotels in downtown Placid, you can strap on your skis and just head out for the woods. There's even guided inn-to-inn skiing sponsored by some lodgings; check with your host if you're staying in the High Peaks. The Jackrabbit Trail joins with many of the commercial ski-touring areas, and traverses the McKenzie Mountain Wilderness Area between Whiteface Inn and Saranac Lake. Note that dogs are not welcome on groomed portions of the Jackrabbit Trail, nor at the privately owned ski centers.

Besides wilderness trails and informal town ski trails, there are some excellent cross-country-ski areas with meticulously groomed tracks and rental equipment. You'll find a variety of ski areas listed below, and we suggest calling ahead for current information about snow cover. Many of the touring centers offer lessons, and the **Adirondack Mountain Club** (518-523-3441; Adirondak Loj, Lake Placid) schedules backcountry- and telemark-skiing workshops.

CROSS-COUNTRY SKI CENTERS AND TRAIL NETWORKS

LAKE GEORGE AND SOUTHEASTERN ADIRONDACKS

Caroline Fish Memorial Trail (518-494-2722; Rte. 8, Chestertown) 11-km town trail.

Rogers Rock State Campsite (518-543-6161; Rte. 9N, Hague) 10-km ungroomed trails.

Cold, Cold, Cold

In the old days, folks caught unprepared in the wilds occasionally died of "exposure." Today, we call that same condition hypothermia (literally "low temperature"), and it remains a serious concern in cool, moist climates year-round. Even on a summer day, a lightly clad hiker can suffer from hypothermia after being caught in the rain. In winter, unaccustomed strenuous exercise coupled with the wrong kind of clothing can lead to hypothermia.

Hypothermia is caused when the body loses warmth faster than it can produce heat. The normal body-core temperature of 98.6°F decreases to a dangerous level, which happens when the body is inadequately insulated by clothing. Precipitating events can be a dunking in cold water or soaking in steady drizzle. To compensate for heat loss, the body tries to produce more warmth, which burns up energy. As energy reserves dwindle and muscles become exhausted, hypothermia sets in.

Signs of hypothermia arrive in stages: first, the person feels and acts cold. He or she may shiver, have trouble with manual dexterity, or show bluish skin color. Next, shaking becomes uncontrollable, and the person starts to behave erratically, acting sluggish, apathetic, or cranky. The victim may stagger or seem off balance. Some folks refer to the "Umble Rule" — watch out when a companion begins to stumble, mumble, grumble, and fumble.

The final stage of hypothermia is a true medical emergency. The person feels cold to the touch; shivering has stopped; limbs may be frostbitten. The victim may seem uncaring about survival. The treatment of all stages of hypothermia is basically the same — add warmth. Warm the person with your hands, body-to-body contact, a fire. Provide hot liquids: tea, soup, cocoa, or any nonalcoholic beverage. For a person in severe hypothermia, try to prevent further heat loss and get the victim to a medical facility as quickly as possible.

A few ounces of prevention go a long way in avoiding hypothermia. Dress in layers, especially clothing made of wool, polypropylene, or synthetic pile, all of which insulate when wet. ("Cotton kills," forest rangers say.) Bring spare hats, mittens, socks, overpants, windbreaker. Pack plenty of high-energy food and warm liquids. Put an "instant heat" packet in a pocket. Watch out for your friends and be honest about your abilities. Know when to turn back.

Frostbite and its cousin, frostnip, are not hypothermia. The terms refer to flesh actually freezing, and it's usually fingers, toes, ears, nose, or chin that are affected. Frostbite can occur quickly, especially on areas exposed to the wind; look for skin appearing waxy. One test for frostbite is to pinch the affected part gently and watch for the color to change. Unaffected flesh will revert to its normal color, but frozen parts remain whitish and feel hard and cold.

At the first sign of frostbite, warm the affected part at body temperature. You can warm your hands by sticking fingers in your mouth, by placing them in an armpit or between your legs; ears and cheeks can be warmed with a dry hand;

(Continued)

feet can be warmed up with the help of a buddy's body. Do not rub a frostbitten part; you can cause severe tissue damage since there are actual ice crystals in the cells. Don't use temperatures above 110°F for warming, as excessive heat can cause greater damage. (In other words, be very careful using a pocket hand-warmer.) Avoid refreezing any frostbitten parts.

Deep frostbite should not be thawed. It sounds grim, but it's better to walk out on frozen feet than it is to thaw them and then try to shuffle along. Severe frost-bite is a medical emergency that will need evacuation and lengthy hospitalization to repair circulatory damage.

Schroon Lake Ski Trails (518-532-7675) Backcountry skiing in Pharaoh Lake and Hoffman Notch wilderness areas.

Warren County Trails (518-623-5576; Hudson Ave., Warrensburg) 16-km trails along the Hudson River.

HIGH PEAKS AND NORTHERN ADIRONDACKS

Adirondak Loj (518-523-3441; Adirondak Loj Rd., Lake Placid) 12-km back-country trails; connect with numerous wilderness trails; guided tours; lessons; food; lodging.

Bark Eater X-C Ski Center (518-576-2221; Alstead Hill Rd., Keene) 20-km groomed trails; connects with Jackrabbit Trail; rentals; lessons; lodging.

Cascade Ski Touring Center (518-523-9605; Rte. 73, Lake Placid) 20-km groomed trails; connects with Jackrabbit Trail; night skiing; rentals; lessons; ski shop.

Cunningham's Ski Barn (518-523-4460; Main St., Lake Placid) Groomed trails on Lake Placid Club property; connects with Jackrabbit Trail; rentals; lessons; full ski shop.

Dewey Mountain (518-891-2697; Rte. 30, Saranac Lake) 20-km groomed trails; night skiing; lessons; guided tours.

Lake Placid Lodge (518-523-2700; Whiteface Inn Rd., Lake Placid) 20-km groomed trails; full shop; lessons.

Mount Van Hoevenberg (518-523-2811; Rte. 73, Lake Placid) 50-km groomed Olympic trails; connects with Jackrabbit Trail; rentals; lessons; ski shop.

NORTHWEST LAKES

Big Tupper Ski Area (518-359-3651; Rte. 30, Tupper Lake) 15-km groomed trails; rentals; ski shop.

Cranberry Lake Trail (315-386-4000; Rte. 3, Cranberry Lake) Backcountry trails.

Deer Pond Loop (518-359-3328; Rte. 30, Tupper Lake) 15-km backcountry loop.

CENTRAL ADIRONDACKS

Adirondack Woodcraft Ski Touring Center (315-369-6031; Rondaxe Rd., Old Forge) 15-km groomed trails; night skiing; rentals; ski shop.

Fern Park Recreation Area (315-357-5501; South Shore Rd., Inlet) 20-km groomed trails; night skiing.

Garnet Hill Cross-Country Ski Center (518-251-2821; 13th Lake Rd., North River) 50-km groomed trails; connects with trails in Siamese Ponds Wilderness Area; rentals; lessons; ski shop; food; lodging.

Gore Mountain (518-251-2411; Peaceful Valley Rd., North Creek) 10-km groomed trails; rentals; ski shop; food.

Lapland Lake (518-863-4974; Storer Rd., Benson) 40-km groomed trails; rentals; lessons; ski shop; food; lodging.

Long Lake (518-624-3077) Backcountry trails; excellent map available for Long Lake and Raquette Lake area trails.

McCauley Mountain (315-369-3225; McCauley Mtn. Rd., Old Forge) 20-km groomed trails; rentals; lessons; food.

Speculator Cross-Country Ski Trails (518-548-4521; Elm Lake Rd., Speculator) Backcountry trails.

CROSS-COUNTRY-SKI OUTFITTERS AND SHOPS

HIGH PEAKS AND NORTHERN ADIRONDACKS

Blue Line Sport Shop (518-891-4680; 82 Main St., Saranac Lake) Ski rentals and sales; sporting goods; maps.

Eastern Mountain Sports (518-523-2505; 51 Main St., Lake Placid) Cross-country, telemark, and backcountry equipment; gear; guidebooks; maps.

High Peaks Cyclery (518-523-3764; Saranac Ave., Lake Placid) Cross-country, telemark and backcountry equipment for sale and rent; snowshoe and skate rentals; outdoor gear and books.

The Mountaineer (518-576-2281; Rte. 73, Keene Valley) Cross-country, telemark, and backcountry equipment; gear; guidebooks; maps.

NORTHWEST LAKES

Tip Top Sport Shop (518-359-9222; 40 Park St., Tupper Lake) Downhill and cross-country-ski equipment; skates.

CENTRAL ADIRONDACKS

Beaver Brook Outfitters (518-251-3394; Rte. 28, Wevertown) Cross-country-ski and snowshoe sales and rentals; outdoor clothing; guidebooks.

Boardertown (518-251-3111; Main St., North Creek) New in winter 1998, with backcountry skis, cold-weather clothing, and snowboards.

Cunningham's Ski Barn (518-251-3215; Rte. 28, North Creek) Downhill and cross-country-ski sales and rentals; clothing.

Free Spirits Adventures (518-924-9275; Rte. 30, Wells) Telemark lessons; guided backcountry trips; cross-country and camping gear; wooden skis.

Inlet Ski Touring Center (315-357-6961; South Shore Rd., Inlet) Racing and touring equipment; trails connect with Fern Park.

Kindred Spirits (518-251-5131; Four Corners, Olmstedville) Cross-country skis and snowshoes; clothing; guidebooks; trail information.

Mountainman Outdoor Supply (315-357-6672; Rte. 28, Inlet) Hiking, camping, and cross-country-ski gear.

Sporting Propositions (315-369-6188; Main St., Old Forge) Downhill and cross-country ski-sales and rentals; clothing.

BEYOND THE BLUE LINE

Fall Line Ski Shop (518-793-3203; Quaker Rd., Glens Falls) Downhill and cross-country-ski sales and rentals.

Inside Edge (518-793-5676; 624 Upper Glen St., Glens Falls) Downhill and cross-country-ski sales and rentals; racing supplies.

Syd & Dusty's Outfitters (518-792-0260; Rtes. 9 & 149, Queensbury) Downhill and cross-country-ski equipment; outdoor gear.

Wooden Ski and Wheel (518-561-2790; Rte. 9, Plattsburgh) Cross-country-ski equipment; outdoor gear.

SKIING: DOWNHILL AND SNOWBOARDING

Skiing has been a part of Adirondack life since the 1930s. Weekend ski trains from New York's Grand Central once brought thousands of folks to North Creek, where they could "ride up and slide down." The "ride up" was in

Skiers at an old-time Adirondack lodge used one very long pole for downhill runs.

Courtesy of *Adirondack Life* magazine

school buses equipped with wooden ski racks mounted on the outside, and the "slide down" was on twisty trails carved out of the forest near Barton Mines, across from the present-day slopes on Gore Mountain.

Today there are a couple of high-profile mountains with challenging slopes and extensive snowmaking: Whiteface and Gore, both operated by the Olympic Regional Development Authority. There are also a number of nice little mountains where the emphasis is on family fun rather than on the trendiest gear. A few towns, like Indian Lake and Newcomb, operate free downhill areas for residents and guests. Of course, you won't find manmade snow there, and you'll have to remember dormant skills for managing a poma lift or a rope tow, but you can have a blast with the kids and beat the crowds.

Naturally downhill season in the Adirondacks depends on the weather. Often snowmaking begins in November, and some trails may open by mid-December, but it can be Christmas week before the snow is reliable throughout an entire ski area. Many people prefer spring conditions when there's corn snow and bright sunshine. Whatever the weather, it's not a bad idea to call ahead for the ski conditions before you go.

Compared to ski areas in Vermont or the Rockies, the Adirondack ones seem undeveloped. The emphasis at the hills is on skiing, not on hot-tub lounging, nightlife, or après-ski ambiance. At the base of a mountain, you won't find condos or designer restaurants; for fancy meals and lodging, you have to go to town. Listed below are some downhill ski areas within the Adirondack Park.

Price Code

Downhill Ski Areas	**Inexpensive**	**Moderate**	**Expensive**
(Weekend lift tickets for an adult)	**under $15**	**$15–$25**	**over $25**

LAKE GEORGE AND SOUTHEASTERN ADIRONDACKS

HICKORY HILL
518-623-2825.
Hickory Hill Rd., off Rte. 418, Warrensburg NY 12883.
Summer address: Box 9004, Schenectady NY 12309.
Trails: 14 (1 beginner, 7 intermediate, 6 expert).
Lifts: 1 rope tow; 1 T-bar; 2 poma lifts.
Vertical drop: 1200 ft.
Snowmaking: No.
Tickets: Inexpensive.
Open: Sat.–Sun. 9am–4pm.

In the late 1940s, Hans Winbaur and friends began carving out slopes on a conical mountain overlooking the Schroon and Hudson rivers near Warrensburg. Today, Hickory retains a folksy, hand-hewn approach, and in fact, it was the first ski area in the country to be owned and operated by its stockholders — a cooperative downhill area. Volunteers work on the trails, service the lifts, and raise money to keep the hill afloat.

Runs named Windfall, Hare, Grand Teton, and Topnotch are steep, expert slopes, but there are gentler ridge trails and traverses for intermediates. There's a certified ski school, a base lodge, and a professional patrol. Hickory Hill depends on natural snow cover, so call ahead.

HIGH PEAKS AND NORTHERN ADIRONDACKS

MOUNT PISGAH
518-891-0970.
Mt. Pisgah Rd., off Trudeau
    Rd., Saranac Lake NY
    12983.
Trails: 1 main trail; some
    side trails.
Lifts: 1 T-bar.
Vertical drop: 300 ft.
Snowmaking: Yes.
Tickets: Inexpensive.
Open: Tues.–Sun.; week-
    days 3–9pm; Sat. 9am–
    6 pm; Sun. 12–6pm.

If you've read *The Bell Jar*, you're acquainted with Mount Pisgah. Sylvia Plath skied there in the fifties and chronicled her spectacular tumble in the book. Since then, the hill was operated on-again, off-again until the late 1980s, when volunteers rebuilt the hill, and by their efforts encouraged public officials to revitalize the slope. The mountain today is still very much a family ski area, with a friendly atmosphere and slopes geared to intermediate skiers. One section called "Suicide" falls somewhere between a modest drop-off and a mini-headwall; 10-year-olds think it's awesome.

There's snowmaking covering most of the hill, thanks to local fundraising efforts, and a ski school, patrol, and base lodge. Pisgah is one of the few places left in the Adirondacks where you can enjoy night skiing; local residents often hit the slopes after work, when a lift ticket (good from 6–9pm) costs about $6.

Whiteface Mountain has the highest vertical drop in the Northeast and more than 60 trails.

Nancie Battaglia

**WHITEFACE
    MOUNTAIN**
518-946-2233.
Rte. 86, Wilmington NY
    12997.
Trails: 65 (17 expert, 25
    intermediate, 17 novice).
Lifts: 9 chairlifts (7 double
    chairs, 2 triple chairs).
Vertical drop: 3216 ft.
Snowmaking: 93%.

New York governor Averill Harriman dedicated Whiteface Mountain, a state-owned facility, in 1958; the event was marred slightly when the chairlift he was riding came to a dead halt, and Harriman had to be rescued by ladder from his lofty perch. Not to worry, modern skiers — Whiteface lifts are totally reliable now.

The Olympic mountain has the longest vertical drop in the East and lots of intense, expert skiing.

Tickets: Expensive.
Open: Daily 9am–4pm.

Cloudspin, one of the black-diamond trails, is long and hard with big bumps; Wilderness, another toughie, is the site of international mogul competitions. Intermediate skiers have dozens of challenging trails, with the three-mile-long Excelsior at the top of the list. Whiteface is big enough — but not a place you can get lost in — to accommodate scads of skiers without building up long lift lines.

There's an excellent play-and-ski program for tots and a first-rate ski school led by Ed Kreil. Whiteface also sponsors races ranging from low-key events like the Cocoa Butter Open to Olympic qualifiers.

There are three lodges for food, drink, and discussing the slopes, plus a full ski shop with rentals for skiers of all sizes and abilities. Although a weekend adult ticket is more than $35, there are sizable mid-week discounts, special promotions, and ladies' days.

NORTHWEST LAKES

Big Tupper Ski Area often has great snow cover and few crowds.

Nancie Battaglia

BIG TUPPER SKI AREA
518-359-7902.
Country Club Rd., off Rte.
  30, Tupper Lake NY
  12986.
Trails: 23.
Lifts: 4 (3 double chairs;
  rope tow).
Vertical drop: 1152 ft.
Snowmaking: 100%.
Tickets: Moderate.
Open: Mid-Dec., 9am–4pm
  daily; some night skiing.

Overlooking Big Tupper Lake, on Mount Morris, is a solid family ski area that's had a roller-coaster history. Since the early sixties, when the mountain was first developed, Big Tupper has been through several operators, from local town government to a New Jersey hot-dog magnate.

The mountain is mostly intermediate terrain. Headwalls launch many routes that fade to long, gentle run-outs. When there's good snow cover, skiers looking for steep, narrow chutes and difficult pitches can try from the top of the number-one chair. At the base lodge, there's a cafeteria, bar, ski shop, ski-school office, picnic tables, and a fireplace; the rental shop is in a separate building.

Big Tupper was among the first Blue Line hills to welcome telemark skiers and snowboarders, and sponsors occasional races on weekends.

CENTRAL ADIRONDACKS

GORE MOUNTAIN
518-251-2441.
Peaceful Valley Rd., off Rte.
  28, North Creek NY 12853.
Trails: 41.
Lifts: 9 (1 4-person gondola,
  1 triple chair, 5 double
  chairs, 1 J-bar).
Vertical drop: 2100 ft.
Snowmaking: 90%.
Tickets: Expensive.
Open: Daily 9am–4pm.

Near North Creek, the cradle of North Country alpine skiing, is the other state-owned Adirondack ski hill: Gore Mountain, which opened in the early sixties. Beginning in 1984, Gore has been managed by the Olympic Regional Development Authority, as is Whiteface Mountain. Since that time, snowmaking has been installed over most of the mountain and trails have been widened.

Gore is intermediate heaven, with wide-open cruising runs, such as Showcase, Sunway, and Twister, on the lower part of the mountain, accessible from the high-speed triple chair. Mogul mavens and expert skiers can find good sport on Chatiemac and Hawkeye. Gore is home to New York's only gondola; folks agree it's a real blessing on blustery winter days.

The mountain has an excellent nursery, a ski-and-play program for preschoolers, and a ski school for all ages. The base lodge has a cozy lounge, but the cafeteria is cavernous. There's a full ski shop and rentals on the ground floor. Citizen racers can join in NASTAR competitions every weekend, while snurfer wannabes can take snowboarding lessons.

MCCAULEY MOUNTAIN
315-369-3225.
McCauley Mtn. Rd., off
  Bisby Rd., Old Forge NY
  13420.
Trails: 14 (3 expert, 5
  intermediate, 6 novice).
Lifts: 5 (1 double chair,
  2 T-bars, 1 rope tow, 1
  poma lift).
Vertical drop: 633 ft.
Snowmaking: Yes.
Tickets: Inexpensive.
Open: Daily 9am–4pm.

Hank Kashiwa, the international racing star and ski designer, learned his first snowplow turns here; his brilliant career is something folks in Old Forge still talk about. Actually, the Town of Webb school has produced three U.S. Olympic ski-team members, thanks to good coaches and the welcoming intermediate slopes at the local hill.

This little mountain has heaps of natural snow, due to a micro-climate that can produce 200 inches or more during an average winter. Helmers and Olympic, both of which have snowmaking, are the most difficult slopes. Intermediates can sample Upper God's Land, a ridge trail; Sky Ride, a wide route serviced by the double chair; or the gentle, sweeping Challenger. The lift crew feeds the deer here, so even non-skiers can enjoy a visit. You'll find all the amenities at McCauley: a ski school, rentals, food and drink.

OAK MOUNTAIN
518-548-7311.
Elm Lake Rd., off Rte. 30,
Speculator NY 12164.
Trails: 13.
Lifts: 3 T-bars.
Vertical drop: 650 ft.
Snowmaking: No.
Tickets: Inexpensive.
Open: Fri.–Sun. 9am–4pm.

Just a yodel away from Speculator's busy corner is Oak Mountain, built in 1948. Norm and Nancy Germain run an exemplary family ski hill here that offers diverse slopes for intermediates and novices. There are steep woodland trails, broad gentle runs, and a few options in between. Telemarkers love the place.

Townsfolk work as lift attendants in exchange for skiing privileges; the nearby public schools offer free ski lessons here for students. There's a base lodge that resembles an overgrown cabin, with dozens of wooden picnic tables, and overall, the philosophy of the place — that downhill skiing is for everybody — remains as clear today as it was forty years ago.

BEYOND THE BLUE LINE

There's good skiing just outside the Adirondack Park, too. Near Glens Falls, you'll find **West Mountain** (518-793-6606; West Mtn. Rd., Queensbury), with 23 trails and 1000-foot vertical. **Titus Mountain** (518-483-3740; Rte. 30, Malone) has 26 trails, 1200 vertical feet, and snowmaking on 90 percent of the runs. To the west, **Snow Ridge** (315-348-8456; off Rte. 26, Turin) has 22 trails and gets about 250 inches of natural snow a year. Snowmaking has been installed on some trails.

SNOWMOBILING

Deep blankets of snow, miles of old roads, active clubs, and support from town trail-maintenance programs add up to excellent snowmobiling in many parts of the park. A hub of snowmobile activity is Old Forge, which issues more than 12,000 snowmobile permits each winter. (Permits are available from the Tourist Information Center on Rte. 28 in the center of town.) Trails in Old Forge spread out like a river with numerous tributaries. You can connect with the Inlet trails to the east, or the Independence River Wild Forest and Big Moose trails to the north, and Forestport and Boonville routes to the south. These trails meet still other trails, so that you can continue further east from Inlet to Indian Lake or Speculator, and then from Speculator to Wells, or you can go from Inlet to Raquette Lake, and then on to Long Lake and Newcomb. Confused? There's information listed below to help you track down maps and brochures, or even find a guide.

Besides the Old Forge–Inlet area, which receives more than 15 feet of snow during an average winter, there are more than 400 miles of snowmobile trails in the Tupper Lake–Saranac Lake–Lake Placid area, and near Cranberry Lake, there are scores of miles of trails. Many trail networks throughout the park cross private timberlands as well as the state forest preserve. Public lands designated as wild forest areas are open to snowmobiling; wilderness areas are not. (You'll find descriptions of these areas near the end of this chapter.)

As with any winter pursuit, planning and preparation help make a successful outing. Know your machine; carry an emergency repair kit and understand how to use it. Be sure you have plenty of gas. Travel with friends in case of a breakdown or other surprise situation. Never ride at night unless you're familiar with the trail or are following an experienced leader. Avoid crossing frozen lakes and streams unless you are *absolutely certain* the ice is safe. Some town or county roads are designated trails; while on such a highway, keep right, observe the posted snowmobile speed limit, and travel in single file.

Your basic pack should contain a topographic map and compass as well as a local trail map; survival kit with matches, flashlight, rope, space blanket, quick-energy food, and something warm to drink; extra hat, socks, and mittens. Although a sip of brandy may give the illusion of warming you up, alcohol impairs circulation and can hasten hypothermia. And an arrest for snowmobiling under the influence carries with it severe penalties.

SNOWMOBILE RENTALS AND GUIDES

Guided snowmobile tours are a new service here, and for getting around unfamiliar territory during a full day's riding, a knowledgeable leader is a real asset. In some communities, you can rent a sled, but this service is not widespread. For example, in Lake Placid you can rent snowmobiles from **Adirondack Snowmobile Rentals** (518-523-1388) and **Lake Placid Sports Unlimited** (518-523-3596); **Adirondack Adventure Tours** (518-523-1475) offers guided expeditions.

To explore the wild forest around Cranberry Lake, contact **Woods Adventure Rentals** (315-848-5005). The company rents snowmobiles and offers a guide service for day trips.

Near Old Forge, several dealers rent snowmobiles: **Old Forge Sports Tours** (315-369-3796) and **Big Moose Yamaha** (315-357-2998, Eagle Bay). **Don's Polaris** (315-369-3255; Rte. 28, Old Forge) and **Smith Marine** (315-369-3366, Old Forge) sell and repair sleds.

For information about snowmobiling in specific areas, contact county and town tourist-information offices listed in Chapter Eight, *Information*.

SWIMMING

There are so many fine places to swim in the Adirondacks it's almost easier to list where you can't swim: Ausable Chasm and High Falls Gorge spring to mind. Most of the towns in the park offer clean, safe, free beaches with lifeguards on duty in July and August, and many of the public campgrounds described earlier in this chapter have excellent swimming areas with guards. If you want to visit a state campground just for swimming and picnicking, the day-use fee is about $5 per carload.

WHITEWATER RAFTING

Whitewater rafting on the Hudson River is prime in spring and fall.

Nancie Battaglia

The wild, remote Upper Hudson River provides some of the East's most exhilarating whitewater: nearly 17 miles of continuous Class III-V rapids. From about 1860 to 1950, river drivers sent logs downstream every spring to sawmills and pulp mills, and they followed along behind the churning, tumbling timber in rowboats to pry logjams loose. Since the mid-1970s, the Hudson's power has been rediscovered for recreational purposes, with several rafting companies making the trip from the Indian River, just south of Indian Lake, to North River.

Reliable water levels are provided by a dam release below Lake Abanakee, courtesy of the Town of Indian Lake. Releases begin about April 1 and last through Memorial Day, and most years, there are summer and fall seasons, with scheduled dam releases on weekends.

Although you don't need whitewater paddling experience to enjoy a trip down the Hudson, you do need to be over age 14, in good physical condition, and a competent swimmer. The outfitters supply you with wetsuit, paddle, life jacket, and helmet; they also shuttle you to the put-in, give on-shore instructions in safety and paddling techniques, and supply a hot meal at the end of the trip. Rafters should bring polypropylene underwear to wear under the suits; wool hats, gloves, and socks; sneakers; and dry, warm clothing for after the trip. (Springtime Adirondack air can be chilly, and the water temperature is truly frigid).

A licensed guide steers each raft and directs the crew. This trip is not for passive passengers; you're expected to paddle — sometimes hard and fast — as the guide instructs. The Hudson Gorge is an all-day adventure, containing four to five hours of strenuous exercise, with the 1997 price $65–$85 per person.

Several rafting companies also offer short, fun trips on the Sacandaga River near Lake Luzerne. These junkets float 3.5 miles and last about an hour. Dam releases make the stream navigable all summer, and the cost is about $15 per person. On the other end of the spectrum is the Moose River from McKeever to Port Leyden; this is a 14-mile beast absolutely for experienced whitewater paddlers only. The Moose is runnable after spring ice-out, and the charge is about $80–$95 per person.

WHITEWATER OUTFITTERS

ARO (1-800-525-RAFT; Box 649, Old Forge) Trips on the Hudson and Moose rivers in spring; Black and Sacandaga rivers in summer.

Adirondack Wildwaters Inc. (1-800-933-2468 or 518-696-2953; Box 801, Corinth) Hudson River trips in spring; Moose River trips in Apr.

Adventure Sports Rafting Company (1-800-441-RAFT; Main St., Indian Lake) Hudson River trips in spring and fall.

Hudson River Rafting Company (1-800-888-RAFT or 518-251-3215; Rte. 28, North Creek) Hudson River trips in spring and fall; Sacandaga River trips in summer; Moose River trips in Apr.

Middle Earth Expeditions (518-523-9572; Cascade Rd., Lake Placid) Hudson River trips in spring; overnight float-in fishing trips in fall.

W.I.L.D./W.A.T.E.R.S. Outdoor Center (518-494-7478; Rte. 28, The Glen) Hudson River trips in spring; Moose River trips in spring and fall as water levels allow; Sacandaga River trips in summer.

WILDERNESS AREAS

"Where man is only a visitor who does not remain," is a phrase contained within legislation that defined the 15 wilderness areas of the Adirondack Park in the early 1970s. These portions of the forest preserve are 10,000 acres or larger and contain little evidence of modern times. Wilderness areas are open to hiking, cross-country skiing, hunting, fishing, and other similar pursuits, but seaplanes may not land on wilderness ponds, nor are motorized vehicles welcome. Listed below are Adirondack wilderness areas.

Nancie Battaglia

View near Indian Falls in the High Peaks Wilderness Area.

LAKE GEORGE AND SOUTHEASTERN ADIRONDACKS

Pharaoh Lake: 46,000 acres; E. of Schroon Lake hamlet. Extensive trail system; 36 lakes and ponds; lean-tos; views from Pharaoh and other nearby mountains.

HIGH PEAKS AND NORTHERN ADIRONDACKS

Dix Mountain: 45,000 acres; S.W. of Keene Valley. Adjacent to High Peaks wilderness; rock climbing at Chapel Pond; views from Noonmark, Dix, and many other mountains.

Giant Mountain: 23,000 acres; between Elizabethtown and Keene. Roaring Brook Falls; extensive hiking trails; views from Rocky Peak Ridge, Giant, and other mountains.

High Peaks: 226,000 acres; between Lake Placid and Newcomb. Excellent trail network; rock climbing at Wallface and other peaks; small lakes and ponds; views from Mount Marcy, Algonquin, and numerous other summits. Some interior destinations (Lake Colden and Marcy Dam) and peaks are very popular, to the point of being overused; more than 12,000 people climb Mount Marcy every year.

Jay Mountain: 7,100 acres; E. of Jay. Difficult access due to surrounding private lands; no official trails at this writing.

McKenzie Mountain: 38,000 acres; N. of Ray Brook. Trails for hiking and cross-country skiing; Saranac River; views from McKenzie and Moose mountains.

Waterfalls

Throughout the Adirondacks, the combination of streams and rivers and mountainous terrain provides numerous waterfalls. Some are spectacularly high, like T-Lake, which is taller than Niagara; others, like Buttermilk Falls, near Long Lake, are just a two-minute walk from the car. Listed below are just a few of the cascades you can visit.

Falls name	Description	Nearest town
Auger Falls	Gorge on the Sacandaga River; easy hike from Rte. 30	Wells
Blue Ridge Falls	On The Branch; visible from Blue Ridge Rd.	North Hudson
Bog River Falls	2-tier falls at Big Tupper Lake; visible from County Rd. 421	Tupper Lake
Buttermilk Falls	Raquette River; easy hike	Long Lake
Cascade Lake Inlet	Rock falls above Cascade Lake; 4-mile hike from Big Moose Rd.	Big Moose
Falls Brook	1-mile hike	Minerva
The Flume	On West Branch Ausable River; visible from Rte. 86	Wilmington
Hanging Spear Falls	Opalescent River; remote wilderness	High Peaks
High Falls	Oswegatchie River; remote	Cranberry Lake
Raquette Falls	Raquette River; remote	Tupper Lake
Rockwell Falls	Sacandaga River	Lake Luzerne
Shelving Rock	On Knapp estate; 4-mile hike	Pilot Knob
Split Rock Falls	Boquet River; access from Rte. 73	Elizabethtown
T-Lake Falls	Steep; remote	Piseco
Wanika Falls	Chubb River; remote	Lake Placid

Sentinel Range: 23,000 acres; between Lake Placid and Wilmington. Small ponds for fishing; few hiking trails; views from Pitchoff Mountain. This area is remote and receives little use.

NORTHWEST LAKES

St. Regis Canoe Area: 20,000 acres; W. of Paul Smiths. 58 lakes and ponds for canoeing; views from St. Regis and other mountains; trail network for hiking and cross-country skiing.

CENTRAL ADIRONDACKS

Blue Ridge: 46,000 acres; S. of Blue Mountain Lake. Contains several miles of the Northville–Lake Placid Trail for hiking and cross-country skiing; Cascade, Stephens, Wilson, Mitchell, and other trout ponds.

Five Ponds: 101,000 acres; between Cranberry Lake and Stillwater Reservoir. Numerous ponds; canoeing on the Oswegatchie River; many acres of old-growth forest; some hiking trails. This area receives little use. Extensive damage from 1995 storm blowdown of thousands of trees; inquire locally about trail conditions.

Ha De Ron Dah: 27,000 acres; W. of Old Forge. Small ponds and lakes; hiking and cross-country-ski trails around Big Otter Lake. This area receives little use.

Hoffman Notch: 36,000 acres; between Minerva and the Blue Ridge Rd. Ponds and trout streams; a few hiking trails. This area is used mostly by fishermen and hunters.

Pepperbox: 15,000 acres; N. of Stillwater Reservoir. Few trails; difficult access; mostly wetlands; excellent wildlife habitat.

Pigeon Lake: 50,000 acres; N.E. of Big Moose Lake. Numerous lakes, ponds, and streams; trails for hiking and cross-country skiing.

Siamese Ponds: 112,000 acres; between North River and Speculator. Canoeing on Thirteenth Lake; Sacandaga River and numerous trout ponds; trails for hiking and cross-country skiing.

Silver Lake: 105,000 acres; between Piseco and Wells. Silver, Mud, and Rock lakes; southern end of the Northville-Placid trail. This area receives little use.

West Canada Lakes: 157,000 acres; W. of Speculator. Cedar, Spruce, West Canada lakes, and 160 other bodies of water; portions of the Northville-Placid trail and other hiking trails. One of the largest roadless areas in the Northeast.

WILD FOREST AREAS

More than a million acres of public land in the park are designated as wild forest, which are open to snowmobile travel, mountain biking, and other recreation. Some of the wild forest areas are listed below.

LAKE GEORGE AND SOUTHWESTERN ADIRONDACKS

Lake George: On both the E. and W. shores of the lake, N. of Bolton Landing. Contains the Tongue Mountain Range on the west, and the old Knapp estate, with 40+ miles of hiking and horse trails, on the east.

Wilcox Lake: W. of Stony Creek. Miles of snowmobile trails and old roads; ponds and streams for fishing.

CHAMPLAIN VALLEY

Hammond Pond: Between Paradox and Moriah, with old roads for hiking and ponds for fishing.

HIGH PEAKS AND NORTHERN ADIRONDACKS

Debar Mountain: Between Loon Lake and Meacham Lake. Horse trails; hiking; fishing in the Osgood River.

Saranac Lakes: W. of Saranac Lake village. Excellent canoeing; island camping.

NORTHWEST LAKES

Cranberry Lake: Between Cranberry Lake and Piercefield. Snowmobile and hiking trails; trout ponds.

CENTRAL ADIRONDACKS

Black River: Between Otter Lake and Wilmurt. Ponds and streams.

Blue Mountain: N.E. of Blue Mountain Lake. Contains part of the Northville–Placid trail; Tirrell Pond; views from Blue Mountain.

Ferris Lake: Between Piseco and Stratford. Dirt roads for mountain biking and driving through by car; numerous ponds and streams.

Independence River: S. of Stillwater Reservoir. Dirt roads; Independence River; snowmobile trails; beaver ponds.

Jessup River: Between the south end of Indian Lake and Speculator. Miami and Jessup Rivers, and Lewey Lake; views from Pillsbury Mountain; trails for snowmobiling, hiking, and mountain biking.

Moose River Plains: Between Indian Lake and Inlet. Dirt roads; numerous ponds and streams; Cedar River and Cedar River Flow; primitive car-camping sites; snowmobile trails. If you want to see moose, this is the place.

Sargent Ponds: Between Raquette Lake and Long Lake. Trout ponds; hiking trails; canoe route between Raquette Lake and Blue Mountain Lake.

Shaker Mountain: E. of Canada Lake. Dirt roads; hiking, cross-country skiing and mountain-biking routes.

Vanderwhacker Mountain: N.W. of Minerva. Fishing on the Boreas River; views from Vanderwhacker Mountain.

WILDLIFE

Viewing the bears at the town dump was a time-honored Adirondack pastime for generations of tourists, but local landfills closed during the early 1990s and ended this quaint practice. To be honest, watching a sow and her cubs rip through garbage bags wasn't all that pleasant an experience. Nowadays, the Adirondack Park offers a great variety of wildlife in their natural habitats to observe.

With marsh and mountain, field and forest to explore, experienced birders might be able to see a hundred different species in day. (Back in the 1870s, young Theodore Roosevelt and a friend compiled and published a bird guide to the northern Adirondacks listing some 90+ native birds they had seen.) In late spring, warblers in all colors of the rainbow arrive, and the best places to watch for them is along edges where habitats meet, such as woods on the border of a wetland, or along the edge of a brushy field. A variety of songbirds, including kingbirds, flycatchers, grosbeaks, waxwings, thrushes, wrens, and sparrows all nest here.

Many interior lakes and ponds are home to kingfishers, ducks, herons, and loons; listen and watch for that great northern diver in the early morning and at dusk. Peregrine falcons and bald eagles, absent from the park for much of the 20th century, have been reintroduced. Cliffs in the High Peaks are now falcon eyries, and you may be able to spot a bald eagle or two in the Northwest Lakes part of the park. In the evening, listen for owls: the barred owl, known by its call, "Who cooks for you, who cooks for you," is quite common. In the fall, look up to see thousands of migrating Canada and snow geese.

Small mammals are numerous: varying hares, weasels, mink, raccoons, fisher, pine martens, otters, bobcats, porcupines, red and gray fox. Coyotes, with rich coats in shades of black, rust, and gray, can be seen in fall, winter, and spring, and their yips and yowls on a summer night can be thrilling to the backcountry campers' ears. About 50 lynx from the Northwest Territories have been released in the High Peaks in the past few years, in an attempt to restore the big cats to their former range.

Whitetail deer are seemingly everywhere, especially in the early spring before the fawns are born. A couple dozen moose (mainly bulls) have wandered into the park; a few cows and calves are sighted each year. The first "moose crossing" signs in New York were put up in October 1997 between Speculator and Indian Lake.

Many of the state campgrounds are good places to observe wildlife, especially aquatic birds and mammals. Ask the caretaker about where to see resident otters, ducks, loons, ospreys, and you may be rewarded with a wonderful vacation experience.

Don't Touch That Critter!

In recent years rabies cases have been reported in the northern and southeastern corners of the Adirondacks. The disease seems to be spread by raccoons, foxes, and skunks in upstate New York.

If you come across a wild animal acting unafraid or lying passively, by all means stay away from it. Don't touch dead creatures you may find. However, humans are not at great risk for rabies exposure since contact with sick wildlings can be avoided.

Dogs must be inoculated against rabies. Keep your pet under control when traveling through the woods, and don't let Fido run loose.

CHAPTER SEVEN

Woodsy Whimsy to Practical Gear
SHOPPING

Nancie Battaglia

The guideboat and pack basket are enduring traditional Adirondack artifacts.

Adirondack style — favored by ordinary folks who chose substance over style and function over form — predates the Ralph Lauren look by a century. Today, in shops across the park, you can get hearty woolens and practical gear without worrying whether you are setting or following the trend.

Emblematic of the region's classic designs is the always-in-season Adirondack chair, available from woodworkers in shops large and small. You can get the country seat in basic pine or beautiful native hardwoods, with rockers or anatomically curved backs, as a settee or porch swing, or even with hinges so the whole thing folds for storage.

Rustic furniture, from simple tables to sculptural headboards, remains an authentic product crafted by artisans who search the woods for the right piece of crooked yellow birch, the perfect shaggy cedar sapling. For a song (almost), you can purchase a rustic picture frame or you can spend a small fortune on a museum-quality piece. Adirondackana — a term used describe housewares with a woodsy motif, historic collectibles, prints, books, and native crafts — is the specialty of some fine shops that have been in business since the 1950s.

During the past twenty-five years, handcrafts have enjoyed a renaissance here. Typical items range from ash-splint pack baskets to batik camp shirts patterned with north woods wildlife to contemporary jewelry depicting miniature fishing lures. Some artisans rely on wood to fire their kilns, or Adirondack wool for their yarns, or even quills from native porcupine for their jewelry. Other craftspeople are here for quiet lifestyles and natural inspiration. Items can be purchased in shops and galleries, at artisans' studios and fairs, all of which are described further in this chapter.

For book lovers, there are shops offering contemporary novels, trashy paperbacks for a rainy day, wholesome stories for kids, and a plethora of how-to, where-to, and why-to publications. If you can't find it on the shelves, just ask — these independent bookstores can order most anything in print. For out-of-print books you'll find several shops, and there's even a mail-order seller who specializes in horror and fantasy fiction. In some emporiums, you'll find books combined with other things like health foods, tobacco, or hardware, making for an excellent afternoon's browsing.

Dozens of antique shops are located in the park, with concentrations around Warrensburg, Chestertown, the Champlain Valley, and Lake Placid. From Stickley rockers to postcards, moose antlers to Georgian silver, squeeze boxes to cheese boxes, there's bound to be the dealer who has just what you're look-ing for at a fair price. There are some first-rate antique shows, which you'll find listed under "Fairs and Flea Markets."

General stores are still the real item in North Country towns, supplying the goods for daily life from fresh milk to rain ponchos to crescent wrenches, and maybe even a wedding present. We like to think that the definition of an authentic general store would be a place where you could buy truly every-thing — from socks to dessert — you'd need for a week in the wilds.

The waters of the Adirondack Park attract many small-craft aficionados to special gatherings and to the fine traditional-boat exhibit at the Adirondack Museum (described in Chapter Four, *Culture*). Boatbuilders who make guide-boats — a sleek rowboat — along with craftsmen who build everything from ultralight canoes to runabouts are listed in this chapter.

The one thing you won't find inside the Adirondack Park is the modern sub-urban shopping mall. For that consumer experience you need to go south, to Aviation Mall (off I-87, Glens Falls), or north, to Champlain Centres (off I-87, Plattsburgh), or west, to Watertown, Utica, Syracuse, and beyond. Schroon Lake and Lake Placid have old-fashioned main streets that you can stroll for serious window shopping; in recent years the historic village Essex has blos-somed into a delightful shopper's destination with galleries and boutiques fea-turing quality crafts, antiques, and gifts. Canada Street, Lake George's main drag, is a day-glo kaleidoscope of t-shirt shops, ice cream stands, and souvenir joints; if you can't decide what to get the folks back home there's a psychic advisor who might be able to help. A few towns like Ticonderoga, Tupper Lake, Saranac Lake, and Lake Placid have plazas with grocery, discount, liquor, and hardware stores, but in general, Adirondack shopping is a relaxed, folksy pastime.

ADIRONDACKANA

The word defines all kinds of material things that complement the country-side and evokes textures: bark, wood grain; smells: balsam, cedar; tastes:

Wildwood, in Old Forge, features regional books, ephemera, antiques, and crafts.

Nancie Battaglia

maple, apple; forest colors: deep green, gold, sienna. For a real sampling of Adirondackana, you need to travel to the heart of the park.

HIGH PEAKS

Keene Valley

The Birch Store (518-576-4561; Rtes. 9N/73, Keene Valley, near the Noon Mark Diner) Antiques, hip clothing, and interesting jewelry combined with traditional Adirondack camp furnishings: blankets, birch-bark baskets and frames, chairs, balsam pillows, and wicker ware in a classy vintage storefront. Open daily June 15–Labor Day, and some fall, winter, and spring weekends.

Lake Placid

Adirondack Decorative Arts & Crafts (518-523-4545; 104-6 Main St.) Delightful new shop with a huge inventory — everything from birch-bark-patterned table linens to one-of-a-kind twig furniture, oiled canvas jackets, bark picture frames, jewelry, woodsy cabinet hardware, and even a full-size rustic doghouse. Open all year; definitely worth a visit.

Adirondack Store and Gallery (518-523-2646; 109 Saranac Ave., W. of Cold Brook Plaza) This place launched the Adirondackana trend decades ago. If you're looking for anything — pottery, wrapping paper, doormats, sweaters, stationery, cutting boards — emblazoned with loon, trout, pinecone or birch motifs, search no further. There's an excellent selection of Adirondack prints by Winslow Homer and Frederic Remington; antique baskets and rustic furniture; camp rugs and blankets; woodsy ornaments for the Christmas tree, including minute Adirondack chairs. Open daily year-round.

Adirondack Trading Company (518-523-3651; 91 Main St., next to With Pipe and Book) Doodads from the woods: cedar-scented sachets, rustic doll-house furniture, pine-cone-covered picture frames, silk-screened totebags shaped like fish; flannel night shirts printed with leaping deer silhouettes; goofy bear-foot slippers. Tables, bookshelves, and dressers with painted tops and white-birch legs and trim are reasonably priced. Open daily year-round.

CENTRAL ADIRONDACKS

Old Forge

Moose River Trading Company (315-369-6091; Rte. 28, Thendara) Pack baskets, canvas hats, Duluth packs, maps, compasses, bug dope, camp cookware and blankets, Adirondack chairs, and Guide's Coffee — what more could you need for an Adirondack expedition or creating your own Great Camp room? Open year-round; mail-order catalog, too.

Wildwood (315-369-3397; Main St., 1 block from Old Forge Hardware) Ash-splint baskets, great selection of stuffed animals, guideboat paddles, rustic furniture, Navajo rugs, whimsical jewelry, wooden toys, and practically every book that mentions the Adirondacks — from Upton Sinclair's autobiography to Ian Fleming's *The Spy Who Loved Me*. Rooms full of antiques, prints, postcards, and photographs, and old books. Open daily Memorial Day–Columbus Day; Mon.–Sat. fall, winter, and spring.

ANTIQUES

George Jaques, in Keene Valley, sells twig furniture, advertising art, and old sporting goods.

Nancie Battaglia

While traveling along rural routes in the Northeast, we just expect to find barns full of milk-painted country furniture, salt-glazed crocks, and marvelous hand tools. But these artifacts don't always relate to the territory we're passing through for reasons of history, culture, and climate. When you're antiquing in the Adirondacks, keep a thumbnail sketch of the region's past in your mind, and that will guide you to old things true to the countryside.

Expect to find artifacts relating to logging and farming days and good-quality mass-produced 19th-century furniture. Local pottery, except in the far southern part of the park is quite rare; Redford glass, made in the Saranac River valley during the early 1800s, is highly prized and extremely hard to find. Vintage rustic furniture, which was discarded willy-nilly in the fifties as camp owners modernized, is scarce, but Old Hickory pieces have the right look and feel and are widely available. If you're on track for a pair of snowshoes or antlers to hang at home, you shouldn't have any trouble finding them here.

High Tor, just east of Schroon Lake, is a beautiful home packed with antiques.

Nancie Battaglia

Many shops stock wood engravings and hand-tinted etchings of Adirondack scenes; these prints — many of them by Winslow Homer or Frederic Remington — which appeared in *Harper's Weekly*, *Every Saturday*, and other magazines, are usually inexpensive. Stereo views of the grand hotels, postcards from 1890-1930, and photographs by George Baldwin, H.M. Beach, "Adirondack" Fred Hodges, and others are charming and not too dear. For photographs of the lakes, mountains, and resorts by Seneca Ray Stoddard, a contemporary of William Henry Jackson and Matthew Brady, you can expect to pay more, but the images are exceptional. Another name on the list for ephemera fans is Verplanck Colvin: mountain panoramas, diagrams, and maps from his 1870-90 surveys are meticulous curiosities.

Another aspect of the Adirondack past to keep in mind is that the area has been a tourist destination since the Civil War. There's a brisk trade in historic souvenirs and small things relating to bygone transportation networks: embossed-brass luggage tags from steamboat and stagecoach lines are one example. Besides items designed to catch a visitor's eye or track his or her property, you can find objects that summer folk brought with them from back home or around the world to decorate camps great and small. These 19th-century part-time residents amassed an eclectic variety of knick-knacks, musical instruments, rugs, silver, and china that have become part of the antique scene as modern families spurned the elephant-foot humidors, Japanese lanterns, and other peculiar things the Victorians adored.

A few publications can help you find antique dealers: *Antiques, Collectibles, Handcrafts* (Box 19, Olmstedville NY 12857) describes shops in the North Creek–Riparius–Olmstedville area. Likewise, the brochure *Crafts, Antiquing & Much More* (518-563-1000; Clinton County Chamber of Commerce, Box 310, Plattsburgh) lists thirty northern-tier shops. Or consider a trip south to Fulton County (information 1-800-676-3858), where there are numerous shops in the Sacandaga and Mohawk basins. In Glens Falls, not too far from I-87, *Glenwood Manor* (518-798-4747; Quaker Rd.) is a group undertaking with 40 dealers, who have filled four dozen rooms with quality antiques; the mansion is open year-round.

The best fair is unquestionably the *Adirondack Antiques Show* at the Adirondack Museum (518-352-7311; Rte. 28/30, Blue Mtn. Lake) in September; dealers from across the country flock there with their absolute best woodsy wares. Also recommended is the July show and sale benefiting the Adirondack Medical Center (518-891-1990; Harrietstown Hall, Saranac Lake NY 12983). Both affairs feature dozens of booths showcasing primitive furniture, decoys, jewelry, books, glass, clocks, dolls, and of course, Adirondackana. Additionally, there's the *Adirondack Memorabilia Show* (518-585-2696), organized by Craig Lonergan, a local antique dealer, in Ticonderoga in early August.

Described below are a sampling of the antique shops you'll find in the Adirondack Park. Most are open several days a week in July and August, and on weekends in spring and fall; some are open year-round. Many dealers frequently travel to shows, so it's always a good idea to call ahead.

LAKE GEORGE AND SOUTHEASTERN ADIRONDACKS

Adirondack

Country Cottage Antiques and Gifts (Carl Pratt; 518-494-2051; 9 Church St.) Oriental rugs, country furniture, and collectibles. Open daily July–Aug.; weekends in spring and fall; call ahead.

Bolton Landing

Black Bass Antiques (Henry Caldwell and Kate Van Dyck; 518-644-2389; Lake Shore Dr.) Books, antique fishing tackle, Lake George souvenirs and photographs, general Adirondack items. Call ahead.

Chestertown

Atateka Books and Collectibles (Donna and Mark Walp; 518-494-4652; Friends Lake Rd.) Old and rare books, amusing souvenirs, toys, and advertising art. Open weekends May–Oct., or by appointment.

The Attic Antiques (Ruth and Bill Aiken; 518-494-2078; Rte. 9 at Loon Lake) A big shop with kitchen primitives, art and Depression glass, china, books, paper ephemera, some furniture. Open summer; call ahead.

Stuff & Things Antiques (John Eagle; 518-494-3948; Friends Lake Rd.) Country furniture; Native American items; unusual international folk art. Open May–Nov.

Lake George

Ralph Kylloe Antiques and Rustics Gallery (518-696-4100, Lake Luzerne Rd.) Established in 1995, enormous shop with exceptional rustic furniture, quality smalls, and sporting antiques. Open year-round; worth a special trip.

Waterborne (Skip and Lynn Gauger; 518-656-9248; Brayton La.) Antique boats, motors, marine art. By appointment.

Schroon Lake

High Tor (Gloria and Irwin Diamond; 518-532-9835; Rte. 74 3 mi. E. of Northway Exit 28) Delightful century-old house filled with furniture, glass, books, linens, mirrors, games, and prints from the Victorian era through Art Deco. Open May–Nov.

Warrensburg

Donegal Manor Antique & Gift Center (518-623-3549; 117 Main St.) Behind Donegal Manor Bed and Breakfast; Irish linen, furniture, coins, postcards, books, pocket watches; Victorian jewelry, glass, prints. Open year-round; daily in summer.

Field House Antiques (Virginia Field; 518-623-9404; 179 Main St.) In the carriage house you'll find furniture, country ware, toys, china, and glass. Open year-round; daily in summer; call ahead.

Fine Finish (Peter and Pam Bombard; 518-623-2428; Rte. 28, 2.5 mi. N.W. of Warrensburg) Antique furniture; restoration. Open year-round.

Ed and Pearl Kreinheder (518-623-2149; 197 Main St.) Rare books; country furniture and accessories. Open year-round, Mon.–Sat. Call ahead.

Riverside Gallery (Lenore Smith; 518-623-2026; 2 Elm St., 1 block W. of Rtes. 9 & 28) Old prints; paintings; reproduction furniture; picture framing. Open year-round Mon.–Sat.

Tamarack Shoppe (518-623-3384; 148 Main St., at the bandstand) Fiesta ware, jewelry, glass, books, and some furniture, mixed in with new brass, table linens, rugs, and imported china. Open daily, year-round.

CHAMPLAIN VALLEY

Elizabethtown

Pleasant Valley Collectibles (Janice and Conrad Hutchins; 518-873-2100; Upper Water St.) "Interesting old stuff from a pack-rat's attic — everything priced to sell." Open by chance or appointment.

Essex

Huston's (518-963-8647; Main St.) Nautical antiques. Open daily late June–mid-Sept.

Margaret Sayward's Antiques & Untiques (518-963-7828; South Main St.) Furniture, glassware, clocks, collectibles. Open daily June–Oct., winter and spring by chance or appointment.

Summer Shop (Colin Ducolon; 518-963-7921; Rte. 22) Painted furniture, early pressed glass, 19th-century textiles, coin silver. Open June–Oct.

Third Time Around (Donna Lou Sonnett; 518-963-7222; Main St.) Antique quilts, paintings, pottery; quilt and fabric restoration. Open June–Sept.; call ahead for restoration work.

Ticonderoga

Lonergan's Red Barn Antiques (Craig Lonergan; 518-585-4477; Rte. 9N) Old barn packed to the roof beams with things that you've been looking for — books, china, furniture, photos, prints, Lake Champlain souvenir plates, Fiesta ware, crocks, tinware, trunks, farm implements, horse-drawn equipment, guns — or, as the flyer says, "Useful Stuff for Man and Beast." Open daily Memorial Day–Columbus Day: weekends in spring and fall.

Past Lives Antiques (518-585-9066; 111 Montcalm St.) Vintage clothing and linens, used books, kitchenware, some furniture. Open year-round.

Robin Hill Antiques (518-585-6675; Roger St.) Oil lamps, vintage jewelry, pottery, furniture. Open Thurs.–Sun. in summer or by appointment. Closed winter.

Willsboro

Ben Wever's Farm (Dare Van Vree Wever; 518-963-8372; 221 Mountain View Dr.) Ten rooms of antiques in a beautifully restored farmhouse: pine, cherry, walnut, and mahogany furniture; fine china, porcelain, and silver; rugs; paintings; lamps; glass; Adirondackana, Americana, and Victoriana. Open daily late June–Labor Day; also Memorial Day weekend.

Brown House Antiques (Suzanne Medler; 518-963-7396; Main St.) Six rooms of linens, prints, pine and mahogany furniture, china, books, Fiesta ware, toys and dolls, wicker, Adirondack collectibles. Open late June–Aug. Tues.–Sat; weekends in Sept. by chance.

HIGH PEAKS AND NORTHERN ADIRONDACKS

Au Sable Forks

Don's Antiques (Marge and Don Denette; 518-647-8422; North Main St.) Furniture, Depression and patterned glass, clocks, stoneware, postcards, "ancestral paraphernalia." Open year-round by chance or appointment.

Bloomingdale

Germaine Miller (518-891-1306; Rte. 3) Country and small Adirondack furniture, painted cupboards, Majolica and Quimper, china, glass, silver. By appointment.

Sign of the Fish Studio & Gallery (Henry and Virginia Jakobe; 518-891-2510; Rte. 3) Furniture, books, paintings and prints, glass, china from the 19th century to the 1950s. Open July–Aug., or by appointment.

Clayburg

Peg's Antiques (Peg and Bob Defayette; 518-293-7062; Rte. 3) Furniture, kitchenware, tools, primitives, jewelry, lamps, dolls, Shaker reproductions. Open by chance or appointment.

Keene Valley

George Jaques Antiques (518-576-2214; Main St., Keene NY 12942) Rustic furniture, advertising art and signs, antique taxidermy, porch furniture, pack baskets. Open Memorial Day–Columbus Day.

Lake Placid

Cassidy's Antiques North (Linda Cassidy; 518-523-9482; Alpine Mall, 120 Main St.) Old rustic furniture, jewelry, carvings, camp-style decorative items, prints. Open year-round.

Heritage Hill Antiques (Mrs. A.E. Dunn; 518-523-2435; Crestview Plaza) Estate jewelry, postcards, prints. Open year-round; weekends only in Jan.

Lake Placid Antique Center (518-523-3913; 103 Main St.) Group shop with several dealers: furniture, books, lamps, advertising art, prints, toys, woodenware. Open daily year-round.

Lake Placid Antiques & Craft Center (Elizabeth Bauer; 518-523-0055; 121 Cascade Rd.) Large new group shop with about a dozen dealers; mini-shops with sporting collectibles and presentation trout-fly sets by Fran Betters and highly realistic replicas of catch-and-release fish by Mountain Wildlife Studio. Open year-round.

Log Cabin Antiques (Greg Peacock; 518-523-3047; 86 Main St.) Furniture, prints, kitchenware, Adirondackana, some reproduction stuff mixed in. Open year-round.

O'Donnell's Antiques (518-523-4770; 71 Saranac Ave.) New shop with country pottery, furniture, toys, and glass. Open year-round.

Old Friends Mercantile (518-523-0125; 52 Saranac Ave.) Interesting accumulation of vintage clothing, antiques, used furniture, rustic smalls, carved bears, and souvenirs. Open year-round.

Alan Pereske (home phone 518-891-3733; shop address 81 Saranac Ave.) Quality oak, pine, and rustic furniture; paintings and prints of local interest; glass, toys; ephemera. Open weekends spring and fall. Mon.–Sat. summer.

Loon Lake

The Old Art Gallery (518-891-3249; Loon Lake Golf Course) Bins of 19th-century engravings and lithographs plus some framed pieces. Open daily mid-May–Oct.

Red Barn Antiques (Roberta and Jay Friedman; 518-891-5219; Onchiota Rd.) Furniture, oil lamps, glassware, tools, sheet music, postcards, prints, jewelry, clocks in a grand old barn. Open July–early Sept., plus some spring and fall weekends.

NORTHWEST LAKES

Tupper Lake

Nice Twice (Jenny Matlock; 518-359-3256; 95 Park St.) Glass galore at reasonable prices plus good used household items. Open year-round.

CENTRAL ADIRONDACKS

Inlet

Lake View Antiques (Barb and Walt Wermuth; 315-357-4722; Rte. 28) Clocks and clock repair; house full of furniture, paper, postcards, china, Oriental rugs. Open late June–Sept.

Johnsburg

Carriage Shed (518-251-2140; Crane Mt. Rd.) Antiques, linens, country furniture, collectibles; call ahead for directions.

Long Lake

Ethel's House (Ann Stewart; 518-624-4242; Rte. 28) Jewelry, glass, kitchenware, quilts, vintage clothing, linens, baskets, tools, prints. Open Apr.–Christmas; daily Memorial Day–Columbus Day, weekends after.

Minerva

Mountain Niche Antiques (John and Kathy Feiden; 518-251-2566; Rte. 28N, 2 mi. N. of Minerva post office) Excellent assortment of country furniture, textiles, books, prints, tools, pottery, glassware. Open most days year-round; call ahead.

Mayfield

The Antique Lover (Terry and Dick Peters; 518-661-6424; Rte. 30) Kitchenware, glass, china, woodenware, postcards, dolls. Open spring–fall, by chance or appointment.

Northville

Red Barn (518-863-4828; 202 N. Main St.) Furniture, prints, collectibles, baskets. Open spring–fall, by chance or appointment.

Wheels of Time (Joan Crean; 518-863-2267; 112 Van Anham Ave.) General line of antiques and collectibles. Open weekends May–June; Weds.–Sun. July– Aug.

Old Forge

Antiques & Articles (Ed Diamond; 315-369-3316; 19 Main St.) Oak, wicker, rustic, and pine furniture; baskets; books; Fiesta ware, Depression glass; toys. Open daily July–Aug.; fall weekends.

Old Stuff and Such (Rte. 28 across from Adirondack Bank) Kitchen items, glass, and smalls; Memorial Day–Labor Day.

Wildwood (315-369-3397; Main St.) Adirondack postcards, prints, fishing tackle; maps, books; regional ephemera; advertising art; toys; glass and china. Open year-round.

Olmstedville

Board 'n' Batten (Floss and Bob Savarie; 518-251-2507; Main St.) Furniture, country items, Adirondack postcards, buttons, steins; focus on quality glass and pottery. Open daily July–Aug.; or by chance or appointment.

Riparius

Clen's Collectibles (Donalda and Clennon Ellifritz; 518-251-2388; River Rd.) Two shops; general line of antiques and smalls; Adirondack postcards and prints. Open year-round by chance or appointment.

Speculator

Newton's Corners Antiques (Pam and Rick Murray; 518-548-8972; Rte. 8) Kitchen cupboards and tables, linens, pottery and glass, jewelry, prints, quilts. Open year-round; closed Sun. and Weds. Call ahead in fall and spring.

ART GALLERIES AND PAINTERS' STUDIOS

The best 19th-century American painters came to the Adirondacks to interpret wild scenery on paper and canvas, and many artists still rely on the great outdoors for inspiration. Listed here you'll find local artists in residence as well as fine arts galleries representing painters from different eras and regions.

CHAMPLAIN VALLEY

Essex

Cupola House Gallery (518-963-7222; S. Main St.) Regional artists, photographers, and craftspersons in changing exhibits; occasional shows of antique furniture. Open spring–fall.

Westport

Atea Ring Gallery (Atea Ring; 518-962-8620; Sam Spears Rd.) A modern professional fine-arts gallery like you'd expect to find in a major city, located instead in an out-of-the-way farmhouse. One-person and group exhibitions of paintings, quilts, prints. Past shows have included works by Harold Weston; realist Paul Matthews; primitive paintings by Edna West Teall (who was the Grandma Moses of Essex County); and Lake Champlain fish decoys. Open June–Sept.

Willsboro

East Side Studio (Patricia Reynolds; 518-963-8356; 390 Point Rd.) Watercolor and oil landscapes of Lake Champlain and the Adirondacks; lovely flower paintings from the artist's extensive perennial gardens; usually a hundred or so works on hand. Open by chance or appointment year-round.

HIGH PEAKS AND NORTHERN ADIRONDACKS

Keene

Heritage Gallery (Bruce and Annette Mitchell; 518-576-2289; Keene NY 12942; corner Spruce Hill and Hurricane Rds.) Oil and watercolor paintings of Adirondack and Vermont scenes; limited-edition wildlife, floral, and landscape prints. Open Mon.–Sat. June–Nov. 14.

Saranac Lake

Small Fortune Studio (Timothy Fortune; 518-891-1139; 71 Main St.) Realistic Adirondack landscapes by an internationally regarded artist; works range from tiny, charming scenes to massive triptychs. Open year-round Tues.–Sat.

NORTHWEST LAKES

Cranberry Lake

End of the Pier Studio (Jean Reynolds; 315-848-2900; Rte. 3, at The Emporium) Watercolor paintings of Cranberry Lake and Adirondack vistas; limited-edition prints. Open by chance or appointment.

Gabriels

Point of View Studio (Diane Leitheit; 518-327-3473; Hunt Building, Rte. 86) Meticulous pen-and-ink drawings of noteworthy Adirondack buildings; special commissions. Call ahead.

Tupper Lake

Casagrain Studio and Gallery (Gary Casagrain; 518-359-2595; Rte. 3, across from Massawepie Cooperative Area, 10 mi. W. of Tupper Lake Village) Oil paintings and limited-edition prints of Adirondack scenes and wildlife. Open year-round; call ahead.

CENTRAL ADIRONDACKS

Edinburg

Lakehouse Studio (Constance Dodge; 518-863-2201; S. Shore Rd.) Portraits by appointment only.

Old Forge

Gallery North (315-369-2218; Main St., at the Ferns Emporium) Limited-edition wildlife and Adirondack prints, posters, and woodcarvings; picture framing. Open year-round.

Wevertown

Art Perryman (518-251-2769; Rte. 8) Wildlife sketches and prints; realistic wildlife carvings from miniatures to full size. By appointment.

BOATBUILDERS

Chris Woodward, at Hathaway Boat Shop, in Saranac Lake, repairs a guideboat.

Nancie Battaglia

The interconnected waterways of the region led to the development of a specialized craft, the Adirondack guideboat. Traditional guideboats, which first appeared after the Civil War, are smooth-skinned rowboats with quarter-sawn cedar or pine planks, and have naturally curved spruce roots for ribs. These delicate-looking craft were fast on the water and easy to carry between ponds, lakes, and rivers. In the 19th century, a handmade boat cost $30 or $40.

Beside guideboats, a number of local boatbuilders have developed their own special designs, from ultralight pack canoes to cold-molded multipurpose sport boats. Listed below you'll find a variety of water-craftsmen; it's always a good idea to call ahead. Also, you may find that there's a waiting list of other prospective buyers. Beautiful things take time to create.

HIGH PEAKS AND NORTHERN ADIRONDACKS

Keene

Pisces Paddles (Dave Kavner; 518-576-2628; Rte. 73) Traditional beaver-tail or bent-shaft wooden canoe paddles ($75-$85); meticulously detailed model guideboats and canoes for your curio cabinet ($500-$700).

Saranac Lake

Hathaway Boat Shop (Christopher Woodward; 518-891-3961; 9 Algonquin Ave.) A long line of boatbuilders has occupied this shop on the edge of town, including Willard Hanmer, whose boats are displayed at the Adirondack Museum. Chris learned the trade from Carl Hathaway, who was taught by Willard himself. Traditional wooden Adirondack guideboats; boat repairs. Traditional guideboats with oars and yoke: $7,500-$10,000.

Spencer Boatworks (Spencer Jenkins; 518-891-5828; Bloomingdale Rd.) Inboard wooden boats built along classic runabout lines with modern epoxy lay-up; models include cruisers and utility boats 18 to 26 feet long; prices $38,000-$92,000. Also wooden boat and inboard-motor repairs.

NORTHWEST LAKES

Lake Clear

Boathouse Woodworks (James Cameron; 518-327-3470; Upper St. Regis Lake) Traditional wooden Adirondack guideboats built to order; 16-foot guideboat with oars and yoke: $6,000-$7,000. Seat caning; boat restoration.

Tupper Lake

Spruce Knee Boatbuilding (Rob Frenette; 518-359-3228; Rte. 30) Rushton-design wooden canoes and rowboats, guideboats, and sailboats all built to order; wooden boat repairs; seat caning. New boats start at $3,000; traditional guideboats with complete outfit: $7,000 and up.

CENTRAL ADIRONDACKS

Indian Lake

John B. Spring (518-648-5455; Rte. 28) New wood-and-canvas canoes in 15-foot Rushton designs and 17-foot traditional models; $3,000 and up. Wooden boat repairs; seat caning.

Long Lake

Adirondack Goodboat (Mason Smith; 518-624-6398; North Point Rd.) This craft, which won the "Great Versatility Race" at Mystic Seaport's annual small-boat gathering, is a car-toppable multipurpose (row, sail, or motor) wooden boat, built with modern materials for easy maintenance and strength without weight. Other models are the Lakesailer and the Chipmunk canoe; kits available. Price range: $1,700-$5,500.

Olmstedville

Hornbeck Boats (Peter Hornbeck; 518-251-2764; Trout Brook Rd.) Nessmuk (George Washington Sears) pioneered the go-light outdoor movement in the 1880s, and Pete has brought his designs into the 20th century. Kevlar pack canoes in 9-, 10 $^1/_2$-, and 12-foot lengths, perfect for tripping into remote ponds, weigh only 12-19 pounds; Kevlar guideboats and ultralight sea kayaks are available by special order. Price range: $550-$2,000.

BOOKS

Within the Adirondack Park, there are about a dozen independently owned bookstores. Each place has its own personality: some highlight nature books; others offer art supplies and crafts too.

CHAMPLAIN VALLEY

Elizabethtown

L.W. Currey, Inc. (Lloyd Currey; 518-873-6477; Water St.) Dealer of rare science fiction, horror, and fantasy books. For serious collectors — by appointment only or mail order.

Ticonderoga

Dragonfly Books and Crafts (Bonnie Davis; 518-585-7543; 214 Montcalm St.) Children's books; regional guidebooks and histories; used books; antiques and crafts. Open year-round.

Fort Ticonderoga (518-585-2821; off Rte. 74) In a huge log cabin at the entrance to the museum, if you go beyond the bins of souvenirs, you'll find books, prints, monographs, maps, and audiotapes pertinent to 18th-century military history. Open daily mid-May–mid-Oct.

HIGH PEAKS AND NORTHERN ADIRONDACKS

The Keene Valley Book Store sells books for children and adults all year-round and has a coffee bar to boot.

Nancie Battaglia

Keene Valley

Keene Valley Book Store (518-576-4736; Rte. 73) Restored farmhouse with an impressive selection (10,000 titles) of regional and children's books; contemporary novels, how-to, nature guides, and cheerful service. Coffee bar, Adirondack folk music tapes and CDs, too. Open daily in summer; closed mid-week fall–spring.
The Mountaineer (518-576-2281; Rte. 73) Good selection of outdoor, international adventure travel, nature and Adirondack titles; topo maps. Open year-round Mon.–Sat.

Lake Placid

The Bookstore Plus (518-523-2950; 89 Main St.) Racks of paperbacks; good how-to guides; contemporary fiction; regional histories and guidebooks; cookbooks; children's books; coffee-table books; art supplies; stationery and cards. Buy a book here and you get a bonus — crisp $2 bills in change. Open year-round Mon.–Sat.

Eastern Mountain Sports (518-523-2505; 51 Main St.) Adirondack and outdoor guidebooks, camping cookbooks, and adventure travel tales; maps; gear and garb. Open year-round Mon.–Sat.; daily in summer.

Nature Unlimited (518-523-TREE; 59 Main St.) Books, nature tapes, science toys, rocks, and minerals. Open Mon.–Sat. all year.

A New Leaf (518-523-1847; Hilton Plaza, Main St.) New Age and self-help books; cards and stationery; tea, coffee, and cappuccino. Open daily year-round.

With Pipe and Book (Julie and Breck Turner; 518-523-9096; 91 Main St.) Landmark shop with new and rare Adirondack books; a huge selection of used books; antique postcards, prints, and maps; pipe tobaccos and imported cigars. Worth a visit just to browse books from their lovely porch overlooking Mirror Lake. Open year-round Mon.–Sat.

Saranac Lake

North Country Community College (518-891-2915; Winona Ave.) College bookstore; general interest; magazines. Open fall–spring Mon.–Sat.

NORTHWEST LAKES

Paul Smiths

Paul Smith's College Bookstore (518-327-6314; Rte. 30, Paul Smith's College, below the snack bar) Regional guides and histories; forestry books; topo maps; magazines. Open year-round Mon.–Sat.

Tupper Lake

Hoss's Country Corner (518-359-2092; 111 Park St.) Adirondack titles; outdoor recreation and natural history guides; cookbooks; Christian books; maps; clothing; gifts. Open year-round Mon.–Sat.

CENTRAL ADIRONDACKS

Blue Mountain Lake

Adirondack Museum Gatehouse Shop (518-352-7311; Rtes. 28/30) Complete assortment of Adirondack histories and guidebooks; books on antique boats and furniture; children's books; Adirondack folk music and storytelling on tape and CD; prints, postcards, stationery, and gifts. Open daily late May–Columbus Day. Mail-order catalog available.

Long Lake

Hoss's Country Corner (518-624-2481; Rte. 30) Adirondack histories and guidebooks, Christian books and tapes, children's nature books, general store. Hoss's sponsors Adirondack book-signing parties in July and August showcasing dozens of regional authors — worth a visit. Open year-round Mon.–Sat.

Old Forge

Old Forge Hardware (315-369-6100; Main St.) Way in the back of this enormous emporium is a huge bookstore with Adirondack histories and guidebooks, cookbooks, nonfiction, children's books, paperbacks, and art supplies. Open year-round Mon.–Sat.; daily in summer.

Wildwood (315-369-3397; Main St.) Adirondack titles, cookbooks, natural histories, novels, photography books, posters, art postcards, large selection of old books. Open year-round Mon.–Sat.; daily in summer.

Speculator

Charles Johns Store (518-548-7451; Rte. 30) Between fresh produce and the deli counter are aisles of regional books, maps, and posters. Open daily, year-round.

BEYOND THE BLUE LINE

At Aviation Mall, on Aviation Road just off I-87, in *Glens Falls*, you'll find **Lauriat's** (518-761-0139), with an excellent selection of regional books as well as the latest best-sellers, extensive reference books, cookbooks, children's books, books on tape. Open daily, year-round.

In *Saratoga Springs*, **Craven Books** (518-583-0025; 440 Broadway) stocks thousands of titles, along with maps, magazines and cards; the regional section features folklore, history, guides, and natural history. Open daily year-round. Also in Saratoga, **Lyrical Ballad** (518-584-8779; Phila St.) has a great assortment of old books and prints.

Several regional publishers specialize in books of local interest and have mail-order catalogs: *Countryman Press* (802-457-1049; Box 175, Woodstock VT 05091), *North Country Books* (315-735-4877; 18 Irving Place, Utica NY 13501), *Syracuse University Press* (315-443-5534; 1600 Jamesville Ave., Syracuse NY 13244-5160), and *Purple Mountain Press* (1-800-325-2665; Box E-3, Fleischmanns NY 12430).

CLOTHING

Hunting for designer bargains in "shop till you drop" mode is best pursued outside the Adirondack Park. Here you'll find classic woolens, practical sportswear, and outer gear. Lake Placid's Main Street, which has a pleasant parade of shops and outlets, is described here; also listed below you'll find haberdasheries plus interesting new places and clothing designers.

LAKE GEORGE AND SOUTHEASTERN ADIRONDACKS

Bolton Landing

Bolton Babies (518-644-2826; Rte. 9N) Handmade infants' and toddlers' clothing, toys, and educational games. Open Memorial Day–Labor Day.

Bolton Bay Traders (518-644-2237; Main St.) Quality sportswear for men and women, including Merrill and Nike hiking boots; Columbia, Big Dog and Sierra Designs jackets, shirts, pants, and shorts; outdoor guidebooks. Open year-round.

Lake George

Janet Vito Boutique (518-668-2601; 283 Canada St.) Batik and tie-dye summer dresses; sportswear for women. Open Weds.–Mon. year-round.

CHAMPLAIN VALLEY

Crown Point

Fritelli & Lockwood (518-597-3910; Rte. 22) Handwoven chenille and woolen fabrics made into tailored jackets, vests, and ties. By appointment only.

Natural Goods and Finery, in Essex, sells handmade clothing.

Nancie Battaglia

Essex

Natural Goods & Finery (Sharon Boisen; 518-963-8109; Main St.) Handmade cotton dresses; lovely fragrances and personal-care products. Open daily mid-June–mid-Sept.

HIGH PEAKS AND NORTHERN ADIRONDACKS

Lake Placid

The Adirondack Store & Gallery (518-523-2646; 109 Saranac Ave.) Hand-knit sweaters and hand-woven jackets; Pendleton woolens. Open Mon.–Sat year-round; daily Memorial Day–Labor Day.

Alphabet Soup (518-523-7170; 28 Main St.) Exceptionally cool kids' clothes, maternity wear. Open Mon.–Sat. all year.

The Bear Haus (518-523-3848; 23 Main St.) Men's and women's clothing, swimwear, and skiwear; Royal Robbins, Obermyer, and other quality labels. Open Mon.–Sat. year-round.

Eastern Mountain Sports (518-523-2505; 51 Main St.) Outdoor clothing and footgear by Woolrich, Patagonia, Merrill, Nike, and EMS. Open Mon.–Sat. year-round; daily in summer.

Far Mor's Kids (518-523-3990; 1 Main St.) "Far Mor" means grandmother in Swedish; picture an indulgent, tasteful granny and you've got a glimpse of this shop. Designer infant and children's clothes; educational toys and puzzles; quilts. Open year-round.

The Gap (518-523-4651; 55 Main St.) Hip outfits for all ages in flannel, denim, fleece, and khaki. Open daily year-round.

The In Step (518-523-9398; 35 Main St.) Designer shoes, stockings, and bags, featuring wool clogs to Mootsie's Tootsies. Open Mon.–Sat. year-round.

Ruthie's Run (518-523-3271; 11 Main St.) Men's and women's clothing, from Cambridge Dry Goods, Ruff Hewn, Tango, and such. Open Mon.–Sat. year-round.

Where'd You Get That Hat? (518-523-3101; 155 Main St.) The question friends back home are bound to ask. . . . Headgear of all descriptions; great selection of Converse high tops. Open year-round.

Saranac Lake

Cinderella's (518-891-4431; 44 Broadway) Handmade fashions for infants to teenagers; special-occasion dresses. Open Mon.–Sat. year-round.

T.F. Finnigan (518-891-1820; Main St., near the Adirondack Bank) Men's clothing, including Cross Creek, Nautica, B.D. Baggies; formal-wear rental and sales. Open Mon.–Sat. year-round.

Michelle Gannon, in Tupper Lake, creates silk batik scarves, vests, and shirts with wildlife motifs.

Nancie Battaglia

Northern Light (Mercado del Sol, Rte. 86 across from Casa del Sol) Imported sweaters and clothing. Open Mon.–Sat. year-round.

NORTHWEST LAKES

Tupper Lake

Michelle Gannon (518-359-7151; Moody Rd.) Batik camp shirts, vests, tapestries, and scarves adorned with terrific hand-painted Adirondack wildlife. By appointment only.

Hoss's Country Corner (518-359-2092; 111 Park St.) From outerwear to expedition underwear for men, women, and children, plus outdoor supplies. Open Mon.–Sat. year-round.

Upper St. Regis

Lynn Cameron Collections (518-327-3470; Upper St. Regis Lake) Looking for the perfect gown for some enchanted evening? Lynn designs and sews meticulous reproductions of antique clothing, specializing in dance attire. By appointment only.

CENTRAL ADIRONDACKS

Old Forge

Sporting Propositions (315-369-6188; Main St.) Tennis, golf, ski, and sports apparel by Izod, Black Diamond, and other brands. Open Mon.–Sat. year-round.

Stuff from Other Countries (no phone; Main St.) Cotton and silk clothing from Guatemala, India, etc. Open Memorial Day–Columbus Day.

BEYOND THE BLUE LINE

They call it the "Million Dollar Half Mile," and it's just a quick toss of the gold card from *Lake George Village*. Four separate plazas on both sides of U.S. Rte. 9 (near its intersection with Rte. 149) add up to outlet heaven for the dedicated shopper. On the west side of the road is **French Mountain Commons Outlet Center** (518-792-1483); on the east is **Log Jam Factory Stores** (518-792-5316), **Adirondack Factory Outlet Mall**, and **Lake George Plaza Factory Stores**. You'll find everything from Fieldcrest towels and Oneida flatware to lingerie and Ralph Lauren men's and women's wear.

In *Plattsburgh*, the north and south **Champlain Centres** (518-561-8660) are close to the Northway and contain chains like Sears and Penneys plus dozens of other clothing stores. Off I-87 close to the Canadian border is **Miromar Factory Outlet Center** (518-298-3333) with 40-some shops.

CRAFT SHOPS

Functional handmade items have always been part of Adirondack life; in the last few decades, the region has attracted contemporary craftspeople from outside, and encouraged local folks to rediscover old-time products. Part of this renaissance has been nurtured by the Adirondack North Country Association (ANCA), a non-profit group that published the first "Craft Trails" map highlighting studios and stores more than fifteen years ago and operated a huge store in Lake Placid for several years. For a free copy of the map, write to ANCA (183 Broadway, Saranac Lake).

Listed below you'll find craft shops showcasing a variety of media. Many of the studios are in private homes, so it's a good idea to call ahead. Further on in this chapter you'll find fiber and fabric artists and basket makers; carvers of wood, plaster and other materials; and furniture makers.

LAKE GEORGE AND SOUTHEASTERN ADIRONDACKS

Bolton Landing

Trees (518-644-5756; Rte. 9N) Adirondack chairs; wooden toys, baskets, balsam items; regional books, prints, and photos. Open mid-June–Columbus Day.

Chestertown

Harness Shop Artisans (518-494-3295; Main St.) Quilts, carvings, toys, jewelry from more than a hundred craftspeople. Meet selected artists on Mondays and Thursdays in July and August. Open daily July–Oct.; Nov.–June Fri.–Sun.

Miss Hester's Emporium (518-494-7940; Main St., next to the Main St. Ice Cream Parlor) Songbirds made by local carvers, quilts and wallhangings, baskets, antiques, cards, and gifts. Open year-round.

Diamond Point

Hearthside Artisans II (518-668-2172; Rte. 9N) Quilts, pottery, woodenware, toys, Christmas items and handcrafted goods by some 65 area artisans. Open Thurs.–Sun. spring and fall; daily June–Oct.

CHAMPLAIN VALLEY

Elizabethtown

River Run Gifts (518-873-6574; Water St.) Paintings by regional artists; local crafts and toys. Open daily mid-June–Oct.

Studio Showcase (518-873-6836/2311; Water St.) Baskets, handmade clothing, jewelry, and toys. Open Mon.–Sat. mid-May–Oct.

Essex

Adirondack Spirit (518-963-4541; Main St.) Tasteful collection of kitchenware, table linens, pottery, glass, and items for children. Open daily June–mid-Oct.

Cupola House (518-963-7222; S. Main St.) Quilts, folk art, prints. Open June–Sept.

The Store in Essex (518-963-7551; 1 Main St.) This 1810-vintage stone building next to the Lake Champlain ferry landing houses an eclectic assortment of contemporary jewelry and clothing, African masks and baskets, designer glass and pottery plus gourmet food from Vermont and the Adirondacks. Definitely fun. Open daily mid-May–late Oct.

Sugar Hill Pottery (Judith Koenig; 518-963-7068; Main St.) Hand-thrown stoneware pottery. Open daily late May–Columbus Day.

Ticonderoga

Hancock House Gallery (518-585-7868; Moses Circle) Works by local artists; historical souvenir items. Open Weds.–Sat. year-round.

Wadhams

New Moon Pottery (Joe Dinapoli; 518-962-4045; Youngs Rd.) Contemporary stoneware, raku, and porcelain in a historic carriage barn.

Westport

Artifacts and Westport Trading Co. (Kip Trienens; 518-962-4801; Main St.) Bark and twig baskets, pottery, jewelry, contemporary furniture, stained glass, and eclectic crafts. Open year-round, most of the time.

Gallery at the Arts Council (518-962-8778; 23 N. Main St.) Juried Adirondack art and crafts at the office of the Arts Council for the Northern Adirondacks. Call ahead for hours.

The Store in Essex has an eclectic assortment of contemporary crafts.

Nancie Battaglia

HIGH PEAKS AND NORTHERN ADIRONDACKS

Jay

Jay Crafts Center (Lee Kazanas and Cheri Cross; 518-946-7824; Rte. 9N) Pottery lamps, bowls, vases, and dinnerware made by Lee and Cheri; wooden toys; ash-splint baskets; silver jewelry; prints; custom matting and framing. Open Apr.–Dec.

Youngs' Studio and Gallery (Sue and Terrance Young; 518-946-7301; Rte. 86) Wonderful pottery made by Sue; limited-edition etchings of Adirondack landscapes by Terry; other local crafts. Open year-round Tues.–Sat.

Keene

North Country Taxidermy (518-576-4318; Rte. 73) You can't miss this place — there's usually a full-size stuffed creature out front. If you'd like to buy a souvenir antler or two, there are boxes full of them. Bearskin rugs are a specialty. Open year-round.

Lake Placid

Adirondack Crafts Center (518-523-2062; 93 Saranac Ave.) More than 250 upstate New York craftspeople are represented here. Jewelry made of silver, porcupine quills, semiprecious stones, butterfly wings, and feathers; designer clothing for dolls, children, and adults; leather bags and backpacks; quilts; handmade paper; woodcarvings of fish, birds, folk figures; baskets; pottery; rustic and contemporary painted furniture; prints; photographs; stationery. Open Mon.–Sat. year-round; daily in July–Aug.

Caribou Trading Co. (518-523-1152; Hilton Plaza, Main St.) Pottery, jewelry, kites and mobiles, woodenware, handwovens. Open year-round.

Guadalupe's Mexican Imports (518-523-9845; 132 Main St.) Tinware, glass, textiles, pottery, sweaters, and jewelry from Mexico and Central America. Open Mon.–Sat. year-round.

Guadalupe's, in Lake Placid, features Mexican pottery, tinware, and clothing.

Nancie Battaglia

Nature Unlimited (518-523-8733; Main St., near the Gap) Polished rock plates, paperweights, bookends, etc.; jewelry; nature toys. Open year-round.

Po Polsku (518-523-1311; 12 Saranac Ave., at the Ramada Inn) Folk crafts imported directly from Poland: embroidered clothing; wooden boxes and plates; dolls and toys; textiles; paper cutouts. Open year-round; daily in summer. Catalog available.

Loon Lake

Kate Mountain Pottery (518-891-0049; Kate Mountain Lodge) Functional stoneware. Open Weds.–Sat. afternoons June–Labor Day; fall weekends.

Saranac Lake

Kate Mountain Pottery (518-891-2726; 41A Main St.) Stoneware with graceful Adirondack motifs. Open Mon.–Sat. summer and fall.

Smith's Taxidermy (518-891-6289; 15 Broadway) Rustic furniture by Thomas Phillips and the Smith brothers; antler chandeliers, pottery, baskets. Open year-round.

Wilmington

Handycraft Store (518-523-2966; Rte. 86) Rustic furniture, pine-cone baskets and figures, Adirondack chairs, animal puppets, wallhangings, quilts. Open daily Memorial Day–Labor Day; weekends in fall.

NORTHWEST LAKES

Childwold

Leather Artisans (Tom Amoroso; 518-359-3102; Rte. 3) Classic leather hand-bags, wallets, belts, and backpacks made on the premises; quality crafts. Open year-round.

CENTRAL ADIRONDACKS

Blue Mountain Lake

Blue Mtn. Designs (Lory Wedow; 518-352-7361; Rte. 30) Blue Mtn. Lake's old-time schoolhouse is packed with contemporary jewelry, fine rustic and camp-style furniture, wrought iron, woodenware, pottery, handwovens, silk-screen prints, photographs, etchings, stationery, candles, toys, leather, and clothing. Also Lory creates custom-cast hardware for Adirondack guideboats. Occasional crafts demonstrations in summer. Open daily mid-May–mid-Oct.; weekends before Christmas.

Cedarwood, in Blue Mountain Lake, has woodcarvings, baskets, kitchen items, antique postcards, and toys.

Nancie Battaglia

Cedarwood Gift Shop (518-352-7306; Rte. 28 next to the post office) Hip jewelry, funky pottery, Adirondack and nature books, posters, cards, candles, and calendars; housewares. Open daily June–Sept.

Red Truck Clayworks (Bill Knoble; 518-352-7611; Rtes. 28/30, S. of the Blue Mtn. Lake Service Center) Platters, bowls, vases, and place settings in a gorgeous variety of glazes and geometric designs, plus large-format photographs, handmade musical instruments, and works by local artists. Open daily mid-June–Labor Day, plus some spring and fall weekends. Also, check out Bill's studio in Chestertown (518-494-2074; Darrowsville Rd.)

Indian Lake

Wilderness Lodge (518-648-5995; Starbuck Rd.) Paintings and photographs by local artists, plus lamps and pictorial panels made of thin slices of native rocks. By appointment or peruse the crafts during dinner; Wilderness Lodge is a restaurant open year-round by reservation.

Lake Pleasant

Cabin Clayworks (Barbara Higgins; 518-548-4506; Rte. 8) Functional pottery; demonstrations. Open June–Aug.; call ahead.

Long Lake

Mountain Medley (Ed Wight; 518-624-4999; Rte. 30 next to Hoss's Country Corner) Adirondack chairs, stoneware pottery, rocking horses, loon and Canada goose planters, lamps, and more all made by Ed, plus baskets, jewelry, quilts, dolls, toys, candles, and so on from regional artisans. Open daily mid-June–mid-Oct.

Mayfield

Havlick Snowshoe Co. (Richard Havlick; 518-661-6447; Rte. 30) Handmade snowshoes and snowshoe furniture, Adirondack pack baskets, and outdoor gear. Open daily, year-round.

Northville

Adirondack Country Store (518-863-6056; 252 N. Main St.) Rambling old home filled with quality local crafts: hickory and oak rockers made by Amish woodworkers, quilts, handwovens, jewelry, hand-spun yarns, baskets, pottery, toys, decoys, Adirondack books. New in 1997 is a small but excellent mail-order catalog. Open daily Memorial Day–Columbus Day; Tues.–Sun. Columbus Day–Dec. and Apr.–Memorial Day; winter weekends.

Old Forge

The Artworks (315-369-2007; Main St.) Cooperative gallery featuring North Country artisans. Ash-splint baskets, stained glass, hooked rugs, woodcarvings, patchwork quilts and pillows, toys, and jewelry. Open year-round.

The Broom Man (315-369-6503; 1146 Main St.) Handmade brooms, rakes, and pitchforks; hand-loomed rugs; sweaters; baskets; wagons. Open daily Memorial Day–Labor Day; weekends in spring and fall.

Hand of Man Gallery (315-369-3381; Main St., near the Town of Webb school) Trendy glass, pottery, and jewelry; handmade lampshades, turned woodenware. Open daily Memorial Day–fall.

Mountain Peddler (315-369-3428; Main St.) Quilts, tinware, baskets, woodenware, gifts. Open year-round; daily Memorial Day–Columbus Day.

Olmstedville

Kindred Spirits (518-251-5131; at the Four Corners) Baskets, quilts, toys, books, pottery, woodenware, plus quality outdoor gear and occasional live music in summer. Open year-round.

Raquette Lake

Sagamore Bookstore (315-354-9905; at Sagamore Lodge) Rustic furniture and miniatures; ash-splint baskets, stained glass, wrought iron, carved and painted shelf fungus, handmade paper. Available by special order are place settings of the Vanderbilts' woodsy china, reissued by Syracuse China in 1997. Open daily Memorial Day–Labor Day; spring and fall weekends.

FAIRS AND FLEA MARKETS

For a true shopping adventure, consider the outdoor extravaganzas: from May through Columbus Day, many Adirondack communities sponsor craft fairs and flea markets. At one end of the spectrum are juried craft shows with high-quality items, while flea markets and town-wide garage sales escape succinct categorization as to just what you can expect to find. But that's the fun of those affairs — nosing past the velvet paintings and tube socks to discover a box of stereo views of Ausable Chasm. Listed below are some annual events arranged by region and date; check local newspapers for information about other festivals. The "Inside & Out" calendar of events in *Adirondack Life* is another good source of information.

LAKE GEORGE AND SOUTHEASTERN ADIRONDACKS

Arts Festival of Beauty (518-623-9814; Main St., Warrensburg) Paintings and crafts of all kinds, early July.

Hobby Fair (518-532-7675; Town Park, Schroon Lake) 50+ craft booths, music, rustic-furniture building and other demonstrations, third Sat. in July. Also that day in Schroon Lake, the Community Church Bazaar, on Rte. 9.

Riverview Arts & Crafts Festival (518-696-3423; Lakeside Park, Lake Luzerne) Craft fair, third Sat. in July.

Bolton Library Book Sale (518-644-2233 or 644-3831; Rte. 9N, Bolton Landing) Late July.

Quality Antique Show–Under the Big Top (518-644-3831; Bolton Central School Ballfield, Bolton Landing) Antique show with 30+ dealers, first weekend in Aug.

World's Largest Garage Sale (518-623-2161; throughout Warrensburg) The traffic backs up to Northway Exit 23 for this town-wide blow-out; more than 500 dealers, plus many local families offer a bewildering array of items for sale. Plan to walk once you get to town; there are shuttle buses from the parking lots. First weekend in Oct.

CHAMPLAIN VALLEY

Marigold Festival (518-962-8383; Main St., Westport) Craft fair on the library lawn, games and events for children. Memorial Day weekend.

Old-Time Folkcraft Fair (518-963-4478; Paine Memorial Library, Willsboro) Last Sat. in July.

Adirondack Memorabilia Show (518-585-2696; Heritage Museum, Ticonderoga) Ephemera and antiques show; flea market; craft fair, first Sat. in Aug.

Champ Day (518-546-7261; Main St., Port Henry) Craft-and-food fair with activities for children celebrating "Champ," Lake Champlain's legendary monster, first Sat. in Aug.

Downtown Essex Day (518-963-4287; Main St., Essex) Craft fair, games, and races, first Sat. in Aug.

HIGH PEAKS AND NORTHERN ADIRONDACKS

Craftfest (518-891-1489; The Lodge, Lake Clear) Juried craft show featuring furniture, pottery, baskets, jewelry, stained glass, and more, third weekend in July.

Peak of Summer Country Fair (518-946-2255; Wilmington Town Park, Wilmington) Craft fair and games for children, third Sat. in July.

Adirondack Antiques Show and Sale (518-891-4141; Harrietstown Town Hall, Main St., Saranac Lake) A high-summer tradition and one of the best around. Late July.

Kiwanis Crafts Fair (518-946-2551; Village Green, Jay) Outdoor craft fair, second weekend in Aug.

Artisans' Studio Tours (518-946-2445) Craftspeople in the Jay–Wilmington–Upper Jay area open their studios to the public, in mid-Aug.

High Peaks Arts and Antiques Show (518-576-4719; Marcy Airfield, Keene Valley) Large assortment of crafts and regional antiques in late Aug.

Adirondack Antiques Auction (518-523-2445; Horse Show Grounds, Lake Placid) Boats, rustic furniture, camp kitsch, prints, and photos in late Sept.

NORTHWEST LAKES

Backwoods Craft Fair and Flea Market (315-848-2391; Rte. 3, Cranberry Lake) Dozens of local artisans selling their wares and demonstrating their skills plus flea market, third weekend in July.

Eastern Star Flea Market (518-359-2542; Municipal Park, across from the A&P, Tupper Lake) More than 300 dealers — everything from Adirondack ephemera to used furniture and new footwear, plus fried dough, sausage-and-pepper sandwiches, and other delicious, artery-clogging carnival chow, third weekend in Aug.

CENTRAL ADIRONDACKS

Neighbor Day (315-369-6411; Arts Center, Old Forge) Craft fair with music, special exhibitions, chicken barbecue, and events for children, second Sun. in June.

Central Adirondack Craft Fair (315-369-6411; sponsored by the Arts Center, Old Forge) Craft fair with 75+ exhibitors, first weekend in July.

Caroga Historical Museum Craft Fair (518-835-4400; Caroga Historical Museum, London Bridge Rd., Caroga Lake) Annual outdoor craft fair, second Sat. in July.

Antique Show and Sale (518-624-3077; Town Hall, Long Lake) Mid-July.

Arts in the Park Craft Fair (315-357-5501; Arrowhead Park, Inlet) Outdoor craft fair, third weekend in July.

Speculator Flea Market (518-548-4521; Ballfield, Speculator) 50+ vendors, third Sat. in July.

Piseco Craft Fair (518-548-8732; Piseco Community Hall, Piseco) 50+ craft booths, last Sat. in July.

Adirondack Gem and Mineral Show (518-251-2612; Gore Mt. Ski Area, Peaceful Valley Rd., North Creek) 20+ rock dealers, plus gem-cutting demonstrations and lectures, first weekend in Aug.

Heart of the Park Craft Fair (518-624-3077; Mount Sabattis Park Pavilion, Long Lake) Craft fair "under the big top," first Sun. in Aug.

TWIGS Arts and Crafts Show (518-548-4521; Rte. 30, Speculator) 75+ craftspeople, second Thurs. in Aug.

Town-wide Garage Sale (518-624-3077; throughout Long Lake) Long Lake introduces drive-by shopping, second Sat. in Aug.

Rustic Furniture Makers' Fair (518-352-7311; Adirondack Museum, Blue Mtn. Lake) Showcase of more than 40 rustic furniture builders, early Sept. Museum admission required for fair visitors.

Adirondack Antiques Show (518-352-7311; Adirondack Museum, Blue Mtn. Lake) Ephemera, quilts, furniture, photographs from some 90 dealers, on the grounds of the Adirondack Museum, late Sept.

Antique Show & Sale (315-369-6411; Arts Center/Old Forge) First weekend in Oct.

FIBER AND FABRIC; BASKETS AND BALSAM

Fiber arts encompass more than things made of thread and yarn; handmade paper relies on wood and other plant fibers, while traditional and modern baskets use wood splints, grasses, leaves, and ropes. The needle arts in the true Adirondack sense of the word include sweet-smelling pillows and sachets; balsam fir (*Abies balsamea*) needles are gathered, dried and stuffed into calico fabric bags and pillows. Listed below you'll find an assortment of quilters, basket makers, paper makers, spinners, weavers, and balsam crafters from across the park. (Check under "Clothing" in this chapter for handmade ready-to-wear items.) If you'd like to visit sheep, goat, and rabbit farms, there's an annual **Washington County Wool and Fiber Tour** held on the last weekend in April; Glens Falls newspapers usually publish a map of participating farms. If you'd like to experience an old-fashioned balsam bee — from chopping the needles to hand-stitching pillows — the **Big Moose Community Chapel** (315-357-5841; Big Moose Rd.) holds one in late July; the extra-fresh pillows are sold at the annual bazaar, held on the first Saturday in August.

North of the Adirondack Park border, on the St. Lawrence River, is Akwesasne, home of many Mohawk families, an excellent place to look for baskets woven of ash splints and sweetgrass. The **Akwesasne Cultural Center Museum** (315-346-2240; Rte. 37, Hogansburg) has a shop selling all kinds of baskets, from tiny thimble cases to full-size pack baskets, plus moccasins decorated with beadwork and porcupine quills. Call for hours and directions; a group of Mohawk artisans is putting together a catalog of fine crafts.

LAKE GEORGE AND SOUTHEASTERN ADIRONDACKS

Putnam Station

Hawk Mountain Crafts (518-547-9511; Box 28) Angora and mohair yarns from their own goats.

Warrensburg

Blue Heron Designs (Charlene Leary; 518-623-3189; Truesdale Hill Rd.) Fine handwovens and women's clothing from her fabrics. Call ahead.

CHAMPLAIN VALLEY

Crown Point

Fritelli & Lockwood Textiles (518-597-3910; Rte. 22) Colorful and elegant handwoven fabrics made into tailored jackets, vests, and scarves, available from retail craft shops in the region. By appointment.

Elizabethtown

Studio Showcase (518-873-6836/2311; Water St.) Baskets made by six different weavers; handmade clothing, jewelry and toys. Open Mon.–Sat. mid-May–Oct.

Essex

Pioneer Weave (Mary Beth Brennan; 518-963-8067) Traditional finely woven rag rugs in assorted sizes and made to order; available at Natural Goods & Finery and Third Time Around, both in Essex. Call ahead.

Willsboro

Alice Wand and Dennis Kalma (518-963-4582; 44 Spear Rd.) Handmade paper sculptures and wall pieces. Call ahead.

HIGH PEAKS AND NORTHERN ADIRONDACKS

Lake Placid

Quaker Mtn. Studio (Annoel Krider; Box 163) Exceptional tapestries and naturally inspired rugs. Works displayed at the Lake Placid Lodge. Commissions by appointment.

Newcomb

Upper Hudson Woolery (Judy Blanchette; 518-582-2144; Rte. 28N) Hand-spun yarns from Judy's own sheep; hand-knit sweaters; spinning wheels; spinning lessons. Open daily year-round.

Saranac Lake

Asplin Tree Farms (518-891-5783; Rte. 86) The best-smelling store in the Adirondacks, filled with balsam pillows and products. Open daily June 1–Dec. 24.

NORTHWEST LAKES

Paul Smiths

Adirondack Mountain Basketry (Tracy Santagate; 518-327-3665; HCR Box 37) Willow and reed baskets; traditional Adirondack ash-splint pack baskets; lessons. By appointment only; mail-order brochure available.

Tupper Lake

Edith Mitchell (518-359-7830; 4 Wawbeek Ave.) Traditional and contemporary quilts in all sizes by one of the leading artists in the Adirondacks. By appointment only.

Thomas and Judy Phillips (518-359-9648; Star Rte. 2) Ash-splint melon, apple, and potato baskets in various sizes; big-bellied pack baskets. By appointment only.

Molly Sheren (518-359-2982; HCR 2, Upper Saranac Lake) Tapestries; textile conservator. By appointment only.

Genevive Sutter (518-359-2675; Raquette River Dr.) Choice pictorial quilts of North Country scenes and historic sites. By appointment only.

CENTRAL ADIRONDACKS

Blue Mountain Lake

Woven with Wood (Tracy Meehan; 518-352-7721; Durant Rd.) Ash-splint baskets including fine Shaker-style baskets; workshops; demonstrations; by appointment.

Indian Lake

Homemade Quilts and Crafts (Kathleen Herrick; 518-648-5360; Rte. 28) Tied quilts, patchwork pillows, dolls, baskets, balsam pillows. Open daily Memorial Day–Columbus Day; other times by chance or appointment.

Long Lake

Adirondack Basket Case (Patty Farrell; 518-624-2501; Rte. 28N at Northwoods Garden Center) Ash-splint baskets of all sizes and styles. Open daily in summer; weekends in fall and winter.

Mountain View Farm (Donna Adams; 518-624-2521; Adams Park Rd., off Walker Rd.) Hand-spun yarns from Donna's sheep and angora rabbits; sweaters, vests, and afghans; spinning lessons and demonstrations. Open year-round; call ahead.

FURNITURE

R egional woodworkers create furniture in a variety of styles, from Shaker-inspired designs, to rugged sculptural pieces, to the straightforward Adirondack chairs that now come in an infinite range of permutations. You can find camp and home furniture in the craft shops described above, or you can go to the workshops listed below. Several of the rustic workers have brochures or catalogs that you may request by mail; if you're planning to visit an individual's shop, call ahead. Note that many studios are in private homes, so don't expect a large ready-made inventory on hand.

If you think you'd like to try to build your own rustic furniture, several arts centers listed in Chapter Four, *Culture*, offer hands-on workshops. Also, Ed Smith, a woodworker from Diamond Point, has collected rustic furniture plans from early 20th-century magazines and published them in a 64-page booklet, *How to Build Rustic Furniture*. The book is $7.95 plus $1 shipping and handling, from Smith Brook Press, RR 1 Box 217D, Diamond Point NY 12824.

LAKE GEORGE AND SOUTHEASTERN ADIRONDACK

Bolton Landing

Thomas W. Brady, Furnituremaker (518-644-9801; 87A North Bolton Rd.) Elegant contemporary furniture in cherry, walnut, and figured maple: screens, bedsteads, desks, blanket chests, tables, and chairs, some with painted motifs or in Shaker designs. Color flier available; open year-round by appointment only.

Chestertown

Chester Creek Woodworks (518-494-0003; Friends Lake Rd.) Furniture and useful wooden ware. Open weekends or by appointment.

Diamond Point

Pine Plank (Don Farleigh; 518-644-9420) Adirondack chairs, benches, and tables in pine. Open year-round Tues.–Sun.

Schroon Lake

Adirondack Rustics Gallery (Barry Gregson; 518-532-9384; Charley Hill Rd.) Rustic tables, chairs, settees, beds, corner cupboards, and sideboards, made

Barry Gregson, from Schroon Lake, works on a rustic settee.

Nancie Battaglia

of burls, cedar, white-birch bark, and assorted woods. Clocks, frames, and selected items by Jerry and Jessica Farrell, Jean Armstrong, and others. Worth a special trip; open summers Tues.–Sat.; call ahead.

CHAMPLAIN VALLEY

Crown Point

Adirondack Fairie Furniture (518-597-3946; Ironville) Miniature rustic scenes. Call ahead.

Crispin Shakeshaft (518-597-3304; RR 1, Box 24) Clean, simple rustic beds, tables, chairs, and interior details for new homes. Call ahead.

Keeseville

Willsboro Wood Products (518-834-5200; Ausable St.) Sturdy and comfortable beds, tables, chairs, dressers, mirrors, benches, and settees made of white cedar; you've seen these in the L.L. Bean catalog. Color catalog available; open Mon.–Fri. year-round.

Mineville

Essex Industries (518-942-6671; Pelfisher Rd.) Canoe and guideboat accessories: backrests, caned seats, yokes; folding canvas camp stools and shopping bags. Flier and price list available; open Mon.–Fri. year-round.

HIGH PEAKS AND NORTHERN ADIRONDACKS

Keene

Hurricane Mountain Industries (518-576-2015; Hurricane Rd.) Amusing rustic clocks with wildlife dioramas, lamps, desks, chairs. Call ahead.

Lake Placid

Adirondack Furniture (David Hall; 518-523-2697; 105 Saranac Ave.) Cherry, maple, and birch tables, chairs, desks, dressers, beds, picture frames, and mirrors. Open year-round.

North Country Wood Works (518-523-4531; Rte. 86 W. of town) Unfinished pine Adirondack chairs, tables, wall cabinets, shelves, planters. Open Mon.–Sat. year-round.

Newcomb

Truly Adirondack Crafts (Bruce Wight; 518-582-3581; Rte. 28N) Rustic coat hooks, towel bars, etc., plus simple furniture. Call ahead.

Saranac Lake

Adirondack Antler Art (Charles Jessie; 518-891-5383; McKenzie Pond Rd.) Chandeliers, lamps, and sconces made from moose and whitetail deer antlers. Call ahead.

Vermontville

Forest Murmurs (Glenn Bauer; 518-327-9373; RR 1, Box 77) Wall secretaries and shelves with antlers; birch-bark signs for your home or camp; lamps, mirrors, frames, and sconces. Price list and brochure available; open summer weekends; call ahead.

NORTHWEST LAKES

Paul Smiths

Train Brook Forest (David Woodward; 518-327-3498; Easy St.) Travel trunks and document boxes made of wood and leather; wrought-iron fireplace screens with wildlife silhouette designs; fireplace accessories; iron lighting fixtures in Arts-and-Crafts designs. Open year-round; by appointment only.

Tupper Lake

Jean Armstrong (518-359-9983; Big Wolf Lake) Rustic boxes, frames, and furniture, fungus art. Summer only, by appointment.

Thomas and Judy Phillips (518-359-9648; Star Rte. 2) Ash-splint baskets with sculptural branch handles; twig-style and birch-bark chairs, tables, benches, and beds; cedar outdoor furniture; rustic furniture restoration. Price list available; open by appointment only.

Michael Trivieri (518-359-7151; Moody Rd.) Burl bowls and tables; woodcarvings; mantels. By appointment.

CENTRAL ADIRONDACKS

Indian Lake

Backwoods Furnishings (Ken Heitz; 518-251-3327; Rte. 28) A Paul Bunyan-size log chair arches over Ken's driveway, marking the home of one of the originators of the Adirondack rustic revival. Twig, birch-bark, and cedar beds, tables, sideboards, settees, rockers, and custom orders. Ken's furniture has been featured in *House Beautiful*, *House and Garden*, *Gourmet*, and many other publications. Color brochure available; open year-round by appointment only.

LeBlanc Woods (518-648-6188; Rte. 30) Functional rustic tables, lampshades, frames, mirrors; canoe restoration. Call ahead.

Long Lake

Cold River Gallery (Jamie Sutliffe; 518-624-3581; Deerland Rd.) Painted arch-top trunks; carved furniture, mirrors and frames with wildlife designs; custom doors and signs. Open year-round by appointment only.

Mountain Medley (Ed Wight; 518-624-4999; Rte. 30) Curved back, classic, and child-size Adirondack chairs in stock or by special order. Open daily late June–Columbus Day.

North Country Designs (James Howard; 518-624-3813; Newcomb Rd.) Bark-and-twig hutches, desks, corner cupboards; burl tables, rocking chairs. Open year-round.

Mayfield

Sampson Bog Studio (Barney and Susan Bellinger; 518-661-6563) Twig mosaic and birch-bark tables, desks, wall shelves, benches with fine hand-painted details and graceful lines. Call ahead.

Adirondack chairs and porch rockers are made in this Old Forge shop.

Minerva

Rustic Homestead (Tom Welsh; 518-251-4038; Box 68) Benches, tables, chairs, and lamps made from yellow birch, cherry, and other woods. Call ahead.

Old Forge

Old Forge Woodmaker (315-369-3535; Main St.) Adirondack chairs and benches; tables, bookshelves, and wooden toys. Open Weds.–Mon. Memorial Day–Labor Day; weekends in spring and fall.

Speculator

Jerry's Wood Shop (518-548-5041; Rte. 30) Adirondack chairs and settees that fold for storage; picnic tables; lawn furniture. Open daily year-round.

Wevertown

Old Farmhouse Rocker Shop (518-251-3226; Rte. 28) Amish hickory furniture and balsam pillows. Call ahead.

GENERAL STORES

In a town that shall remain nameless, there's an abandoned cobblestone building with a sign proclaiming that it's the "Shop of Three Wonders: Wonder Where It Came From, Wonder What It Costs, and Wonder How Long It's Been Here." Those kinds of intellectual exercises make an expedition to a real general store fun. Chances are you'll find odd things like nail pullers and chick-feeding troughs right alongside the glass percolator tops and sugar shakers and an aisle over from the suspenders and boot socks, around the corner from the chips and salsa. Don't worry about the dust; don't be afraid to ask the price. If you can't find it here, you can probably live without it.

Some general stores really take the word "general" to heart, so that you can pick out a nice graduation gift as well as the fixings for an afternoon picnic, including sunglasses, bug dope, and sustenance. Each shop has its own personality, and they all occupy a hallowed place within the community.

LAKE GEORGE AND SOUTHEASTERN ADIRONDACKS

Adirondack

Adirondack General Store (Joan and Dick Lomnitzer; 518-494-4408; East Shore Dr.) There's a fine line between country-looking places that try too hard and end up cutesy, and those authentic country stores that mix the antique and the modern — and turn out charming. This place, which was the company store for a tannery dating back to the 1850s, hits the nail on the head. You can hang out by the wood stove when it's cold, read the paper on the porch when it's warm, buy a nice gift, or get milk, eggs, bread, and such for camping in Pharaoh Lake Wilderness Area. The deli is very good, Joan's homemade soups are scrumptious, and if there are any pies left, grab one. They're the best around. Open year-round.

Brant Lake

Daby's General Store (518-494-4039; Rte. 8) Along with the Freihofer's donuts, videos, cold beer, and wristwatches are display cases and shelves with 1940s-vintage dolls, old bottles and toys, fancy knives (for looking at, not for sale). You can find just about everything here, and even if you only buy some Popsicles, the view down Mill Pond toward the cobblestone library perched out over the water is worth the trip. Open year-round.

Chestertown

The Crossroads (518-494-3821; Rte. 8, near Northway Exit 25) Carhartt heaven! Woolrich blankets and clothing, hiking boots, groceries, beer, maps, magazines, fishing and hunting gear — all discounted. Open year-round.

HIGH PEAKS AND NORTHERN ADIRONDACKS

Bloomingdale

Norman's Wholesale Grocery (518-891-1890; Rte. 3) Norman's has been in the same family since it began in 1902, and display drawers still have ornate hardware and lettering declaring "Socks and Mittens" or "Silks and Laces." For retail customers, the stock is mainly convenience-store items, but the place still feels very much like the old times when the stagecoach stopped here. Open year-round.

NORTHWEST LAKES

Cranberry Lake

The Emporium (315-848-2140; Rte. 3) Tiny place crammed with souvenirs, maps, fishing tackle, announcements of coming attractions, canned goods, frozen treats, and t-shirts, but there's even more — the Emporium is a marina with gas pumps, water taxi, and a big long weathered wooden dock. This kind of place used to be common in the Adirondacks, and the Emporium is one of the few lakeside general stores that remains. Open daily year-round.

CENTRAL ADIRONDACKS

Batchellerville

Olde Country Store (518-863-2110; S. Shore Rd.) Since 1912 — everything from homemade box lunches to beachwear. Open year-round.

Indian Lake

Pine's Country Store (518-648-5212; Rte. 28) Clothing, garden equipment, extensive hardware and houseware selection. Open year-round.

Long Lake

Hoss's Country Corner in Long Lake has everything from live lobster to antique quilts.

Nancie Battaglia

Hoss's Country Corner (John and Lorrie Hosley; 518-624-2481; corner Rtes. 30 & 28N) Exemplary modern general store with aisles of groceries, fresh meats and deli items; Woolrich clothing for men and women, camp furnishings; stuffed animals; quilts, rugs, and baskets galore; cold beer; topo maps; Adirondack, outdoor, children's, and Christian books; jewelry; soaps and candles; out-of-town newspapers; film . . . the list is nearly endless, as is the rambling frame building that goes up, down, and around. Open Mon.–Sat. year-round.

Minerva

Murdie's General Store (518-251-2076; Rte. 28N) If you're on the Teddy Roosevelt Memorial Highway retracing his 1901 midnight ride to the presidency, and find that you need gas, nightcrawlers, crusher hat, six-pack, transmission fluid, ice cream, spaghetti, or maps, well, look no farther. Open year-round.

Old Forge

Old Forge Hardware (315-369-6100; Main St.) A visit to Old Forge Hardware is to Adirondack shopping as a trip to the Adirondack Museum is to regional history. This coliseum-size landmark bills itself as the "Adirondacks' Most General Store," a title with which we can't argue. Need a pack basket? Bamboo steamer for your wok? Spar varnish? Snowshoes? Reflective dog collar to fit a Newfoundland? Authentic shade for your antique Aladdin lamp? Spiles for maple sugaring? Replacement handle for your peavey? You can spend an entire day here. Open year-round.

Raquette Lake

Raquette Lake Supply (315-354-4301; downtown) The Dillon family has owned Raquette Lake Supply in one manifestation or another for more than a century. The building is huge, with the post office, a bakery, and the Tap Room on one side; a laundromat on another; the store takes up most of the floor space facing the water. There's a soda fountain, meat counter, dairy case, and groceries, plus toy tomahawks, vintage postcards, and fish poles. This is the only place in the park where you can get honest-to-gosh, cut-from-the-lake ice for your cooler; the huge bluish blocks come with a frosting of sawdust that a quick plunge in the lake rinses off. Open year-round. If you're around in February for the annual ice-cutting weekend, drop by for a glimpse of a time-honored process.

Sabael

The Lake Store (Eris Thompson; 518-648-5222; Rte. 30) Toys, gifts, sports gear, souvenirs, moccasins, and clothing, plus a summertime soda fountain, year-round deli, and all the major food groups. Open year-round.

GLASS

A handful of glass workers ply their trade in the Adirondacks, making custom beveled or stained-glass windows or blown-glass decorative items. You'll find their studios listed below; since many craftspeople work out of their homes, it's always a good idea to call ahead.

LAKE GEORGE AND SOUTHEASTERN ADIRONDACKS

Chestertown

Handblown Glass by Beth Melecci (518-494-2066; Stagecoach Rd.) Blown-glass lamps, vases, and ornaments in subtle, swirling colors; fine crystal decorative pieces. Open year-round, by appointment only.

CHAMPLAIN VALLEY

Westport

Westport Trading (Kip Trienens; 518-962-4801; Main St.) Architectural stained-glass windows, panels, and mirrors in stock or made to order; repairs for antique stained glass. Shop open most of the time, year-round; drop-ins welcome.

HIGH PEAKS AND NORTHERN ADIRONDACKS

Upper Jay

Epic Glassware (Nick Ferro; 518-946-7100; Rte. 9N) Etched glass in hundreds of freehand designs on pitchers, plaques, wineglasses, plates; the pine-cone and pine-tree motifs have an authentic Adirondack look. Custom orders. Shop open Thurs.–Mon., year-round; drop-ins welcome.

CENTRAL ADIRONDACKS

Old Forge

Meyda Stained Glass Studio (315-369-6636; Main St.) Tiffany-style shades, mirrors, planters, jewelry boxes. Open daily Memorial Day–Labor Day.

JEWELRY

Many of the craft shops listed above carry silver, gold, or porcelain jewelry by local artisans; the jewelers and mineral shops described below specialize in contemporary designs or native gemstones.

HIGH PEAKS AND NORTHERN ADIRONDACKS

Lake Placid

Darrah Cooper Jewelers (518-523-2774; 10 Main St., next to the Hilton) Delightful sterling silver and gold charms and earrings representing miniature North Country objects: pack baskets, canoe paddles, guideboats, oars, pine cones, and Adirondack chairs. Also rings, bracelets, and necklaces in precious stones, silver, and gold. Open Mon.–Sat. year-round.

Spruce Mountain Designs (518-523-9212; Box 205) Adirondack wildflowers in sterling silver and gold. By appointment only.

Arthur Volmrich (518-523-2970; 99 Main St.) Amusing earrings and necklaces mixing antique charms, buttons, and stones with modern components; turquoise bracelets and watchbands; custom rings; repairs and resettings. Open Mon.–Sat. year-round.

CENTRAL ADIRONDACKS

Blue Mountain Lake

Blue Mtn. Designs (Lory Wedow; 518-352-7361; Rtes. 28/30) Classic contemporary cast and hand-fabricated silver and 14k gold: rings, earrings, handmade chains, pins, bracelets, Adirondack charms, and necklaces. Also cast hardware for antique boats. Open daily Memorial Day–Columbus Day, plus fall weekends until Christmas.

North River

Gore Mountain Mineral Shop (518-251-2706; Barton Mines Rd., 5 mi. off Rte. 28) Garnet jewelry; faceted gemstones; rocks and minerals from around the world; gem-cutting demonstrations on Sun. and Mon. Open daily late June–Labor Day.

Jasco Minerals (Jim Shaw; 518-251-3196; Rte. 28) Specializing in native garnet, plus fossils and semiprecious stones from around the world; custom jewelry orders. Open daily May–Dec.

OUTDOOR GEAR

Many shops in the Adirondack Park offer sports equipment, outdoor clothing, and camping supplies; you'll find them listed in *Recreation* under specific headings like Camping, Fishing, Rock and Ice Climbing, or Skiing.

SCULPTURE AND WOODCARVINGS

Architectural-design elements, folk-art figures, realistic wildlife, and modern concrete sculpture are just a few of the things shaped by Adirondack hands. Listed below you'll find a sampling of decorative items for indoors and out.

CHAMPLAIN VALLEY

Essex

The Weeping Cherub (Loy Kempster; 518-963-8952; on the alleyway to the Old Dock House Restaurant) Plaster mantels, friezes, ceiling medallions, wall sconces, planters, garden benches, and table supports reproduced from Greek and Roman antiquities, della Robbia sculptures, and 16th- and 17th-century homes; plaster restoration. Catalog available. Open Mon.–Sat. May–Oct.

HIGH PEAKS AND NORTHERN ADIRONDACKS

Bloomingdale

Ralph Prata (518-891-2417; West Main St.) Abstract concrete carvings: free-standing sculptures, wall reliefs, and framed limited-edition works. Brochure available; open by appointment only.

NORTHWEST LAKES

Tupper Lake

Michael Trivieri (518-359-7151; Moody Rd.) Burl bowls and tables; bas-relief sculptures of Adirondack wildlife; commissions. Many of Mike's woodland scenes are prominently featured in the dining room at the Lake Placid Lodge. Call ahead.

CENTRAL ADIRONDACKS

Blue Mountain Lake

Rick and Ellen Bütz, Woodcarvers (518-352-7737; $1/4$ mi. N. of the Adirondack Museum) If you know anything at all about whittling, chances are you are familiar with these Adirondack carvers: Rick is host of the nationally broadcast PBS television series, "Woodcarving with Rick Bütz," and author of several popular books on the subject. The Bützs' shop features wildlife woodcarvings from songbirds to whitetail deer, figures from Adirondack folk tales, and historic St. Nicholas carvings; special commissions are welcome. Call ahead.

Wevertown

Art Perryman (518-251-2769; Rte. 8) Wildlife carvings, prints, and drawings. By appointment only.

CHAPTER EIGHT
Nuts, Bolts, and Free Advice
INFORMATION

Nancie Battaglia

Where's the best view from an Adirondack chair? Ask the organizations listed below.

Consult this chapter to find the answers to questions about important community services and organizations, and for an array of miscellaneous facts and figures.

AMBULANCE, FIRE, STATE AND LOCAL POLICE

There is no unified emergency-assistance system that operates throughout the Adirondack Park. In Warren County, which includes Lake George, Warrensburg, North Creek, Lake Luzerne, Pottersville, Johnsburg, and several other communities, you can dial 911 for help. If you're traveling on I-87, the Northway, there are solar-powered emergency phones spaced about every two miles along the shoulders that automatically contact dispatchers.

Clinton County, which covers the northeastern portion of the Adirondack Park, has enhanced 911 service; this means that when you call, your name and address pop up on a display screen at the safety center. Ticonderoga (585) and Lake Placid (523) telephone exchanges have basic 911 service.

Elsewhere in the Adirondacks, you should dial 0 to reach the operator; stay on the line and you'll be connected to the appropriate agency. If you're lucky enough to have a telephone book nearby when you run into trouble, check the inside front cover for emergency listings for individual towns.

The New York State Police has offices throughout the Adirondacks. If no local officer is available calls are forwarded to a 24-hour central dispatcher. Numbers are:

Chestertown	518-494-3201
Schroon Lake	518-532-7711
Elizabethtown	518-873-2111
Willsboro	518-963-7400
Keeseville	518-834-9040
Ray Brook	518-897-2000
Tupper Lake	518-359-7677
Indian Lake	518-648-5757
Old Forge	315-369-3322

The number for Central New York Poison Control is 1-800-252-5655.

AREA CODES

The area code for the eastern two-thirds of the Adirondacks, including Lake George, Warrensburg, Schroon Lake, Elizabethtown, Westport, Keene, Lake Placid, Saranac Lake, Tupper Lake, Long Lake, Blue Mountain Lake, Indian Lake, North Creek, Speculator, Wells, and Northville is **518**. For communities in the northwestern and west-central Adirondacks, such as Cranberry Lake, Star Lake, Raquette Lake, Inlet, Eagle Bay, Big Moose, and Old Forge, the area code is **315**.

BANKS AND AUTOMATIC TELLER MACHINES

Most days of the week many Adirondack banks still keep the proverbial "banker's hours," so don't count on transactions after 3pm. A few banks are locally owned and independent; several are associates of Fleet or Marine Midland chains, and will honor checks drawn on accounts from member banks.

For a vacation-time cash crunch, some banks may advance money on charge cards. Automatic teller machines are not associated with every bank, as they often are in urban areas; in much of the Adirondack Park ATMs are actually quite rare. However, you can find NYCE Cashere terminals at Stewart's Shops throughout the park. These booths honor NYCE, or can give you an advance on VISA, Mastercard, American Express, or Discover cards, but don't expect the machine to dispense greenbacks. The NYCE terminal furnishes a paper receipt that you present to the cashier, who then gives you the money.

LAKE GEORGE AND SOUTHEASTERN ADIRONDACKS

Evergreen Bank
Main St., Bolton Landing; 518-644-3421
97 Main St., Corinth; 518-654-2311
Canada St., Lake George; 518-668-5486
137 Main St., Warrensburg; 518-623-2666
Corinth, Lake George, and Warrensburg branches have NYCE and Cirrus
    ATMs.

Fleet Bank
2097 Main St., Lake Luzerne; 1-800-228-1281
138 Main St., Warrensburg; 1-800-228-1281

Glens Falls National Bank
Main St., Chestertown; 518-494-2691
Canada St., Lake George; 518-668-5461
Main St., Schroon Lake; 518-532-7121

CHAMPLAIN VALLEY

AlBank (formerly Albany Savings Bank)
Montcalm St., Ticonderoga; 518-585-6066 (24-hour ATM in the foyer for NYCE
and Cirrus cards)
Main St., Au Sable Forks; 518-647-8136

Essex County Champlain National Bank
Main St., Crown Point; 518-597-3322
Court St., Elizabethtown; 518-873-6347
18 Main St., Westport; 518-962-8216
Point Rd., Willsboro; 518-963-4201 (NYCE and Cirrus ATM)

Evergreen Bank
Main St., Keeseville; 518-834-7331

Fleet Bank
S. Main St., Port Henry; 1-800-228-1281
Montcalm St., Ticonderoga; 1-800-228-1281

Ticonderoga Federal Credit Union
Wicker St., Ticonderoga; 518-585-6725 (24-hour drive-up ATM for NYCE cards)

HIGH PEAKS AND NORTHERN ADIRONDACKS

Adirondack Bank
60 Main St., Saranac Lake; 518-891-2323
53 Church St. Extension, Saranac Lake; 518-891-2323
Cold Brook Plaza Extension, Lake Placid; 518-523-3344
All branches have ATMs connected to the NYCE, Cirrus, Pulse, Discover,
Cashere, and Plus systems.

Albank
Emmons & Cook St., Dannemora; 518-492-2561
Saranac Ave., Lake Placid; 518-523-9535
Rte. 28N, Winebrook Hills, Newcomb; 518-582-2711
55 Broadway, Saranac Lake; 518-891-2900
Dannemora, Lake Placid, and Saranac Lake branches have 24-hour ATMs for
NYCE, Plus, and Cirrus systems.

Essex County Champlain National Bank
Rte. 73, Keene; 518-576-9515

Marine Midland Bank
70 Main St., Saranac Lake; 518-891-3711

National Bank & Trust Co.
81 Main St., Lake Placid; 518-523-9544. (24-hour ATM for NYCE, Plus, TX, and
Cirrus cards)
Cold Brook Plaza, Lake Placid; 518-523-9544
2 Lake Flower Ave., Saranac Lake; 518-891-2050

NORTHWEST LAKES

Albank
402 Park St., Tupper Lake; 518-359-2917

Community Bank
Rte. 3, Star Lake; 315-848-3344

Grand Union
Ames Plaza, Tupper Lake; 518-359-9197. NYCE cardholders can receive cash at the service desk between 9am and 9pm.

Tupper Lake National Bank
75 Park St., Tupper Lake; 518-359-3344
3 Main St., Tupper Lake; 518-359-2709

CENTRAL ADIRONDACKS

Adirondack Bank
Codling St., Old Forge; 315-369-3153
24-hour ATM in the lobby for NYCE and Cirrus cards.

Albank
Rte. 28, Indian Lake; 518-648-5711
Rte. 30, Long Lake; 518-624-5161
Main St., North Creek; 518-251-2441

City National Bank
231 Bridge St., Northville; 518-863-2101 (NYCE, Cirrus, Plus, and Cashere 24-hour ATM at the side entrance)

Fleet Bank
Main St., Old Forge; 1-800-228-1281 (24-hour ATM in lobby connected to Cirrus and NYCE)

Marine Midland Bank
Rte. 30, Speculator; 518-548-7211

National Bank & Trust Co.
Main St., Northville; 518-863-4341

BIBLIOGRAPHY

Diverse authors have been inspired by the Adirondacks, from Robert Louis Stevenson, who completed the *Master of Ballantrae* when he was a tuberculosis patient in Saranac Lake, to Nathanael West, who penned part of *Miss Lonelyhearts* during a sojourn in Warrensburg. Sylvia Plath chronicled her ski accident at Mt. Pisgah in *The Bell Jar*. Alix Kates Shulman spent a season as a

For curling up with an Adirondack book, nothing beats a quiet spot at a state campground.

Nancie Battaglia

waitress in Lake Placid; her *Memoirs of an Ex-Prom Queen* has plenty of juicy details about a wild summer in the mountains. Ian Fleming's *The Spy Who Loved Me* is set in a dreary motor court near Lake George; L. Sprague DeCamp's horror-fantasy *The Purple Pterodactyls* has a definite Adirondack flavor. Mystery writer John D. McDonald, of Travis McGee fame, even wrote a book about his cats spending their summers in Piseco.

The two lists that follow are collections of recent books and out-of-print volumes that may be read at several local libraries. The latter books don't circulate; an appointment may be necessary in order to peruse a special collection. For a list of libraries with special sections of Adirondack literature, consult Chapter Four, *Culture.* For where to buy Adirondack books, check Chapter Seven, *Shopping.*

BOOKS YOU CAN BUY

Literary Works

Banks, Russell. *Cloudsplitter.* NY: HarperFlamingo, 1998. 540 pp., $27.50. Novel about abolitionist John Brown and his sons.

Cooper, James Fenimore. *The Last of the Mohicans.* Numerous paperback editions. NY: Bantam Classics, 1982. 384 pp., $3.50.

Doctorow, E.L. *Loon Lake.* NY: Random House, 1980. 258 pp., $11.95.

Dreiser, Theodore. *An American Tragedy.* Paperback editions available. NY: Signet Classics, 1964. 832 pp., $4.95.

LaBastille, Anne. *Woodswoman.* NY: E.P. Dutton, 1976. 277 pp., $7.95.

White, William Chapman. *Just About Everything in the Adirondacks.* Syracuse, NY: Syracuse University Press, 1994 reprint. 100 pp., illus., $9.95.

Anthologies

Jamieson, Paul. *The Adirondack Reader*. Glens Falls: Adirondack Mountain Club, 1989 (2nd edition). 544 pp., $18.50. An excellent introduction to the region, with selections spanning two centuries of Adirondack history, literature, and commentary.

Tefft, Tim, ed. *Of the Summits, Of the Forests*. Morrisonville, NY: Adirondack Forty-Sixers, 1991. 352 pp., photos, index, $18.50.

Architecture and Decorative Arts

Kaiser, Harvey. *Great Camps of the Adirondacks*. Boston: David Godine, 1986. 240 pp., color photos, maps, index, $35.

Kylloe, Ralph. *Rustic Traditions*. Layton, UT: Gibbs Smith Publishers, 1993. 175 pp., color photos, furniture makers' directory, index. $39.95.

Folklore

Bethke, Robert D. *Adirondack Voices: Woodsmen and Woods Lore*. Logging songs and stories. Reprinted by Syracuse University Press, 1994. 150 pp., photographs, music notations, index, $14.95.

Thompson, Harold W. *Body, Boots and Britches*. Syracuse, NY: Syracuse University Press, 1979. 538 pp. Folklore and folk music of northern New York.

Ward, Vaughn. *I Always Tell the Truth (Even When I have to Lie to Do It!)* Tall tales by members of the Adirondack Liars' Club. Greenfield, NY: Greenfield Review Press, 1990. 116 pp., $9.95.

History

Bond, Hallie. *Boats of the Adirondacks*. Blue Mountain Lake, NY: Adirondack Museum, 1995. 334 pp., $49.95.

Brumley, Charles. *Guides of the Adirondacks*. Utica, NY: North Country Books, 1994. 320 pp., photos, list of guides, index, $35 cloth, $20 paper.

Donaldson, Alfred L. *A History of the Adirondacks*. 2-volume set originally published in 1921; reprinted Fleischmanns, NY: Purple Mountain Press, 1993. 766 pp., $58.95.

McMartin, Barbara. *The Great Forest of the Adirondacks*. Utica, NY: North Country Books. 1994, 266 pp., photos, charts, index, $27.50.

Schneider, Paul. *The Adirondacks*. NY: Henry Holt, 1997. 340 pp., $25 cloth. Well-written retelling of regional history.

Steinberg, Michael. *Our Wilderness*. Glens Falls, NY: Adirondack Mountain Club, 1991. 112 pp., photos, $14.95. Billed as a history for ages 10 and up, this book is also an excellent summary for adults.

Terrie, Philip G. *Contested Terrain*. Blue Mountain Lake and Syracuse, NY: Adirondack Museum and Syracuse University Press, 1997. Political history contrasting the real vs. imagined Adirondacks.

Todd, John. *Long Lake*. Pittsfield, MA: 1845; reprinted in 1997 by Purple Mountain Press. Glimpses of pioneer life; perfect companion to *Contested Terrain*.

Natural History

North Country Books, in Utica, publishes a series of field guides on native birds, mammals, trees and shrubs, wildflowers, and mushrooms. All of the books are paperbacks with numerous color photos; prices are $12.95 each for the mushroom and wildflower guides, and $13.95 each for the bird, mammal, and tree guides.

DiNunzio, Michael. *Adirondack Wildguide*. Elizabethtown, NY: Adirondack Conservancy/Adirondack Council, 1984. 160 pp., illus., $14.95.

Terrie, Philip G. *Wildlife and Wilderness: A History of Adirondack Mammals*. Fleischmanns, NY: Purple Mountain Press, 1993. 176 pp., photos, index. $14.50, pap.

Photographic Studies

Farb, Nathan. *100 Views of the Adirondacks*. NY: Rizzoli Press, 1988. 168 pp., color photos, $45.

Oppersdorff, Mathias. *Adirondack Faces*. Syracuse, NY: Syracuse University Press/Adirondack Museum Book, 1991. 108 pp., $34.95.

Winkler, John. *A Bushwhacker's View of the Adirondacks*. Utica, NY: North Country Books, 1996. 118 pp., $27.50. Color photographs of the High Peaks.

Recreation

There are two main sources for Adirondack guidebooks for hiking, snowshoeing, and cross-country skiing: the Adirondack Mountain Club (ADK), based in Lake George, NY, and North Country Books, out of Utica, NY. The *Forest Preserve Series* by various ADK authors covers seven different regions of the park, from the High Peaks to the Northville–Lake Placid Trail; these $14.95 pocket-size paperbacks have plenty of detail and each comes with a separate topo map showing trails. North Country Books distributes the *Discover the Adirondacks Series*, written by historian/hiker Barbara McMartin. These are more lively to read, with notes on the human and natural history of a particular destination, and cost between $9.95 and $14.95.

Two new guidebooks intended for young readers by Barbara McMartin are *Adventures in Hiking* and *Fun on Flatwater*, available from North Country Books; new in 1998 is *Kids on the Trail*, equal parts how-to and where-to, published by the Adirondack Mountain Club. If you can't decide on which region to trek, Barbara McMartin has also written *Fifty Hikes in the Adirondacks: Short Walks, Day Trips, and Extended Hikes Throughout the Park*, published by Backcountry Publications in Woodstock, VT ($12.95).

Aprill, Dennis. *Good Fishing in the Adirondacks*. Woodstock, VT: Backcountry Publications, 1992. 224 pp., photos, maps, $15.

Goodman, Tony. *Classic Adirondack Ski Tours*. Lake George, NY: Adirondack Mountain Club, 1996. 127 pp., maps, index. $10.95.

Jamieson, Paul and Morris, Donald. *Adirondack Canoe Waters: North Flow*. Lake George, NY: Adirondack Mountain Club, 1994. 368 pp., maps, index, $15.95.

McKibben, Halpern, etc. *25 Bike Rides in the Adirondacks: Bicycle Adventures in the East's Largest Wilderness*. Woodstock, VT: Backcountry Publications, 1995. 174 pp., $13.

Mellor, Don. *Climbing in the Adirondacks: A Guide to Rock & Ice Routes*. Lake George, NY: Adirondack Mountain Club, 1996. 318 pp., photos, maps, index, $24.95.

Travel

Folwell, Elizabeth and Godine, Amy. *Adirondack Odysseys*. Lee, MA and Blue Mountain Lake, NY: Berkshire House Publishers and the Adirondack Museum. 220 pp., $16.95. Guide to museums and historic sites from the Mohawk Valley to the St. Lawrence River.

Stoddard, Seneca Ray. *The Adirondacks Illustrated*. Glens Falls, NY: Chapman Historical Museum, 1983. Reprint of 1874 guidebook. 204 pp., illus., index, $15.

BOOKS YOU CAN BORROW

Barnett, Lincoln. *The Ancient Adirondacks*. NY: Time-Life Books, 1974. 184 pp., photos, index. An excellent introduction to the Adirondack Park by a Westport resident and former *Life* magazine editor.

Colvin, Verplanck. *Report on a Topographical Survey of the Adirondack Wilderness of New York*. Albany, NY: 1873. Sounds dull, but it reads like an adventure story. Many engravings and maps.

Deming, Philander. *Adirondack Stories*. Boston, MA: 1880. Gritty short stories.

Jerome, Christine. *An Adirondack Passage*. NY: HarperCollins, 1993. 230 pp., photos, $20. Wonderful essay about a long canoe trip.

CLIMATE AND WEATHER INFORMATION

Nine months of winter and three months of poor sledding" sums up an Adirondack year if you happen to ask a native in, say, mud season. A typical twelve months has about 190 days of sub-freezing temperatures. The western Adirondacks, including Old Forge, Eagle Bay, Big Moose, Inlet, and north to Cranberry Lake and Star Lake, get considerably more snow than the

Courtesy of the Barry Collection, Lake Placid Center for the Arts

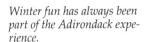

Winter fun has always been part of the Adirondack experience.

eastern Adirondacks, with about *ten feet* falling in an average winter from lake-effect storms.

Spring in the Adirondacks can be elusive. March is winter, despite the date of the vernal equinox. April weather bounces between brief flashes of hot and dry, or sustained snow and cold, or mixtures of mild and moist. May tends to be reliably above freezing during the daytime, although in 1976, nearly two feet of snow fell on May 19. June temperatures can be sweltering, with plenty of bug activity.

July and August days are usually in the 70s and 80s, with occasional hotter spells, but evenings cool off pleasantly. Early September often brings the finest dry weather for outdoor activities, with highs in the 70s and lows in the 50s.

Fall can be brilliantly sunny, providing great leaf-peeping opportunities from about September 20 through October 15, depending on the elevation. Or autumn can be dismally rainy, with the only chance to see fall colors by looking in mud puddles. There's a toll-free hotline for fall foliage reports, 1-800-CALL-NYS.

Generalities about the weather are one thing; getting an accurate forecast is another. There is no nearby National Weather Service station. Predictions for Albany or Syracuse need temperatures to be adjusted downwards by five or ten degrees, with a corresponding change for precipitation — 40 degrees and rain for the Capital District usually means subfreezing temperatures and sleet or snow in the Adirondacks.

The Lake Placid radio station, WIRD (105.5 FM), has a weatherman on staff who provides good information for the area from Tupper Lake to Keene; there's a 24-hour telephone weather report available at 518-523-1363. North Country Public Radio WSLU-FM (see below for frequencies), broadcasting out of St. Lawrence University, in Canton, airs extensive forecasts that cover much of the Adirondacks. The "Eye on the Sky" weather update from Vermont Pub-

lic Radio, WVPR (107.9 FM), tends to be fairly reliable for the eastern Adirondacks. The Albany television station, WRGB, also has a weather forecast at
518-476-WRGB, which covers the southern Adirondacks.

On the World Wide Web, **rainorshine.com** shows five-day forecasts for Lake
George and Lake Placid, and the North Country Public Radio home page
(http://www.ncpr.org) links to weather information.

GUIDED TOURS

There are hundreds of licensed Adirondack Guides for fishing, hunting,
hiking, and climbing trips; you'll find information about them in Chapter
Six, *Recreation*. Several communities in the Champlain Valley have self-guided
walking and driving tours for historic-preservation buffs; check "Architecture," in Chapter Four, *Culture,* for the details. Guided bus tours of the
Olympic facilities are available from Lake Placid Sightseeing Tours, on Mirror
Lake Dr., 518-523-4431.

HANDICAPPED SERVICES

Disabled New York residents can get free passes to state-operated camping, swimming, and golf facilities, and historic sites. Write to Office of
Parks and Recreation, Agency Building 1, Empire State Plaza, Albany, NY
12238 for an application.

Some of the nature trails at the Visitor Interpretive Centers, at Paul Smiths
and Newcomb, are designed for the mobility-impaired. The Adirondack
Mountain Club (see "Bibliography," above) has appendices on appropriate
trails for wheelchairs in some of its hiking guidebooks.

Cultural institutions, such as the Adirondack Museum, libraries, and arts
centers are generally accessible; some historic buildings are not. Chapter Four,
Culture, provides more information. Restaurants that are accessible are
described in Chapter Five; lodgings with handicapped facilities are listed in
Chapter Three.

HEALTH CENTERS AND HOSPITALS

LAKE GEORGE AND SOUTHEASTERN ADIRONDACKS
Bolton Health Center, 518-644-9471; Cross St., Bolton Landing
Chester Health Center, 518-494-2761; Main St., Chestertown

Glens Falls Hospital, 518-792-5261; 100 Park St., Glens Falls
Schroon Lake Health Center, 518-532-7120; North Ave., Schroon Lake
Warrensburg Health Center, 518-623-2844; Main St., Warrensburg

CHAMPLAIN VALLEY
Champlain Valley Physicians Hospital Medical Center, 518-561-2000; Beekman St., Plattsburgh
Elizabethown Community Hospital, 518-873-6377; Park St., Elizabethtown
Mineville Health Center, 518-942-6661; Hospital Rd., Mineville
Moses-Ludington Hospital, 518-585-2831; Wicker St., Ticonderoga
Ticonderoga Health Center, 518-585-6708; Old Chilson Rd., Ticonderoga

HIGH PEAKS AND NORTHERN ADIRONDACKS
Adirondack Medical Center, 518-523-3311; Church St., Lake Placid (formerly Placid Memorial Hospital)
Adirondack Medical Center, 518-891-4141; Lake Colby Dr., Saranac Lake (formerly Saranac Lake General Hospital)
Mountain Health Center, 518-576-9771; Rte. 73, Keene

NORTHWEST LAKES
Clifton-Fine Hospital, 315-848-3351; Rte. 3, Star Lake
Adirondack Health Center (formerly Mercy Health Care), 518-359-3355; 115 Wawbeek Ave., Tupper Lake

CENTRAL ADIRONDACKS
Indian Lake Health Center, 518-648-5707; Rte. 28, Indian Lake
Long Lake Medical Center, 518-624-2301; Rte. 28N, Long Lake
Nathan Littauer Hospital, 518-725-8621; 99 E. State St., Gloversville
North Creek Health Center, 518-251-2541; at Adirondack Tri-County Nursing Home, Ski Bowl Rd., North Creek
Town of Webb Health Center, 315-369-6619; South Shore Rd., Old Forge

LATE NIGHT FOOD AND FUEL

Most towns with more than a few hundred people now have convenience stores open until 11pm or later, offering gas, food and personal-care essentials. From Lake George to Lake Placid to Old Forge, look for Cumber-

B. Folwell

Pig Rock, on Rte. 30 near Speculator, has been a landmark for generations of motorists.

land Farms, Nice n' Easy, Stewart's Shops, or Sugar Creek plazas. Stewart's stores also have cash machines.

MAPS

A standard road-atlas page showing New York State shrinks the Adirondack Park down to a postage stamp and indicates maybe three highways. The Adirondack North Country Association publishes an excellent full-size road map that shows just the park and adjacent counties; send $2.00 (check or money order) and a stamped, self-addressed legal-size envelope to ANCA, 183 Broadway, Saranac Lake NY 12983, to receive one. JiMapco, in Round Lake, NY, publishes individual county maps that are widely available in grocery stores and book shops. The *New York State Atlas and Gazetteer* ($13.95) published by De Lorme Mapping Co., Freeport, ME, uses a topographical map format to show areas in still greater detail; these can be found in most area bookstores.

MEDIA: MAGAZINES AND NEWSPAPERS; RADIO STATIONS

Magazines & Newspapers

Adirondac 518-668-4447; RD 3, Box 3055, Lake George NY 12845; bimonthly magazine. Published by the Adirondack Mountain Club, with articles on local history, outdoor recreation, and environmental issues.

Adirondack Life 518-946-2191; Box 410, Jay NY 12941; Award-winning bimonthly magazine, plus annual *Guide to the Outdoors*. Known for excellent color photography; publishes essays, short stories, columns, and features on history, outdoor recreation, architecture, culture, local life, regional products, politics, and environmental issues by nationally known writers.

LAKE GEORGE AND SOUTHEASTERN ADIRONDACKS

Glens Falls Post Star 518-792-3131; Lawrence and Cooper Sts., Glens Falls NY 12801; daily newspaper covering the Adirondacks from Lake George to Long Lake.

CHAMPLAIN VALLEY

Plattsburgh Press-Republican 518-561-2300; 170 Margaret St., Plattsburgh NY 12901; daily paper covering from Ticonderoga to Saranac Lake to Plattsburgh, with news bureaus in Lake Placid (518-523-1559) and Ticonderoga (518-585-4070).

Valley News 518-873-6368; Denton Publishing Co., Elizabethtown NY 12932; weekly paper for Elizabethtown, Westport, Essex, Keene, and Keene Valley.

HIGH PEAKS AND NORTHERN ADIRONDACKS

Adirondack Daily Enterprise 518-891-2600; 61 Broadway, Saranac Lake NY 12983; daily paper for Lake Placid, Saranac Lake, Paul Smiths, and Tupper Lake area; the *Weekender* has a good regional calendar of events plus local history features.

Lake Placid News 518-523-4401; Mill Hill, Lake Placid NY 12946; weekly paper for Lake Placid, Keene, Keene Valley, and Wilmington.

NORTHWEST LAKES

Tupper Lake Free Press 518-359-2166; 136 Park St., Tupper Lake NY 12986; weekly paper covering Tupper Lake, Piercefield, Cranberry Lake, and Long Lake.

On the Internet

For the past few years, Adirondack organizations, artisans, and tourist destinations have presented information on their services, products, and special events via the Internet. Home pages on the World Wide Web describe everything from ski-jump competitions at Lake Placid to facts about Mount Marcy, New York's highest peak. A sampling of where to look for Adirondack materials in cyberspace follows, but note that this is just the beginning. New listings are filed practically every week. Internet addresses for lodgings and restaurants described in Chapters Three and Five are listed with the phone numbers.

The **Adirondack Mountain Club** (http://www.adk.org) uses its home page to promote outdoor workshops and describe the club's activities and facilities.

Adirondack Mountain Specialties (http://www.icw.com.america/adarndak.html.) is a catalog of fine arts and crafts produced in the North Country, listing New Moon Pottery, in Wadhams, Westport Trading Company, and nature illustrators, for example.

AdirondackNet (http://www.adirondack.net.) has many listings of interest to travelers about golf courses, Lake George boat cruises, whitewater rafting, lodgings, museums, attractions, and so forth in the Lake George region and southeastern Adirondacks, Champlain Valley, and High Peaks.

Adirondacks.com (http://www.adirondacks.com) is the most comprehensive site for regional resorts, real estate, maps, events, and attractions, with links to specific communities and businesses.

The **Mount Marcy** page (http://www.inch.com./~dipper/ny.html.) shows background on this mile-high mountain.

The **Olympic Regional Development Authority** (http://www.orda.org.) describes downhill and cross-country-skiing facilities, bobsled and luge races, speed-skating events, and useful Lake Placid tourist information.

Two Usenet groups, which are bulletin boards on the Internet, show postings covering Adirondack issues: the **backcountry recreation forum** (rec.backcountry) and **upstate New York forum** (alt.cult.ny-upstate).

Watertown Daily Times 315-782-1000; 260 Washington St., Watertown NY 13601; daily newspaper with an Adirondack bureau based in Tupper Lake.

CENTRAL ADIRONDACKS

Adirondack Express 315-369-2237; Box 659, Old Forge NY 13420; weekly newspaper covering from Blue Mountain Lake to Otter Lake.

Hamilton County News 518-548-6898; Rte. 30, Speculator NY 12164; weekly newspaper for Long Lake, Blue Mountain Lake, Indian Lake, Speculator, Wells, Piseco, and Benson.

North Creek News 518-251-3012; Ski Bowl Rd., North Creek NY 12853; weekly paper for Johnsburg, Bakers Mills, Minerva, Olmstedville, North Creek, and North River.

Radio Stations

National Public Radio: Three NPR affiliates reach different parts of the Adirondacks:

WAMC-FM, 90.3, 518-465-5233; Albany NY; also translator WANC, 103.9 (Ticonderoga).

WSLU-FM, 89.5 (Canton), 90.9 (Malone), 91.3 (Blue Mountain Lake and Thousand Islands), 91.7 (Long Lake, Lake Placid, Tupper Lake), 90.5 (Saranac Lake), 88.3 (Peru), 89.9 (North Creek). 315-379-5356; Canton NY. The best news and feature coverage for the entire Adirondack Park by any media outlet.

WVPR, 107.9, 802-674-6772; Windsor, VT. News coverage for the eastern Adirondacks and relatively reliable weather forecasts.

Commercial Radio Stations

WIRD-FM, 105.5, 518-523-3341. Lake Placid. General.

WSCG-FM, 93.5, 518-654-9058. Corinth. Country.

WIPS-AM, 1250, 518-585-2868. Ticonderoga. General.

WNBZ-AM, 1240, 518-891-1544. Saranac Lake. General.

Television Stations

There are no television stations broadcasting from the Adirondacks, and TV reception in areas not covered by cable or translator can be terrible. The Plattsburgh NBC-affiliate, WPTZ, reports on news from Lake Placid, Saranac Lake, and elsewhere in the eastern Adirondacks during the "Today Show" and in evening slots.

REAL ESTATE

Because the population of the region has been fairly stable over the last century, there are often older farmsteads and village homes for sale, as families build new houses to meet their needs. If you're not afraid of the "handyman's special," the Adirondacks could provide some challenges and rewards for you. Townhouses and condominiums are a new local phenomenon, and after intense initial speculation, prices have stabilized at a level that shouldn't be too shocking to a typical New England urbanite. Waterfront — on just about any lake, river, or pond inside the Blue Line — tends to be scarce and pricey: the going rate can be as high as $1000 per running foot of shoreline just for the land. Add a summer cottage, or a real winterized house plus a decent driveway, a boathouse, or a garage, and the figures start to climb.

Even crossroads that don't have grocery stores have real-estate offices. Weekly newspapers usually have some real-estate listings, and many realtors publish bimonthly buyers' guides. *Adirondack Life* magazine has a large real-estate section in each issue.

RELIGIOUS SERVICES AND ORGANIZATIONS

Churches throughout the Adirondacks anchor the communities and provide a network of help and social life along with spiritual guidance. Several local churches are interesting for their architecture and are listed on the National Register of Historic Places; a few seasonal chapels are located on lovely islands accessible only by boat. Some churches even put on great, inexpensive dinners (see Chapter Five, *Restaurants and Food Purveyors*, for advice on chicken barbecues and church suppers). Check the papers for listings of church services. Inside the park, Lake Placid has the only active synagogue; Temple Beth Joseph, in Tupper Lake, is open as a historic building and only occasionally offers services.

ROAD SERVICE

For **AAA** members, there are local offices in Glens Falls, 518-792-0088; Gloversville, 518-725-0811; and Plattsburgh, 518-563-3830. For non-AAA members, some towing and automotive services are listed below:

LAKE GEORGE AND SOUTHEASTERN ADIRONDACKS

Lakeview Automotive, Lake George	518-668-9267
Thomson's Garage, Lake George	518-668-5337
Pottersville Garage, Pottersville	518-494-3631
Warrensburg Car Care, Warrensburg	518-623-2135

CHAMPLAIN VALLEY AND NORTHEASTERN ADIRONDACKS

Chesterfield Truck Stop, Keeseville	518-834-7407
Pierce's Service Station, Lewis	518-873-2065/962-8971 evening
R.B. Motors, Ticonderoga	518-585-7774

HIGH PEAKS AND NORTHERN ADIRONDACKS

Central Garage, Lake Placid	518-523-3378
John's Sunoco Service, Saranac Lake	518-891-5938
Wilmington Service Station, Wilmington	518-946-7138/946-7478 evening

NORTHWEST LAKES

Counter's Garage, Tupper Lake	518-359-9846

CENTRAL ADIRONDACKS

Central Adirondack Garage, Indian Lake	518-648-5565
Chambers Garage, Inlet	315-357-2051
C&H Citgo, Old Forge	315-369-3678
Speculator Auto, Speculator	518-548-8102
Brussel's Thendara Garage, Thendara	315-369-3755

TOURIST INFORMATION

Taking care of visitors is the number-one industry in the Adirondacks and communities have become quite skilled at educating the public about their special offerings. Warren County (which encompasses Lake George and the Southeastern Adirondacks) publishes a handsome guide with a calendar of events, lists of hiking trails, boat-launch sites, museums, libraries, attractions, campgrounds, and much more; call 518-761-6366 for a copy. Likewise, the Lake Placid/Essex County Visitors Bureau (518-523-2445) has an extensive promotional packet.

Franklin County publishes a four-color booklet with general background information plus publications detailing services and outdoor recreation; these are available from the tourism office, at 518-483-6788. Clinton County offers a magazine-size guide, available by calling 518-563-1000. Hamilton County has a series of pamphlets about hunting and fishing, snowmobiling, craft shops, dining, and lodging, available by calling 518-648-5239.

Some local chambers of commerce and visitor information centers are listed below; check out **www.adirondacks.com** for links to these towns.

LAKE GEORGE AND SOUTHEASTERN ADIRONDACKS

Bolton Landing: Rte. 9N, Bolton Landing NY 12814; 518-644-3831
Chestertown-Brant Lake-Pottersville: Main St., Chestertown NY 12817; 518-494-2722
Hague-Silver Bay: Rte. 9N, Hague NY 12836; 518-543-6353
Lake George: Rte. 9, Lake George NY 12845; 518-668-5755
Lake Luzerne: Box 222, Lake Luzerne NY 12846; 518-696-3500
Schroon Lake: Main St., Schroon Lake NY 12870; 518-532-7675
Stony Creek: Box 35, Stony Creek NY 12878; 518-696-2395
Warrensburg: 136 Main St., Warrensburg NY 12885; 518-623-2161

CHAMPLAIN VALLEY

Ticonderoga–Crown Point: Box 70, Ticonderoga NY 12883; 518-585-6619
Westport: General Delivery, Westport NY 12992; 518-962-8383

A friendly farewell from Onchiota.

Willsboro: Box 124, Willsboro NY 12996; 518-963-8668
Essex County Visitors Information Center, Bridge Rd., Crown Point NY 12928; 518-597-4646.

HIGH PEAKS AND NORTHERN ADIRONDACKS

Lake Placid Visitors Bureau: Main St., Lake Placid NY 12946; 518-523-2445
Saranac Lake: 30 Main St., Saranac Lake NY 12983; 518-891-1990 or 1-800-347-1992
Whiteface Mountain: Rte. 86, Wilmington NY 12993; 518-946-2255

NORTHWEST LAKES

Cranberry Lake: Box 506, Cranberry Lake NY 12927; 315-848-2900
Tupper Lake: 55 Park St., Tupper Lake NY 12986; 518-359-3328

CENTRAL ADIRONDACKS

Blue Mountain Lake Association: Rte. 28, Blue Mtn. Lake NY 12812; 518-352-7659
Central Adirondack Association: Main St., Old Forge NY 13420; 315-369-6983
Gore Mountain Region: Main St., North Creek NY 12853; 518-251-2612
Indian Lake: Main St., Indian Lake NY 12842; 518-648-5112
Long Lake: Rte. 28N, Long Lake NY 12847; 518-624-3077
Speculator–Lake Pleasant–Piseco: Rte. 30, Speculator NY 12164; 518-548-4521

IF TIME IS SHORT

A whirlwind tour to see the Adirondacks can mean an awful lot of time spent in the car rather than getting to know a few nice places. Maybe it's best to carefully consider your tastes and concentrate your energy within a forty-mile area.

If you're a history buff and want to stroll through attractive, well-preserved towns and old forts, then head for the Champlain Valley, especially Ticonderoga, Crown Point, Westport, and Essex. If you crave sweeping mountain vistas, aim your sights at the High Peaks, highlighting Keene Valley, Keene, and Lake Placid. If you like quiet lakes, use Upper Saranac, Cranberry, Long, Blue Mountain, Indian, Raquette, Piseco, and First through Eighth lakes, or Lake Pleasant as a base. For a terrific overview — literally — charter a floatplane from Long Lake or Inlet or take a glider ride above the High Peaks from Lake Placid.

Recommended drives include Rte. 22 along Lake Champlain, Rte. 73 between Keene and Lake Placid, Rte. 30 between Long Lake and Lake Pleasant, and the Blue Ridge Rd. between the Interstate 87 (the Northway) and Newcomb. Take a trip up the toll roads on Prospect or Whiteface mountains if you'd love to do a summit without walking more than a few hundred yards. Incidentally, the Northway offers quite possibly the most scenic high-speed road experience in the mid-Atlantic states.

A few suggestions for places to see or stay:

LODGING

The Sagamore Hotel (518-644-9400; Sagamore Rd., Bolton Landing) is at a particularly beautiful spot on Lake George and is a thoroughly luxurious modern resort with a grand 18-hole golf course, gourmet restaurants, spa, and tennis. Do take a cruise on the *Morgan*, a handsome wooden tour boat that leaves from the Sagamore dock.

Lake Placid Lodge (518-523-2700; Whiteface Inn Rd., Lake Placid) is a marvelously elegant rustic hotel with massive stone fireplaces in each room, lovely furnishings, gorgeous views of Lake Placid and the High Peaks, and one of the finest restaurants in upstate New York.

CULTURAL ATTRACTIONS

The Adirondack Museum (518-352-7311; Rtes. 28/30, Blue Mtn. Lake) is open from late May through Columbus Day, and no visit to the Adirondack Park is complete without spending a day here. The scope of the exhibits ranges from classic watercraft to fine arts to folk crafts.

Fort Ticonderoga (518-585-2821; Fort Rd., Ticonderoga) is a handsomely restored fortress that played important roles in the French and Indian Wars and the American Revolution; it's in a beautiful promontory on Lake Champlain. Plan your visit on a nice day so you can enjoy the view. Open early May through late October.

Adirondack Park Visitor Interpretive Centers (518-327-3000, Rte. 30, Paul Smiths and 518-582-2000, Rte. 28N, Newcomb) offer exhibits on the park's natural history; interpretive trails for hiking, skiing, and snowshoeing; and numerous programs for adults and children. Open year-round.

RESTAURANTS

Highwinds Inn (518-251-3760; Barton Mines Rd., North River) has a great view, lovely ambiance, and a small but thoughtful selection of absolutely fresh fish, veal, beef, and vegetables, topped off with exceptional desserts. Closed November and April–May; by reservation only.

Le Bistro Laliberté (518-523-3680; 51 Main St., Lake Placid) has an innovative — but very reasonably priced — menu of new American cuisine and awesome desserts. In the summer you can sit on the private deck overlooking Mirror Lake and watch the sunset. Open year-round.

Tail O' the Pup (518-891-5092; Sara-Placid Hwy., Ray Brook) is a no-frills roadside eatery with good barbecue at great prices; you can't pick a better place to bring the family. Open May through October.

The *William West Durant* (315-354-5532; Pier One, Raquette Lake) is a wonderful tour boat that presents a movable feast as it cruises Raquette Lake, the fourth-largest lake in the Adirondacks. Open May through October.

Nancie Battaglia

A delightfully rustic room at Lake Placid Lodge.

Index

LODGING BY PRICE CODE

RESTAURANTS BY PRICE CODE

RESTAURANTS BY CUISINE

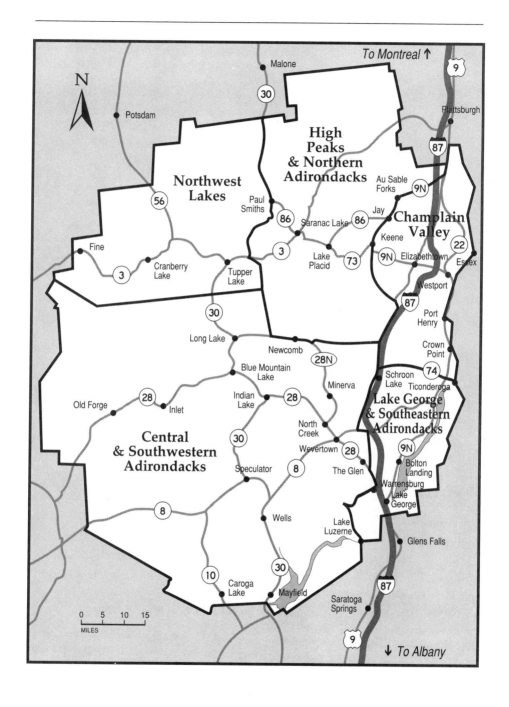

THE ADIRONDACKS IN FIVE REGIONS

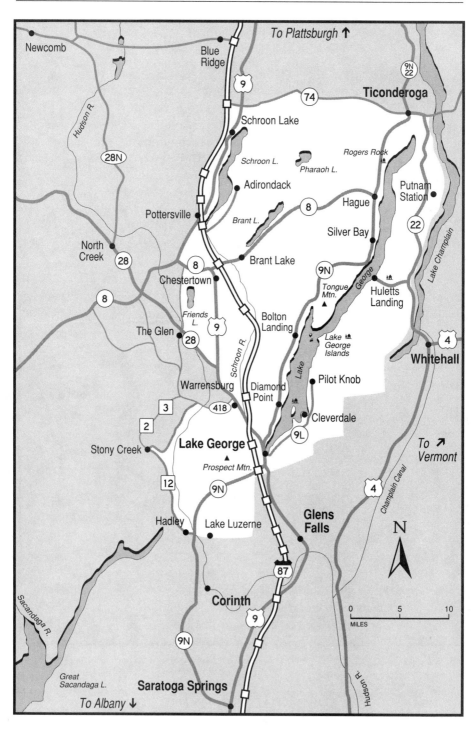

LAKE GEORGE AND SOUTHEASTERN ADIRONDACKS

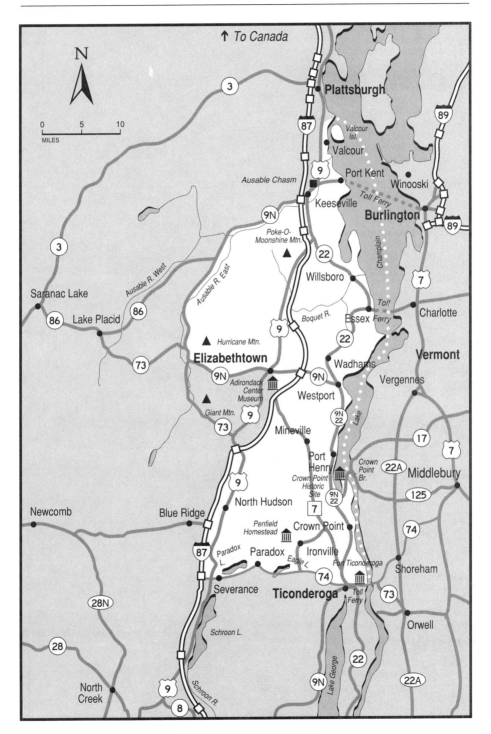

CHAMPLAIN VALLEY

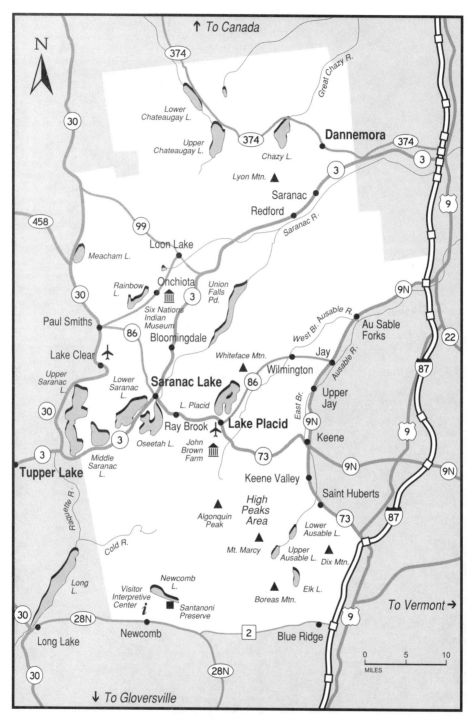

HIGH PEAKS AND NORTHERN ADIRONDACKS

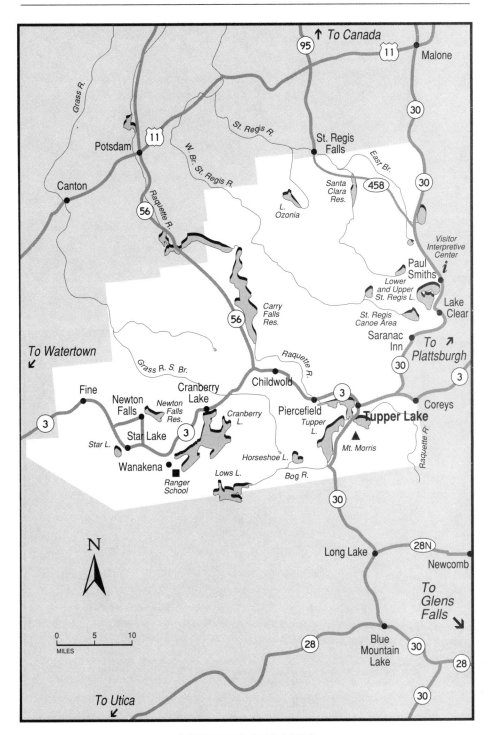

NORTHWEST LAKES

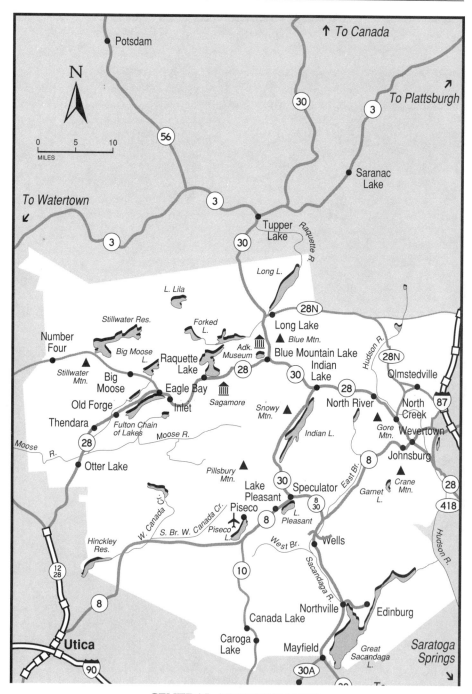

CENTRAL ADIRONDACKS

About the Author

Since moving to the mountains in 1976, Elizabeth Folwell has worked in a variety of Adirondack places, serving as education coordinator of the Adirondack Museum in Blue Mountain Lake, and as executive director of the Adirondack Lakes Center for the Arts, also in Blue Mountain Lake. Currently she is editor of *Adirondack Life* magazine, based in Jay, New York. She also had a brief career as manager of a general store, and worked as a project coordinator for Travelers Aid during the 1980 Winter Olympics in Lake Placid.

While at *Adirondack Life*, she has written numerous pieces on local history, outdoor recreation, and the environment; her freelance articles on adventure travel, regional history, and indigenous crafts in the Northeast, Southwest, and Caribbean have appeared in the *New York Times* travel section, *National Geographic Traveler*, Reader's Digest Books, and other publications. She is the author, with Amy Godine, of *Adirondack Odysseys: Exploring Museums and Historic Places from the Mohawk to the St. Lawrence* (copublished in 1997 by the Adirondack Museum and Berkshire House Publishers).

She lives in Blue Mountain Lake with her husband, Tom Warrington, and two dogs.